WE ARE THE

BAD GUYS

WE ARE THE
BAD GUYS

THE GLOBAL COST OF
AMERICAN POWER,
U.S. IMPERIALISM, FOREIGN POLICY
AND COVERT WARS

Michael T. Lester

We Are The Bad Guys
Copyright © 2025 by Michael T. Lester

ISBNs
Paperback: 979-8-9992556-1-7
Hardback: 979-8-9992556-0-0
eBook: 979-8-9992556-2-4
Audio Book: 979-8-9992556-3-1

Library of Congress Control Number: 2025923808

Published by Ironclad Press

Author's Bio Photograph: Lucy Sukar
Book Cover Artwork: Amanda Hamati

DEDICATION

To all the true patriots in the world who still honor
liberty, justice, accountability, and equality.

ACKNOWLEDGMENTS

First and foremost, I want to thank my wife Sahar, without whose constant encouragement, support, patience, understanding, and editing, this book would never have been possible. We spent many hours discussing and sharing our different experiences and perceptions as children and young adults growing up and living in different parts of the world. Through that sharing and her introduction to many others outside of the United States, what I was only feeling or suspecting was confirmed and even expanded. Seeing the world through other people's eyes is the best way to examine your own views.

I would also like to thank Jon Olson for his insights and meticulous editing of the first drafts of this book.

TABLE OF CONTENTS

INTRODUCTION

I'm an American.

I was raised in the Midwest in Minnesota.

I graduated from the U.S. Naval Academy with a degree in history, and then became an officer and pilot in the United States Marine Corps.

I was proud to "defend my country", "show the flag" and "support democracy."

In 1989 I was part of a naval deployment during the Philippine coup attempt and deployed again to the middle east for Desert Shield and Desert Storm.

I was helping to protect the greatest country in the world from those who challenged it or wanted to challenge our freedoms or our way of life.

Slogans and quotes from earlier patriots rang in my head.

> *"I regret that I have but one life to give for my country."*
> *"Give me liberty or give me death."*
> *"Freedom isn't free."*
> *"If you want peace, Prepare for war."*

But I slowly started feeling that something was off. I started to notice that what we were doing, and how we were doing it, didn't really match what we said we were doing, or why we said we were doing it.

I started to notice that the looks on the faces of the local population weren't those of gratitude, or of liberation, or even of freedom or happiness. They were looks of resignation and distrust.

Because of that, I started talking to locals more and listening to their stories, and what I slowly recognized through those conversations was that the reasons I was told we were in these other countries, what we were doing, and why we were doing it, wasn't correct, or at the very least wasn't complete. I recognized a fundamental disconnect between the official reasons for our presence and reality.

This clash between what I was told and what I saw created cognitive dissonance. My brain couldn't hold these contradictory truths at the same time. The only way to remove this dissonance was by digging into the information more deeply until one piece of information maintained its truth, and the other started to crumble.

Consequently, I spent the last 20 years using my training as a historian to study the history and the background of many of the events that have shaped the world and the United States. I didn't concentrate on the event itself or the popular narrative. Instead, I investigated why key players acted as they did and the circumstances surrounding these events. In other words, I tried to look at events through the eyes not only of an American, but also through the eyes of the people local to the event.

It was through this process that I slowly came to realize:

We are the Bad Guys.
Or at the very least, we are perceived to be the bad guys.

This is a monumental revelation that challenges everything most Americans believe about our country's role in the world, and quite frankly, it's one that many Americans will not be able to accept. Many are unable to accept anything that conflicts with their lifelong beliefs and they just dismiss it with a wave of the hand and a comment of "that's not true," or even more directly "I don't believe that."

I have taken this journey over many years and many hours of research both academically and in person in other countries. I am sharing what I have found with you in the hopes that you might examine the facts and also come to the realization that much of what we have been told, and much of what we believe as Americans, just isn't true.

The first step in solving a problem is recognizing that there is one. Once we recognize a problem, we can work on solving it. In this case, that means making this country what it has the potential to be.

This book aims to expose an issue that is hidden by design. An issue that is keeping the United States from being in reality, what it claims to be in speech, and through that exposure, take a first step in embarking on a path of repair.

My goal is to expose and break some of the molds that keep us as a nation from becoming the shining example of democracy, freedom, and justice that so many of us believe we already are.

Americans are good people, but America as a country is engaged in worldwide activity that does not display the compassion or the empathy that we claim to have. It engages in activities that the rest of the world considers despotic, uncaring, and imperial. This statement is not my opinion. International media consistently portrays America as a harbinger of coercion and destruction.

How can we view ourselves one way while much of the rest of the world views us completely differently? If presented with the same information, most large groups will come to the same, or very similar, conclusions. If they don't, it means that they don't have the same information, or individuals or small groups hold more decision-making power than the large group does. In the case of the United States and its international actions, my research suggests that it is a little of both—and that is much of what this book explores.

This book will examine why "the truth" as we know it, is not the whole truth and because of that, why many people's opinions and beliefs are not formed from a position of knowledge or experience. In fact, we'll examine how many people's opinions and beliefs are crafted for them. We'll look at examples of how the United States has taken action that contrasts with our slogans, contrasts with our shared national persona, and even contrasts with our beliefs. Once enough of us are aware of what is taking place both to us and in our name, then we can work together to change for the better.

This book challenges you to examine what you think you know from a different perspective by providing information and perspective that might not align with what you've been taught.

Let me show you how this pattern of incomplete information works with a simple example most Americans learned in school.

In elementary school in the United States, most children are taught that "Columbus discovered America." Then in high school they learn that Columbus wasn't the first one to discover America; the Vikings had discovered it centuries earlier. Then in College, if they study history, they learn that Columbus didn't even see or set foot on what is today known as the American mainland. The closest he came was during his fourth voyage (did you know he made four voyages to the Americas?) when he was exploring the northern parts of Central America.

They may have learned that Columbus, an Italian, was sponsored by Spain because Spain wanted to find a faster route to Asia, but they probably didn't learn that Spain didn't care about discovery. They wanted to increase trade, spread Christianity, and gain territorial advantage over other countries. In fact, when Columbus landed in the Bahamas in 1492, he thought he was all the way in India, and so he called the people there "Indians." That is why we still use that term today.

But did you learn that in 1500, eight years after "discovering" America, Columbus was arrested for tyranny, brutality, and corruption and extradited back to Spain in chains? Did you learn that he was later released and died just six years later in 1506, stripped of prestige, feeling betrayed and neglected, largely out of both public and royal favor, without title, without the vast riches he believed he had earned, largely forgotten, widely discredited, and a social outcast?

When you know all the facts, it changes your perspective from the energetic, happy, explorer-hero setting out to find new lands, to an almost hypocritical missionary brute who stayed one-step ahead of the law until his actions caught up with him.

Which was he? Maybe a little of both. History is seldom clear cut. But it helps to know the whole truth so you can discuss an event or person logically from a position of knowledge and make informed decisions.

This pattern of progressive revelation—learning more complete truths as we dig deeper—applies to much larger issues than Columbus, and we're going to use that approach to examine the United States we think we know.

The narrative most of us have been taught is one of American dominance, benevolence, kindness, and international support. But that narrative doesn't fit what most other people are taught in other countries. When I travel and discuss history or current events with citizens of other countries, they frequently look at me with a confused expression and ask, "How can you not know this?"

That's an excellent question. How *can* we not know?

The answer is that we live in various information bubbles. The information that we receive in those bubbles influences what we think we know and subsequently how we think. In fact, some of the statements made in this book might be perceived by a reader to be incorrect or exaggerated because they don't fit the narrative that they've been taught. To address this, I've meticulously referenced every fact, statistic, and claim in the endnotes using both primary and secondary sources. I encourage everyone to check the references and investigate anything they disagree with.

This book will give you new perspectives to U.S. involvement in international events and in domestic actions. It will give you a contrasting perspective of the stories or history that you think you already know. By doing that, hopefully it will motivate you to find out more, become more informed, and better equipped to make decisions and formulate opinions on current events and U.S. actions.

Now let's start talking about The United States that we think we live in…

PART I:

THE AMERICAN BUBBLES

Americans live inside carefully constructed bubbles of manufactured reality that obscure how information and power operate in our society.

The Information Bubble ensures citizens receive carefully constructed narratives rather than factual analysis. *The Government Bubble* maintains the fiction that elections determine national policy while in fact, corporate and foreign interests write legislation. *The Military Bubble* portrays aggressive interventions as defensive necessities while obscuring the costs of perpetual warfare. *The Law Enforcement Bubble* frames systematic oppression as public safety while protecting property and power rather than people.

Together, these bubbles create a curated worldview where American actions are always justified, and American power is always benevolent. Because of these bubbles, U.S. citizens can't see their country as others do, not as a beacon of freedom, but as an empire whose primary exports are violence, debt, and manipulation.

The first part of this book exposes the architecture of American self-deception, examining how each bubble operates and what realities they conceal. Breaking free requires confronting uncomfortable truths about institutions we've been taught to revere, and that is the first step toward genuine reform.

CHAPTER 1:
THE NATIONALISTIC BUBBLE

United States citizens live in a nationalistic and geographic bubble.

We are bordered on the east and west by oceans and by only one country to the north and one to the south. Events in the other 193 sovereign countries recognized by the United Nations[1] are noticed little by most Americans because…well…they are "over there".

GEOGRAPHIC IGNORANCE

A National Geographic survey showed that **77% of Americans couldn't point to Afghanistan on a map**[2] even though over 775,000 Americans were sent there to fight, 20,000 came home injured, and 2,461 never came home at all.[3]

When we can't locate other countries on a map, we laugh it off with 'I'm terrible at geography,' as if ignorance about places where we send troops is somehow charming. We also somehow believe that ignorance is acceptable while simultaneously believing that we should have opinions on what the United States does in these foreign countries or why we are even involved there.

Another survey in 2019 conducted by the Council on Foreign Relations and the National Geographic Society[4] revealed that in geography and world events, U.S. adults had a very "limited knowledge about these topics." In the survey most adults scored at or below the 50% level. That's an "F" in every grading system.

Regarding its role in the world, the same survey revealed that "Americans divide evenly as to whether the United States should reduce or not reduce its role in the world. On international actions, U.S. adults overwhelmingly prefer multilateral action with other countries' support (88 percent) over unilateral action (6 percent)."

Given our geographic isolation from other countries, it's not difficult to understand why most Americans have such a poor grasp of world geography and events. Since we don't often travel to other countries or do business with them directly, events that take place outside of the United States are typically of little interest to most Americans. The information that we do receive is highly censored and massaged to provide more entertainment and "engagement" than it is an actual coverage of news, but we'll cover this in more detail later.

THE FREEDOM MYTH

There's a scene in the opening of *The Newsroom*, a show that flirts with truth more often than most networks dare, where a college student asks a panel, "What makes America the greatest country in the world?"

One of the panelists answers with a rousing "Freedom and Freedom... so let's keep it that way!"

The audience cheers and applauds. Cue the red, white, and blue pride swelling in the room.

But here's the thing: that applause wasn't for a *truth*. It was for a *belief*.

Americans are raised to believe that freedom is not just an American value, it's an exclusively American one. That they, and they alone, know what it is to be free. But like many foundational myths in this country, the facts don't line up with the story.

Before we go further, let's stop and ask: What do we even mean when we say "freedom"?

It's a word we toss around with conviction, but most people can't define it beyond a gut feeling. And that gut is often reacting to decades of repetition, not reflection.

TWO KINDS OF FREEDOM

British philosopher Isaiah Berlin offered one of the clearest frameworks in his 1958 essay "Two Concepts of Liberty."[5] He broke "freedom" into two parts:

- **Freedom from**, what he called *negative liberty*. It's the absence of constraints. No one is forcing you to do something.

- **Freedom to**, or what he called *positive liberty*. It's about empowerment. You're allowed to do something because no law or system is preventing you.

Both are essential. And both are often in tension.

This tension is built into the American system. Our Constitution doesn't give us rights, it recognizes that we already have them. That's a crucial distinction. The First Amendment doesn't say, "You now have freedom of speech." It says, "Congress shall make no law... abridging the freedom of speech." The right exists. The government is just told to keep its hands off, so we grow up believing we are free until someone can prove otherwise.

But here's where it gets tricky. There are two ways to design a system. Either everything is allowed unless explicitly forbidden, or everything is forbidden unless explicitly allowed.

America claims to follow the first model. But more and more, we're quietly inching toward the second.

THE SLOW EROSION OF LIBERTY

Change doesn't always knock at the front door. Sometimes it slips in through the back window.

Psychologists call it "change blindness"[6]—the inability to notice gradual shifts over time. You don't see what's being taken from you until the space where it used to live is empty.

In theory, Americans cherish the principle: "Your right to swing your fist ends where my nose begins." But what happens when your "fist" is a protest, a post, a press release? What happens when that protest is silenced, that post is taken down, or that press release never reaches the public?

Legally, freedom is easy to uphold between individuals. But once corporate power, state bureaucracy, or surveillance technologies enter the equation, the balance breaks. The bigger the entity, the harder it is for the average person to maintain their ground.

THE EXCEPTIONALISM MYTH

Americans, from the time they are born, are told that "America is the greatest country in the world," that we are the "Defenders of Democracy", and the "Champions of human rights."

Unfortunately, the facts don't support any of these statements. This is a bold statement, and some people may take offense to it, but the very fact that questioning this statement evokes a visceral reaction only strengthens the argument that the statement is more emotionally based than factual.

As Americans, we are so accustomed to these statements that we stop questioning them. "America is the greatest country in the world." Of course it is. End of discussion. But what if I said to a fellow American "Minnesota is the greatest state in the union." People in Minnesota might agree, but people who live in the other 49 states would probably have a different opinion. The logical response to a statement like "Minnesota is the greatest state in the union" is to ask, "Why do you say that?" or "What makes it so great?" And that is exactly what many non-Americans do if an American makes the claim that America is the greatest country in the world. Unfortunately for Americans, the claim is difficult, if not impossible, to defend.

The truth is that there is absolutely no evidence to support the statement that the United States is the greatest country in the world.

INTERNATIONAL REALITY CHECK

Freedom of Speech? A study in 2025 concluded that the United States ranked 9th in personal freedom of speech with Norway and Denmark taking the number 1 and 2 positions.[7]

Freedom of the Press? If you look at freedom of the press—the freedom of news outlets to publish articles that might be critical of the country, the current administration, or groups of individuals—Norway and Denmark retain the number 1 and 2 positions, but **the United States drops to 44th!** Finland, Germany, France, Belgium, Jamaica, Taiwan, and Argentina all have more freedom of the press than the United States does.[8]

Freedom of Religion? A Pew Research study on religious freedom ranks the U.S. 9th in religious freedom.[9]

A Free Democracy? If you look at all the things that make a country a democracy (civil liberties, electoral process, political culture, etc.), most Americans will be surprised the United States ranks 29th in the world and is categorized as a **"Flawed Democracy."** The top 9 countries (Norway, New Zealand, Iceland, Sweden, Finland, Denmark, Ireland, Switzerland, and Netherlands) all have an overall "Democracy Score" of 9.0 or above on a 10-point scale. The United States has a score of 7.85, flanked by Chile and Malta.[10]

THE NUMBERS DON'T LIE

Let's put this in more numbers that might shock you.

The World Population Review, along with organizations like Reporters Without Borders, ranks countries based on key freedoms, including freedom of speech.[11] One of their metrics is a composite score of key freedoms like "freedom of speech," "freedom of press," "freedom of expression," and others. It is an overall view of the sum of all freedoms in a country.

Take a guess where the United States ranks out of 180 countries.

Top 10?

Top 20?

Try 55th.

Yes, 55th! As of 2025, we barely crack the top third.

That means countries like South Africa, Chile, Namibia, the Czech Republic, and Canada offer their citizens more freedom to speak, publish, and dissent than the United States does. That's not opinion. That's data.

But data doesn't always survive the American echo chamber. Many people respond to these numbers with disbelief and comment:

"That can't be right."
"Those rankings are biased."
"Fake News."
"Well, yeah, but we still have it better than most."

In the chapters that follow we're going to examine why they, or maybe even *you,* might say that.

FREEDOM IN DECLINE

Here's the part that should worry everyone, regardless of your political leaning:

In 2021, the U.S. scored 78 out of 100 in its Freedom of Speech index. By 2025, that number dropped to under 68.[12]

That's a 15% decline in just four years.

We're not expanding freedom. We're shrinking it. Slowly. Methodically. Almost invisibly.

And the damage isn't just in censorship or overregulation. It's in the perception that we're still free, even as the scaffolding of freedom is being quietly dismantled right under our feet.

The next time someone shouts "freedom!" with chest-pounding certainty, ask them:

Freedom to do what? Freedom from what? And how do you know it's still there? Because patriotism built on myth is not patriotism; it's denial.

The facts reveal that despite our lifelong belief to the contrary, it's difficult to support the claim that America is the greatest country in the world. In fact, in most international affairs we are, or at the very least are perceived to be, the bad guys.

CHAPTER RECAP – THE NATIONALISTIC BUBBLE

This introduction sets the stage by showing how Americans live inside nationalistic and geographic bubbles—separated by oceans, cushioned by myths of greatness, and largely ignorant of the wider world. Surveys reveal that most citizens can't even locate countries where American troops fight and die, yet they hold strong opinions about U.S. involvement abroad. This ignorance isn't harmless; it's cultivated by isolation, repetition, and carefully curated narratives of exceptionalism. The belief that America is "the greatest country in the world" persists not because of evidence, but because questioning it feels like betrayal.

The truth is harder: in rankings of democracy, press freedom, and civil liberties, the U.S. lags far behind the image it projects. This contradiction, the gap between who we think we are and who we actually are, is the foundation of the bubbles we'll now examine.

In the next chapter, we begin with the **Patriotism Bubble**, where love of country is often distorted into blind loyalty, and where dissent—the very essence of a functioning democracy—is too often mistaken for disloyalty.

CHAPTER 2:

THE PATRIOTISM BUBBLE

Patriotism is a word invoked often, sometimes recklessly, in American life.

In political debates, media soundbites, and everyday conversations, it is used less as a measure of devotion to principle and more as a weapon to silence dissent.

Criticize the government, and someone will quickly respond, "That's not very patriotic." That shuts down discussion, shifts focus, and creates the illusion that loyalty to a political party or a particular leader defines love of country.

But this is a dangerous distortion. To understand patriotism, we need to strip the slogans from it and return to its roots.

PATRIOTISM MISUSED

Not everyone agrees on what "patriotism" means. For some, it means flying the flag, reciting the pledge, or cheering at a military parade.

For others, it means holding government accountable when it fails its citizens. The tension between these interpretations is not new, but in contemporary political discourse, the meaning of patriotism has been blurred to the point of contradiction.

When one citizen says patriotism means obedience to authority, and another insists it means resistance to tyranny, disagreement is inevitable.

The result is not only division but also confusion. Citizens end up talking *at* one another instead of *with* one another, believing they are arguing about the same concept when in truth they are speaking entirely different languages.

This misuse of patriotism has consequences. It reduces meaningful debate into shallow accusations and fosters division where questioning government policy becomes labeled as "un-American," and where dissent is confused with disloyalty.

Yet American history proves that dissent has always been a crucial element of true patriotism. The abolitionists who opposed slavery, the suffragists who demanded equal rights for women, and the civil rights activists who confronted segregation were all accused of being unpatriotic in their time.[1]

Today, we recognize their courage as the truest form of devotion to country, a refusal to accept injustice in silence. We need to apply that recognition to ourselves today.

TRUE VS. FALSE PATRIOTISM

True patriotism is rooted in principle. It is not blind obedience to the state, nor is it unconditional loyalty to a political figure.

False patriotism, by contrast, is about performance—loud slogans and empty gestures, unmoored from responsibility.

Mark Twain captured this distinction when he wrote:

> "The modern patriotism, the true patriotism, the only rational patriotism is loyalty to the nation all the time, loyalty to the government when it deserves it."[2]

This principle guided America from its very founding. If patriotism were defined by obedience to authority, America would never have been born.

The colonists who resisted British rule did so in the name of higher principles. Their resistance was not treason; it was patriotism in its purest form because it sought to align government with justice, liberty, and the rights of the people.

To be a patriot, then, is not to stand by government unconditionally but to call it back to its founding promises and principles.

False patriotism, on the other hand, thrives on symbols while neglecting substance. It is the individual who waves a flag but turns away from injustice. It is the politician who wraps themselves in national colors while betraying the principles the colors are meant to represent. It is the citizen who confuses "loyalty to power" with "loyalty to principle," and in this way, false patriotism serves as a shield for corruption, and silences those who demand accountability.

True patriotism, by contrast, demands courage. It requires questioning authority, even when doing so is unpopular. It requires sacrifice, not in empty gestures but in the willingness to engage with uncomfortable truths, and it requires a love of country strong enough to confront its flaws rather than deny them.

THE FOUNDERS' PATRIOTISM

The American Revolution was not led by conformists but by dissenters. Thomas Jefferson, in the Declaration of Independence, affirmed the right of the people "to alter or to abolish" a government destructive of their rights.[3]

This was not a rejection of patriotism, but its highest expression. George Washington warned against blind allegiance in his Farewell Address, urging citizens to remain vigilant against government overreach—a concept modern scholars have characterized as opposing 'unthinking loyalty.'[4]

James Madison echoed the same idea when he declared that "the advancement and diffusion of knowledge is the only guardian of true liberty."[5]

Patriotism, for the founders, required not passive acceptance but active engagement. It demanded that citizens remain informed and ready to hold leaders accountable.

Consider Thomas Paine, whose pamphlet "Common Sense" galvanized colonial resistance. He didn't shy away from criticizing the government, and he argued boldly that the people had a duty to reject tyranny in all forms.

"Government," Paine wrote, "even in its best state, is but a necessary evil; in its worst state, an intolerable one."[6] His words reveal that the founders' conception of patriotism was never blind loyalty but principled resistance.

PATRIOTISM VS. NATIONALISM

Confusion often arises when patriotism is conflated with nationalism. Though the two are related, they are not the same.

Patriotism is devotion to principles: liberty, justice, equality before the law. Nationalism is devotion to power: loyalty to the party or the nation-state above all else, often regardless of whether it honors those principles.

The patriot says: "I love my country because it seeks to uphold truth and justice."

The nationalist says: "My country is always right, even when it commits injustice. My country right or wrong! Love it or leave it!"

This difference is critical. Nationalism demands silence in the face of wrongdoing; patriotism demands accountability.

The twentieth century offers abundant warnings about what happens when nationalism overtakes patriotism: authoritarian regimes, wars of aggression, and suppression of dissent.[7] We'll explore examples of these later in this book.

Nationalism places the privilege of a few above the principles of democracy for all. President Dwight D. Eisenhower observed this thread early in America and warned, "A people that values its privileges above its principles soon loses both."[8]

Contrasting nationalism, patriotism values accountability over comfort, principle over power, and insists that justice applies to all.

PATRIOTISM AND ACCOUNTABILITY

To be a patriot is to accept responsibility. Citizens cannot love their country by ignoring its failures. They love their country by insisting it live up to its highest ideals.

Abraham Lincoln reminded Americans during the Civil War that the Union's cause was not merely survival, but an opportunity ". . . for us the living, rather, to be dedicated here to the unfinished work which they who fought here have thus far so nobly advanced. . ."[9] Those phrases, and quite candidly the entire Gettysburg Address, captures the essence of true patriotism: progress toward principles, not preservation of power.

This accountability requires courage. It is easier to wave a flag than to confront injustice. It is easier to shout slogans than to demand reform, but empty displays of loyalty are not patriotism; they are theater. True patriotism requires sacrifice, not of conscience, but of comfort. It asks citizens to do the difficult work of engaging, questioning, and, when necessary, resisting.

Early proponents of democracy recognized this duty. As Wendell Phillips observed in 1852, "Eternal vigilance is the price of liberty," reflecting the founders' belief that citizens must remain actively engaged.[10] Vigilance does not mean paranoia or suspicion but an active, engaged citizenry willing to challenge authority when it strays from principle.

In this sense, patriotism is not passive emotion but active responsibility.

PATRIOTISM IN MODERN AMERICA

In modern America, patriotism is too often reduced to symbols. Wearing a pin, standing for an anthem, or echoing political slogans has replaced the hard work of holding leaders accountable.

That is not patriotism. That is performance. Symbols matter, but without substance, they are hollow.

After September 11, 2001, America witnessed a surge of symbolic patriotism. Flags flew from every porch, and unity was palpable. Yet that moment also revealed the dangers of confusing symbolism with substance. In the name of "patriotism," policies were enacted that eroded civil liberties, launched wars under questionable pretenses, and silenced critics as "un-American."[11]

That was not patriotism. That was nationalism cloaked in patriotic language. True patriotism would have demanded both security and liberty, both strength and accountability.

To love America is to love its principles more than its power. It is to insist that justice applies to all, that liberty cannot be selective, and that equality under the law is not negotiable. It is to use America's power for good for everyone, not just a select few.

When politicians equate patriotism with obedience, they invert its meaning. A silent citizenry is not patriotic; it is complicit.

Patriotism without accountability is nationalism, and nationalism has no place in a republic built on liberty.

The highest form of loyalty is not loyalty to power or a person, but loyalty to principle. That is the patriot's duty. That is America's unfinished work to which Lincoln referred.

I question what our government is doing because I want to hold them accountable to the principles on which this country was founded and which I fought to defend. The government represents me. When our country does something, as a patriot, I know that I am responsible. You cannot be a patriot if you are uninformed, if you put party or person over country, or you disagree with what the country is doing, but don't take action to correct it, or you try to divorce yourself from the country by saying or thinking "well, that is the country, not me."

CHAPTER RECAP – PATRIOTISM OR PERFORMANCE?

This chapter unraveled the **Patriotism Bubble**, showing how a word meant to inspire unity and accountability has been twisted into a tool of division and silence. Too often, patriotism is reduced to flags, slogans, and unquestioning loyalty, while true devotion to country—the kind practiced by abolitionists, suffragists, civil rights leaders, and even the Founders themselves—requires vigilance, dissent, and sacrifice. The difference between patriotism and nationalism is not academic; it is the difference between a republic that can self-correct and an empire that collapses under its own delusions.

True patriotism demands that citizens remain informed, engaged, and courageous enough to challenge their leaders when principles are betrayed. False patriotism demands conformity and punishes dissent. Which one we choose will define America's future.

With this foundation set, the next chapters move from the patriotic illusion to the **Information Bubble**, where the way we see the world—and even how we define truth—is filtered, framed, and manipulated. Understanding how information is controlled is the next step toward reclaiming genuine patriotism rooted in knowledge, not performance.

CHAPTER 3:
THE INFORMATION BUBBLE:
INTRODUCTION

There is an old parable about a group of blind men and an elephant. It goes like this:

A group of blind men heard that a strange animal, called an elephant, had been brought to the town, but none of them were aware of its shape and form. Out of curiosity, they said: "We must inspect and know it by touch, of which we are capable." So, they sought it out, and when they found it, they groped about it. The first person, whose hand landed on the trunk, said, "This being is like a thick snake." For another one whose hand reached its ear, it seemed like a kind of fan. As for another person, whose hand was upon its leg, said, the elephant is a pillar like a tree-trunk. The blind man who placed his hand upon its side said the elephant, "is a wall." Another who felt its tail, described it as a rope. The last felt its tusk, stating the elephant is that which is hard, smooth and like a spear.

What each man described was both true and false. It was true to a degree but since it didn't describe the whole animal it was false in total.

This is a simple example of why people may disagree on events. Each person believes that they know the truth and that the other person is mistaken, and each believes this based on facts that they believe can't be questioned. But each person's view of "the truth" is different because although it is based on facts, it's based on a subset of all of the facts. Because of this we get into weird discussions of "facts" and "alternative facts." "Alternative facts" is just a way of saying "facts that aren't included in the original analysis." A fact is a fact. The truth is comprised of all available facts, and even then "the truth" is subject to framing and interpretation, as we'll discuss later.

HOW PERCEPTION SHAPES REALITY

Each of us perceives and communicates information in different ways based on our experience, knowledge, emotions, and biases. Let's look at a simple example so that we can understand what I'm talking about:

Imagine standing in the same place at the same time with two other people watching a sunrise, and all three of you wrote down what you saw. The three of you might write something like:

1. I saw a beautiful sunrise displaying God's majesty.

2. The sun didn't rise. The earth rotated and slowly revealed the sun.

3. While enjoying the cool morning, I was blinded by the ridiculously bright sun.

Each of these statements is factual and true, but they leave the reader with completely different impressions and feelings about the event.

This demonstrates one way that information can be distorted. By funneling people's attention toward specific aspects of an event and using emotional expressions while suppressing or omitting other aspects, one can manipulate perception without ever lying outright.

When an authority or media outlet chooses to emphasize certain details while ignoring or downplaying others, they create **a curated version of reality.** The version of reality that they present might be technically correct, but it's no longer whole. Like a photo cropped to hide what's outside the frame, the story becomes biased not by fabrication, but by **strategic omission**. By doing this on a national scale, a nation's view of the world can be narrowed, distorted, and ultimately controlled.

THE ROLE OF BIAS AND SUBJECTIVITY

Subjectivity plays a powerful role as well. Every piece of information we consume has already passed through someone else's lens—the journalist, the anchor, the editor, the headline writer, or the application algorithm. Personal beliefs, institutional loyalties, political affiliations, and corporate and unconscious biases all affect what gets emphasized and what gets ignored.

An unconscious bias is a hidden assumption, stereotype, or mental shortcuts we use in our brain to shape how we interpret people, events, and information.[1] It's subconscious and we aren't directly aware of it. These biases work silently in the background, filtering what we notice, how we weigh evidence, and which perspectives we give more credibility to. The harm comes from the fact that, when left unexamined, unconscious bias narrows our field of vision. We see patterns that confirm what we already believe (confirmation bias), we dismiss inconvenient details that challenge the narrative we believe, and we unconsciously favor narratives that feel familiar or comfortable to us. This distorts our understanding of an event or topic because what we think we know becomes less about objective truth, and more about our blind spots that we never bothered to notice.

Two news outlets may report on the same bombing, the same protest, or the same policy decision, but through selective framing, tone, and focus, they can lead the audience to entirely different conclusions. In the same way three people can describe the same sunrise in wildly different ways, media presenters can describe the same event as a triumph, a tragedy, or a threat depending on the agenda they serve.

THE MECHANICS OF INFORMATION CONTROL

What makes this curation of information so dangerous is that the audience usually doesn't realize that they're being guided. Omitted facts don't announce their absence. Framing doesn't come with warning labels, and subjective language often hides behind an illusion of objectivity. This is how information control and opinion shaping works, not by banning information outright, but by **saturating citizens with selective truths** until they forget what balanced information even feels like. It's not about forcing belief but about **limiting the range of acceptable belief** so that people are manipulated to "choose" the sanctioned narrative themselves. And once the boundaries of belief are set, control of opinion and approval of action don't require violence, it just needs repetition.

Psychologists use a number of terms to refer to the intentional shaping of opinion, beliefs, and behaviors, including: "Behavioral Conditioning," "Psychological Manipulation," "Social Engineering," "Narrative Control," and of course, "Propaganda," and "Indoctrination."[2,3] Regardless of the label or the specific method, shaping opinions and beliefs typically follow some well-documented steps.

The first step to effectively manipulate another person's beliefs, attitudes, and opinions is isolation.[4] That doesn't mean that the person needs to be physically isolated (although that often makes it easier); it means that they must be mentally isolated. They need to get their information from highly curated sources that support the desired narrative. Any opposing ideas need to be immediately discredited, ridiculed, and diminished, by force if necessary. The United States by its very geography is isolated from the rest of the world, and now with most of the information we receive being filtered specifically for each of us individually by algorithms, especially through social media, we isolate ourselves, or at the very least allow ourselves to be isolated without dissent.

After isolation, the subject needs to be conditioned through the twin concepts of **repetition** and **cognitive overload.** The subject needs to be relentlessly exposed to the same messages and slogans while simultaneously being overloaded with information so they don't have the time to effectively analyze what they are being told. **Over time, repetition creates familiarity, and over even more time, familiarity feels like the truth.** We will examine this in more detail in the next chapter.

Herbert A. Simon, an economist and Nobel Laureate, concisely summed up how repetition and cognitive overload affect the individual:

> "What information consumes is rather obvious: it consumes the attention of its recipients. Hence a wealth of information creates a poverty of attention and a need to allocate that attention efficiently among the overabundance of information sources that might consume it."5

And if people aren't paying attention, the human brain readily accepts whatever information is presented with little question.

After the isolation and repetition, all that is left is **Conditional Love and Reward, and Maintenance and Reinforcement.** If the subject repeats the desired message, they are rewarded. If they reject the message, they are framed as disloyal, ignorant, or traitorous. Most of us have seen this kind of activity in the news.

HISTORICAL EXAMPLES OF INFORMATION MANIPULATION

In this context, the opinion or position of a person doesn't matter as much as the environment in which they are expressing that opinion or position. In the United States, we vote for new administrations every four years. As the administration changes, so does the environment and consequently how a message is received. The exact same message will be praised by one group and then derided by the other.

Historical examples demonstrate this pattern clearly. When Colin Kaepernick first knelt during the national anthem to protest police brutality, he was widely vilified by media outlets and political commentators as unpatriotic during the 2016–2020 administration.[6] Yet only a few years later, during the 2020–2024 administration, the same act was widely praised as courageous and principled, with public officials, corporations, and even the National Football League acknowledging that he had been right to speak out.[7] Similarly, when the Pentagon Papers—classified documents exposing years of government deception about the Vietnam War—were first published in 1971, government officials denounced their release as treasonous and even sought to block their publication.[8] But after the New York Times Co. v. United States Supreme Court ruling upheld the right to publish them, they came to be celebrated as a landmark of investigative journalism and press freedom.[9] This shows that it is often not the content of a message that determines how it is received, but the political environment in which it is delivered.

CHAPTER RECAP — FRAMING OUR PERCEPTION

This chapter introduced the concept of the information bubble by showing how perception shapes reality. Through parables, examples, and historical cases, we saw that truth is rarely a complete picture. Instead, it is filtered by experience, bias, omission, and strategic framing. Media outlets, political leaders, and even algorithms curate what we see and how we interpret it, not by inventing lies, but by presenting partial truths that feel whole. When facts are emphasized selectively, when bias hides in headlines, and when repetition turns familiarity into "truth," perception itself becomes a tool of control.

This chapter established the groundwork: reality as presented to us is never neutral, it is always filtered. The mechanisms may be subtle, but their consequences are profound. With this foundation in place, we now turn to the next step, understanding the specific manipulation techniques that power the information bubble and keep entire societies within its grip.

CHAPTER 4:

THE INFORMATION BUBBLE:

MANIPULATION

Understanding how information is manipulated requires examining the specific tools used to shape perception. Three techniques stand out for their effectiveness and widespread use: omission of facts, framing and language, and repetition of key messages. Each works differently, but together they form a powerful arsenal for controlling public opinion.

OMISSION OF FACTS

What you don't know *can* hurt you or control you. By omitting critical facts, an incomplete narrative becomes the only narrative, and it can be just as powerful as outright lies when it comes to shaping perception. By selectively presenting only certain details while leaving out others, a communicator can construct a version of reality that feels truthful but is fundamentally distorted. This manipulation is often subtle, making it difficult for the audience to recognize that anything is missing.

For example, reporting on a protest without mentioning the reason behind the protest can frame participants as unruly rather than standing up for high principles, or reporting that country "B" attacked country "A" without mentioning that country "A" had previously attacked country "B" multiple times thus framing country "B" as the aggressor.

Leaving out context, contradictions, or consequences limits the listener's ability to form a complete understanding, allowing the presenter to steer opinion while appearing neutral. In this way, omission becomes a tool for quiet control, crafting a partial truth that conceals the full picture.

For example:

- In the lead-up to the **Iraq War**, intelligence agencies from multiple countries, including the U.S., Britain, and Israel, shared similar flawed assessments about Iraq's weapons of mass destruction capabilities.[1] Media coverage emphasized these intelligence claims while giving insufficient attention to dissenting voices and weapons inspectors who questioned the evidence. The omission of skeptical analysis helped create widespread public support for the war.

- During the **Cold War**, Americans heard endless stories about the evils of communism, but little about U.S.-backed coups, embargoes, or the exploitation of other nations happening at the same time.

- In 2021, initial media reports described Border Patrol agents as "whipping" Haitian migrants, based on photographs that appeared to show whips but were actually horse reins. While major outlets later issued corrections when investigations found no evidence of whipping, the initial framing dominated the news cycle.[2]

Omitting facts is a form of dishonesty, but because the public doesn't know what is missing, they accept what is presented as the truth. This is why knowledge is so important. Only when you know the whole story can you tell when someone is leaving parts out.

FRAMING AND LANGUAGE

The way information is presented matters as much as the information itself. Words carry weight. Consider the difference between these two statements:

- "Protesters are fighting for democracy."
- "Rioters are threatening national stability."

The event may be the same, but the framing changes everything. Governments and media frequently use language to shape public perception:

- A "coup" becomes a "regime change."

- "Bombing campaigns" are labeled as "defensive operations."

- Opposing voices are dismissed as "radicals," "terrorists," or "foreign agents."

- The reporting side's soldiers are "murdered" while opposition side's just "died" or "were eliminated."

- The reporting side's citizens and soldiers captured by the opposition are "hostages" while the opposition's citizens and soldiers they capture are "detainees."

This last point may seem irrelevant to some, "Tomato, Tomahto," but words really do matter. "Hostages" implies civilians or soldiers taken by a militant, terrorist, or criminal group to coerce political action, while "detainee" refers to any person deprived of their liberty by a government, military, or police force. By using the different words, the legitimacy or illegitimacy of a group is implied.

There is a wonderful joke that demonstrates this perfectly:

When a visitor to a town in Alabama spotted a dog attacking a boy, he grabbed the animal, pulled it off the child, and in order to save the child, ended up killing the attacking dog with his bare hands.

A local reporter witnessed the entire event and told the visitor that the next day's headline would scream **"Valiant Local Man Saves Child by Killing Vicious Animal."**

"I'm not from this town," the visitor said.

"Then," the reporter said, "it will say **'Alabama Man Saves Child by Killing Dog.'"**

"Actually," said the man, "I'm from New Hampshire."

"In that case," the reporter grumbled, "the headline will be **'Yankee Kills Family Pet.'"**

By controlling language, institutions shape public perception and influence both how people interpret events and how they react to them.

REPETITION OF KEY MESSAGES

Whether in a propaganda playbook or a corporate sales manual, **repetition is a core tactic** for shaping beliefs and driving behavior. Repeating a message, especially when the same message is delivered through multiple channels, makes the message more familiar, more believable, and eventually, more accepted. Psychologists refer to this as the "illusory truth effect,"[3] where repeated statements are more likely to be perceived as true, even if they're false. In high-pressure persuasion environments, from cults to political campaigns to marketing funnels, repetition is used to wear down resistance, reinforce desired narratives, and create emotional associations. It isn't always about logic or evidence but about **embedding the message so deeply** that it becomes second nature, something you feel rather than question.

Politicians, advertisers, and propagandists have mastered this technique.

- During the 2003 Iraq War, Americans were bombarded with the phrase **"Saddam has WMDs"**. The repetition was so relentless that, even years later, some Americans still believed Iraq had weapons of mass destruction.

- During the COVID-19 pandemic, false claims that **"Vaccines contain microchips for government tracking"** spread repeatedly through social media. Despite overwhelming scientific evidence to the contrary, surveys indicated that a significant portion of the population believed these claims.[4]

- Hitler was portrayed as the only man who could restore German greatness. Phrases like *"Ein Volk, ein Reich, ein Führer"* (**"One people, one empire, one leader"**) were repeated endlessly to unify national identity under Hitler's authoritarian figure.

- In Maoist China during "The Cultural Revolution," citizens were required to memorize and recite quotes every day from Mao's "Quotations of Chairman Mao" (also known as "The Little Red Book"). Posters, songs, and public events constantly repeated Maoist slogans like *"Serve the People"* and *"The East is Red."*

- The U.S. Military Psychological Operations Field Manual (*specifically FM 3-05.301 Psychological Operations Process Tactics, Techniques, and Procedures*)[5] recommends repetition of consistent messages through leaflets, broadcasts, and influencers to reinforce desired attitudes or behaviors in target populations.

- David Ogilvy, in *Ogilvy on Advertising*, emphasizes "branding through consistent repetition" of slogans, colors, and benefits.[6]

- Robert Cialdini, in his book *Influence*, highlights "consistency and commitment"—where repeated exposure leads people to internalize ideas and act on them.[7]

Repetition works because the human brain craves certainty. Familiar ideas feel safe, true, and reliable. New or conflicting information feels uncomfortable. This works even better if the message is repeated by different sources.

The power of repetition in propaganda was well understood by Nazi leaders, though the specific techniques they employed have often been misrepresented in popular culture. The concept of the "big lie" was actually first described by Hitler in *Mein Kampf*, not as a technique he advocated, but as something he accused his enemies of using.[8]

CHAPTER RECAP - TOOLS OF MANIPULATION

This chapter mapped the core tactics that turn partial truths into public consensus. First, omission trims away context, contradictions, and causes, leaving a clean, persuasive fragment that feels complete. Second, framing and language load the dice, where "protester" becomes "rioter," "coup" becomes "regime change," and the same event can be praised or condemned depending on the chosen words. Third, repetition makes familiarity feel like truth through the illusory truth effect, as slogans and talking points echo across platforms.

Across examples, from Iraq War messaging to pandemic claims, from advertising playbooks to military manuals, the pattern holds: repeat, simplify, saturate, and let emotion do the rest. Audiences seldom see what went missing, and bias hides inside neutral-sounding headlines, anchors, and algorithms. The result is consent shaped by selection, tone, and the drumbeat of sameness rather than by balanced evidence.

With the mechanics clear, Chapter 5, "Controlling Information", follows the pipeline back to its source: how gatekeepers control access, consolidate media, rebrand news as entertainment, and deploy labels like "conspiracy theory" to police the boundaries of acceptable belief.

CHAPTER 5:

THE INFORMATION BUBBLE:

CONTROL

Understanding how information is controlled requires examining three levels: direct source control, corporate consolidation, and rhetorical dismissal. Each operates differently but serves the same purpose—limiting what enters public discourse and how it's interpreted.

CONTROLLING SOURCES OF INFORMATION

When all available information comes from a single source, or sources that echo the same message, people's beliefs become uniform.

For example:

- The North Korean government restricts citizens to only state-run media. The government decides what people see, hear, and know. Internet access is **banned** for the general public; instead, a closed intranet called "Kwangmyong" is used.[1] Citizens are taught to worship the Kim family, and possession of foreign media (especially South Korean) may be punishable by death.

- In China, a vast system of online censorship and surveillance, dubbed the **Great Firewall**, is maintained to control information. Topics like Tiananmen Square, Uyghur genocide, or Taiwan independence are heavily censored. Foreign social media platforms (e.g., Twitter, Facebook, Google) are banned, and domestic equivalents are monitored.[2]

- The British passed laws like the Vernacular Press Act (1878)[3] in India to suppress local-language newspapers critical of colonial rule. Anti-colonial leaders and writers were arrested or exiled for publishing "seditious" material.

- Israel maintains a **military censor** that reviews security-related stories before publication. In 2024, the censor completely banned 1,635 articles and partially redacted 6,265 others. Foreign journalists operating in Israel must obtain press credentials and agree to censorship rules.[4] Major news outlets, including CNN, have developed internal review processes for Israel-Palestine coverage, routing stories through Jerusalem-based teams that operate under these constraints.[5]

- In Saudi Arabia all media is state controlled; criticism of the royal family or Islam is criminalized. Social media users, journalists, and activists (e.g., Jamal Khashoggi) have been imprisoned or killed. Foreign media is filtered or blocked entirely.[6]

Even in democracies, the illusion of choice can be manufactured through media conglomeration. In the United States, thousands of media outlets appear diverse, yet ownership is highly concentrated. As of the mid-2020s, just a few large corporations dominate most major news platforms:

- Nexstar Media Group, Sinclair Broadcast Group, and Gray Television collectively control nearly 40% of all local TV stations in the country, reaching the majority of U.S. households[7].

- In print media, the top 25 newspaper chains employ about 40% of all U.S. print and digital journalists, with chains like Gannett and Lee Enterprises owning hundreds of local newspapers[8] [9].

This consolidation allows a small number of corporate gatekeepers to shape much of the national narrative, often marginalizing dissenting or local voices despite the appearance of abundant choice.

AMERICAN ~~NEWS~~ ENTERTAINMENT

When a handful of corporations control what we see, hear, and read, the incentive shifts. News becomes a product, and we, the public, become the commodity. The goal is no longer to inform but to attract eyeballs, hold attention, and sell that attention to advertisers. Truth, in this model, is incidental. Accuracy and depth take a backseat to whatever keeps people clicking and scrolling. When you begin to understand that, you also begin to see why certain stories are told endlessly, while others vanish without a whisper.

It is important to understand that these companies are not in the business of informing you; they are in the business of holding your gaze. If a story happens to tell you something useful along the way, that is incidental. The real commodity is your attention, packaged and sold to advertisers at the highest possible price. Newsrooms are forced to serve two masters: the public's right to know and Wall Street's demand for growth. One of those masters is always fed. The other gets the scraps.

A democracy cannot thrive on information designed to be addictive rather than enlightening. And yet that is exactly where we find ourselves: a media environment optimized for outrage and fear, stripped of nuance, because that's what sells. It is a model that feeds on division and ignorance, even as it pretends to inform. We should not mistake this for a public service. It is, at its core, a sales pitch disguised as news, and it is eroding the very foundation of an informed Republic.

Let's look at two shows on television and online that are on opposite sides of the political spectrum and claim to be providing Americans with "the truth." Those, of course, would be Fox News on the right, and MSNBC on the left.

Fox News built its empire by declaring itself the antidote to "liberal media," and for millions of conservatives it became the only voice they trust. Daytime programming wears a neutral mask, but the network's prime-time stars—Hannity, Ingraham, and others—shape the conversation with opinion disguised as fact. Behind the scenes, even the hosts acknowledge this. The Dominion Voting Systems lawsuit revealed internal communications where network personalities privately contradicted claims they were making on-air about election fraud. When sued, Fox didn't argue "we told the truth." Instead, it argued that no one should expect these shows to be factual at all, with their own lawyers calling them "hyperbolic" and "entertainment."[10]

MSNBC is the mirror image from the other side of the aisle. It is the network liberals love to trust. Like Fox, it packages information for entertainment and loyalty, not depth or accuracy. Prime-time personalities—Maddow, O'Donnell, Reid—speak to progressive concerns with a similar formula: a narrow selection of stories framed to confirm their audience's worldview. MSNBC doesn't have the same market dominance Fox enjoys, but it uses the same structure: a thin veneer of daytime "news" followed by evening blocks that are mostly opinion.

Together, these two channels are not simply reporting on America's political divide; they are creating it and deepening it. They thrive on outrage because outrage keeps viewers engaged. They package ideology as journalism and callously let truth become a casualty in the chase for ad dollars and market share. Their defenders will say that they are just reflecting what the audience wants. That might be true, but that is precisely the problem. When news organizations are driven by ratings and profit instead of curiosity and truth, democracy itself becomes the collateral damage.

"CONSPIRACY THEORY": THE EASIEST WAY TO BURY THE TRUTH

We've been conditioned to tune out certain phrases. Say the words **"conspiracy theory"** and watch how quickly minds shut down. Eyes roll. Ears close. The phrase has become a rhetorical kill switch, an easy way to discredit uncomfortable facts before they're even examined. You don't have to prove the claim wrong. You just have to label it.

But what if that instinct to dismiss, to scoff, to ridicule, is part of the very conditioning the term was designed to create? If a fact threatens power, but can't be disproven, the next best strategy is to brand it delusional. A fringe fantasy. A danger to "national security." We aren't encouraged to investigate truth. We're encouraged to feel, especially fear, ridicule, or scorn, and then walk away.

Most of us frequently encounter these conversation enders or "Thought terminating cliches," but we don't think of them as being used to stop the conversation. Some of the phrases that have this effect are: "Conspiracy Theory," "Antisemitic," "Sexist," "Anti-American," "Foreign Agent," "Fake News," "Radical," "Extremist," or "Fringe."

Consider just a few examples that were once widely written off as baseless conspiracy theories, until they weren't:

- **COINTELPRO** (FBI Surveillance of Civil Rights Leaders)[11] Civil rights leaders like Martin Luther King Jr. and Malcolm X were often accused of paranoia for claiming that the government was surveilling them. Turns out, they were right. In 1971, antiwar activists broke into an FBI office in Media, Pennsylvania, and discovered classified documents exposing COINTELPRO—a covert FBI operation designed to infiltrate, disrupt, and discredit civil rights and anti-war groups across the country.

- **MK-Ultra** (CIA Mind Control Experiments)[12] For decades, rumors swirled that the CIA was conducting secret mind control experiments on American citizens using drugs like LSD. The idea sounded like science fiction. But in 1975, the Church Committee hearings and Freedom of Information Act requests unearthed thousands of CIA documents proving MK-Ultra was real. The program involved illegal and unethical testing on unwitting people, including U.S. citizens and Canadian psychiatric patients.

- **The Tuskegee Syphilis Study**[13] Between 1932 and 1972, nearly 400 Black men in Alabama were told they were being treated for "bad blood." In truth, the U.S. Public Health Service was observing the progression of untreated syphilis in these men while deliberately withholding treatment. When the story was first whispered, it was dismissed as inflammatory nonsense. But in 1972, a whistleblower leaked proof to the press, and the horrifying truth was confirmed.

- **NSA Mass Surveillance** (Revealed by Edward Snowden)[14] Before 2013, the idea that the U.S. government was spying on its own citizens at scale was mostly relegated to the realm of conspiracy theorists. Then Edward Snowden leaked thousands of classified documents proving that the NSA was collecting phone metadata and internet activity from millions of Americans, often illegally and without warrants. What had been mockable speculation became undeniable fact.

These aren't anomalies. They're patterns. And they remind us that skepticism of power isn't paranoia, it's survival. The only way a lie persists is if no one's willing to challenge it. When a fact is uncomfortable, disruptive, or embarrassing to those in charge, it will almost always be labeled a "conspiracy theory," "fake news," or "anti-American" before it's ever honestly debated.

As you continue reading this book, I challenge you to pause when you feel a reflexive dismissal. Ask yourself: Why do I feel that way? Who benefits from me shutting this down? Then go look. Truth doesn't fear inspection. Lies do.

CHAPTER RECAP — CONTROLLING THE NARRATIVE

This chapter revealed how power is maintained not only by shaping messages but by limiting access to competing voices. From North Korea's closed networks to America's concentrated media giants, we saw how gatekeepers curate what enters public consciousness. The control does not always come through overt censorship, but often through the commodification of news itself, where entertainment and profit take precedence over accuracy and depth. In this system, truth is whatever keeps viewers watching, advertisers buying, and dissent minimalized.

We also examined how labels such as "conspiracy theory" or "fake news" operate as rhetorical kill switches, silencing uncomfortable facts before they can be weighed. What was once dismissed as fringe paranoia—COINTELPRO, MK-Ultra, Tuskegee, NSA surveillance—later emerged as documented reality. The lesson is clear: information control thrives not on proving lies true, but on teaching us which truths to ignore.

As we move forward, the next chapter, *Illusions of Choice*, explores the digital age where algorithms, psychology, and the illusion of free thought create a subtler but no less powerful cage, one in which we believe we are choosing freely while our choices are being engineered for us.

CHAPTER 6:

THE INFORMATION BUBBLE:

ILLUSIONS

Understanding modern information control requires examining how choice itself becomes an illusion. Rather than banning information outright, sophisticated systems create the appearance of free selection while carefully constraining what options are available. This occurs through three interconnected mechanisms: algorithmic curation, psychological manipulation, and consequences for dissent.

THE DIGITAL AGE: ALGORITHMS AND THE NEW INFORMATION GATEKEEPERS

Most people assume that what they see online is a reflection of the world, but in truth, it's a reflection of what the algorithm wants them to see. Social media platforms like Facebook, YouTube, TikTok, and X (formerly Twitter) use complex algorithms designed to maximize engagement, not accuracy or balance. These algorithms track every click, share, pause, like, and comment, then feed users more of what they're likely to respond to.[1]

This means if a person watches one video critical of a political figure or issue, the algorithm will likely serve them similar content, over and over, regardless of whether the content is factual, biased, or inflammatory. If they watch two or three videos similar to the first, the algorithm strengthens their bias for this type of video and starts to provide similar videos as a greater and greater percentage of their overall viewing. The algorithms are constantly evaluating what videos you watch or what news you read, how long you spend on that article or video, and modify the next video you see or article you read based on that analysis.

These algorithms exist for a simple reason: profit. The longer users stay on a platform, the more ads they see, and the more data they generate, the more advertising they can sell. Algorithms are engineered to exploit emotional reactions, especially outrage, fear, and tribal identity, because these emotions drive more engagement than reasoned discussion. Content that provokes strong feelings is more likely to be clicked, shared, and commented on, so the algorithm prioritizes it. This creates a feedback loop where extreme or sensational content is rewarded, while moderate, nuanced, or balanced views are buried.

The result is that each user lives in a **personalized information bubble**, curated by invisible systems they don't control or even fully understand. Someone with a conservative lean might be pushed deeper into nationalist or anti-globalist content, while a progressive user may be fed constant reminders of systemic injustice or political hypocrisy. Over time, the user starts to believe that their view is not only correct, but widely shared, because everything they see seems to confirm it. Contradictory perspectives become rare, suspect, or completely absent. This can radically distort how people perceive global politics, making foreign nations seem more threatening, allies more untrustworthy, or certain conflicts more clear-cut than they really are.

Perhaps most dangerously, algorithmic filtering gives the illusion of being informed, while narrowing the scope of awareness. Complex geopolitical realities, like the nuances of the Israel-Palestine conflict, U.S. interventions abroad, or the motivations behind economic sanctions, are often reduced to emotionally charged memes, sound bites, or cherry-picked headlines. Users may never encounter the full context or alternative viewpoints, not because they are censored, but because the algorithm deems them less clickable. In this way, algorithms don't just show us what we like, they shape what we believe, and by extension, how we vote, whom we trust, and what kind of world we think we're living in.

WHY INFORMATION CONTROL WORKS: THE PSYCHOLOGY OF TRUST

Digital algorithms succeed because they exploit fundamental aspects of human psychology. Understanding these psychological shortcuts helps explain why even well-intentioned people can be systematically misled about complex issues.

Why do people trust certain sources of information? It often comes down to three psychological shortcuts: authority, consistency, and social proof.

1. **Authority:** We tend to believe experts, leaders, and institutions, even when they lie.

2. **Consistency:** Repeated messages feel reliable, regardless of accuracy.

3. **Social proof:** If everyone around us believes something, we are more likely to believe it is true.

These cognitive biases are deeply rooted in how humans assess truth in uncertain environments. We instinctively believe figures of authority, experts, leaders, and institutions, because, historically, doing so improved our chance for survival. Similarly, when we hear the same message repeatedly, we tend to believe it is more reliable—the *illusory truth effect* we discussed above. And when the people around us believe something, we often adopt the same belief, not because we've critically assessed it, but because we fear social exclusion or assume the group must know something we don't.

Each of these tendencies reflects a logical fallacy when misapplied: *appeal to authority*, *argumentum ad populum* (appeal to the majority), and *repetition bias* are not evidence of truth, they're evidence of influence. In formal logic, truth is independent of the source, frequency, or popularity of a claim. A proposition is either true or false based on its relationship with reality, not who says it, how often it's said, or how many people believe it. Yet, these logical missteps are routinely and intentionally exploited. Media outlets, politicians, and influencers use repetition to build trust, present themselves as authorities, and highlight social consensus to manufacture legitimacy.

Those who shape information understand these weaknesses and use them strategically. A government-controlled news outlet, a charismatic leader, or a viral campaign doesn't need to lie outright, they simply need to present selected truths with confident authority, repeat them often, and show the masses agreeing. This combination is powerful enough to override critical thinking, especially when the population is stressed, afraid, or distracted.

In these conditions, people don't evaluate claims, they *absorb narratives*. And once a narrative is embedded through authority, consistency, and social proof, even contradictory evidence can be ignored or dismissed.

THE ILLUSION OF FREE THOUGHT

The most effective form of control is when people believe they are acting of their own free will. Information control achieves this not by demanding obedience, but by shaping the boundaries of perception, guiding people to certain conclusions while giving them the illusion of independent thought. When people feel they've come to a decision on their own, whether it's supporting a war, distrusting a movement, or condemning a whistleblower, they are more likely to defend that belief and reject alternative views. This is not coercion in the traditional sense. It's **manufactured consent**, where public opinion is shaped through curated facts, filtered narratives, and emotional appeals.

Consider the Iraq War example again. Millions of Americans supported the 2003 invasion not because they were coerced, but because they believed Saddam Hussein had weapons of mass destruction. They were shown maps, satellite images, and confident testimony from top officials. Major media outlets echoed these claims, rarely challenging the intelligence. As a result, Americans felt they were making an informed, rational choice. But that choice was made inside a bubble of carefully selected and incomplete information. When the truth came out, that the WMDs didn't exist and that intelligence had been manipulated or misrepresented, many people struggled to reconcile the betrayal. Some refused to believe it at all.

This illusion of free thought is dangerous because it feels empowering. People defend their views passionately, often unaware that those views were seeded by external forces through repetition, authority, and group consensus. When individuals believe they've independently reached a conclusion, they become more resistant to correction. This makes opinion-based control far more effective than force. It doesn't spark rebellion. It creates loyal defenders of the very system that misled them.

THE COST OF DISSENT

When someone does break from the accepted narrative, the system often responds not with debate, but with exclusion. In the United States, there have been multiple instances where civil liberties were restricted or access to the country was denied based solely on a person's political beliefs or opinions. These responses serve not only to punish dissent but also to discourage others from straying outside the approved boundaries of discourse, for example:

- **Ismail Ajjawi (2019):** A Palestinian student admitted to Harvard was denied entry to the U.S. after customs officials searched his phone and found political posts critical of the U.S. on his contacts' social media feeds. Ajjawi himself had not posted them. After eight hours of detention and interrogation about his religious practices, his visa was revoked. He was eventually admitted after widespread publicity and legal intervention.[2]

- **James Dyer (2018):** The British journalist reported being subjected to questioning by a U.S. Customs and Border Protection agent while entering the United States, who asked if he was part of the "fake news media" after seeing his journalist visa—highlighting the scrutiny journalists can face when traveling to the U.S.[3]

- **Norman Finkelstein:** A Jewish academic known for his critiques of Israeli policy and U.S. complicity was effectively blacklisted from academia and faced significant travel restrictions, including being banned from entering Israel for 10 years.[4]

- **U.S.–Mexico Border Database (2019):** Documents leaked to NBC 7 San Diego revealed that U.S. authorities created a secret database of nearly 60 individuals, including about 10 journalists, covering migrant caravans. These journalists were flagged for heightened screening at border crossings, with some subjected to secondary inspections, interrogations, and even temporary detentions. The database included their photos, personal details, and notes about their reporting activity, highlighting how constitutionally protected journalism can be treated as suspicious activity by government agencies.[5]

- **Edward Snowden and Chelsea Manning:** While their cases involved the illegal release of classified material, the intensity of legal action and public condemnation they endured was shaped heavily by narrative framing. Almost no attention was given to the activity they exposed. The focus stayed on their actions, not the events that led to their actions.[6]

- One of the most concerning examples of this is **The Canary Mission.** The Canary Mission is a controversial online blacklist that profiles and publishes detailed dossiers on students, academics, and activists, primarily those critical of Israel or those in support of Palestinian rights. It operates anonymously and has been linked to efforts that harm individuals' careers and reputations, often without recourse.[7]

These examples demonstrate how punishment for political opinions operates not only through formal legal channels but also through travel restrictions, visa denials, surveillance, and narrative manipulation. Dissent becomes not only unwelcome, but increasingly costly on a personal and professional level.

CHAPTER RECAP — THE CAGE OF CHOICE

This chapter on illusions of choice revealed how modern information control operates through the illusion of choice rather than overt censorship. Digital algorithms create **personalized information bubbles** that feel like diverse information landscapes while actually narrowing perspective. Psychological shortcuts—authority, consistency, and social proof—make people believe they're thinking independently while actually absorbing narratives shaped by others. When individuals do challenge approved thinking, they face consequences ranging from travel restrictions to professional blacklisting.

The result is a system where people feel free while being systematically constrained. Unlike traditional propaganda, which demands belief, this approach makes people want to believe. It turns citizens into willing participants in their own manipulation, defending views they think they chose independently through **manufactured consent**.

This sets the stage for examining how these subtle manipulation techniques connect to more overt propaganda systems. The next chapter, *The Propaganda Bubble*, explores how governments and institutions use both traditional and modern methods to shape public opinion, creating unified narratives that serve power while appearing to emerge naturally from informed public discourse.

CHAPTER 7:

THE PROPAGANDA BUBBLE

The United States is a master of propaganda, both at home and abroad. Of course, like we discussed above and because of "framing the message," we don't call it "propaganda." It's only propaganda and indoctrination if others do it. Through a combination of media, entertainment, and education though, the U.S. attempts to shape perceptions of itself on both the national and international stage by crafting a narrative of moral superiority and justifiable actions.

HOLLYWOOD AS A PROPAGANDA TOOL

Hollywood plays a significant role in promoting U.S. values and foreign policy. War films like "American Sniper" and "Zero Dark Thirty" depict American soldiers as heroes fighting for freedom, while enemies are often portrayed as faceless terrorists or tyrants. These films subtly shape public perception, glorifying U.S. military actions, and downplaying their consequences.

If you pay attention to films from different decades, you'll notice that the "bad guys" change to fit what is going on in politics at the time. Let's look at that, period by period:

1900s-1930s: The "Yellow Peril" and Anti-Chinese Sentiment

The Chinese Exclusion Act of 1882 was the first significant U.S. law restricting immigration based on race, reflecting widespread anti-Chinese sentiment.

Notable Films:

- *The Mysterious Dr. Fu Manchu* (1929): Introduced the character of Dr. Fu Manchu, a Chinese villain embodying Western fears of the "Yellow Peril."

- *The Mask of Fu Manchu* (1932): Portrayed Fu Manchu as a megalomaniac threatening Western civilization and stating that he wanted to "Kill the white man and take his women!"

These films popularized the idea of the insidious Asian villain, contributing to anti-immigrant attitudes and justifying policies that excluded people in these groups. It also fueled domestic support for the U.S. placing American citizens of Japanese descent into concentration camps in 1942 (but we called them "relocation centers").[1]

1940s-1950s: The Red Scare and Anti-Communist Hysteria

The onset of the Cold War and McCarthyism fueled fears of communist infiltration, leading to widespread suspicion of Soviet influence.

Notable Films:

- *The Red Menace* (1949): Depicted communists as deceitful and dangerous, aiming to undermine American values.

- *I Was a Communist for the FBI* (1951): Portrayed a protagonist infiltrating communist groups, highlighting internal threats.

These films reinforced anti-Soviet sentiments, legitimizing domestic surveillance and loyalty programs.

1980s: The Height of Cold War Tensions and Arab Villainy

U.S.-Soviet relations remained strained, and Middle Eastern conflicts, such as the Iran hostage crisis, influenced public perception.

Notable Films:

- *Rambo: First Blood Part II* (1985): Portrayed Vietnamese and Soviet forces as brutal antagonists.

- *Iron Eagle* (1986): Depicted Arab nations as aggressors, reinforcing negative stereotypes.

These films solidified the image of Soviets and Arabs as primary villains, reflecting and shaping public fears.

1990s: Post-Cold War and the Rise of the Middle Eastern Terrorist Trope

The Gulf War and increasing attention to Middle Eastern politics influenced Hollywood narratives.

Notable Films:

- *True Lies* (1994): Featured Arab terrorists as the main antagonists, blending action with comedy.

- *Executive Decision* (1996): Portrayed Islamic extremists hijacking a plane, echoing real-world anxieties.

These portrayals reinforced the association between Arabs and terrorism, contributing to Islamophobic sentiments.

2000s: Post-9/11 and the Intensification of Anti-Muslim Stereotypes

The September 11 attacks led to the "War on Terror," significantly impacting media representations.

Notable Films:

- *The Kingdom* (2007): Depicted FBI agents investigating a terrorist attack in Saudi Arabia, highlighting Middle Eastern terrorism.

- *Body of Lies* (2008): Focused on CIA operations in the Middle East, portraying complex Arab characters but often reinforcing stereotypes.

These films continued the pervasive image of Arabs as a threat but also started to expand the definition of a "bad actor" to anyone of the Muslim faith from any country, influencing public opinion and policy.

2010s-2020s: Resurgence of Anti-Chinese Sentiment

Rising tensions with China over trade, technology, and global influence have led to renewed scrutiny.

Notable Films:

- *The Great Wall* (2016): Faced criticism for cultural appropriation and reinforcing Western savior narratives in a Chinese setting.

- *3 Body Problem* (2024): Heavily featured Chinese military leadership as deceptive, authoritarian, and ruthless, particularly in scenes depicting China's Cultural Revolution. Chinese critics claimed it advanced "American cultural hegemony" and maintained stereotypical villains while ignoring modern China's progress.[2]

THE MEDIA AND FRAMING

We covered the idea of "Framing" earlier. Framing is one of the most subtle and powerful tools in shaping how we understand the world. It's not just about what facts are presented, but how those facts are packaged, what language is used, which details are emphasized, and what context is omitted. In American media, framing often aligns with national interests, creating narratives that defend allies, vilify enemies, and present U.S. actions as inherently moral or necessary.

Strategic omission and selective framing create double standards that influence public opinion:

- When allies commit atrocities, like Saudi Arabia did when it murdered the critical journalist Jamal Khashoggi in their own embassy, the media used soft language, describing the murder as a "mistake" or an "unintended consequences." But when Alexander Litvinenko, a former Russian KGB agent that defected to the UK was assassinated using poison, the media decried it as "A brazen act of international murder."

- When Israel bombs Gaza, the US portrays it as "defensive military operations," but when Russia bombs Ukraine, the US portrays it as "indiscriminate targeting of civilians."

- When Israeli military members die, they are reported as having been murdered, but when Palestinian civilians are killed by the Israeli military, they are reported as just "dying," or being "made unalive."

- When there were protests about the government in Egypt and Venezuela, Egypt was framed as a "Complex Political transition," while Venezuela was framed as an "Authoritarian Crackdown."

- When the Soviets invaded Afghanistan (1979-1989) US media portrayed it as a "Brutal, imperialist occupation" to "prop up a puppet regime and crush Afghan resistance."[3] When the United States invaded Afghanistan (2001-2021) the US Media portrayed it as a "just and necessary response" to terrorists and portrayed US actions as both "just self-defense and a moral duty."[4]

This selective framing creates a double standard that influences public opinion. Americans view U.S. actions as justified, even when in violation of international law, while condemning similar actions by others.

EDUCATION AND PATRIOTISM

From a young age, Americans are exposed to patriotic propaganda through education. History textbooks often gloss over U.S. injustices, such as the genocide of Native Americans, slavery, and imperialism while emphasizing the country's achievements. The narrative is one of exceptionalism: America is a beacon of freedom, democracy, and justice.

This indoctrination creates a population less likely to question their government's actions, because they have been taught to see their country as inherently good. In the second section of this book we'll investigate some of the United States actions throughout the years with information and perspectives not taught in our government sponsored schools.

THE WEALTHY ELITE & THE FOURTH ESTATE

For centuries, people have relied on one institution above all others to speak truth to power: the press. Long before there were satellite feeds, podcasts, or cable news tickers, the idea of a free press was considered so essential to liberty that it earned a title of its own. They called it **the Fourth Estate.**

The term originated in 18th and 19th century Europe, when "estates" referred to the three pillars of society: the clergy, the nobility, and the common people. The press was dubbed the Fourth Estate because it wielded influence powerful enough to rival the other three. Its role was to hold power accountable, expose corruption, and ensure that ordinary citizens were informed enough to stand their ground against kings, parliaments, and later, presidents and parliaments.[5]

That's the ideal. But ideals are fragile. And in the United States today, the Fourth Estate has been bent, bought, and co-opted.

Instead of being a check on the powerful, much of our modern media has become a tool for them. The very institutions that were supposed to question power now depend on their finance and influence for their survival. A handful of massive corporations own the majority of what Americans watch, read, and hear. When ratings and advertising revenue become the lifeblood of news, stories stop being chosen for their importance and start being chosen for their ability to hold attention. Narratives aren't shaped to uncover the truth, they're shaped to protect the interests of shareholders, sponsors, and political allies.

The result is a press that often mirrors the priorities of those already in power or those seeking it. Instead of pulling back the curtain, it helps draw it. The watchdog becomes a guard dog, protecting the very people it was meant to confront.

CONTROLLING THE NARRATIVE

In the United States, a small group of corporations—such as Comcast, Disney, Warner Bros. Discovery, Paramount, and News Corp—control the majority of media outlets.[6] This consolidation allows powerful interests to influence not just what stories are told, but how they are framed, and which ones are ignored altogether. The following examples illustrate how this plays out in real-world news coverage:

- **Occupy Wall Street (2011):** Despite massive protests highlighting income inequality and corporate greed, major networks delayed and minimized coverage, with some anchors even mocking the movement's message.

- **Bernie Sanders' Campaign Coverage (2016):** Sanders consistently polled high and drew record crowds, but mainstream media like MSNBC and CNN gave him a fraction of the airtime compared to candidates like Hillary Clinton and Donald Trump, both of whom had stronger corporate ties. Studies showed Sanders received only 20 minutes of coverage on major networks compared to Trump's 327 minutes.[7]

- **Standing Rock Protests (2016-2017):** The Indigenous-led resistance to the Dakota Access Pipeline received minimal early coverage, despite widespread public support and environmental stakes. Coverage only spiked after violent confrontations made the issue harder to ignore.

- **Flint Water Crisis vs. Celebrity News:** During key months of the Flint water contamination scandal, major networks devoted more time to stories like the

Kardashians' personal lives and celebrity divorces than to the poisoning of an American city's water supply.

These patterns reveal a troubling reality: when media ownership is concentrated in the hands of those with deep financial and political interests, public attention is steered away from the structures of power and redirected toward distractions.

MANUFACTURING CONSENT

Political thinker Noam Chomsky argued in his book *Manufacturing Consent* that propaganda in democratic societies does not require censorship or force. Instead, it operates subtly, through media institutions that shape public perception by deciding which topics are worthy of attention and how those topics are framed, and those decisions are made based on what kind of advertising revenue they can sell.

Rather than telling people what to think directly, the media tells them **what to think about**, and just as importantly, what to ignore. Coverage of major events is often filtered through a lens that reinforces the priorities of corporate and political elites. For instance, economic crises are often explained in terms of individual irresponsibility, such as overspending, poor budgeting, or a supposed decline in work ethic. Meanwhile, structural causes like deregulation, corporate monopolies, or exploitative labor practices receive minimal scrutiny.

This framing doesn't just distort public understanding of events, it also affects policy responses. When the public is led to believe that poverty or unemployment is the result of laziness or poor choices, they are less likely to support social safety nets, labor reforms, or corporate accountability measures. Conversely, narratives that challenge elite power structures, like calls to tax the wealthy, regulate financial markets, or expand workers' rights, are often marginalized, ridiculed, or ignored altogether.

The result is a public that feels informed but is in reality deeply misled. **Manufacturing consent** doesn't mean the absence of disagreement—it means that the boundaries of disagreement are controlled. You can debate tax rates but not question corporate ownership of media. You can argue about immigration policy but not the economic and military forces that displace people in the first place. In a truly free society, the press would interrogate the powerful and give voice to the voiceless. But in a system where profit, access, and political influence dominate, the media too often functions not as a check on power, but as its amplifier.

THE PSYCHOLOGICAL POWER OF PROPAGANDA

Propaganda works because it exploits human psychology. People are more likely to believe information that aligns with their existing beliefs, especially when it comes from trusted sources. Propaganda reinforces these biases, creating a feedback loop that is difficult to escape.

FEAR AND SAFETY

Fear is one of the most powerful levers in the propaganda playbook, and it is often deployed through a tactic known as *FUD*—Fear, Uncertainty, and Doubt. Propagandists use FUD to manipulate beliefs by presenting certain groups, countries, or ideologies as imminent threats to security, identity, or societal order. This strategy is especially effective because it bypasses logical analysis and activates emotional survival instincts. When people are afraid, they stop asking critical questions. They become more susceptible to black-and-white thinking, more loyal to authority figures promising safety, and more willing to trade away their freedoms for the illusion of protection.

FUD has been central to many major decisions in recent history. After 9/11, the U.S. government used fear of terrorism to justify The USA Patriot Act, widespread surveillance programs, indefinite detentions, and wars in multiple countries, despite the lack of direct links between those actions and improved safety.[8]

During periods of social unrest or economic decline, politicians and media outlets often amplify fear of crime, immigration, or political extremism to consolidate control or justify harsher policies. This manipulation is rarely about the actual danger, it's about manufacturing a public mood conducive to compliance.

The brilliance of FUD is that it doesn't have to offer a convincing argument, only a disturbing question: "What if the worst happens?" Once that doubt takes root, people will often abandon their principles in pursuit of security, no matter how illusory it may be.

Look at the following messages by some of our elected officials:

President George W. Bush (Republican) -- Post-9/11 Security Measures

Following the September 11 attacks, President George W. Bush's administration emphasized the threat of terrorism to justify various security measures. In a 2002 speech, he stated:

"We cannot wait for the final proof—the smoking gun—that could come in the form of a mushroom cloud."[9]

This statement was used to advocate for the Iraq War, despite debates over the existence of weapons of mass destruction.

Representative Alexandria Ocasio-Cortez (Democrat) -- Climate "12 Years" Warning (2019)

Discussing climate change, AOC said:

"The world is going to end in 12 years if we don't address climate change."

This line, from a Martin Luther King Jr. Day event, was intended to emphasize urgency, but it was widely interpreted literally. Scientists have warned of severe climate consequences, but not that the entire world would end in that specific timeframe. This presented a worst-case scenario as if it were a near certainty, framing the policy debate around existential panic rather than measured projections.[10]

Representative Louie Gohmert (Republican) -- "Terror Babies" Conspiracy (2010)

In a 2010 interview on CNN and in a speech on the House floor, Rep. Louie Gohmert (R-TX) claimed that foreign Muslim terrorists were sending pregnant women to the U.S. so their babies could be born as American citizens, then later return to commit terrorist acts:

"It appeared they would have young women come over here who are pregnant. They wouldn't even have to pay for the baby. And then they would return where they could be raised and coddled as future terrorists."[11]

This baseless claim relied on fear and xenophobia, attempting to stir public anxiety about immigrants and Muslims as long-term threats hidden in plain sight. No evidence was ever produced, but the fear lingered.

GROUPTHINK AND CONFORMITY

Propaganda thrives not only on emotion and fear, but also on one of the most deeply ingrained aspects of human psychology, the tendency to conform to social norms. We are social creatures by design, and our sense of identity, safety, and even morality is heavily shaped by the beliefs of those around us. Propagandists understand this and deliberately exploit it to reinforce dominant narratives.

When a certain viewpoint is echoed repeatedly by peers, institutions, and authority figures, it becomes less a matter of individual belief and more a marker of group belonging. Agreeing with the prevailing view feels safe, socially rewarded, and even virtuous. Dissent, on the other hand, can lead to isolation, ridicule, or punishment. In this way, propaganda doesn't always need to convince, it just needs to surround.

This effect is especially potent in tightly controlled environments, such as authoritarian regimes, high-control religious groups, or even modern digital spaces governed by algorithms. In these spaces, alternative viewpoints are not only challenged, but they are also often actively suppressed. Whistleblowers are discredited or criminalized. Journalists who stray from the accepted narrative may lose access or face legal threats. On social media, dissenting opinions are buried by platform bias, brigading, or content moderation policies that claim to fight "misinformation" but often silence legitimate critique. As a result, the public is exposed to a narrow range of thoughts that appears overwhelmingly supported, when in fact it may be artificially propped up. This can lead to the **spiral of silence**, where individuals who hold minority or contrary views stay quiet out of fear, which in turn reinforces the illusion that everyone agrees.

This psychological pressure is self-reinforcing. When people see no public dissent, they assume none exists, or worse, that it's morally wrong to disagree. They begin to censor themselves to avoid being ostracized. Over time, people don't just act like they believe the dominant narrative, they internalize it. The boundaries of acceptable thought shrink, not through force, but through culture. Propaganda succeeds best not when it forces everyone to say the same thing, but when it convinces people that they arrived at a belief on their own. And by aligning truth with popularity, it erodes the very foundation of critical thinking, replacing it with conformity masked as consensus.

HOW YOU CAN RECOGNIZE PROPAGANDA

Recognizing propaganda requires effort. It requires critical thinking and a willingness to question accepted narratives.

Resisting propaganda also requires consuming diverse sources of information. To resist propaganda, you need to actively seek out independent media, international news outlets, and dissenting voices. Like the parable of the elephant, the more perspectives you have, the harder it becomes for propaganda to shape your reality.

You can use the technology available today to do this easily, but you must make the choice to do that. Instead of watching Fox News or MSNBC all day long, try reading articles on an application called "Ground News" that aggregates dozens of news sources and displays a "Bias Bar" that depicts how the news sources are leaning.

CHAPTER RECAP - THE BATTLE FOR TRUTH AND CONTROL

The Propaganda Bubble revealed how information warfare operates through entertainment, education, and media to shape public perception. From Hollywood's evolving villains that mirror political priorities to news media's double standards in framing identical actions, from childhood patriotic indoctrination to corporate control of information flow, we saw how **manufactured consent** creates the illusion of informed public opinion while actually serving elite interests.

The most effective propaganda doesn't force belief—it makes people want to believe. It exploits fear through FUD tactics and social conformity through the **spiral of silence**, creating environments where dissent feels dangerous and agreement feels virtuous. Understanding these psychological mechanisms—from **strategic omission** to **manufacturing consent**, is the first step toward independent thought.

Propaganda is not just a tool of manipulation; it is a weapon in the battle for truth and control. The powerful and wealthy use it to maintain control, shape perceptions, and silence dissent. The truth can be hidden by propaganda, but it is not so easily erased.

By questioning narratives, seeking alternative viewpoints, and educating ourselves, we can reclaim our ability to think independently.

The antidote to propaganda is awareness. Once you see how it operates, you can never unsee it, and that is the first step toward true freedom.

But propaganda doesn't just control what we think about politics and war, it shapes how we see ourselves and our place in the world. The next chapter, *The Lifestyle Bubble*, explores how the same manipulation techniques are used to define success, happiness, and the "good life," keeping us chasing goals that serve the system rather than our own wellbeing.

CHAPTER 8:

THE LIFESTYLE BUBBLE

From kindergarten to cable news, from sitcoms to schoolbooks, we've been spoon-fed a single message dressed up in different costumes: America is the best place to live. The freest. The happiest. The most successful. We're told we've cracked the code on how life should be lived: a blend of hard work, opportunity, and reward so magical that the rest of the world envies us. But what if that message isn't just flawed, what if it's deliberately misleading?

This isn't about bashing American people. It's about bursting the bubble we've all been trapped in.

Let's call it what it is: it's indoctrination. It's a cultural narrative so deeply embedded that questioning it feels like betrayal.

But a belief system that demands silence or shame for those who question it is a fragile one. So, let's question it. Let's ask: In reality, are Americans the happiest people in the world? Do we really enjoy the best lifestyle?

THE MANUFACTURED MIRAGE

Turn on American television and you're immersed in a world of beaming smiles, pristine kitchens, limitless products, and perfectly trimmed lawns. The underlying message? This is the good life. The dream.

Meanwhile, news about other countries is often filtered through a lens of chaos, poverty, or authoritarianism. We see only the riots in France, not the universal healthcare. The floods in Bangladesh, not the community resilience. The protests in Finland, not their world-class education system.

Even our entertainment reinforces this **manufactured mirage**. Pay close attention to Hollywood films and you'll notice that scenes set in the United States are typically vibrant and colorful, while many scenes in other countries appear dull and dreary. This isn't accidental, it's the intentional application of visual filters designed to make the United States look better than it is and other countries look worse than they are.

This distorted view creates a false comparison: America's best moments against the world's worst. And from that contrast, a delusional superiority takes root.

THE NUMBERS DON'T LIE

According to the World Happiness Report 2024, the United States ranks 23rd in global happiness—not even in the top 20 happiest countries. Finland claims the top spot, followed by Denmark, Iceland, Sweden, and the Netherlands. Even countries like the Czech Republic and Lithuania outrank us.[1]

These aren't statistical flukes reflecting momentary mood swings. They represent consistent patterns measured through serious, objective factors: GDP per capita, social support, healthy life expectancy, freedom to make life choices, generosity, and perceptions of corruption. In other words, the basic building blocks of a good life.

The Organisation for Economic Co-operation and Development (OECD) data reveals similar gaps. Countries like Norway, Switzerland, and New Zealand regularly outperform the U.S. not just in happiness, but in healthcare quality, education outcomes, workplace safety, work-life balance, and trust in government institutions.

Here's what that looks like in concrete terms:

- **Work-Life Balance:** Americans work an average of 1,791 hours annually compared to 1,356 hours in Germany and 1,511 in France.[2] Paid vacation isn't legally guaranteed. Parental leave remains abysmal compared to other developed nations.

- **Healthcare:** We spend more per capita on healthcare than any other country, nearly twice the OECD average, yet 27.5 million Americans lack health insurance.[3] Surely since we spend more on healthcare, we must have a higher life expectancy, right? Unfortunately, that isn't true. The U.S. ranks 49th in the world behind countries like Cuba, Estonia, and Saudi Arabia.[4] Medical bankruptcy affects approximately 530,000 families annually, a phenomenon virtually unknown in other developed countries.[5]

- **Education:** Student loan debt exceeds $1.7 trillion nationally.[6] Public school funding varies dramatically by zip code, creating vast inequalities in educational opportunity.

- **Safety:** The United States experiences more mass shooting events than any other developed nation. Police killings claim over 1,000 lives annually, with rates significantly higher than comparable countries.[7] Globally, the United States ranks 137th in safety with Iran ranking 138th.[8]

And yet, through all of this, we're told: Be grateful. You live in the greatest country in the world.

THE PSYCHOLOGY OF EXCEPTIONALISM

How do you maintain a myth in the face of overwhelming evidence? Through repetition and emotional conditioning. **American exceptionalism** isn't taught as an idea open to debate, it's presented as self-evident truth.

From our pledge of allegiance to political speeches, we hear it constantly: America is the land of freedom. The defender of democracy. The shining city on a hill. This language isn't descriptive; it's prescriptive. It tells us what to feel, not what to examine.

There's psychological power in that messaging. People resist hearing that they've been deceived. It's more comfortable to cling to familiar stories than confront uncomfortable alternatives. Admitting our nation sells a dream it doesn't fully deliver requires emotional work most would rather avoid.

THE REAL COST OF THE LIE

Living inside this bubble has tangible consequences. It blinds us to possibilities for improvement. If we're already the best, why change?

But consider this reality: while other countries invest systematically in public well-being, Americans are increasingly isolated, overworked, indebted, and anxious. Life expectancy declined for three consecutive years before the pandemic and continues stagnating.[9] Social trust has eroded to historic lows. We spend more on defense than the next ten countries combined yet can't fix aging water systems or adequately house our veterans.[10]

The myth of **lifestyle superiority** also feeds foreign policy arrogance. If we believe our way is inherently best, we justify exporting it, by force when necessary. And when other nations resist, they're labeled backward, ungrateful, or dangerous.

BREAKING THE BUBBLE

So what now?

The goal isn't wallowing in cynicism or rejecting our identity. It's reclaiming truth. Acknowledging where we fall short so we can demand better. Looking beyond curated images of American life and asking: what do people in other countries understand that we don't?

They understand that community matters. That safety nets represent collective strength, not weakness. That education, healthcare, and leisure aren't luxuries but necessities for a society to flourish and grow.

They know happiness isn't built on shopping malls, military might, or chest-thumping nationalism. It's built on connection, dignity, and trust.

Deep down, we know this too. But too often we get distracted by sports, entertainment, advertising, work pressures, and daily survival concerns.

We need to pop the bubble not to hate our country, but to love it more honestly. Not to burn the flag, but to stop hiding behind it. Not to diminish America, but to become as forthright about our shortcomings as we are about our accomplishments.

If we do this, we can begin building a version of the American dream that's actually attainable for everyone willing to work for it, and one that doesn't require delusion to sustain it.

CHAPTER RECAP—POPPING THE "BEST LIFE" MYTH

This chapter dismantled the American lifestyle story we're sold from childhood: that we are the happiest, freest, and most successful people on earth. International measures of well-being place the U.S. outside the top tier, while everyday realities, overwork, medical debt, student loans, underfunded schools, and endemic violence, reveal harsher truths. Media framing compounds the illusion, spotlighting America's brightest moments against other countries' darkest days.

When a nation can no longer admit its faults, it loses the ability to fix them. The cost of this myth is real, it numbs us to reforms that could genuinely improve lives and feeds foreign-policy arrogance that exports problems along with supposed solutions.

Bursting this bubble isn't about self-loathing; it's about honest love of country and building a better, more truthful American dream.

Next, we examine an even more personal myth: the belief that individual willpower writes our destiny. In "The Self-

Determination Bubble," we confront how class, race, geography, trauma, and systematically unequal opportunities shape the "choices" we think are entirely free.

CHAPTER 9:

THE SELF-DETERMINATION BUBBLE

This is the **myth of American self-determination**. The belief that our lives are built from pure willpower. That if you want something badly enough, you'll get it. And if you don't? Well, that must be on you.

But here's the truth: the game is rigged long before we even know we're playing.

By the time a child chooses their first backpack, the zip code they were born into has already shaped their options. Their family's wealth, or lack of it, has already bought or denied them access to opportunities. Their ethnicity has already begun to influence how teachers, police, doctors, and employers will treat them.

We don't live in a meritocracy. We live in a system that **repackages luck and legacy as merit** and then blames the unlucky for losing.

THE STORIES WE'RE SOLD

We grow up on a steady diet of bootstrap mythology: Billionaires who started in garages. Celebrities who slept in cars. Athletes who came from "nothing" and made it big. These stories are elevated to near-mythic status and held up as proof that success is just a matter of grit, hustle, and personal drive. "If they did it, so can you," we're told. It's meant to inspire, but it often distorts reality instead.

What's left unsaid speaks even louder: If you haven't made it, it's your fault. Maybe you didn't work hard enough. Maybe you didn't want it badly enough. Maybe you made the wrong choices. But that line of thinking ignores the structural realities most people face—lack of access, generational debt, systemic bias, or the randomness of opportunity. It also ignores a deeper psychological truth: **people often confuse privilege with merit.**

A powerful study by psychologist Paul Piff at UC Berkeley painfully demonstrated this. Participants were asked to play **a rigged game of Monopoly**.[1] One player, chosen at random, was given a clear advantage. They received more starting money, higher payouts for passing "Go," and the ability to roll two dice instead of one. To no one's surprise, the advantaged players won. The surprising reveal from the experiment was how the winners explained their victory. Instead of acknowledging the head start, they credited their "success" to smart strategy and skill. They acted more dominant, took more space, even ate more of the snacks provided to players. The inequality was scripted from the start, but the winners internalized their win as self-earned.

That's how systemic advantage works. It hides in plain sight and rewires how people view themselves and others. Those with privilege come to believe they deserve their place. Those without it are told to try harder. And when that doesn't work, they're told it's because of some flaw in their character. This is the lie embedded in the stories we're sold—not just that anyone can make it, but that those who don't must have failed because of an internal character flaw. In reality, working hard but not reaching the pinnacle in a system designed to elevate a few and exhaust the rest is not a failure. Surviving that system with your integrity intact is a kind of success that no myth can capture.

WHAT REALLY SHAPES YOUR DESTINY

Like Dorothy did in The Wizard of Oz, let's pull back the curtain and see who is moving the levers...

1. Family Wealth and Class

In America, your starting line matters more than your stride.

We love the myth that hard work alone determines success, but the data tells a different story. If you're born into the bottom 20% of income earners, your chances of reaching the top 20% are about 7.5%. In other words, more than 9 out of 10 people born at the bottom stay there or close to it.[2] That's not economic mobility. That's a caste system with better marketing.

Wealth opens doors that most people never even see. It buys access to high-quality early education, private tutoring, safe neighborhoods, well-funded public schools, Advanced Placement courses, extracurriculars, and college admissions coaching. It buys unpaid internships at prestigious institutions, social capital, and alumni networks. According to Opportunity Insights, children whose parents are in the top 1% of income are 77 times more likely to attend an Ivy League school than those from the bottom 20%.[3]

Poverty, on the other hand, comes with invisible shackles. It brings housing instability, food insecurity, underfunded schools, higher exposure to violence, and chronic stress. It forces families to make trade-offs between healthcare and rent, between after-school programs and a second job. It buys anxiety, fewer choices, and an early education in survival rather than opportunity. While we celebrate the few who escape poverty, research from the Pew Economic Mobility Project shows that over 70% of those born into the bottom fifth of the income ladder never reach the middle class.[4]

A notable example of privilege shaping outcomes is **the "marshmallow test"** conducted by psychologist Walter Mischel in the 1960s.[5] Children were given a choice: eat one marshmallow immediately or wait 15 minutes and receive two marshmallows. Some children ate their marshmallow immediately while others waited for the larger reward. The researchers followed these children into middle age and found that those who delayed gratification had better life outcomes, including higher SAT scores and lower body mass index. The researchers interpreted this to mean that self-control was a key predictor of success—a logical conclusion at the time.

However, in 2018 the study was replicated by Tyler Watts and challenged the earlier conclusion.[6] By analyzing a more diverse sample and controlling for factors like family background and early cognitive ability, they found that the ability to delay gratification was not a strong predictor of later success. Instead, socioeconomic status played a more significant role. Children from wealthier families were more likely to wait for the second marshmallow not necessarily because they had more self-control, but because their environment taught them that waiting would pay off. In contrast, children from less affluent backgrounds had learned that immediate rewards are more reliable, and promises for future rewards frequently don't materialize, making their choice to eat the marshmallow immediately a rational response to their circumstances.

Additionally, research on cross-class friendships has shown that social networks play a powerful role in shaping opportunity. A large 2022 study conducted by researchers at Harvard and other institutions analyzed anonymized Facebook data from millions of Americans and found that low-income individuals who formed friendships with higher-income peers earned significantly more in adulthood. Those relationships were also associated with greater economic mobility across generations.[7] The study concluded that economic connectedness, friendships and ties that cross income groups, was a stronger predictor of upward mobility than neighborhood wealth, school quality, or even demographic background.

These findings underscore the importance of considering environmental and socioeconomic factors when assessing behavior and success. They challenge the notion that individual traits like willpower are solely responsible for life outcomes and highlight the role of systemic inequality in shaping opportunities and choices.

We love rags-to-riches stories because they comfort us. They reinforce the belief that the system is fair. But statistically, most rags stay rags, not because people didn't try, but because the race was rigged before they even stepped onto the track. Conversely, most wealthy families stay wealthy, not solely because of their hard work and personal acumen, but because the system was rigged in their favor from the beginning. Until we acknowledge that, we'll keep mistaking privilege for merit and luck for virtue.

2. Education Isn't the Equalizer You Think It Is

We're told education is the great equalizer. But in the U.S., it's often the great divider.

Public schools in the United States are primarily funded through local property taxes, which means that communities with higher property values can allocate more resources to their schools. According to the National Center for Education Statistics, in the 2020-21 school year, 44% of public school revenues came from local sources, predominantly property taxes, while only 11% came from federal sources.[8] This funding structure creates significant disparities: affluent districts can afford modern facilities, experienced teachers, and a wide array of extracurricular activities, while under-resourced districts often struggle with outdated materials, overcrowded classrooms, and limited programs.

Efforts to address these inequities have had mixed results. The Elementary and Secondary Education Act of 1965 aimed to provide federal funding to support disadvantaged students, but subsequent studies have shown that even with programs like Title I, which is designed to assist low-income schools, the highest-poverty schools often receive less funding per student than their more affluent counterparts. For instance, a Department of Education report found that in 2004-05, the highest-poverty schools received an average of $558 per low-income student, compared to $763 in the lowest-poverty schools.[9]

Further complicating the issue, policies like the No Child Left Behind Act of 2001 introduced standardized testing as a measure of accountability. While intended to improve educational outcomes, this approach often penalized underperforming schools without providing the necessary support to address underlying challenges. By 2010, 38% of schools were failing to make adequate yearly progress, up from 29% in 2006.[10]

In essence, the current education system, influenced by local funding disparities and federal policies, often reinforces existing inequalities rather than mitigating them. Addressing these challenges requires a comprehensive reevaluation of how educational resources are allocated and how success is measured across diverse communities.

3. Race, ZIP Code, and Policing

Where you're born in America doesn't just shape your future, it can predict your lifespan. The legacy of discriminatory housing practices (called "redlining"), segregated schooling, and mass incarceration has entrenched disparities that continue to disadvantage entire communities. Black and Brown Americans navigate systems historically designed to marginalize them, often facing punitive responses to their efforts to advance.

Consider life expectancy: as of 2021, Black Americans had a life expectancy of 70.8 years, compared to 76.4 years for White Americans, a gap of nearly six years. For American Indian and Alaska Native populations the disparity is even more pronounced with a life expectancy of 65.2 years. These differences are not merely statistical; they reflect systemic inequities in healthcare access, environmental conditions, and socioeconomic status. Multiple studies have shown that these results are not due to genetics; they are overwhelmingly due to environment.[11]

Historical practices like redlining have had lasting health impacts. Communities that were once redlined continue to experience higher rates of chronic diseases such as asthma, hypertension, and diabetes. For instance, residents of formerly redlined neighborhoods are nearly four times as likely to die from asthma compared to those in non-redlined areas.

The G.I. Bill of 1944, heralded for creating a prosperous middle class, largely excluded Black veterans due to discriminatory practices. While the bill's benefits were theoretically available to all veterans, systemic racism in housing and education meant that Black veterans were often denied access to the very opportunities that propelled their White counterparts into economic stability.

The War on Drugs further worsened racial disparities. Policies implemented during this era led to the mass incarceration of people of color, particularly Black men. At its peak, nearly one in three Black men born in 1981 were projected to be imprisoned at some point in their lives. Although this rate has declined to one in five for those born in 2001, the disparity remains stark.[12]

These systemic issues underscore a broader truth: success in America is often less about individual effort and more about the circumstances into which one is born. Addressing these disparities requires a concerted effort to dismantle the structural barriers that perpetuate inequality.

4. Trauma and Health

Chronic stress doesn't just weigh on the mind—it reshapes it. For children, especially those growing up amid poverty, racism, abuse, or instability, this stress can leave lasting imprints on brain development, behavior, and physical health.

The landmark Adverse Childhood Experiences (ACE) study revealed a direct link between early trauma and outcomes like depression, addiction, incarceration, and premature death. Subsequent research has deepened our understanding of how these experiences affect the developing brain. For instance, chronic exposure to stress hormones like cortisol can alter the architecture of brain regions responsible for learning, memory, and emotional regulation. This means that children exposed to sustained adversity may face challenges in academic achievement and social interactions.

Moreover, the prevalence of ACEs is alarmingly high. According to the CDC, approximately 61.5% of students have experienced emotional abuse, and 31.8% have faced physical abuse, but these experiences are not evenly distributed. Children from marginalized communities often face a higher burden. For example, Black children living in poverty encounter increased instances of stress and trauma, which can lead to alterations in brain development as evidenced by MRI studies. These changes are associated with mental health issues like PTSD, anxiety, and depression later in life.[13]

Despite these findings, the prevailing narrative in American society often overlooks the impact of early adversity. We celebrate stories of resilience without questioning why such resilience was necessary in the first place. This perspective ignores the systemic factors that contribute to chronic stress and its effects on children.

Addressing the consequences of chronic stress requires a comprehensive approach that includes early intervention, trauma-informed care, and policies aimed at reducing socioeconomic disparities. By acknowledging and addressing the root causes of chronic stress, we can create environments that support healthy development and break the cycle of adversity.

OUR CHILDREN ARE FEELING IT

There's a cost to living inside a contradiction.

We tell people they're free while their lived experience says otherwise. And the result? **Despair.**

Youth mental health is collapsing.

The youth mental health crisis in the United States has escalated dramatically over the past decade. Between 2007 and 2018, suicide rates among individuals aged 10-24 increased by nearly 60%, with particularly sharp rises among adolescent girls and Black youth. In response, the U.S. Surgeon General issued a 2021 advisory declaring youth mental health a national crisis, emphasizing that the decline in well-being was evident even before the COVID-19 pandemic.[14]

Several interrelated factors contribute to this crisis:

- **Economic Stress and Inequality**: Young people face significant financial pressures, including student debt, high housing costs, and job insecurity. A Deloitte survey found that 46% of Gen Z individuals feel stressed most of the time, with financial concerns being a major factor.[15]

- **Climate Anxiety**: The looming threat of climate change has led to widespread psychological distress among youth. A global survey revealed that nearly 60% of young people aged 16-24 are extremely worried about climate change, with many reporting that this anxiety affects their daily lives.[16]

- **Social Media and Digital Exposure**: Excessive use of social media platforms has been linked to increased feelings of inadequacy and depression among adolescents. The constant exposure to curated images and information can erode self-esteem and contribute to mental health issues.[17]

- **Systemic Inequities**: Structural factors such as racism, poverty, and housing instability disproportionately affect marginalized communities. Youth experiencing housing instability, for instance, have higher rates of anxiety and depression and face significant barriers to accessing mental health services.[18]

Deep down, people know. They know the ladder is missing rungs. They know the game is fixed. They know that working multiple jobs and still living paycheck to paycheck isn't personal failure, but younger generations have less ability to cope with these contradictions.

Recent studies indicate that today's youth, particularly Generation Z (born between 1997 and 2012), exhibit lower resilience compared to previous generations. This diminished resilience is linked to many factors, including economic instability, climate anxiety, social media exposure, and broader societal shifts.

- **Comparative Studies on Resilience**: Research comparing Generation Z to Generation X (born between 1965 and 1980) found that Gen Z individuals demonstrate lower resilience levels. For instance, a study published in Current Psychology revealed that Gen Z participants were less resilient and more susceptible to stress during the COVID-19 pandemic compared to Gen X counterparts.[19]

- **Longitudinal Mental Health Trends**: A longitudinal study examining adolescents over a 20-year span reported that current adolescents exhibit higher and increasing levels of depressive symptoms and social anxiety compared to those from two decades ago. The study highlighted that the odds of being consistently at risk for depressive symptoms were 3.64 times higher in the current adolescent cohort.[20]

- **Workplace Stress and Resilience**: A comparative study on workplace stress found that Gen Z employees reported higher levels of stress and lower resilience scores than Generation X employees. The study emphasized the need for targeted interventions to bolster resilience among younger workers.[21]

THE WAY OUT ISN'T MORE HUSTLE, IT'S MORE TRUTH

So, what do we do?

First, we stop lying. We stop pretending that success is purely personal, and we stop calling systemic injustice a lack of effort.

Then we build something better.

We demand universal healthcare so that health isn't a luxury available only to those who can afford it. We fight for equitable school funding that doesn't punish kids for being born in the wrong zip code. We push for comprehensive student debt relief, living wages that actually cover the cost of living, and housing policies that treat shelter as a human right rather than an investment commodity.

We advocate for criminal justice reform that emphasizes rehabilitation over punishment, environmental policies that address climate anxiety with concrete action, and mental health services that are accessible to all young people regardless of their family's ability to pay.

We build a society where freedom is not a privilege distributed according to wealth and circumstance, it's a shared foundation that gives everyone the tools, the support, and the safety to rise.

Because real freedom doesn't mean stepping over others to reach the top. It means creating a world where everyone has genuine opportunities to thrive, where choices are real rather than theatrical, and where success isn't predetermined by the lottery of birth.

Until then, "the freedom to choose" will remain just a fantasy for the few, and a burden for the rest.

CHAPTER RECAP—THE RIGGED GAME OF CHOICE

This chapter stripped away the myth of self-determination. We are told that success is a matter of grit, hustle, and smart decisions, but the truth is that the race is rigged before most people even start. Family wealth, zip code, race, trauma, and social networks quietly shape our destinies while we're told it's all about "personal responsibility." Rags-to-riches stories comfort us by making the exception feel like the rule, while in reality, generational poverty persists, privilege masquerades as merit, and systemic barriers block the path for most.

Education, often touted as the great equalizer, is exposed as a great divider, funded by property taxes that guarantee wealthy neighborhoods perpetuate advantage while poorer ones fall further behind. Policing, housing discrimination, and mass incarceration reinforce inequalities. Even health outcomes and mental resilience are shaped by environment and systemic stress rather than individual willpower. What looks like "choice" is too often theater, with the real options fenced off before we know they exist.

The chapter left us with a hard truth: until we confront the structures that define opportunity, "self-determination" remains more myth than reality. Next, we'll examine the very system that enforces these inequities—how our democracy actually functions, where our tax dollars really go, and whether our voices are truly heard in "The Government and Taxes Bubble."

CHAPTER 10:

THE GOVERNMENT & TAXES BUBBLE

To live in America is to live under the impression that your voice matters and your money is spent wisely. We are taught that we have a representative democracy "of the people, by the people, for the people." That our taxes, though painful, fund shared infrastructure: roads, schools, defense, and a safety net for those in need.

But peel back the patriotic rhetoric, and what you find is a broken system where democracy is distorted by lobbying, elections are manipulated by money, and tax dollars are redirected toward interests that frequently exclude the American people.

This is the government and tax bubble, the myth that we fund and live under a functional, fair, and self-correcting democratic system. In reality, the U.S. government increasingly serves a permanent ruling class of corporations, foreign lobbies, and entrenched power brokers, while the average American pays more and receives less.

A FLAWED DEMOCRACY

In theory, American citizens elect leaders who serve their interests. In practice, we vote in a system that is heavily shaped by money. As of 2024, running a successful congressional campaign costs millions, and a presidential campaign requires well over a billion dollars.[1]

This high-stakes fundraising model ensures that candidates are often more accountable to corporate donors and political action committees (PACs) than to voters. Princeton researchers Martin Gilens and Benjamin Page found that economic elites and organized interest groups have substantial independent impacts on U.S. policy, while average citizens have virtually none.[2]

That's not democracy. That's **plutocracy with better branding**.

It's important to think this through. Billions are spent on elections, but where does that money go? It shouldn't be surprising that the overwhelming majority goes to media companies. In the 2024 election cycle, $12.3 billion was spent with 72% of that flowing to media outlets, a 30% increase over 2020.[3] Major media corporations recorded substantial revenue increases from election advertising, creating a system where those who report on elections have strong financial incentives to maintain the expensive status quo.

Additional research regarding our election system reveals troubling but unsurprising insights. Candidates who spend the most money typically win. In House races between 2000-2024, **the top spender won about 93-95% of elections**; in Senate races, around **82-88%**. This pattern has been consistent over multiple election cycles.[4]

This is the American system today. Winners aren't the most qualified or those with the best plans for America. They are the ones with the most money. That is the very definition of plutocracy.

WHERE DO OUR TAXES REALLY GO?

The average American works over a quarter of the year just to pay taxes, a sum that feeds into the largest government budget on earth. But despite the immense pool of revenue, public services in the U.S. lag behind those in countries with far lower tax burdens.

Federal spending breaks down roughly as follows: Social Security and Medicare consume about 38% of the budget, defense spending accounts for approximately 15%, interest on the national debt takes 13%, and various other programs divide the remainder. What's notable is how little goes toward education (2%), transportation (2%), or other infrastructure that directly benefits citizens' daily lives.

As a country, every year we spend more money than we have. Where do we get that additional money? We borrow it and call the result "the national debt." Since 1980, our debt has grown exponentially regardless of which political party controls government. We require Congress to stay within a debt limit, but Congress keeps voting to raise that limit, and the national debt keeps growing because we keep spending money we don't have.

This creates a vicious cycle: as debt grows, interest payments consume an ever-larger share of the budget, leaving less money for actual government services while requiring even more borrowing to maintain current spending levels.

FOREIGN AID FOR THE WEALTHY

One of the most jarring contradictions in American taxation is our pattern of **foreign aid to wealthy nations**. It's noble to aid those in genuine need—sending food to drought-stricken regions or medical supplies during epidemics is dignified and necessary. But that's not primarily what we do.

We send the largest portions of our foreign aid to countries that often have higher standards of living than many American communities. For decades, Israel has been the largest recipient of U.S. foreign aid, receiving over $3.8 billion annually despite having achieved developed-nation status.[5] According to OECD data, Israel's economic indicators in areas like healthcare access and education outcomes now match or exceed those of average Americans.[6]

So why are we subsidizing a prosperous foreign state while our own infrastructure crumbles and veterans experience homelessness? The answer lies in the influence of lobbying organizations like AIPAC (American Israel Public Affairs Committee) and the broader pro-Israel lobbying network, which exerts significant influence over U.S. foreign policy and congressional appropriations. Similar dynamics apply to other wealthy aid recipients like Jordan and Egypt, where aid serves strategic rather than humanitarian purposes.

This isn't about the worthiness of any particular country, it's about the contradiction of borrowing money to fund other nations while neglecting domestic needs.

THE SCATTERED PIE: FEDERAL ALLOCATION BY POLITICAL FAVOR

Federal spending isn't just misguided, it's inefficient by design.

One of the least discussed but most costly features of American governance is the practice of **geographic equalization** in budget allocations. In simple terms: Congress ensures **every state gets a slice**, regardless of whether that state needs it or whether the expenditure makes strategic sense.[7]

Why? Because every senator and representative wants to bring "jobs" and "funding" back home. The result is a national budget that looks more like a patchwork of political favors than a rational spending plan. We build military bases, federal laboratories, and transportation projects in low-population, strategically unimportant areas simply because their representatives have seniority or political leverage.

As an example, look at the **F-35 Fighter Jet Program.** The F-35 program, the most expensive weapons system in history and has components manufactured in nearly every state precisely to make it "too politically big to fail." This strategic distribution ensures continued funding despite the program's consistent cost overruns and performance issues. The logic is simple: cut the program, and representatives lose jobs in their districts, which loses them votes.

This isn't national defense. It's taxpayer-funded job insurance for politicians, and it results in weapons systems that cost more and perform worse than they should.

A NATION DROWNING IN DEBT

At the time this book was written, the United States carries a national debt exceeding **$36 trillion and growing rapidly**.[8] This isn't theoretical, it's a compounding crisis. Interest payments alone are now the **third-largest federal expenditure**, after Social Security and defense.[9]

Here's the terrifying part: we are approaching a point where **interest payments could exceed federal revenue** in certain economic scenarios. When that happens, the U.S. government would be forced to either slash services drastically (including Medicare, Social Security, and education), raise taxes across the board, or face default. None of those options bode well for average citizens.

Economists call this a **fiscal death spiral**: when debt grows faster than the economy and interest payments outpace revenues, the system becomes mathematically unsustainable. We're not there yet, but current trends point in that direction without significant policy changes.

TAX BURDEN: RISING AND REGRESSIVE

Despite popular belief, American tax policy has become increasingly regressive. While the ultra-rich benefit from tax loopholes, capital gains advantages, and offshore strategies, the working and middle classes shoulder a growing share of the burden.

Consider these realities:

The top 1% of earners often pay a smaller effective tax rate than many middle-income Americans, thanks to capital gains treatment and various deductions.[10] The Social Security tax is capped at approximately $160,000 of income, meaning someone earning $160,001 pays the same dollar amount into the system as a billionaire. Sales taxes disproportionately affect the poor, who spend a larger portion of their income on necessities.

Meanwhile, tax cuts like the 2017 Tax Cuts and Jobs Act shifted wealth upward by slashing corporate taxes from 35% to 21%, while providing only modest and temporary relief to middle-income earners.[11] The corporate tax cuts were permanent; the individual tax cuts expire.

WHAT COULD THAT MONEY DO INSTEAD?

It's not just that we waste tax dollars, it's that we deny ourselves a better society in the process.

What would it look like to redirect even a portion of the $877 billion military budget toward education, healthcare, or infrastructure?

For perspective, according to policy research organizations: Just $70 billion annually could fund tuition-free public college for all Americans.[12] $100 billion could create comprehensive universal childcare.[13] $300 billion could accelerate the transition to renewable energy infrastructure.[14]

But we don't fund those things adequately. Why? Because they don't generate campaign donations, lucrative defense contracts, or maintain global military presence.

THE MYTH OF CONSENT

The greatest illusion of all is that we consent to this system. That by voting every two or four years, we have somehow endorsed these spending priorities. But true consent requires understanding and genuine alternatives. Neither is provided in our current system.

Budgets are passed in omnibus bills that few legislators read completely. Lobbyists draft legislation that benefits their clients. Both major parties ensure the fundamental structures remain intact, offering voters the choice between two flavors of the same basic system, both funded by similar corporate interests.

This isn't democracy failing, it's democracy being captured by interests that profit from its dysfunction.

POPPING THE BUBBLE

We cannot fix what we refuse to acknowledge. And we cannot claim to live in a functioning democracy when the mechanics of governance serve corporate and foreign interests while extracting wealth from everyone else.

Bursting the tax and government bubble means demanding: transparent budgeting with clear explanations of spending priorities and their justifications. Campaign finance reform that reduces the influence of corporate money on elections. A reallocation of spending toward infrastructure, education, and healthcare that directly benefits citizens. Strategic rather than political foreign aid that serves clear humanitarian or national security purposes. Fiscal responsibility that prioritizes future generations over current political convenience and defense contractor profits.

This isn't a radical vision. It's a return to what government was supposed to be: a steward of the people's will and wealth, not a redistribution mechanism that flows money upward to elites and outward to foreign interests.

Until that happens, American taxpayers will continue subsidizing a system that serves everyone except them, while being told they should be grateful for the privilege.

CHAPTER RECAP—DEMOCRACY FOR SALE

This chapter cut through the patriotic veneer of American governance, revealing that what we call democracy often functions as plutocracy. Elections hinge less on ideas than on cash, with candidates who raise the most money nearly guaranteed to win. Lobbyists and corporations, not ordinary citizens, dictate policy, while media companies profit from the billions poured into campaigns every election cycle.

Taxes, meanwhile, flow into a system riddled with inefficiency, foreign aid to wealthy nations, and bloated contracts for defense projects designed more to spread jobs across voting districts than to meet genuine security needs. The debt spiral grows unchecked while tax burdens shift toward working families and away from the wealthy. Vital public investments, education, healthcare, infrastructure, are starved while military contractors and political donors are endlessly fed.

The greatest illusion is that we "consent" to this system through periodic elections, when in truth our choices are constrained by money and entrenched power. Bursting this bubble means demanding transparency, fiscal responsibility, and governance that serves citizens rather than elites.

But the story doesn't end with domestic politics and spending. Next, we'll examine the largest beneficiary of this broken system: a trillion-dollar war machine sold to us as defense but operating as empire, industry, and ideology in "The Military Bubble."

CHAPTER 11:

THE MILITARY BUBBLE

No empire admits it's an empire.

And yet, the United States maintains more military outposts around the world than any empire in history.[1] With patriotic slogans and Hollywood narratives, we disguise military expansion as freedom-fighting, and global intimidation as defense. We don't call it occupation; we call it presence. We don't admit it's about control; we say it's about democracy.

This is the military bubble, the carefully crafted illusion that America's vast and growing military footprint is necessary, benevolent, and beneficial. But beneath the camouflage of flags and medals lies an inconvenient truth: our military has become less about protection and more about projection—projection of power, projection of ideology, and projection of profit.

THE EMPIRE NOBODY TALKS ABOUT

The U.S. currently operates **over 750 military bases** in **more than 80 countries**. By comparison, all other countries combined operate fewer than 30 military bases outside their borders.[2]

According to the Department of Defense, nearly 200,000 active-duty U.S. troops are stationed overseas.[3] Germany, South Korea, and Japan host tens of thousands each. These bases are not temporary deployments—many have been there for decades, becoming permanent fixtures of American presence.

This is not a defense force, this is a global occupation. And most Americans have no idea it exists.

THE MONETARY BLACK HOLE

As this book is being written in 2025, Congress approved **$1.01 trillion** in military spending, including both direct and indirect spending. That exceeds the military budgets of the next ten countries combined, including China and Russia,[4] and accounts for 37% of all military spending worldwide.[5]

Despite this massive budget, Pentagon audits repeatedly reveal billions lost to waste, fraud, or "unaccounted-for" transactions. In fact, the Pentagon has never passed a full financial audit, despite being required by law since 1990.[6] Billions simply disappear into the bureaucratic void while contractors profit and oversight fails.

Where does it all go? Not primarily to soldiers or veterans. It flows to defense contractors, Lockheed Martin, Raytheon, Boeing, Northrop Grumman, whose CEOs earn tens of millions while lobbying Congress to keep wars and weapons contracts flowing.

The people actually fighting for our country and risking their lives are so low paid that many of the junior ranks fall below the national poverty level and qualify for the Supplemental Nutrition Assistance Program (SNAP), colloquially known as "Food Stamps."[7]

EXPORTING DEMOCRACY BY DRONE

From Vietnam to Iraq, from Libya to Afghanistan, U.S. military interventions have consistently left nations in ruins, leadership in chaos, and regional stability in tatters. Despite the rhetoric of promoting democracy and freedom, most of these wars have failed to achieve their stated objectives, created power vacuums exploited by extremists, and cost trillions of dollars plus hundreds of thousands of lives.

- **Vietnam (1955-1975):** Over 58,000 American deaths and millions of Vietnamese killed. The war ended with U.S. withdrawal and a unified communist Vietnam.[8]

- **Iraq (2003-present):** Justified by nonexistent weapons of mass destruction, the invasion toppled Saddam Hussein but led to civil war, the rise of ISIS, and over $2 trillion in spending.[9] Military troops are still stationed Iraq.

- **Afghanistan (2001-2021):** America's longest war. Two decades, 2,400 U.S. military deaths, and over $2.3 trillion spent, only to see the Taliban retake control within days of U.S. withdrawal.[10]

- **Libya (2011):** U.S. and NATO forces helped topple Muammar Gaddafi, transforming Libya into a failed state plagued by ongoing civil war and humanitarian crisis.[11]

In each case, America left behind less democracy and more disorder, while defense contractors profited from both the destruction and attempted reconstruction.

THE MILITARY-INDUSTRIAL COMPLEX: BUILT FOR PERPETUAL WAR

The United States doesn't just fight wars, we manufacture them. That's not metaphor; it's infrastructure.

President Dwight D. Eisenhower, himself a five-star general, warned against this in his 1961 farewell address when he coined the term **"military-industrial complex"** and cautioned:

> "We must guard against the acquisition of unwarranted influence... The potential for the disastrous rise of misplaced power exists and will persist."[12]

That was over 60 years ago. Today, the complex he warned about has become the system itself.

The American war machine is no longer just a tool of foreign policy, it *is* our foreign policy. War, or more precisely the tools of war, has become one of America's most profitable exports. The U.S. is the world's largest arms exporter, responsible for over 40%

of global weapons sales.[13] We don't just respond to conflicts; we fuel them by arming multiple sides and ensuring no region ever runs out of ways to destroy itself.

PEACE IS BAD FOR BUSINESS.

The U.S. doesn't just prepare for conflict; we manufacture weapons in anticipation of theoretical threats. When there's no war to fight, we find new buyers, create new dependencies, and build new justifications for military expansion.

This system is embedded throughout American society:

- Defense contractors spread jobs across every congressional district, making military spending cuts politically dangerous
- Entire towns and states depend economically on weapons manufacturing
- We flood allied countries with surplus equipment, then sell ourselves newer, more expensive replacements
- Local police departments receive military-grade equipment as if preparing for warfare rather than community policing

THE COST OF GLOBAL CONTROL

Imagine if those trillions had been spent differently—if the money used to bomb foreign cities was used to build domestic infrastructure:

$300 billion could repair every public school in America.[14] $100 billion could effectively end homelessness.[15] $200 billion could create universal pre-K and childcare.[16] $500 billion could fund a comprehensive Green New Deal to transform our energy infrastructure.[17]

Instead, we build more jets, more bombs, more bases, while American infrastructure crumbles and social services are starved of funding.

FOREIGN MILITARY AID: SUBSIDIZING WEALTHY ALLIES

While military spending spans the globe, some of its most questionable investments involve aid to wealthy nations that arguably don't require assistance for survival.

Every year, the U.S. sends $3.8 billion in military aid to Israel, locked in by a 10-year memorandum regardless of America's debt levels or domestic crises.[18] This supports the Israeli ongoing military operations that often violate international law, while the U.S. receives little tangible benefit in return—no energy resources, no security guarantees for Americans, no favorable trade arrangements.

Similar patterns exist with other wealthy allies receiving substantial military aid while American communities lack basic services. The aid serves strategic and political purposes rather than humanitarian ones, often creating regional dependencies that require ever-increasing American involvement.

BASES AND BLUNDERS: GLOBAL GARRISONING GONE WRONG

Maintaining 750+ military bases isn't just expensive, it's often counterproductive. In Okinawa, Japan, decades of protests have erupted over U.S. military presence due to environmental pollution, crime, and land disputes. In South Korea, American bases remain sources of local tension that undermine the alliances they supposedly strengthen.

In Africa, where the U.S. has expanded military operations under AFRICOM, increased drone strikes and counterterrorism training have correlated with greater regional instability, not less. American military presence often generates the very resistance it claims to fight, creating dependency while fueling nationalist backlash.

WHO BENEFITS? (NOT YOU)

U.S. military expansion serves a narrow circle of beneficiaries:

Defense contractors profit from perpetual conflict and weapons sales. Politicians receive campaign donations and patriotic talking points. Foreign allies receive advanced weaponry and funding with minimal accountability.

Meanwhile, Americans foot the bill while enduring crumbling infrastructure, expensive healthcare, student debt, and eroding social services. The average taxpayer pays over $2,300 annually toward military spending, more than for Medicare, more than for education.[19]

THE MYTH OF SECURITY

Supporters argue military dominance keeps America safe. But examine our actual threats: the 2008 financial collapse, the COVID-19 pandemic, domestic terrorism, infrastructure failures, and cyber attacks. A trillion-dollar defense system didn't, and couldn't, prevent any of these.

Real national security involves public health, economic stability, education, and trust in institutions. In all these areas, America is failing while pouring resources into military hardware designed for conflicts that rarely materialize as expected.

ARSENAL OF THE UNFREE

The United States has become the arsenal of the unfree, arming dictators, fueling conflicts, and building war machines that guarantee our continued relevance in global instability. We don't just defend democracy; we subsidize repression worldwide. We don't just protect allies; we ensure their dependency on American weapons systems.

This represents warfare as commerce, destruction as export, violence as economic policy. Every bomb sold, every fighter jet delivered, every contract signed reinforces America's role not as the world's peacekeeper, but as its primary arms dealer.

BREAKING FREE FROM THE WAR ECONOMY

The military bubble survives because it's embedded in our economy and culture. We've created a system too big to disarm, too profitable to abandon, and too politically entrenched to challenge. Defense spending feeds GDP, underwrites technological innovation, and maintains global economic hegemony.

But empires don't fall from external enemies, they collapse under the weight of their own contradictions and unsustainable commitments. We face a choice: continue inflating the military bubble while domestic needs go unmet, or redirect resources toward building a society actually worth defending.

Bursting the military bubble means cutting unnecessary overseas commitments, closing redundant bases, ending blank-check military aid, and investing in human needs rather than warfare capabilities. We have the resources; we lack only the political courage to use them differently.

The question isn't whether we can afford to change course, it's whether we can afford not to.

CHAPTER RECAP—WAR AS AN INDUSTRY

This chapter revealed America's military machine as less about national defense than global dominance, profit, and political dependency. With over 750 bases worldwide and trillion-dollar budgets, the U.S. operates an empire it refuses to acknowledge. From Vietnam to Afghanistan, military interventions launched for claims of democracy and freedom consistently end in instability and lucrative contracts for weapons manufacturers.

The "military bubble" persists because war has become integral to American economics and culture. Defense contractors spread jobs across every state to ensure congressional support.

Politicians equate military spending with patriotism while taxpayers pay more for warfare than for education, healthcare, or infrastructure combined. The military-industrial complex Eisenhower warned about has become the system itself, one where peace threatens profits and perpetual conflict drives economic growth.

Military aid to wealthy allies illustrates the distortion, as billions flow overseas while American infrastructure deteriorates. The result is a war economy that manufactures conflicts to sustain itself, turning America into the world's primary arms dealer rather than its peacekeeper.

But this logic of force and control doesn't stop at national borders. Domestically, similar patterns emerge in how we police our own communities. Next, we'll examine how American law enforcement, rooted in slave patrols and strike-breaking, has evolved into a system that serves power and property while often endangering the communities it claims to protect in "The Law Enforcement Bubble."

CHAPTER 12:

THE LAW ENFORCEMENT BUBBLE

The American public has been sold a carefully packaged idea: that law enforcement exists to protect and serve. That police officers are community guardians, neutral arbiters of peace and justice. But behind the badge and blue lies a more complicated, and more troubling, truth.

The law enforcement bubble is the collective illusion that American policing is designed for the safety of its citizens. In reality, it's an institution structured to protect power, property, and the status quo, not people. And often, it does so at the direct expense of the very communities it claims to serve.

THE HERO MYTH: MANUFACTURING MARTYRS

Perhaps no aspect of the law enforcement bubble is more carefully constructed than the hero myth—the narrative that police officers are brave protectors risking their lives daily to keep us safe. This mythology serves powerful political purposes, justifying massive budgets, militarized equipment, and immunity from accountability. But like most propaganda, it crumbles under factual scrutiny.

The Bureau of Labor Statistics tracks occupational fatalities across all industries, providing objective data on workplace dangers. According to their most recent comprehensive analysis, police work doesn't crack the top 20 most dangerous jobs in America. In fact, it ranks around 50th in occupational mortality rates.[1]

Police officers experience 14 deaths per 100,000 workers annually, a rate that sounds significant until compared to other occupations we consider routine:

- **Delivery drivers:** 27.7 deaths per 100,000 (nearly twice as dangerous as police work)

- **Farmers and agricultural workers:** 24.7 deaths per 100,000

- **Construction workers:** 13.6 deaths per 100,000 (nearly identical to police)

- **Maintenance workers:** 15.1 deaths per 100,000

- **Truck drivers:** 26.9 deaths per 100,000

The most dangerous jobs in America include logging workers (111 deaths per 100,000), fishing workers (77 deaths per 100,000), and aircraft pilots (58 deaths per 100,000).[2] Amazon delivery drivers face nearly double the mortality risk of police officers, yet we don't build shrines to UPS workers or grant them qualified immunity for mistakes made under pressure.

Even more revealing: **most police deaths result from traffic accidents and health issues, not criminal violence**. According to the National Law Enforcement Officers Memorial Fund, vehicle crashes and medical emergencies consistently account for more police deaths than shootings or assaults.[3] The "thin blue line" narrative of officers standing between civilization and chaos simply doesn't match the statistical reality of police work.

THE RESPONSE MYTH

The hero narrative also obscures a fundamental truth about policing: **police primarily respond to crimes after they occur, rather than preventing them**. Despite popular mythology about officers patrolling neighborhoods and deterring criminal activity, research consistently shows that police presence has minimal impact on crime prevention.

Studies analyzing police patrol effectiveness find that increasing police presence in an area typically reduces crime by only 2-5%, a modest improvement that comes at enormous financial cost.[4] Most crimes occur in private spaces (homes, businesses) where police patrols are irrelevant, or they happen so quickly that response time is meaningless.

The average police response time for emergency calls ranges from 7-14 minutes in most American cities, long after crimes have concluded.[5] For property crimes, domestic violence, and most violent encounters, police arrive to document what happened, not to prevent it from happening.

This reality explains why countries with far fewer police officers per capita often have substantially lower crime rates than the United States. The correlation between police spending and public safety is weak at best, suggesting that other factors, education, economic opportunity, mental health services, community cohesion, have greater impact on crime prevention.

MEDIA MANUFACTURING

The hero myth receives constant reinforcement through entertainment media that portrays police as action heroes saving innocent victims from immediate danger. Television shows, movies, and news coverage systematically overrepresent the dramatic, violent aspects of police work while ignoring the routine traffic enforcement, report-taking, and property protection that comprises most police activity.

This media representation creates public expectations about police work that have little connection to reality. Citizens expect officers to be crisis counselors, mental health professionals, social workers, educators, and community mediators, roles for which they receive minimal training and often prove counterproductive.

The disconnect between mythological expectations and actual police functions helps explain why police encounters so often escalate unnecessarily. Officers trained for combat scenarios respond to mental health crises, family disputes, and social problems with techniques designed for enemy suppression rather than community service.

POLICING POWER, NOT PEOPLE

From its inception, American law enforcement has been built around the defense of property and the enforcement of social hierarchy. Early municipal police departments in the northern United States arose during labor strikes and civil unrest, not to protect workers, but to protect factory owners and corporate interests. In the South, modern policing evolved from slave patrols designed to capture runaway slaves and suppress uprisings.

That foundational DNA hasn't changed.

Today, police are far more likely to be deployed for property crimes, protests, and demonstrations than to prevent or respond to violent crimes against individuals. During the 2020 George Floyd protests, police nationwide responded with military-style tactics to demonstrations against police violence, illustrating the paradox in full: law enforcement is most aggressive when the legitimacy of law enforcement itself is questioned.

FAILURES TO PROTECT CITIZENS

If the role of police were truly to protect citizens, we'd expect that priority to be reflected in outcomes. But across the country, law enforcement fails repeatedly to protect the public from genuine harm:

- **Rape kit backlogs** in major cities mean thousands of sexual assault cases go untested and unresolved for years.[6]

- The **Uvalde, Texas school shooting (2022)** exposed officers unwilling to breach a classroom while children were being murdered.[7]

- At **Parkland (2018)**, an armed school officer remained outside during a mass shooting.[8]

Meanwhile, police killings have become a significant cause of death for young Americans, particularly young Black men. According to analysis of police violence data, **Americans face substantially higher risk of death from police encounters than from terrorist attacks,** a stark indication of where the real dangers to public safety lie.[9]

Unarmed civilians are killed in their own homes during no-knock raids. Mental health crises are met with bullets instead of counselors. Traffic stops turn fatal for minor infractions, disproportionately affecting Black and Brown Americans.

These are not aberrations. They are the predictable results of a system trained to control rather than care.

PROTECTING PROPERTY AND GOVERNMENT

Time and again, police demonstrate that their core allegiance is to institutions and property, not individuals. During the Standing Rock protests, militarized police units protected oil pipeline construction at the expense of Indigenous communities and environmental concerns. During the Occupy Wall Street movement, peaceful protesters were forcibly removed to defend financial institutions and business districts.

When Enron, Lehman Brothers, or Purdue Pharma executives devastate the economy or cause thousands of deaths through corporate malfeasance, no one is dragged from boardrooms in handcuffs. But steal a backpack, sell loose cigarettes, or sleep in the wrong stairwell? That's where police show their teeth.

The disparity reveals the system's true priorities: protecting wealth and power, not public welfare.

THE RISE OF POLICE MILITARIZATION

In recent decades, American law enforcement has undergone a dramatic transformation—not into peacekeepers, but into paramilitary units. Thanks to the **1033 Program**, which transfers surplus military equipment to police departments, even small towns now possess armored vehicles, grenade launchers, and tactical gear.[10]

According to the ACLU, over 80% of SWAT deployments in America are for serving warrants, primarily for nonviolent drug offenses, not hostage situations or terrorism.[11] The militarization budget tells the story: in 1990, $5 million in military equipment was transferred to police. By 2020, over $1.8 billion in military-grade gear flowed to law enforcement—a budget larger than many countries' entire military expenditures.[12]

Militarization changes not only how police look, but how they act. Communities become war zones, civilians become suspects, and de-escalation disappears entirely from the tactical playbook.

COMPARATIVE METRICS: A GLOBAL OUTLIER

The U.S. doesn't just have more police equipment, it has a fundamentally different approach to law enforcement than other developed nations, with dramatically different results.

Police Officers: The United States isn't the most heavily policed nation, but it is by far the most armed and aggressive in enforcement style.

Table 1: Police Officers per 100,000 People

Germany	297
United States	238
United Kingdom	211
Canada	186
Japan	207

Crime Rates: Despite comparable or higher police presence, U.S. violent crime rates far exceed other developed nations. [13]

Table 2: Violent Crimes Per 100,000 People

United States	398
United Kingdom	124
Canada	109
Germany	61
Japan	15

Law Enforcement Spending: The U.S. spends the most on law enforcement: [14]

Table 3: Law Enforcement $ Per Capita

United States	500
Canada	340
United Kingdom	320
Germany	280
Japan	230

Despite higher spending and extensive police presence, America experiences significantly more violent crime. This isn't a funding issue—it's a design flaw in the philosophy of policing.

PROFIT-DRIVEN ENFORCEMENT

Perhaps the most glaring example of systemic corruption is **civil asset forfeiture**, where police can seize property they *suspect* is connected to a crime, even if the owner is never charged. The department that seizes assets often keeps the proceeds, while property owners must pursue expensive legal action to recover their belongings, even when no charges are filed.

This creates perverse incentives where departments focus on drug busts, highway stops, and seizures over solving rapes, murders, or assaults. According to the Institute for Justice, police seized over **$68 billion** through civil asset forfeiture from 2000 to 2019.[15] Most citizens never recover their property due to the complexity and cost of legal proceedings. In 2024 80% of the property seized was accomplished through administrative processes, i.e. without charges and without court involvement. Only ½ of 1% of the property seized was ultimately returned to its owner.[16]

It's important that you understand this clearly: your property can be taken without criminal charges, without trial, and without conviction. Even when no charges are filed, recovering seized assets requires hiring lawyers to sue the police for their return, all while your taxes continue paying their salaries.

INCARCERATION FOR PROFIT

The United States leads the world in incarceration—not in prosperity, innovation, or freedom, but in caging its own citizens. With less than 5% of the world's population, the U.S. holds nearly

25% of the world's prisoners.[17] Even authoritarian regimes like Iran and Saudi Arabia incarcerate fewer people per capita.[18]

Table 4: Imprisoned People Per 100,000

United States	664
United Kingdom	134
Canada	104
Germany	69
Japan	36

This isn't about being "tough on crime"—it's about profit. Incarceration has become a business model. Private prison companies like CoreCivic and GEO Group generate billions annually operating facilities where keeping beds filled is literally part of their financial strategy. States sign contracts guaranteeing **minimum occupancy rates,**[19] meaning taxpayers pay penalties if prisons aren't sufficiently full—regardless of actual crime levels.

Freedom becomes a liability to their bottom line.

Prison labor, paying mere cents per hour, supports industries from food packaging to military equipment production. It's legalized exploitation masquerading as rehabilitation. We don't just arrest people to improve public safety—we arrest them to maintain cash flow.

The result is harsh sentencing laws, mandatory minimums, and a criminal justice system that punishes poverty, race, and addiction while leaving white-collar criminals largely untouched. We don't have a justice system—we have a profit system dressed up as justice.

CRIMES AGAINST CITIZENS VS. CRIMES AGAINST POWER

Law enforcement systematically underinvests in solving crimes against individuals while aggressively pursuing offenses that threaten property or authority. Only 33% of reported rapes result in arrest.[20] Only 50% of murders are solved in many cities.[21]

Contrast this with the fact that over 80% of drug arrests are for possession rather than trafficking, disproportionately targeting poor communities while major dealers and corporate drug crimes receive minimal attention.

Policing prioritizes control over justice, order over safety, and profit over protection.

THE DOUBLE STANDARD

A system that fails to solve violent crimes while succeeding at seizing cash, cars, and homes isn't broken—it's functioning exactly as designed, just not for ordinary citizens' benefit.

The predictable results include: Black Americans being 3 times more likely to be killed by police than whites,[22] low-income communities facing disproportionate surveillance and arrests,[23] and peaceful protests for accountability being met with increased violence.

Meanwhile, mass shooters, white-collar criminals, and violent police officers often face minimal consequences.

WHAT LAW ENFORCEMENT COULD BE

Alternative models exist. Imagine public safety focused on preventing harm rather than punishing symptoms—where mental health professionals respond to crises, schools employ counselors instead of armed officers, and community investment replaces surveillance.

The $130 billion spent annually on U.S. law enforcement could instead fund after-school programs and youth employment, addiction treatment and housing support, unarmed responders for nonviolent emergencies, and actual investigation of violent crimes.

These aren't radical concepts. Countries **like Norway, the Netherlands, and Japan** implement such approaches, achieving incarceration rates and police violence levels that are fractions of America's rates.

POPPING THE BUBBLE

To burst the law enforcement bubble, we must stop asking how to improve policing and start examining what it's actually designed to accomplish. When a system consistently protects wealth over wellness, suppresses dissent over disorder, and profits from punishment, it's not malfunctioning—it's operating according to its true purpose.

Reform tinkers at the edges while leaving fundamental structures intact. Real change requires reimagining public safety from the ground up, starting with honest acknowledgment of whom current systems actually serve.

The myth that police exist to serve ordinary people collapses under examination. The data reveals the truth: law enforcement in America functions as a mechanism for protecting power, not people.

What remains is the urgent question: who does the law actually serve, and who does it silence? Until we're willing to answer honestly, American law enforcement will remain exactly what it is—not a shield for communities, but a sword for those who wield power over them.

CHAPTER RECAP: PROTECTING POWER, NOT PEOPLE

This chapter exposed the central myth of American policing: that law enforcement exists to "protect and serve" ordinary citizens. In reality, from its origins in slave patrols and strike suppression to today's militarized SWAT teams and profit-driven prisons, the system has always prioritized guarding property and preserving hierarchy over public safety.

The hero myth portrays police as brave protectors risking their lives daily, but Bureau of Labor Statistics data reveals police work ranks around 50th in occupational mortality, less dangerous than delivery driving, farming, or construction work. Most police deaths result from traffic accidents, not criminal violence, while their primary function involves responding to crimes after they occur rather than preventing them.

Police respond aggressively to protests but hesitate during mass shootings. They clear homeless encampments, seize assets through civil forfeiture, and fill private prison beds while rape kits gather dust and violent crimes go unsolved. America spends more, arrests more, and imprisons more than any peer nation, yet genuine safety and justice remain elusive for most communities.

This isn't a system that failed to achieve its stated goals, it's one that functions exactly as designed. It protects wealth, enforces compliance, and generates profit, often at the direct expense of the people it claims to safeguard. Reform addresses symptoms while leaving the fundamental structure intact.

With the Information, Government, Military, and Law Enforcement bubbles now revealed, our focus turns outward. These same patterns of control, exploitation, and manufactured consent extend far beyond U.S. borders, reshaping economies, cultures, environments, and security systems worldwide. In Part II—*Collateral Damage: The Cost of American Power*—we examine how American empire affects the rest of the world, starting with the economic mechanisms that ensure global dependency and extraction.

PART II:

COLLATERAL DAMAGE: THE COST OF AMERICAN POWER

The United States, with its resources, economy, military, and population has a unique opportunity in the world to be the leader in democracy, human rights, environment protection, and safety. It has the opportunity to truly make the world a better place both now and in the future.

Unfortunately, that opportunity, more often than not, is missed or consciously squandered.

In this section, we'll examine areas where the United States could be a leader in advancing global initiatives, or a leader in setting the example for other countries by advancing initiatives domestically, but instead has elected to either ignore those opportunities, or worse, act in a short-sighted manner that promotes more long-term harm than good.

We'll examine environmental issues, modern warfare, gender and human rights, and look at how all of this affects both American and world citizens each day and how it will likely affect our children and grandchildren.

CHAPTER 13:

ECONOMIC AND FINANCIAL IMPERIALISM

You are told that America's wealth is the result of ingenuity, hard work, and free enterprise. You are told that the dollar is strong because the United States is trustworthy, stable, and moral. But scratch the surface, and the story collapses. The truth is that American prosperity has always been tied to empire, not just with guns and soldiers, but with banks, loans, and contracts. Economic power has been America's quiet weapon, the velvet glove that covers the iron fist.[1]

This is not leadership. This is not principled free markets. It is domination dressed up as opportunity. Washington doesn't just play in the global economy, it rigs the game. The United States promises development, then delivers dependency. It preaches freedom, then chains nations to debt. It tells the world to play fair, while it controls the rules, the referees, and the scoreboard.[2]

And when the bills come due? It isn't Wall Street that pays. It isn't American corporations that carry the cost. It's the people in Jamaica, or Greece, or Venezuela— mothers, farmers, children, who are forced to live under austerity, who lose jobs, food subsidies, pensions, and futures, all because American bankers and politicians decided their survival was less important than profit.[3] That is not "spreading democracy." That is empire.

In America, we are proud of our lifestyle and standard of living, but we seldom consider that our standard of living is achieved at the expense of others.

THE DOLLAR AS EMPIRE

If you want to understand how America became the most powerful nation on earth, forget the flag and the military parades. Look at the dollar. Follow the money. The **dollar empire** is America's true foundation. That statement isn't metaphorical, it's literal.[4]

111

Since World War II, the U.S. dollar has been the world's reserve currency. Countries trade in dollars, borrow in dollars, and hoard dollars because Washington and Wall Street have made sure no alternatives are available.[5] When oil is sold, it is sold in dollars. When banks collapse, they are rescued in dollars. The global financial system is a dollar system, and America sits at the center of it like a spider in a web.[6]

This arrangement means that every financial crisis funnels back into U.S. power. When nations owe debts in dollars, they don't just owe money, they owe obedience. If they resist, Washington cuts off access. If they disobey, sanctions follow. And if they collapse, the International Monetary Fund (IMF) and World Bank are waiting with loans that look like lifelines but act like nooses.[7]

Think about that: America controls the money everyone else needs just to survive. That isn't free enterprise. That isn't fair play. It is control, plain and simple. It is empire without soldiers, conquest without invasion.[8] And the world has been paying the price for decades.

THE IMF AND WORLD BANK: COLONIALISM IN A NEW SUIT

When Americans hear about the IMF or the World Bank, they picture smart economists in suits, parachuting in to help poor countries climb out of poverty. The branding is brilliant. Who could be against a "World Bank"? Who doesn't want an "International Monetary Fund"? The names sound like lifelines. But to the nations forced to deal with them, they feel like shackles.[9]

The IMF and World Bank don't rescue economies. They conquer them. They offer loans with one hand while writing surrender terms with the other. The price is always the same: slash food subsidies, cut wages, fire teachers and nurses, sell public utilities, privatize national resources, and open markets wide to foreign corporations.[10] These "structural adjustment programs" don't heal economies, they hollow them out.

And here's the part Washington doesn't say out loud: these institutions are not neutral referees. They were built by the U.S. and its allies at Bretton Woods in 1944 to lock in American dominance after World War II.[11] The U.S. is the biggest shareholder in both the World Bank and the IMF. It controls the voting shares, appoints the leadership, and sets the terms. When the IMF speaks, it speaks with an American accent.[12]

Once a country takes the deal, it's trapped. Loans pile on loans. Interest compounds. Old debts are rolled into new ones with even harsher conditions attached.[13] Development turns into dependency.

John Perkins, who worked as what he called an "economic hitman," admitted that his job was to convince leaders to accept loans they could never repay. While critics have questioned some of Perkins' specific claims and called him a "conspiracy theorist," his former colleagues have confirmed the basic dynamics he describes. Einar Greve, his supervisor at Chas. T. Main, agreed that "what John's book says is, there was a conspiracy to put all these countries on the hook, and that happened."[14] Perkins described the goal: "These loans were intended to make them dependent on the United States and its corporations."[15] That isn't aid. That isn't partnership. That is colonialism, updated, rebranded, and enforced with contracts instead of cannons.

WHO OWNS THEM AND HOW THEY PROFIT

The IMF and World Bank present themselves as international institutions, accountable to all nations. But peek behind the curtain and you'll see they answer to a very small circle. Ownership isn't spread equally across the globe, it's concentrated in the hands of the wealthiest countries, and within those countries, in the hands of political **and financial imperialism** elites who benefit from keeping the system exactly as it is.[16]

The United States is the largest shareholder in both institutions. That means Washington wields veto power over major decisions, from loan approvals to policy frameworks.[17] The presidents of the World Bank have always been American, handpicked by the White House. The IMF's managing directors are traditionally European, a bargain struck at Bretton Woods to cement Western dominance over the so-called global economy.[18] The world is told these are multilateral institutions. In reality, they are Western-controlled banks with global branding.

And they profit handsomely. The IMF lends money at interest to governments in crisis, creating a cycle where old debts are paid off with new loans. The World Bank funds "development projects", dams, highways, power plants, that often enrich foreign contractors more than the local communities they claim to serve.[19] Nations are left with debt and environmental wreckage, while corporations walk away with contracts worth billions.

This isn't charity. It's business. And the families who control the world's largest financial firms, the same banks and corporations with outsized influence in Washington, London, and Brussels, benefit twice: once from the contracts, and again from the interest payments on the loans that financed them.[20]

Perkins put it bluntly: "The system is built by the corporatocracy, a small group of people who run the biggest corporations, banks, and governments. They shape policies to serve their own wealth and power."[21] That corporatocracy sits behind the IMF and World Bank, pulling the strings while telling the rest of the world it's all for their own good.

DEBT AS A WEAPON

Empires used to control nations with armies. Today, they do it with debt. The IMF and World Bank don't need to fire a single shot, they just send a loan agreement. And once a country signs, the trap snaps shut.[22]

Debt as a weapon is not neutral. It's a tool of control. When a country owes billions in U.S.-backed loans, its leaders lose the freedom to act in their people's best interest. Every decision, on food subsidies, public health, schools, even clean water, must pass through the filter of "creditworthiness."[23] And who decides what counts as responsible? The very bankers and bureaucrats who profit from keeping nations on the hook.

The cruel brilliance of this system is that it looks voluntary. Countries ask for loans. They agree to the terms. But in reality, there's no choice. When currencies collapse, when oil prices crash, when sanctions cut off trade, nations have nowhere else to turn. And Washington makes sure of it by dominating global finance and shutting out any alternatives.[24]

Once indebted, nations are forced into austerity: cutting social spending, privatizing state industries, and opening markets to foreign corporations. These structural adjustment programs gut public services while flooding economies with imports, destroying local industries in the process.[25] People pay twice, once in higher prices for basic goods, and again in lost jobs. Meanwhile, U.S. corporations swoop in to buy privatized assets at fire-sale prices.[26]

Perkins described this tactic with chilling clarity: "Economic hit men arrange huge loans... but the money never actually reaches the countries. Instead, it flows to U.S. corporations. The country is left holding the debt, plus the interest, plus the burden of obedience."[27] Debt doesn't just enslave economies, it ensures political loyalty. Leaders who resist risk financial strangulation, coups, or worse.

Debt is the perfect imperial weapon because it doesn't look like conquest. There are no tanks in the streets, no flags raised over capitals. But the result is the same: sovereignty surrendered, resources extracted, lives diminished. Only this time, the chains are invisible, numbers in a ledger that bind nations as tightly as iron ever could.[28]

ECONOMIC IMPERIALISM IN ACTION

Jamaica: When Jamaica gained independence in 1962, it inherited big dreams but little capital. By the 1970s, global oil shocks and falling bauxite prices left the government desperate for help. The IMF stepped in, but help came with conditions. To get loans, Jamaica was forced to slash food subsidies, cut wages, and privatize industries.[29] Farmers who once fed their communities couldn't compete with cheap U.S. imports. Local businesses collapsed under the weight of foreign goods flooding the market. By the 1980s, instead of thriving, Jamaica was drowning in debt, with unemployment soaring and social services gutted. Bob Marley sang about liberation, but the island lived under financial occupation.

Greece: Fast forward to 2008. The global financial crisis crushed economies across Europe, but Greece became the poster child of debt dependency. The IMF, European Central Bank, and European Commission swooped in with bailout packages. But these weren't rescues, they were ransom notes. In exchange for loans, Greece had to cut pensions, slash healthcare, and sell off public assets.[30] Athenians saw hospitals closed, suicides rise, and youth unemployment skyrocket above 50 percent.[31] Greece was turned into a laboratory for austerity, where ordinary people paid the price for Wall Street's crash. The so-called "rescue" didn't save Greece, it saved French and German banks, who were paid off with the loans, while leaving Greece shackled with debt for generations.

Venezuela: Venezuela tells a different but connected story. For decades, U.S. banks and oil companies dominated its economy. When Hugo Chávez tried to break free in the early 2000s, redirecting oil profits toward healthcare, housing, and education, Washington responded with economic warfare. Sanctions choked off access to credit, froze assets abroad, and cut Venezuela from international markets.[32] These measures didn't just target leaders, they devastated ordinary citizens, fueling shortages of medicine and food.[33] In Venezuela, debt and sanctions worked hand in hand: punish independence, enforce compliance, and send a warning to any other nation daring to challenge U.S. financial hegemony.

Across these cases, the pattern is clear: whether through IMF austerity, European bailouts, or sanctions, the United States wields financial power as a weapon. Nations don't fall because they are weak, they fall because the system is designed to make them fall.

SANCTIONS AS ECONOMIC WARFARE

When America wants to punish another country, it doesn't always send troops. It sends bankers. Sanctions are the modern siege weapon, a way to starve nations into obedience without ever firing a bullet. Washington dresses them up as "targeted" measures, claiming they hit corrupt leaders or rogue regimes. In reality, they devastate ordinary people while strengthening the very elites they claim to weaken.[34]

Cuba has lived under a U.S. embargo for more than sixty years. What started as punishment for daring to nationalize American-owned sugar and oil refineries has become a generational blockade.[35] Children grow up with medicine shortages, farmers can't access equipment, and families are forced to improvise everything from car parts to medical tools. Washington calls it policy. Cubans call it survival.

Iran has been hammered with sanctions designed to cut it off from the global banking system. These measures crippled its ability to import medicine, food, and essential goods, hitting cancer patients and children long before politicians or military leaders felt the squeeze.[36] Sanctions don't just punish governments; they punish populations into desperation.

And then there are tariffs, sanctions by another name. Donald Trump bragged that tariffs were his weapon of choice, slapping them on steel, aluminum, and hundreds of billions in Chinese imports.[37] He boasted that trade wars were "easy to win." But who paid the price? American farmers crushed by retaliatory tariffs, consumers facing higher prices at Walmart, and global supply chains rattled into chaos. Like IMF austerity or World Bank loans, Trump's tariffs were framed as protecting American workers, but in practice they deepened global economic instability and extended Washington's leverage over trade partners.[38]

Whether it's sanctions on Cuba, blockades on Iran, asset freezes in Venezuela, or tariffs on China, the message is the same: obey, or suffer. Sanctions are war by another name. They don't fall from the sky like bombs, they seep into hospitals, markets, and kitchens, breaking societies from the inside out. That's not foreign policy. That's collective punishment on a global scale.[39]

FINANCIAL CRISES AS WEAPONS

Most people think financial crises are accidents, storms no one can control. But for Washington, crises are opportunities. When markets collapse, currencies crash, or debt spirals out of control, the U.S. steps in not as a savior, but as a conqueror. Crises become weapons, used to force nations into dependency and submission.[40]

Take Latin America in the 1980s. When U.S. interest rates spiked under Paul Volcker, debt across the region suddenly became unpayable. Mexico, Brazil, Argentina, all plunged into crisis. The IMF arrived with its "solutions": structural adjustment, austerity, privatization. In reality, these were surrender terms. Whole economies were remade in Washington's image while U.S. banks were bailed out and foreign corporations picked up state industries for pennies.[41]

Asia saw the same playbook in 1997. Currency speculation, fueled in part by U.S.-backed financial institutions, triggered the Asian Financial Crisis. Thailand, Indonesia, and South Korea turned to the IMF for help, only to be told to gut social programs, raise interest rates, and sell off national assets.[42] Millions lost jobs, wages collapsed, and poverty spiked. Yet American and European investors scooped up failing companies at bargain prices. What was called "recovery" looked a lot more like looting.

Perkins warned of this dynamic: "Economic hit men don't create crises by accident, they exploit them. Debt is a tool. Crises are opportunities. And the victims never see it coming until it's too late."[43] Washington understands this better than anyone. In the empire of finance, instability isn't a bug, it's a feature.

Financial crises may look like natural disasters, but they function like precision-guided weapons. They break nations open so American capital can march in. And when the dust settles, the winners are always the same: Wall Street, Washington, and the corporations that feed off collapse.[44]

THE HYPOCRISY OF FREE MARKETS

America never stops preaching about free markets. It tells the world that capitalism is about open competition, a level playing field, and equal opportunity. It scolds other nations for protecting their industries or subsidizing their workers. But behind the curtain, the U.S. does the exact same thing, and worse. The "free market" is a slogan, not a reality. It's a tool used to discipline weaker nations while America quietly breaks every rule it wrote.[45]

Washington insists that other countries tear down tariffs, open borders to imports, and let foreign corporations buy up local industries. But when its own interests are at stake, America throws out the rulebook. U.S. agribusiness, for example, receives billions in subsidies every year.[46] That cheap, subsidized grain floods markets in Mexico and Africa, bankrupting local farmers who can't compete. Free markets for them, corporate welfare for us.

The same hypocrisy shows up in trade. American leaders demanded that China liberalize its economy, but when Chinese exports grew too strong, Donald Trump launched a trade war with tariffs on hundreds of billions in goods.[47] Suddenly, "free trade" didn't apply. It never really did. Markets are free only as long as America wins.

Intellectual property is another battlefield. U.S. corporations demand global enforcement of patents on medicines, even in countries where people die because they can't afford them.[48] During the COVID-19 pandemic, Washington blocked efforts by India and South Africa to waive vaccine patents, ensuring that pharmaceutical giants kept their monopoly profits while billions in the Global South went unvaccinated.[49] Free markets, once again, meant freedom for corporations, and death for the poor.

Again, Perkins summed it up: "The system is built on double standards. We sell free markets as if they were holy, but what we really want is control. Free markets are only free when they serve us."[50]

The hypocrisy of free markets isn't a side effect of empire. It is the empire. America waves the banner of freedom while quietly keeping its hand on the scale. And when other nations protest, they're told it's economics. But it's not. It's domination, wrapped in the language of liberty.[51]

BRICS: THE SLOW REVOLT AGAINST THE DOLLAR

Empires don't last forever. Even financial empires crack when the rest of the world grows tired of playing by someone else's rules. That's why BRICS—the bloc of Brazil, Russia, India, China, and South Africa—was formed. At its heart, BRICS represents a rebellion against the dollar system, a collective attempt to escape America's financial chokehold, though progress has been slower and more limited than many anticipated.[52]

For decades, Washington has used the dollar as both carrot and stick. Trade in dollars, borrow in dollars, and stay inside the system or face sanctions, exclusion, and economic strangulation. BRICS nations, some of the largest and fastest-growing economies on Earth, saw the trap. They realized that as long as the dollar remained the world's reserve currency, the United States would always sit in the driver's seat. So they began building alternatives: development banks, trade agreements in local currencies, and discussions of a shared reserve currency.[53]

However, the reality of BRICS progress has been more modest than the rhetoric suggests. At the 2024 BRICS summit in Russia, members continued discussions about creating a potentially gold-backed currency called "the Unit," but no concrete timeline emerged.[54] India's External Affairs Minister S. Jaishankar stated in March 2025: "I don't think there's any policy on our part to replace the dollar. The dollar as the reserve currency is the source of global economic stability."[55] Internal disagreements and diverse economic interests have slowed coordination.

Still, if BRICS alternatives eventually take hold, the implications for the U.S. economy could be significant. The "exorbitant privilege" of the dollar—the ability to print money, run deficits, and still have the world accept it—could erode.[56] Imagine oil sold in yuan or a BRICS currency instead of dollars. Demand for U.S. Treasury bonds would shrink. American borrowing would become more expensive. The empire's invisible subsidy, the world's faith in the dollar, would start to vanish.[57]

That's why American politicians are concerned. They dismiss BRICS in public but work to undermine it in private. Expanding sanctions, pressuring allies, destabilizing member states, these aren't coincidences. They're preemptive strikes against a threat more dangerous than any foreign army: the potential loss of dollar supremacy.[58] Without it, Washington can't fund endless wars, can't prop up its deficits, and can't dictate global terms.

The rise of BRICS, while slower than anticipated, still signals the cracks in America's economic empire. Whether these initiatives succeed or stumble, their very existence represents a declaration from the Global South that they will no longer automatically accept financial imperialism. For the first time in decades, the world is daring to imagine life after dollar dominance. And that is the empire's greatest fear.[59]

CHAPTER RECAP

Empires of the past ruled with armies. America rules with money. It waves the banner of free markets and development, but behind the curtain it enforces dependency, debt, and domination. The **dollar empire** is not just a currency, it's a weapon. The IMF and World Bank are not neutral arbiters, they are instruments of control. And financial crises are not accidents, they are opportunities to tighten the leash.[60]

The rhetoric is always about helping. Loans are called "assistance." Sanctions are called "pressure." Austerity is framed as "reform." But strip away the language and the truth is unmistakable: these are acts of war by other means.[61] The casualties aren't soldiers on battlefields, but workers laid off, children pulled out of schools, patients left without medicine, and families forced into poverty so that foreign creditors can be paid.

And the hypocrisy runs deep. Washington demands open markets but shields its own industries. It insists others play by the rules, then rewrites them whenever it suits American corporations. It claims to defend democracy, yet it uses economic weapons to punish any nation that dares pursue independence. Financial imperialism doesn't just break economies, it breaks the promise of sovereignty itself.[62]

While critics have questioned some of his specific claims, John Perkins' basic assessment remains accurate: "We were building an empire. And we were doing it with debt, contracts, and corruption instead of armies."[63] His confession is not an exception. It is the rule. This is how the system works, and how it was designed to work.

The cost of American power is not measured in dollars or balance sheets. It is measured in lost futures, in silenced democracies, in lives cut short. Debt as a weapon is the invisible chain. Sanctions are the silent siege. And the empire of finance ensures that the poorest pay the price so that the richest can remain in control.[64]

Yet as we move toward the next chapter on "Digital and Surveillance Imperialism," remember that this economic dominance requires something more than just financial muscle. It requires control of information itself. The empire of finance needs an empire of data to survive and expand. In the next chapter we'll examine how America has weaponized the digital revolution, turning the internet from a tool of liberation into an instrument of control, surveillance, and manipulation that makes economic domination easier to maintain and harder to resist.

CHAPTER 14:

DIGITAL AND SURVEILLANCE IMPERIALISM

America sells the internet as freedom. Silicon Valley executives talk about connecting the world, breaking down borders, and giving every voice a platform. Politicians frame technology as democracy's greatest ally. But behind the bright screens and slick slogans, digital power has become one of the sharpest weapons of U.S. imperialism.[1]

The internet was born as a Pentagon project. Surveillance was in its DNA from the start. Today, that legacy lives on through the dominance of U.S. tech giants, Google, Apple, Facebook, Amazon, Microsoft, companies that don't just shape global markets but shape the very flow of information.[2] When a billion people search, stream, or shop, they aren't just making choices. They're feeding the American empire data.

This is **digital imperialism** without borders, empire written in code instead of maps. Every email that passes through Gmail servers, every WhatsApp message, every financial transaction routed through SWIFT or Visa, builds America's control.[3] Washington doesn't need soldiers to occupy your streets when it can occupy your data.

U.S. officials lecture the world about privacy, freedom of speech, and human rights. But they operate the largest surveillance apparatus in human history, one that spies not only on adversaries but on allies, corporations, and ordinary citizens worldwide.[4] The world is told it's free, yet every click, call, and movement is monitored.

Like the economic imperialism we just examined, digital imperialism doesn't look like empire. There are no flags planted, no armies deployed. That's what makes it so effective. It doesn't conquer land. It colonizes minds, memories, and identities. And the scariest part is, most people never even notice it happening or actively invite it.[5]

THE U.S. EXPORT OF SURVEILLANCE TECHNOLOGY

America doesn't just spy at home; it sells the tools of surveillance abroad. What began as Cold War intelligence gathering has morphed into a trillion-dollar industry where U.S. corporations and government agencies export technology that allows foreign regimes to monitor, censor, and control their own populations.[6]

From facial recognition systems to predictive policing software, much of the world's surveillance backbone is built in the United States, or in other countries like Israel, to U.S. specifications. Companies like Palantir, Amazon Web Services, and Microsoft pitch their platforms as tools for efficiency and security, but in practice, they become weapons of repression. Governments from the Middle East to Latin America buy these systems, often financed by U.S. aid programs, and use them to target activists, silence dissent, and suppress opposition.[7]

Washington calls this "capacity building." But the real capacity being built is for control. Just as the School of the Americas trained soldiers to crush insurgencies, Silicon Valley now trains data regimes to crush dissent. And it isn't just authoritarian states. U.S. allies in Europe and Asia eagerly purchase American spyware, cloud systems, and monitoring tools because aligning with U.S. standards means aligning with U.S. power.[8]

Once hooked, these countries can't easily escape. Their databases, infrastructure, and communications systems run on U.S. platforms. Their intelligence agencies depend on U.S. algorithms. Even their law enforcement workflows are designed around U.S. tech. Dependency is no accident. It's the point.[9]

The export of surveillance technology isn't about helping partners modernize. It's about embedding American power so deeply in their systems that it becomes inescapable. When every protest can be tracked, every phone tapped, every social network monitored, America's reach is global, invisible, and permanent.[10]

THE NSA AND GLOBAL SPYING

When Edward Snowden revealed the scope of the National Security Agency's operations in 2013, the world learned what insiders already suspected. The NSA was not just collecting data on terrorists or foreign leaders, it was collecting everything, everywhere, all the time.[11]

The scale was unparalleled in human history. Programs like PRISM gave the NSA direct access to servers of U.S. tech companies, pulling emails, chats, photos, and documents from Google, Facebook, Apple, and Microsoft.[12] Other operations tapped undersea cables that carry the world's internet traffic, vacuuming up billions of communications at once. Even leaders of allied countries were not spared. German Chancellor Angela Merkel discovered that her personal phone had been tapped by Israeli intelligence, America's closest intelligence partner.[13]

The justification was always security. But what kind of security requires monitoring entire populations, storing phone metadata for millions, and mapping social networks across continents?[14] Surveillance at this scale is not about preventing attacks, it is about controlling information and ensuring that no government or corporation operates outside Washington's shadow.

The U.S. defends this by pointing to China or Russia, arguing that authoritarian regimes spy on their people too. But the difference is reach. No other country has the infrastructure, the tech monopolies, or the global access to data flows that America commands. The internet itself is routed through systems the NSA can access, which means the empire of surveillance covers nearly every corner of the globe.[15]

Snowden called it **"turnkey tyranny"**, a system so vast and automated that the flip of a switch could turn mass surveillance into mass repression. The U.S. insists it would never use such power domestically, but history shows otherwise. From COINTELPRO in the 1960s to post-9/11 monitoring of Muslim communities, American surveillance has always turned inward once it was perfected abroad.[16]

The NSA does not just spy, it sets the standard for a world where privacy is impossible, and obedience is assumed. That is digital imperialism, hidden in plain sight.

CORPORATE SURVEILLANCE AND THE BUSINESS OF DATA

If the NSA is the state's surveillance machine, Silicon Valley is its corporate twin. The difference is that when the government spies, it calls it security. When corporations spy, they call it service. Both extract the same thing, your data, and both feed into the same empire.[17]

Google tracks your searches, maps your movements, and predicts your interests before you even type them. Facebook and Instagram catalog your social networks, political views, and private conversations. Amazon records your purchases, your voice through Alexa, and even your reading habits through Kindle. None of this is accidental. Data is the new oil, and U.S. corporations are the drillers, refining every click and swipe into profit and power.[18]

The genius of this system is that it doesn't feel like surveillance. People hand over data willingly, trading privacy for convenience, and become "information donors." You don't feel coerced when you post a photo, use a GPS app, or order groceries online. But every action is stored, analyzed, and monetized, creating a digital shadow of your life that corporations own and sell.[19] And because these corporations are American, Washington can tap into their systems whenever it chooses.

Edward Snowden revealed how the NSA had direct access to corporate servers, but the relationship goes even deeper. Companies like Palantir were built specifically to serve the intelligence community. Amazon hosts CIA and Pentagon cloud services. Microsoft and Google supply facial recognition and predictive analytics to law enforcement agencies. The line between private enterprise and state surveillance is blurred to the point of invisibility.[20]

This model is then exported abroad. Countries that rely on U.S. platforms for communication, commerce, and security are locked into American terms. Their citizens' data flows through U.S. servers, their corporations rely on U.S. infrastructure, and their governments are pressured to adopt U.S. surveillance standards. **Data colonization** is hardwired into the system.[21]

Corporate surveillance is not just about selling ads. It is about cementing control. The same companies that convince you to share photos with friends also shape elections, manipulate markets, and tilt the flow of global information. They are not neutral platforms, they are pillars of empire disguised as apps.[22]

THE WEAPONIZATION OF SOCIAL MEDIA

Social media was sold as liberation. Platforms like Facebook, Twitter, and YouTube promised to give ordinary people a voice, to bypass traditional gatekeepers, and to connect the world in ways once unimaginable. For a moment, it seemed true. The Arab Spring uprisings of 2011 were hailed as the "Facebook Revolution," proof that technology could empower the powerless. But that moment was short lived. The same tools that spread protests also became tools to monitor, manipulate, and mislead.[23]

The U.S. quickly realized that social media was more than entertainment, it was influence. Platforms based in America control what billions of people see and share every day. Algorithms decide which voices are amplified and which are buried. Content moderation, often framed as protecting users, becomes a political weapon. Posts that challenge American interests can be throttled, demonetized, or erased. Voices that align with Washington can be boosted, trending overnight.[24]

Meanwhile, the platforms themselves became data goldmines. Political campaigns mine Facebook profiles to target voters with micro ads. Intelligence agencies analyze Twitter traffic to predict unrest. YouTube's recommendation system, designed to keep people watching, can also steer them toward narratives that shape public opinion. The line between organic conversation and manufactured consent has blurred almost completely.[25]

Foreign governments noticed, and they rushed to use these tools too. Russia deployed troll farms and bots to influence U.S. elections. China built its own platforms, like WeChat and TikTok, to control domestic discourse while projecting soft power abroad. But here is the difference. U.S. platforms are global by default. Facebook, Twitter, Instagram, and YouTube dominate worldwide, making them unmatched channels of cultural and political power.[26]

What looks like free expression often functions as a battlefield. Washington can lean on Silicon Valley companies to silence dissenting voices abroad, just as easily as authoritarian regimes lean on them at home. This is not a neutral marketplace of ideas. It is an empire of influence, where information is weaponized, narratives are engineered, and truth is whatever the algorithm decides to show you.[27]

THE DOUBLE STANDARD OF INTERNET FREEDOM

America loves to brand itself as the defender of internet freedom. U.S. officials lecture the world about China's Great Firewall, Russia's censorship, and Iran's monitoring of dissidents. Washington funds NGOs to promote "digital rights" abroad and condemns authoritarian governments for restricting access. But when those same freedoms threaten U.S. power, the mask comes off.[28]

Consider WikiLeaks. When the organization exposed U.S. war crimes and diplomatic hypocrisy, Washington did not celebrate transparency. Instead, it hunted Julian Assange like a criminal, pressured allies to silence him, and cut off his organization's access to donations and servers.[29] The same government that praises whistleblowers in authoritarian states drove one of its own into exile and prison.

Or take Edward Snowden. His revelations showed that the NSA spied on billions of people worldwide, including U.S. citizens and allied leaders. Instead of reckoning with the abuse, Washington revoked his passport, charged him under the Espionage Act, and forced him into permanent exile. America claimed to defend digital freedom while punishing the man who proved it was a lie.[30]

The double standard is also visible in how U.S. platforms treat dissent. Social media companies are pressured to remove content deemed "foreign influence" or "misinformation," categories that often align neatly with Washington's political interests. Voices critical of U.S. foreign policy can be suppressed, while state-aligned narratives are promoted as fact. Freedom of expression, it turns out, has conditions.[31]

Meanwhile, U.S. companies sell surveillance technology to repressive regimes, quietly enabling the very censorship and crackdowns that American leaders condemn. The same firms that build secure servers for the CIA also provide spyware to governments that disappear journalists.

America does not defend internet freedom. It manages it, using the rhetoric of liberty as a tool to maintain hegemony. When the internet serves U.S. interests, it is a weapon of democracy. When it exposes U.S. crimes, it becomes a threat to national security. The principle is simple, freedom for thee, control for me.[32]

CASE STUDIES: CHINA, THE MIDDLE EAST, AND THE GLOBAL SOUTH

China: China is often cast as America's digital rival, but in many ways, it has simply borrowed from the U.S. playbook. The Great Firewall blocks foreign platforms, ensuring that domestic companies like WeChat, Weibo, and TikTok dominate. The state uses mass surveillance, facial recognition, and censorship to maintain control. Washington condemns these practices as authoritarian, yet forgets that the internet itself was born as a Defense Department (now more openly, "War Department") tool and that U.S. companies pioneered much of this technology.[33] What Beijing does openly, Washington often does in secret.

The Middle East: In the Middle East, American surveillance has been both exported and deployed directly. During the wars in Iraq and Afghanistan, U.S. forces used biometric databases to catalog entire populations, scanning eyes and fingerprints at checkpoints and storing the information indefinitely.[34] These tools did not disappear after the wars. They were handed off to local governments, embedding U.S. surveillance practices into national security systems. In countries like Saudi Arabia and the UAE, U.S. companies sold spyware and monitoring tools that were later used to target dissidents, journalists, and even members of royal families who opposed the regime.[35] America decries repression, yet supplies the tools to enforce it.

The Global South: Across Africa, Asia, and Latin America, U.S. digital imperialism takes a different form. Instead of direct censorship, it comes through dependency. Facebook's "Free Basics" program promised free internet access in poor countries, but only within Facebook's curated ecosystem.[36] Millions of users came online believing Facebook was the internet itself. The catch, of course, was that every click, message, and photo flowed back to U.S. servers. In the name of bridging the digital divide, Washington created new colonies of data.

These case studies show the global reach of American digital imperialism. China builds firewalls, the Middle East buys U.S. spyware, the Global South lives inside American platforms. The methods differ, but the result is the same. Digital power reinforces political power, and in every corner of the world, the balance tilts toward Washington.[37]

PALANTIR: THE PRIVATE SURVEILLANCE EMPIRE

Palantir is not a household name, but it may know more about you than your closest friend. Palantir is not just another tech company, it is a cornerstone of the modern surveillance state. Founded with seed money from the CIA's venture capital arm, In-Q-Tel, Palantir was built from the start to serve intelligence agencies. Today it stands at the crossroads of war and data, simultaneously fueling U.S. military operations overseas and monitoring civilians at home.[38]

Inside the United States, Palantir has been entrusted with unprecedented access to personal data. Its contracts with Immigration and Customs Enforcement (ICE) gave agents the power to track, detain, and deport migrants using data from license plate readers, utility bills, court filings, and social media. Critics say this system enabled family separations and mass raids under Trump's immigration crackdown.[39] The company also holds contracts with the FBI, the Department of Homeland Security, and even the Department of Health and Human Services. During the COVID-19 pandemic, Palantir managed sensitive health records for millions of Americans. A private company, with no public oversight, now sits at the center of America's healthcare, legal, and government data infrastructure.[40]

Palantir's advantage is its status as a private firm. Because it is not technically a government agency, it can gather, process, and cross-analyze personal information in ways that federal agencies cannot legally do. The government then buys the finished product.

This arrangement gives Washington the power of mass surveillance while sidestepping constitutional protections. The public is told their privacy is safe, but in reality, their data is being weaponized by a company accountable only to shareholders.[41]

Abroad, Palantir has expanded operations into conflict zones, raising serious human rights concerns. Since 2015, the company has operated in Israel, partnering with the Ministry of Defense to supply its Gotham and Foundry platforms for military operations.[42] According to investigations by *The Nation* and other outlets, Palantir's technology has allegedly been used to enhance targeting capabilities in military operations, including in occupied Palestinian territories.[43] However, the company has disputed many specific allegations about its Gaza operations, stating that reports contain "numerous incorrect statements."[44]

The controversy intensified after October 7, 2023, when Palantir signed what it called a "Partnership for Battle Tech" with Israeli forces. Critics and some investors have raised concerns about the company's involvement in operations that have resulted in civilian casualties. Norway's largest asset manager, Storebrand, divested its $24 million stake in Palantir in October 2024, citing concerns that the company's work might implicate the fund in violations of international humanitarian law.[45]

Palantir's history is riddled with controversy beyond its international operations. Journalists uncovered its discussions about discrediting activists critical of U.S. corporations, a role that blurred national security with corporate dirty tricks. In New Orleans, Palantir quietly piloted predictive policing technology, raising alarms that biased data would hardwire racial profiling into law enforcement.[46] Its predictive tools, once tested abroad in counterinsurgency campaigns, found their way back home to U.S. streets.

CEO Alex Karp insists Palantir only supports liberal democracies, but the company's record tells a different story. It supplies ICE with deportation tools, the Pentagon with battlefield intelligence, Israeli and other foreign militaries with targeting systems, and the U.S. healthcare system with pandemic data. It is everywhere, invisible yet unavoidable. The government uses Palantir precisely because it is private, because it can do what the state cannot. That makes it more dangerous, not less. Palantir is not just a contractor, it is the outsourced face of empire.

CHAPTER RECAP

Digital technology was supposed to liberate humanity. The internet was supposed to flatten hierarchies, connect the disconnected, and empower the powerless. Instead, it has become one of the sharpest tools of empire. The United States does not just dominate global finance or military power, it dominates the very infrastructure of information. Whoever controls the data, controls the world.[47]

America insists that it stands for freedom, yet it runs the largest surveillance machine in history. It warns against authoritarian firewalls in China, yet spies on its own citizens and allies with tools just as invasive. It condemns foreign propaganda, yet uses social media platforms to engineer narratives that serve its own agenda.[48] This is not hypocrisy by accident, it is strategy by design.

The real genius of digital imperialism is invisibility. Tanks and troops are easy to spot, but algorithms and metadata are not. Occupation in the digital age just requires servers, satellites, and Silicon Valley CEOs. And while many nations resist U.S. military bases, few can escape U.S. digital platforms. Dependence is built into the code.[49]

The consequences are global. In Venezuela and Iran, sanctions cut off online payments. In Africa and Asia, "free" internet means permanent dependence on U.S. platforms. In Europe, allies discover that their leaders' phones are tapped by the

NSA. Everywhere, the message is the same, America decides what freedom looks like, and everyone else has to accept it.[50]

Edward Snowden warned of "turnkey tyranny," a system so vast that the flip of a switch could turn mass surveillance into mass repression. That switch exists today, and Washington holds it. Digital imperialism is not science fiction, it is the present reality, hidden in plain sight.[51]

If the last century was defined by oil and armies, this one is defined by data and algorithms. The empire has adapted, but the logic remains the same. If you control resources, you control people. If you control information, you control the world. The United States has built a digital empire, and like all empires before it, the cost will not be paid in Washington, it will be paid everywhere else.[52]

Yet as we move toward the next chapter on "Cultural Imperialism," remember that digital surveillance and economic control are only part of the story. The most insidious form of empire operates not through force or finance, but through culture itself. In the next chapter we'll examine how America exports its values, entertainment, and worldview, convincing the world not just to submit to American power, but to desire it, embrace it, and see it as their own.

CHAPTER 15:
CULTURAL IMPERIALISM

Empires are not sustained by armies alone. They are sustained by stories, images, and ideas. America's most powerful export therefore is not steel or oil, it is culture. From Hollywood films to Silicon Valley apps, from fast food chains to pop music, the United States has built a global cultural empire that shapes how people think, dream, and even define freedom itself.[1]

This is a kind of soft power. It is control disguised as entertainment. Every Marvel movie, every McDonald's, every iPhone advertisement carries with it a subtle message about what life should look like, what success means, and whose values are universal. In the process, local traditions are challenged, local economies are pressured, and many people are raised on an American worldview.[2]

Washington knows this power and invests heavily in it. Agencies like the U.S. Agency for Global Media fund outlets that broadcast American narratives abroad. Corporations flood markets with English-language content, often drowning out indigenous languages. As we saw in the last chapter, even the internet, supposedly borderless, reflects American priorities through platforms built and governed in California.[3]

The result is dependency, not just on American goods, but on American meaning. It is subtle, but pervasive. Nations begin to measure themselves against U.S. standards, adopting its models of consumerism, governance, and even personal identity. Resistance becomes harder when the very language of aspiration has already been colonized.

Cultural imperialism arrives in screens, in brands, and in lifestyles that are sold as liberation. But make no mistake, it is just as coercive. By reshaping the cultural imagination, America ensures that its empire is not just enforced by power, but desired by those it dominates.[4]

HOLLYWOOD AND THE GLOBALIZATION OF AMERICAN NARRATIVES

Hollywood is not just an entertainment industry, it is a propaganda machine that shapes the way the world sees America, and even how America sees itself. For more than a century, U.S. film studios have dominated global markets, flooding theaters with stories where America is always the hero, freedom always looks American, and villains always look suspiciously foreign.[5]

From World War II newsreels to Marvel blockbusters, Hollywood has consistently aligned itself with Washington's geopolitical goals. During the Cold War, it pumped out anti-communist films that painted the U.S. as a beacon of freedom. After 9/11, action movies glorified counterterrorism and celebrated military technology, often with direct cooperation from the Pentagon. When the Department of Defense provides access to aircraft carriers or fighter jets, it demands script approval. The result is cinema that doubles as recruitment material.[6]

The reach is enormous. American films dominate box offices in Europe, Asia, Latin America, and Africa, often pushing out local cinema. In many markets, a significant majority of films shown are American made, and the scripts aren't neutral. They normalize U.S. military intervention, consumer lifestyles, and a vision of justice that depends on violence. Watching enough Hollywood movies is like receiving a slow drip of imperial ideology disguised as fun.[7]

Even seemingly apolitical genres carry the message. Romantic comedies reinforce consumer-driven versions of love and success. Animated films like *Frozen* or *Toy Story* teach children American ideals about individuality, family, and morality. These cultural exports may feel harmless, but they frame the world through an American lens, leaving little room for alternative perspectives.[8]

The impact is significant, though not always total. Local film industries often struggle to compete against the financial juggernaut of Hollywood. Talented filmmakers may adapt American styles and narratives to get distribution. While local cultures show resilience and creativity in responding to these pressures, the global imagination is significantly shaped by Hollywood storylines, influencing how billions dream, fear, and define possibility.[9]

CONSUMERISM AS CULTURAL WEAPONRY

If Hollywood shapes dreams, consumerism shapes daily life. American brands have become global symbols, not just of products, but of entire ways of living. Coca-Cola, McDonald's, Nike, Apple, these are not just companies, they are cultural ambassadors, spreading a gospel of convenience, speed, and endless consumption.[10]

Every fast-food franchise that opens in Asia or Africa competes with local cuisines. Every mall filled with American clothing chains helps redefine what it means to be fashionable. Every iPhone sold in South America reinforces the idea that modernity itself is American designed. Consumption becomes cultural alignment, where buying a burger or a pair of sneakers feels like participating in the American dream.[11]

The genius of this system is that it creates dependency disguised as choice. Nations reorganize their economies to host American franchises, import American goods, and imitate American marketing. Local businesses struggle to compete, while supply chains stretch across oceans to serve U.S. corporate interests. What looks like development is actually a form of economic surrender, trading sovereignty for Big Macs and Air Jordans.[12]

Washington has always understood the political value of this. During the Cold War, Coca-Cola and Levi's jeans were seen as weapons against communism, symbols of freedom that spoke louder than speeches. Today, the same dynamic continues. American consumer culture is packaged as liberation, even as it can trap people in debt, waste, and unhealthy lifestyles. Behind every golden arch or glowing screen is a quiet lesson: America sets the standard and everyone else must follow.[13]

The environmental and social costs are not immaterial. Industrial agriculture to feed fast food chains contributes to deforestation in Brazil. Factories in Asia produce cheap clothes and electronics for Western markets. Global waste from discarded products accumulates in landfills worldwide. Consumer imperialism doesn't just change tastes, it reshapes landscapes, economies, and lives.[14]

At its core, consumerism as cultural weaponry is about influence. By shaping what people want, America shapes what they value. And by shaping values, it shapes politics. A world that eats American food, wears American clothes, and dreams American dreams is a world more likely to accept American power.

LANGUAGE, MEDIA, AND THE COLONIZATION OF THOUGHT

Empire doesn't just conquer land, it conquers language. Today, English is the global lingua franca, not because it is inherently superior, but because American power made it that way. Speaking English opens doors to jobs, education, and global commerce. Not speaking it can lock entire communities out of opportunity. This isn't enhanced communication, it's cultural dominance.[15]

Media multiplies this effect. American television, music, and digital platforms saturate global markets. Netflix, Disney+, and YouTube distribute American voices and values in dozens of languages, yet the framework remains American. Stories are told

140

through U.S. perspectives, morality is coded in U.S. terms, and even when local cultures are represented, they are often filtered through Hollywood's lens. The medium may translate, but the message remains empire.[16]

Journalism has been influenced in similar ways. Global news agencies like CNN and The New York Times help define which stories are important and how they are framed. Wars become humanitarian interventions when America wages them but acts of terror when others resist. Economic exploitation is called development when orchestrated by Washington, but corruption when practiced by others. As we saw in the American Bubble sections, influence over global narratives allows the U.S. to shape reality itself.[17]

Even education is shaped by this influence. American universities dominate global rankings, and their degrees are treated as tickets to upward mobility. Many nations restructure their curriculums to align with U.S. standards, importing not just knowledge but ideology. Textbooks funded by U.S. agencies promote free-market capitalism, liberal democracy, and consumer culture as universal truths. The classroom becomes an extension of empire.[18]

This cultural colonization is subtle but also powerful. By influencing language, media, and knowledge, America narrows the spectrum of possibility. Alternatives to capitalism, challenges to empire, or critiques of U.S. policy can be dismissed as fringe or illegitimate. The imagination itself becomes influenced, leaving less room to dream of worlds outside America's shadow.[19]

THE WEAPONIZATION OF AID AND NGOS

The United States has mastered the art of using aid and NGOs as cultural weapons, presenting them as humanitarian while quietly aligning them with American interests. The language is compassion, but the purpose is still control.[20]

Foreign aid often comes with strings attached. Nations receiving U.S. assistance are expected to adopt free-market reforms, deregulate industries, or open their borders to American corporations. "Technical assistance" programs reshape education systems, rewrite laws, and rewire economies to fit Washington's vision. The rhetoric is development, but the effect is dependency.[21]

NGOs play a central role in this process. While many do genuine good, others can act as vehicles for American influence. Human rights organizations may highlight abuses by U.S. rivals while overlooking violations by U.S. allies. Democracy promotion groups push electoral systems that benefit pro-Western candidates. Even public health programs can become political tools, with funding contingent on cooperation with U.S. foreign policy.[22]

Examples are well-documented. In Latin America, USAID has been accused of funneling money to groups working to destabilize governments that resisted U.S. economic policies. In Cuba, the agency secretly funded a fake social media platform called ZunZuneo to stir dissent among youth. According to the Associated Press investigation, the platform was "covertly developed as a long-term strategy to encourage Cuban youths to revolt against the nation's government," reaching about 40,000 users before shutting down in 2012.[23] In Eastern Europe, NGOs backed by Washington helped engineer "color revolutions" that replaced governments unfriendly to U.S. interests. These efforts were packaged as grassroots activism, but behind the curtain, the puppeteer was clear.

Aid is also used to export American values directly. Education programs abroad carry U.S. cultural assumptions. Media grants promote narratives favorable to U.S. policy. Agricultural programs often require the use of American seeds, fertilizers, and technologies, creating long-term dependency. What begins as generosity ends as leverage.[24]

The tragedy is that real needs are exploited for political gain. Communities desperate for food, medicine, or education become captive audiences for American ideology. The hungry are fed, but with conditions. The sick are treated, but with strings. Aid becomes less about solving problems and more about remaking societies in America's image.

This is cultural imperialism disguised as compassion. It is not about solidarity, it is about shaping the world's future to mirror Washington's interests.

CASE STUDIES: LATIN AMERICA, AFRICA, AND THE MIDDLE EAST

Latin America: Latin America has long been ground zero for U.S. cultural imperialism. Hollywood movies flood cinemas from Mexico to Argentina, influencing beauty standards, family ideals, and political attitudes. Fast food chains like McDonald's and KFC compete with traditional foods, while Coca-Cola becomes ubiquitous. Aid programs and NGOs reinforce U.S. influence, funding youth groups, media outlets, and education reforms that align with neoliberal policies. The ZunZuneo case in Cuba demonstrates how cultural manipulation can be as aggressive as any military campaign, with USAID secretly creating a social media platform designed to encourage political unrest.[25]

Africa: In Africa, cultural imperialism often rides in on the back of aid. U.S.-funded NGOs promote American norms in education, health, and governance, presenting them as universal. Peace Corps volunteers teach English and Western values in rural schools, often with genuine humanitarian intent but also cultural impact. Western media corporations expand broadcasting networks across the continent, sometimes sidelining local languages and traditions. Meanwhile, American consumer goods dominate many markets, reshaping diets and lifestyles. For many African youth, global modernity becomes associated with adopting

American brands, speaking English, and consuming U.S. media, even when it competes with their own heritage.[26]

The Middle East: In the Middle East, cultural imperialism is layered on top of military intervention. During the occupation of Iraq, U.S. authorities rewired the media landscape, shutting down critical outlets and funding new stations that broadcast pro-Western narratives. American entertainment also filled the void, with satellite TV and social media pushing U.S. values deep into societies still reeling from war. Aid programs promoted "democracy" while ignoring the role of U.S. bombs in creating instability. Even consumer culture became a tool, with franchises and malls springing up in war-torn cities as symbols of progress. Yet the deeper message was clear: modernization equals Americanization.[27]

Across all three regions, the pattern is significant though not always total. Local traditions face pressure, economies are restructured, and cultural sovereignty is challenged. What looks like modernization or development often creates dependency. America doesn't just dominate markets, it influences meaning, shaping how people see themselves and their place in the world. That is the essence of cultural imperialism.

CHAPTER RECAP

Cultural imperialism is the empire you can't see. It works through stories, brands, and values, reshaping how billions of people live, dream, and define themselves. By influencing the imagination, America makes resistance harder, because the very language of aspiration has been shaped by its power.[28]

Hollywood floods screens with American heroes, while local cinemas struggle. McDonald's competes with traditional meals, while health problems spread in its wake. English becomes the language of opportunity, while indigenous tongues are marginalized. Aid programs and NGOs enter communities with promises of help, but can leave behind new loyalties to Washington's worldview. These aren't accidents or byproducts of progress, they're strategies.[29]

The effect is subtle but significant. A child in Kenya may grow up idolizing Captain America instead of local legends. A student in Bolivia may believe progress means speaking English and wearing Nike shoes. A worker in Cairo may spend wages on American fast food, even as local farmers struggle to survive. These daily choices, shaped by cultural imperialism, reinforce an invisible empire that can be harder to resist than military occupation.[30]

Washington frames its cultural exports as gifts—freedom, opportunity, democracy, while condemning other nations for "propaganda." Yet the U.S. has perfected propaganda on a global scale, packaging it in entertainment, fashion, and apps. It's empire with a smile, conquest with a soundtrack.[31]

Cultural imperialism doesn't just challenge diversity, it can entrench dependency. When local economies struggle under the weight of foreign franchises, when schools rewrite curriculums to match American models, when media systems run on U.S. platforms, sovereignty becomes symbolic. Nations may fly their own flags, but their imaginations are significantly influenced by the stars and stripes.[32]

And like all forms of imperialism, the costs are often paid by the vulnerable. Farmers lose markets, indigenous languages decline, youth can be trapped in cycles of debt and consumerism, communities may fracture under the weight of imported values. The gains, meanwhile, flow back to Wall Street and Silicon Valley.

Cultural imperialism influences the most precious resource of all: the human mind. Until nations reclaim their stories, their languages, and their traditions, the empire of culture will remain America's most effective weapon—invisible but everywhere.[33]

As we move toward the next chapter on "Policing and Security Imperialism," remember that cultural influence, while powerful, still requires enforcement. The most successful empires combine soft power with hard power, using cultural attraction to make coercion more palatable. In the next chapter we'll examine how America exports its models of policing and security, turning local law enforcement into extensions of American power while claiming to promote safety and democracy.

CHAPTER 16:

POLICING AND SECURITY IMPERIALISM

America calls itself the land of the free, but look at how it polices both at home and abroad, and the truth is undeniable. The United States has turned law enforcement into an export, a model of control it sells to the world. Whether through military aid, training programs, or private contractors, Washington spreads its version of policing across the globe, leaving behind not safety but fear.[1]

As we covered in the Law Enforcement Bubble, this system is not about protecting people, it is about protecting power. Domestically, U.S. policing grew out of slave patrols and strikebreakers, designed to keep oppressed groups in line. Internationally, the same logic applies. American "security assistance" trains police forces to crack down on dissent, secure corporate interests, and protect regimes friendly to Washington.[2]

Billions of taxpayer dollars are funneled into "security cooperation" each year. Programs like the State Department's Bureau of International Narcotics and Law Enforcement Affairs, or the Pentagon's Section 1206 funding, equip foreign police and militaries with weapons, surveillance gear, and crowd-control training. The rhetoric is stability, but the results are often repression.[3]

From Latin America's drug wars to Middle Eastern counterterror campaigns, U.S.-trained police forces have been notorious for human rights abuses. Amnesty International and Human Rights Watch have documented torture, disappearances, and massacres carried out by units built with American money and expertise.[4] While these programs may sometimes serve legitimate security needs, they too often create dependency and fear, while cementing U.S. influence in every corner of the globe.

147

Policing imperialism is not just about foreign aid, it is also about bringing the battlefield home. The same tear gas used in Baghdad shows up in Los Angeles and Portland. The same armored vehicles deployed in Kabul roll down American streets. What is tested abroad is perfected at home, and what is perfected at home is exported abroad. It is a militarization feedback loop, a global cycle of repression powered by American dollars and American weapons.[5]

This is empire with a badge, a baton, and a body camera. And everywhere it goes, it leaves behind the same message: resistance will be met with force.

THE MILITARIZATION OF DOMESTIC POLICING

Walk through almost any American city and you will see a strange sight: police who look less like public servants and more like soldiers. Armored vehicles roll down suburban streets, officers in camouflage carry assault rifles, and drones hover overhead. This is not policing in the traditional sense, it is occupation.[6]

The militarization of U.S. police accelerated after 9/11, when the so-called War on Terror blurred the line between foreign battlefields and domestic neighborhoods. Federal programs like the Department of Defense's 1033 Program funneled surplus military equipment to local police departments. Everything from grenade launchers to MRAPs, mine-resistant vehicles built for Iraq and Afghanistan, ended up in small-town America. The message was clear: treat communities as potential combat zones.[7]

This equipment did not sit idle. During the 2014 protests in Ferguson, Missouri, following the police killing of Michael Brown, residents faced a heavily militarized response. Images of snipers aiming rifles at unarmed demonstrators shocked the world. While Ferguson Police Department itself had received mostly non-tactical equipment through the 1033 program—including laptops, generators, and unarmored vehicles—the broader law enforcement response involved St. Louis County and other agencies with access to military-grade gear.[8] But for many Americans, especially black and brown communities, this was nothing new. The tactics of counterinsurgency policing abroad had come home. The state did not respond to protest with dialogue, it responded with tear gas, flashbangs, and armored convoys.

The Pentagon insists this gear is necessary to "keep communities safe." But safe for whom? Studies show that heavily militarized police do not reduce crime or increase officer safety, though they also don't necessarily make things worse.[9] However, communities of color are disproportionately targeted, turning neighborhoods into potential warzones. As one report put it, "the use of military equipment changes the mindset of police officers, encouraging them to see citizens as enemies rather than people to protect."[10]

Even beyond protests, militarization shapes daily life. SWAT raids, once reserved for hostage situations, are now used for routine drug searches. No-knock warrants, backed by battering rams and flash grenades, terrorize families in the middle of the night. Innocent people, including children, have been killed in these raids. This is not law enforcement, it is counterinsurgency turned inward.[11]

The irony is that America condemns authoritarian states for using military force against their own citizens. Yet in the U.S., police have become increasingly indistinguishable from soldiers, patrolling their own populations with weapons of war. What is exported abroad comes home again, and the cycle of militarization feeds itself.

EXPORTING POLICING ABROAD

The United States does not only militarize its own streets, it exports its model of policing around the world. Washington calls it "security assistance," but in reality it is training foreign police forces to act as extensions of American power. The U.S. does not just fund weapons and gear, it rewires entire systems of law enforcement to protect U.S. interests, not always the people they claim to serve.[12]

Since the 1960s, the U.S. has run police training programs across Latin America, Africa, and Asia. Under the banner of fighting communism, American advisors taught foreign police how to crush political dissent, infiltrate unions, and suppress uprisings. These programs were not always about building safer societies, they were often about preventing movements that threatened U.S. corporations and Cold War strategy.[13]

The tactics exported abroad were often brutal. In El Salvador, Honduras, and Guatemala, U.S.-trained police units became infamous for torture and death squads during the dirty wars of the 1970s and 1980s.[14] In Colombia, billions in U.S. aid through Plan Colombia equipped police and paramilitary units that committed extrajudicial killings in the name of fighting drugs. Human rights groups documented massacres of peasants accused of collaborating with guerrillas, while U.S. contractors kept the funding flowing.[15]

These practices were not limited to Latin America. In the Philippines, U.S. training and equipment bolstered a "war on drugs" that left thousands dead in extrajudicial police killings. In Bahrain and Egypt, U.S.-supplied crowd control gear was used against protesters demanding democracy during the Arab Spring. In each case, the pattern was similar: Washington claimed it was helping stabilize allies, but in reality, it was often exporting repression.[16]

Security imperialism works because it creates dependency. Once a country adopts U.S. training, weapons, and technology, it cannot easily turn back. Its police forces rely on American gear, its intelligence services depend on American software, and its governments depend on U.S. aid to fund security budgets. The leash is financial, technical, and political all at once.[17]

The U.S. insists these programs are about spreading democracy. But democracy built on riot shields, tear gas, and torture chambers is a contradiction. What America often exports is control, policing the world to keep it safe for empire.

PRIVATE SECURITY AND MERCENARIES

When governments want to avoid accountability, they outsource. The rise of private security contractors has allowed the United States to wage wars and police the globe while dodging the scrutiny that comes with official forces. These companies are the mercenaries of the modern age, operating in the shadows, armed with American weapons, and loyal not to democracy but to profit.[18]

During the wars in Iraq and Afghanistan, private firms like Blackwater, later rebranded as Academi, became infamous for their brutality. Contractors carried out raids, guarded convoys, and even ran prisons. Unlike soldiers, they were not bound by military codes of justice. Their actions often went unpunished, even when they committed atrocities. The 2007 Nisour Square massacre, where Blackwater contractors killed 17 unarmed Iraqi civilians, became a symbol of what happens when war is privatized.[19]

But these companies did not disappear when the wars ended. They found new markets in Africa, Latin America, and the Middle East, offering "security services" to protect oil pipelines, mining operations, and political elites. Their presence blurs the line between policing and corporate enforcement. A community resisting a foreign-owned mine might not face local police, but American-trained contractors paid to suppress dissent.[20]

Domestically, private security has also crept into American life. Corporations hire contractors to monitor protests, track activists, and provide intelligence on labor movements. Reports have shown firms like TigerSwan, staffed by former U.S. special forces, infiltrating Native-led protests against the Dakota Access Pipeline and treating peaceful demonstrators as insurgents.[21] This is the export-import cycle of repression: tactics tested abroad brought home against American citizens.

The appeal of private contractors is simple. They provide deniability. When things go wrong, the government can point to a "rogue company." When abuses are exposed, blame falls on mercenaries, not the state. Yet these firms are licensed, funded, and armed by Washington. Their survival depends on American contracts. The separation is an illusion.

Private security is policing without accountability, empire without responsibility. The U.S. has built a shadow army that enforces its will around the world, answering not to voters or international law, but to balance sheets. In the age of privatized repression, justice is for sale, and the highest bidder always wins.

THE GLOBAL WAR ON DRUGS AS POLICING IMPERIALISM

The so-called War on Drugs has been one of America's most effective tools of policing imperialism. At home, it criminalized entire communities. Abroad, it provided the perfect excuse to militarize policing across Latin America, the Caribbean, and beyond. Washington framed it as a fight against crime, but the deeper purpose was often control.[22]

In Colombia, billions in U.S. aid under Plan Colombia funded police and paramilitary forces that sprayed toxic chemicals over coca fields, displaced peasants, and carried out extrajudicial killings. Human Rights Watch documented "false positives," cases where civilians were murdered and dressed up as guerrillas so police could collect U.S.-funded rewards. The War on Drugs became a war on the poor, with American money paying for body counts.[23]

Mexico's experience tells the same story. Under the Mérida Initiative, the U.S. provided billions in aid, training, and equipment to Mexican security forces. The result was staggering levels of violence, with tens of thousands killed in cartel wars and countless civilians caught in the crossfire. Amnesty International and Mexican human rights groups have accused U.S.-backed police and military units of torture, disappearances, and collaboration with cartels. The war created chaos, but it also deepened Mexico's dependency on U.S. funding and intelligence.[24]

The Caribbean was not spared either. In Jamaica, U.S. pressure for aggressive anti-drug operations culminated in the 2010 Tivoli Gardens massacre, where at least 73 civilians were killed in a raid to capture a drug lord wanted by the United States. Local police forces, trained and equipped with U.S. support, treated an entire community as enemy combatants. This was not policing, it was war.[25]

Back home, the War on Drugs disproportionately targeted Black and Latino communities. Policies like mandatory minimum sentences and stop-and-frisk policing filled prisons with nonviolent offenders. The same racial logic that justified heavy policing domestically was exported abroad, where poor farmers and urban slum dwellers bore the brunt of American drug policy. The war was global, and its casualties were always the most vulnerable.[26]

By framing narcotics as a global security threat, Washington gained the authority to reshape police forces around the world. Entire regions were remade under U.S. doctrine, their sovereignty weakened, their populations terrorized. The War on Drugs was never just about drugs. It was about creating a global policing regime under U.S. command, and its human toll remains incalculable.

COUNTERTERRORISM AND SECURITY TRAINING PROGRAMS

After 9/11, Washington found its perfect excuse to globalize policing under the banner of counterterrorism. Billions of dollars poured into training programs, surveillance networks, and joint security initiatives. Every government was told the same story: partner with America to fight terror, or risk being labeled part of the problem.[27]

The U.S. created sprawling programs like the Anti-Terrorism Assistance Program, the International Criminal Investigative Training Assistance Program, and the State Department's Office of Anti-Terrorism. Through these, American police, FBI agents, and military advisors trained tens of thousands of foreign officers. The curriculum often looked less like community policing and more like counterinsurgency, teaching riot control, surveillance, and interrogation techniques.[28]

This was not always about making allies safer. It was about embedding U.S. power inside their security institutions. Once a country depended on U.S. intelligence, weapons, and trainers, it could not act independently. Its policing strategies, budgets, and even its definition of "terrorism" were rewritten to align with Washington. Political opponents and activists could be labeled terrorists, and the U.S. would provide the tools to suppress them.[29]

One example is Israel. Through joint counterterrorism programs, American and Israeli forces have shared surveillance techniques and crowd-control tactics. Tear gas tested on Palestinians in the West Bank later appeared on American streets in Ferguson and Minneapolis. This cycle of exchange shows how counterterrorism programs blur the line between foreign occupation and domestic repression.[30]

African nations too have become laboratories for U.S. counterterrorism. Under the Trans-Sahara Counterterrorism Partnership and other initiatives, the U.S. has funded police and military units in Niger, Mali, and Nigeria. These units, armed and trained by Americans, have been implicated in coups, massacres, and crackdowns on civil society. Washington calls it stabilization. Local communities call it state terror.[31]

It's ironic. In the name of protecting freedom, America exports tools of repression. Counterterrorism training does not always build democracy, it often builds dependency. The lesson taught is always the same: security is not about protecting people, it is about protecting power, and that power belongs to Washington.

CASE STUDIES: FERGUSON, IRAQ, AFGHANISTAN, AND LATIN AMERICA

Ferguson: In 2014, the world watched as Ferguson, Missouri erupted after police killed Michael Brown, an unarmed Black teenager. The broader law enforcement response involved armored vehicles, sniper rifles, and tear gas from multiple agencies including St. Louis County. The images looked less like a Midwestern suburb and more like Baghdad. And in a way, they were connected. Much of the military-style gear came from programs like the Pentagon's 1033, equipment recycled from America's wars. The tactics came straight from counterinsurgency manuals used in Iraq and Afghanistan.[32]

Iraq: During the U.S. occupation of Iraq, policing and military operations were blurred into one. American contractors and advisors trained Iraqi police forces, who quickly gained a reputation for torture, corruption, and extrajudicial killings. Some of these units doubled as death squads, targeting Sunni civilians under the guise of counterterrorism. The U.S. framed this as "capacity building," but Iraqis understood it as repression, built with American money and oversight.[33]

Afghanistan: In Afghanistan, the U.S. spent billions training police forces that were supposed to bring stability. Instead, they became notorious for extortion, drug smuggling, and human rights abuses. Many Afghans called them worse than the Taliban, because they preyed on the very communities they were meant to protect. When the U.S. finally withdrew in 2021, the Afghan police collapsed almost instantly, proof that the system had no legitimacy without American backing.[34]

Latin America: Latin America has long been a testing ground for U.S. policing imperialism. In El Salvador, U.S.-trained units committed massacres during the civil war, targeting peasants and church leaders who spoke out against injustice. In Honduras, after the 2009 coup, U.S.-funded police were implicated in killings of journalists and activists. In Mexico, the Mérida Initiative turned whole regions into warzones, where U.S.-equipped police battled cartels and civilians alike. Each case shows the same pattern: Washington exports policing in the name of security, but the result is often bloodshed and dependency.[35]

Taken together, these case studies expose the lie at the heart of U.S. policing imperialism. Whether in Ferguson or Fallujah, Tegucigalpa, or Kabul, the model is the same. Arm, train, and militarize forces to suppress dissent and maintain order, not necessarily for the people's benefit, but for empire's.

CHAPTER RECAP

Policing is supposed to mean safety, protection, and justice. But when America exports its policing model, what it often exports is repression. At home and abroad, U.S. policing has never been neutral. It has always been about protecting power, not people. From Ferguson to Fallujah, the pattern is similar: militarize, surveil, and suppress.[36]

The militarization of American policing shows that the tools of empire do not stay overseas. They come back, embedded in local police departments, reshaping communities into potential combat zones. Empire and policing feed each other, a loop of repression with no clear boundary between foreign and domestic.[37]

Private contractors like Blackwater and surveillance firms prove that the state does not even need to carry out repression directly. It can outsource, hiding behind private companies that profit from surveillance and violence while avoiding accountability. The illusion of separation makes it easier for Washington to deny responsibility, even as its fingerprints are everywhere.[38]

The War on Drugs and the War on Terror became excuses to militarize police worldwide, turning public safety into counterinsurgency. Communities were treated as potential enemies, not citizens. Farmers in Colombia, protesters in Honduras, families in Ferguson, all became collateral damage in America's global policing machine.[39]

Washington condemns authoritarian regimes for using force against their citizens, yet arms its own police with tanks and trains foreign police to crush dissent. America lectures the world about democracy, while exporting the tools of repression that make democracy difficult.[40]

The costs are measured in bodies, in children lost to raids, in journalists silenced, in protesters killed, in communities traumatized. They are measured in the erosion of trust, the normalization of militarized policing, and the quiet acceptance that freedom always ends at the edge of a riot shield.[41]

Policing imperialism reveals the heart of empire. It is not just armies or bankers that enforce U.S. power, it is cops, mercenaries, and surveillance contractors. Together they form a global system of control that keeps populations in check and governments in line. What is sold as protection is, in truth, often occupation.[42]

If empire is a cage, policing is the lock. And America has handed out keys to police forces across the world, ensuring that no matter where you live, the knock on your door might echo with the sound of Washington's power.

As we move to the next chapter on "Environmental Imperialism," remember that control extends beyond people to the planet itself. In this next chapter we'll examine how America has turned the environment into both weapon and victim, using ecological destruction as a tool of dominance while ensuring that the costs of its consumption are paid by the most vulnerable communities around the world.

CHAPTER 17:

ENVIRONMENTAL IMPERIALISM

Empires have always exploited land, air, and water, but America has elevated environmental exploitation into a weapon of global control. The U.S. does not just burn more than its share of fossil fuels—it structures the world economy to ensure that others carry the costs. It shifts the burden of climate change onto the Global South, while reaping the profits of extraction, pollution, and endless consumption.[1]

The story is always the same. American corporations mine, drill, and deforest abroad, then leave behind poisoned rivers and scorched earth. When communities resist, Washington calls it progress. When nations protest, they are told to be "responsible partners" in development. Meanwhile, the U.S. military, the single largest institutional polluter in the world, emits more greenhouse gases than most countries combined, and yet is exempt from international climate agreements.[2]

Environmental imperialism is not just about carbon emissions. It is about how America uses climate policy, trade rules, and military might to enforce a system where it consumes the most and suffers the least. Climate refugees flood borders, droughts wipe out harvests, islands disappear beneath rising seas, but Washington refuses to take accountability. Instead, it tells the rest of the world to adapt, while continuing business as usual.[3]

And when global institutions step in, they often carry America's fingerprints. The World Bank funds massive dam projects that displace indigenous peoples. The IMF pushes austerity that cuts environmental protections. Trade deals lock nations into exporting raw materials while forbidding them from protecting ecosystems. The result is a world where environmental costs are socialized, but profits are privatized in American hands.[4]

America's empire is not just political and financial, it is ecological. By treating the planet as a battlefield and the atmosphere as a dumping ground, the U.S. ensures its own prosperity while pushing the costs onto the poor and powerless. The language is sustainability, but the practice is domination.

THE U.S. MILITARY AS THE WORLD'S BIGGEST POLLUTER

When people think about climate change, they picture smokestacks, SUVs, or oil refineries. What they rarely picture is the Pentagon. Yet the U.S. military is the single largest institutional consumer of fossil fuels on Earth, and one of the largest polluters in history.[5]

Every war burns oil. Every fighter jet sortie, every naval patrol, every convoy across the desert guzzles fuel at a staggering rate. The U.S. military uses more petroleum each year than many entire countries. Its global network of bases requires constant shipments of supplies, fuel, and weapons. The empire runs on oil, and the climate pays the price.[6]

Washington lectures the world about cutting emissions, while exempting its military from accountability. In the 1997 Kyoto Protocol negotiations, the U.S. insisted that military emissions be excluded from national reporting. That loophole carried into later climate agreements, meaning that the largest polluter in history never has to fully report its footprint.[7] The Pentagon hides behind national security while poisoning the globe.

U.S. wars in Iraq and Afghanistan left not only political chaos but also ecological catastrophe. Burn pits spewed toxic fumes that sickened soldiers and civilians alike. Bombing campaigns destroyed farmland, poisoned water systems, and created wastelands where cities once stood. These scars remain long after American troops depart—a toxic legacy.[8]

And yet, the military uses climate change as justification for more funding. The Pentagon calls climate a "threat multiplier," arguing that rising seas, droughts, and mass migration create instability that only U.S. power can contain. The logic is circular. America drives the crisis, then claims it must expand its reach to control the fallout. The solution to climate disaster, according to Washington, is more bases, more weapons, more ships patrolling the seas.[9]

The truth is unavoidable. The U.S. military is not just defending the empire, it is destroying the planet to sustain it. The cost is global, but the accountability is nowhere to be found.

RESOURCE WARS AND ENVIRONMENTAL EXTRACTION

Empire is not just about territory, it is about resources. From oil to lithium, from copper to cobalt, the U.S. has waged wars, staged coups, and backed dictatorships to secure access to what powers its economy. Environmental imperialism is not only about pollution, it is about the extraction that fuels the machine.[10]

Iraq is the clearest example. In 2003, the U.S. invaded under the pretext of weapons of mass destruction. What it left with was control over one of the largest oil reserves on the planet. American oil companies signed lucrative contracts while Iraqis lived amid bombed-out infrastructure and poisoned soil. The war killed hundreds of thousands, but for ExxonMobil and Halliburton, it was a windfall.[11]

The same story plays out in Latin America. In Bolivia, Washington opposed Evo Morales when he sought to nationalize lithium reserves, critical for batteries and the renewable energy transition. Morales described it bluntly: "They know we have the largest lithium reserves, and that is what they are after." His ouster in 2019, under pressure from the U.S., cleared the way for corporate access to Bolivia's resources.[12]

Africa too has been carved up for minerals. U.S.-backed interventions in the Democratic Republic of Congo were less about humanitarian concerns than they were about resources: cobalt, coltan, and other rare earth minerals essential for electronics. Local communities faced displacement, violence, and environmental collapse, while Western corporations walked away with the spoils.[13]

This pattern is not accidental. The U.S. economy depends on constant extraction abroad. When countries resist, they are punished with sanctions, coups, or destabilization. When they comply, their ecosystems are sacrificed, their communities displaced, their sovereignty undermined. The U.S. doesn't run on democracy; it runs on oil rigs, strip mines, and deforestation.

Environmental extraction is sold as development, but like other aspects of imperialism, what it develops is dependency. Nations export raw resources and import poverty. America imports wealth and exports destruction. And as the climate crisis deepens, the scramble for resources like lithium, cobalt, and water will only accelerate. The wars of the future will not just be about ideology, they will be about survival, and Washington intends to stay ahead by any means necessary.[14]

CLIMATE REFUGEES AND BORDER MILITARIZATION

The extraction of resources abroad connects directly to another form of environmental violence: the displacement of people who can no longer survive in their homelands. Climate change is not a distant threat, it is already forcing millions from their homes. Rising seas, megadroughts, and superstorms are displacing people across the globe. By 2050, the United Nations estimates that more than 200 million people could become climate refugees. Yet instead of preparing to welcome them, the United States is building higher walls, stronger borders, and deadlier deterrents.[15]

America is one of the largest contributors to global emissions, yet those who suffer the consequences are often from countries that emitted the least. Pacific islanders watch their homes sink beneath the ocean. Farmers in Central America flee droughts and failed harvests. Families in South Asia face deadly heat waves that make survival impossible. These people arrive at U.S. borders not as threats, but as victims of an environmental crisis America helped create.[16]

Washington's answer is militarization. The U.S. has poured billions into border enforcement, expanding detention centers, deploying drones, and contracting private security firms to patrol the frontier. Migrants fleeing climate disasters are criminalized, locked in cages, or deported back to unlivable conditions. What should be a humanitarian response becomes a security response, where the victims of climate change are treated as invaders.[17]

Instead of addressing root causes, the U.S. uses the framing of climate change as a force multiplier to justify expanding its military footprint. Bases in the Pacific are fortified against storms, African commands monitor migration routes, and naval patrols increase in the Arctic as ice melts and new shipping lanes open. Climate disasters become opportunities for empire, not reasons for justice.[18]

The result is a cruel inversion. Those who contributed least to climate change pay the highest price, and those who caused it fortify themselves behind walls and weapons. Climate refugees are not just displaced by storms and droughts, they are displaced by an international system that values borders over lives. America positions itself as a protector, but in truth it is a jailer, locking out the very people it helped drive from their homes.[19]

GREENWASHING AND CLIMATE HYPOCRISY

The United States loves to market itself as a climate leader, but beneath the rhetoric the image crumbles. Politicians boast about clean energy investments, corporations advertise "net zero" pledges, and the Pentagon talks about "greening" its bases. Yet America continues to burn oil, expand drilling, and bankroll industries that profit from environmental destruction.[20]

Take U.S. corporations. Oil giants like ExxonMobil and Chevron spend millions on advertising campaigns that highlight token renewable projects while continuing to pump billions of barrels of crude. Their emissions targets are vague, unenforceable, and riddled with loopholes. This is not transformation, it is branding. Greenwashing allows corporations to appear responsible while locking the world deeper into fossil fuel dependency.[21]

The government does the same. Washington signs climate agreements with one hand while approving new pipelines, oil leases, and fracking projects with the other. During his presidency, Donald Trump pushed this hypocrisy to its limits. He authorized drilling in the Arctic National Wildlife Refuge, one of the most fragile ecosystems on Earth.[22] He opened Nevada's Ruby Mountains to oil and gas exploration despite widespread local opposition.[23] He moved to greenlight mining near Minnesota's Boundary Waters Canoe Area, threatening pristine wilderness and one of the most visited water systems in the United States.[24] These were not isolated decisions, they were signals that protecting corporate profits mattered more than protecting the planet.

Even the Inflation Reduction Act, hailed as America's most ambitious climate legislation, contains subsidies for carbon capture technology that critics say is more about prolonging the life of fossil fuels than replacing them. The rhetoric is clean energy, the reality is fossil capitalism repackaged.[25]

The Pentagon has perfected its own form of greenwashing. It touts biofuels for fighter jets and solar panels on bases, but these are crumbs compared to the massive fuel consumption of its wars and global logistics network. Painting tanks green does not change the fact that the U.S. military is the world's largest institutional polluter. Yet the narrative works, allowing Washington to present itself as climate-conscious while remaining exempt from accountability.[26]

Greenwashing is not harmless, it is strategic. By convincing the public that progress is happening, it delays real change. It protects profits while creating the illusion of responsibility. And it shifts the blame onto individuals, urging people to recycle or drive hybrids while ignoring the structural role of U.S. corporations and the military in driving the crisis.[27]

This hypocrisy undermines global action. Developing nations are lectured about emissions even as U.S. companies extract their resources and the Pentagon burns fuel at wartime levels. America presents itself as the solution to climate change while remaining one of its biggest drivers. The mask of green leadership hides the machinery of environmental imperialism, still running at full speed.

CHAPTER RECAP

Empires leave ruins, and America's empire leaves environmental ruins on a global scale. It is not just the bombs dropped or the oil fields seized, it is the entire system of extraction, pollution, and deception that defines U.S. power. The richest nation consumes the most, emits the most, and then tells the poorest to tighten their belts and adapt.[28]

The U.S. military burns more fuel than most nations and yet remains exempt from climate agreements. Corporations greenwash their destruction, while politicians promise change and then approve new drilling. Washington frames climate change as a threat multiplier, not because it wants to solve it, but because it wants to use it to justify more bases, more weapons, and more control. Environmental collapse is treated not as a crisis to prevent, but as a battlefield to dominate.[29]

For the Global South, the costs are unbearable. Communities are displaced by rising seas, poisoned by mining projects, and trapped in debt by climate loans that demand austerity in exchange for survival. Farmers, fishers, and indigenous peoples pay with their lives, while U.S. corporations profit with their balance sheets. Climate refugees flee storms and droughts only to be met with walls, cages, and drones at America's borders. The cruelty is global, and the hypocrisy is endless.[30]

Despite this reality, the narrative is carefully managed. Slick campaigns from oil giants, Pentagon press releases about biofuels, and White House speeches about green innovation all serve the same purpose—to mask the continuity of empire. America does not lead the world into a sustainable future, it drags the world deeper into dependency, selling illusion while practicing exploitation.[31]

What makes environmental imperialism distinct is its invisibility. Bombs can be counted, sanctions tracked, coups exposed. But climate collapse creeps forward slowly, its victims scattered across continents, its perpetrators hiding behind abstractions like "the economy" or "security." The violence is just as real, but harder to see. That is why it is so effective.[32]

The world cannot confront climate change without confronting empire. As long as the U.S. military remains the planet's biggest polluter, as long as American corporations dictate energy markets, and as long as Washington exempts itself from accountability, there will be no global justice. Sustainability without sovereignty is a lie. Climate leadership without responsibility is a con.

Environmental imperialism reveals the truth about American power. It is not about protecting the planet, it is about protecting privilege. And until that system is broken, the world will continue to burn for the empire's profit.[33]

PART III:

AMERICAN HEGEMONY AND WORLD MANIPULATION

There is a myth Americans grow up believing: that the United States is a beacon of freedom, a global force for good, and a reluctant superpower that intervenes only when democracy needs defending. But the historical record tells a different story, one of calculated interference, covert manipulation, and military dominance executed not for liberation, but for leverage.

The 20th and 21st centuries have been defined by what historians call **American hegemony**, the exercise of power through both overt force and behind-the-scenes engineering. Across the globe, U.S. foreign policy has prioritized economic control, resource access, and geopolitical dominance over the self-determination of nations. Often, the tools of this dominance include military intervention, economic coercion, intelligence-led coups, and propaganda campaigns that reshape entire governments from the shadows.

Much of this manipulation has been justified, at least rhetorically, by two foundational doctrines: the **Monroe Doctrine**

167

(1823) and the **Roosevelt Corollary to the Monroe Doctrine (1904)**. The Monroe Doctrine initially positioned the United States as the protector of the Western Hemisphere, warning European powers against interference. But what started as a defensive posture soon became a pretext for **interventionist imperialism**. By the time Theodore Roosevelt added his corollary, the U.S. had given itself the authority to act as an international police force in Latin America, claiming the right to intervene in any nation that posed a threat to American interests.

That vague phrase, "American interests", would become the legal and moral fig leaf for more than a century of interference.

From toppling democratically elected leaders to installing brutal dictatorships, from bankrolling civil wars to imposing crippling sanctions, the United States has waged a quiet war for control that spans continents. The victims are often invisible to the American public, but not to those who lived under U.S.-backed regimes or suffered the economic devastation of U.S.-engineered austerity.

Sometimes these actions were led by boots on the ground. Other times by the more silent machinery of the CIA, or transnational corporations working in tandem with U.S. foreign policy. Regardless of the method, the result was the same: the subversion of national sovereignty for the sake of American global dominance.

The next section of this book will detail some of this record. Each chapter will focus on a specific country where the U.S. has actively intervened, militarily, economically, or covertly, to shape the political and economic landscape in ways that supposedly advanced American power but left the target nation fractured, impoverished, or enslaved to foreign capital.

These include:
- Hawaii
- Panama

- Iran
- Iraq
- Libya
- Nicaragua
- Haiti
- Guatemala
- Afghanistan

This is not a comprehensive list. To document every case would require volumes. But these examples offer a representative sample of how American hegemony is enforced, not through the consent of the governed, but through the manipulation of systems, the suppression of dissent, and the calculated use of force. They will document how America, while claiming to act for the greater good, has in reality only been selfishly furthering its own agenda at the expense of others.

Let us step beyond the patriotic myths and examine what was done, not in our name, but with our money, under our flag, and without our informed consent.

CHAPTER 18:

HAWAII

THE STOLEN NATION BENEATH THE PALM TREES

Hawaii is often imagined through postcards and honeymoon packages—waves crashing on volcanic cliffs, leis on tanned skin, ukuleles under moonlight. But beneath the surface of this tropical fantasy is a wound that never healed. The real story of how Hawaii became America's 50th state is not one of unity or progress.

It is a story of betrayal.

It is a story of a sovereign nation invaded, a queen deposed, a people silenced.

And it begins long before the ink dried on any annexation resolution.

THE KINGDOM THAT WAS

Before the missionaries, before the sugar barons, before Pearl Harbor, there was the Kingdom of Hawaii, a thriving, sovereign nation.

The Hawaiian people, or *Kanaka Maoli*, had their own government, their own economy, their own spiritual and ecological wisdom. They cultivated taro and sweet potatoes in harmony with the land, managed water systems with precision, and lived under a monarchy that was internationally recognized by the United States, Britain, and France.

MISSIONARIES, MONEY, AND THE MACHINERY OF COLONIZATION

The first American missionaries landed in the 1820s with crosses and good intentions, or so the story goes. But with the gospel came more than Bibles.

It brought a new legal system. A new economic model. And a new ruling class.

Their descendants, white businessmen, didn't just preach salvation. They bought land. They built plantations. And they started reshaping the islands in America's image.

Sugar became the currency of domination. Hawaii's lush lands were turned into profit machines, exporting wealth to the mainland while dispossessing Native Hawaiians from their ancestral homes. The Great Māhele (Division) of 1848[1], advertised as a step toward modernization, in reality handed vast swaths of land to foreigners. Most Native Hawaiians, unfamiliar with Western property law, lost everything.

With land went power, and with power came control.

THE COUP: A QUEEN BROUGHT DOWN AT GUNPOINT

By the late 19th century, American influence had hollowed out the Hawaiian Kingdom from the inside. King Kalākaua was forced to sign the 1887 "Bayonet Constitution"[2] at gunpoint, stripping the monarchy of its authority and disenfranchising Native Hawaiians.

His sister, Queen Liliʻuokalani, took the throne in 1891 determined to restore sovereignty. She drafted a new constitution to return power to her people.

She never got the chance.

In 1893, a group of American businessmen staged a coup d'état, backed by U.S. Marines from the USS *Boston*, deployed under the direction of U.S. Minister John L. Stevens.[3] Liliʻuokalani, facing the threat of bloodshed, surrendered her throne to avoid violence.

But she did not surrender her dignity. And she never surrendered her nation.

> "I yield to the superior force of the
> United States of America... To avoid any
> collision of armed forces and perhaps the

loss of life, I do this under protest, and impelled by said force yield my authority." —Queen Liliʻuokalani

A PEOPLE WHO SAID NO

Despite what the textbooks may suggest, the annexation of Hawaii was not inevitable.

It was resisted. Massively.

In 1897, Native Hawaiians organized "the Kūʻē Petitions"[4], gathering over 21,000 signatures from across the islands rejecting annexation. That was more than half of the Indigenous adult population. It was democracy in action, but Washington didn't care.

Congress didn't vote on a treaty of annexation, which would've required two-thirds approval in the Senate. Instead, they used a legal sleight of hand: "the Newlands Resolution," a joint congressional resolution that bypassed the need for consent from Hawaii's government or its people.

IT WAS A BACKDOOR DEAL MADE DURING WAR FEVER.

America had just entered the Spanish-American War and wanted Hawaii's location for naval supremacy in the Pacific. Pearl Harbor was a crown jewel for military logistics. Sovereignty be damned.

FREEDOM FOR WHOM?

In 1898, President McKinley signed off on annexation.[5]

"We need Hawaii just as much and a good deal more than we did California. It is manifest destiny."

"Manifest destiny" sounds righteous. But it has always meant the same thing:

Take what you want and call it divine.

Hawaii didn't become part of the United States because its people wanted it. It became part of the United States because the right people, wealthy, white, and well-connected, wanted it more.

AFTER THE FALL: THE COST OF BEING COLONIZED

After annexation, Hawaii was stripped not only of its sovereignty but of its soul.

- The Hawaiian language was banned in schools.
- Cultural practices were criminalized or ridiculed.
- Native Hawaiians became strangers in their own land, economically sidelined and politically silenced.

The islands were turned into a playground for investors and a fueling station for the U.S. Navy. The "Big Five" corporations[6], run by American businessmen, controlled nearly every aspect of the economy, from sugar to shipping to banking. Meanwhile, Native Hawaiians labored in the fields that once belonged to their ancestors.

And when the sugar boom faded, tourism took over. Hawaii's image was sold back to Americans as paradise—romantic, exotic, and conveniently apolitical.

But the cost of that fantasy was real: The erasure of culture. The theft of land. The deepening of inequality.

A RECKONING THAT'S STILL COMING

In 1993, a century after the coup, the U.S. government passed "the Apology Resolution."[7] It admitted the overthrow was illegal. It expressed regret. But it stopped short of offering reparations or restoring sovereignty.

It was a start. But apologies without action are just well-worded betrayals.

Today, Native Hawaiians are still fighting. For land. For language. For justice.

Movements like the Hawaiian Renaissance and groups such as Ka Lāhui Hawaiʻi, the Office of Hawaiian Affairs, and many others are reclaiming space, voice, and identity. The struggle is not over, but neither is the spirit of resistance.

CHAPTER RECAP: SO, WHO WERE THE BAD GUYS?

America tells itself a lot of stories. Stories that our nation brings freedom, not occupation. Stories that our nation spreads democracy, not domination. Stories that our nation liberates, never loots.

But Hawaii is an inconvenient truth. A smoking gun that proves the stories false. Hawaii wasn't annexed; it was stolen.

And while the palm trees still sway, and the tourists still come, the land and the people remember.

If we have any interest in justice, we must stop mistaking conquest for destiny. Hawaii was not America's to take, and it still isn't.

The only thing left to decide is whether we'll keep romanticizing a theft, or finally reckon with what was taken, and who we became in the process.

CHAPTER 19:

CUBA

THE ISLAND THAT REFUSED TO BOW

When most Americans think of Cuba, they picture cigars, 1950s cars, and Cold War tension. But Cuba's modern history isn't just frozen in time—it's a live indictment of American foreign policy. From the moment Fidel Castro took power in 1959, the United States launched a campaign to destroy what it saw as an unacceptable experiment in sovereignty just 90 miles off its shores.

BATISTA'S CUBA: A PLAYGROUND FOR THE POWERFUL

Before the revolution, Cuba was a playground for American elites and corporations. Under Fulgencio Batista, a military dictator backed by the U.S., the country was awash in corruption, inequality, and repression. American companies owned more than 70% of Cuba's arable land, operated its electric and telephone utilities, and dominated its sugar industry. The island's wealth was siphoned off while the majority of Cubans lived in poverty.

Havana's coast was dubbed "the Las Vegas of the Caribbean," a neon-lit haven for American mobsters, gamblers, and tourists. Meanwhile, rural Cubans lacked running water, education, and basic healthcare.

Batista's regime was brutal. Political opponents were tortured, elections were rigged or canceled, and dissent was met with violence. The CIA funneled support to Batista, even as he crushed unions and aligned with organized crime.[1]

A REVOLUTION ROOTED IN REALITY

The revolution wasn't a foreign imposition, it was a grassroots uprising. Fidel Castro, Che Guevara, and the 26th of July

Movement ignited a widespread rebellion that resonated with peasants, students, and workers alike. Contrary to U.S. propaganda, the revolution had mass Cuban support.[2] People didn't need outside influence to tell them they were being exploited— they lived it daily.

SOVEREIGNTY MEETS SABOTAGE

After Castro's victory in 1959, he moved quickly to nationalize U.S. owned plantations, banks, and factories. These moves were framed in Washington as "communist aggression," but they were simply acts of sovereignty. Cuba was choosing self-determination over servitude.

The U.S. responded with fury. In 1961, it orchestrated the Bay of Pigs invasion[3], sending CIA-trained Cuban exiles to overthrow Castro. The mission failed spectacularly. It was a humiliation for the Kennedy administration and a galvanizing moment for Cuban nationalism. Castro emerged stronger, and the revolution's legitimacy was cemented in the eyes of many Cubans.

That failure didn't stop U.S. aggression. The CIA launched Operation Mongoose[4], a campaign of sabotage, terror, and over 600 attempts to assassinate Castro. These included exploding cigars, poisoned pens, and other absurdities that bordered on parody, but the intention was deadly serious.

THE MISSILE MISTAKE THAT SEALED CUBA'S IMAGE

The Cuban Missile Crisis of 1962 was the most perilous moment of the Cold War, and it stemmed directly from Cuba's decision to align with the Soviet Union. Isolated, embargoed, and under constant threat of U.S. invasion, Cuba saw an alliance with Moscow as its only path to survival. After the failed Bay of Pigs invasion and ongoing assassination attempts against Castro, Cuba rightly concluded that the United States would stop at nothing to overthrow its government.

The Soviets offered protection in the form of a strategic deterrent: nuclear missiles stationed on Cuban soil. For Cuba, this was a desperate bid for security. For the United States, it was an intolerable provocation—Soviet nukes just 90 miles from Florida. The standoff brought the world to the brink of nuclear war. Ultimately, the Soviets agreed to remove the missiles in exchange for a U.S. promise not to invade Cuba and a secret deal to remove U.S. missiles from Turkey.

But for Cuba, the cost was steep. The decision to host Soviet missiles confirmed American fears that Cuba was merely a puppet of the USSR, damaging its reputation as an independent revolution and giving Washington the pretext it needed to justify six decades of hostility. Aligning with the Soviet Union may have bought Cuba protection, but it cemented its place in the American imagination not as a sovereign nation, but as a Cold War adversary.

AN EMBARGO MEANT TO BREAK THE PEOPLE

Then came the embargo. What began as a limited economic restriction morphed into one of the harshest and most enduring sanctions regimes in modern history. Medicines, food, industrial equipment, all were restricted. The embargo's goal, as stated in internal U.S. memos, was to "deny money and supplies to Cuba... to bring about hunger, desperation, and overthrow of the government."[5]

Read that again. *The United States' continuing goal is "to bring about hunger and desperation..."* Does that sound like the country you were taught about in school? Home of the free? Land of the brave?

SURVIVAL AGAINST THE ODDS

And yet, the Cuban government didn't fall. Despite the hardship, the revolution survived. Cuba developed a robust healthcare system, sent doctors abroad to aid global crises, and

179

maintained some of the highest literacy rates in the developing world. It wasn't perfect, there were political prisons, censorship, and economic inefficiencies, but the country's resilience under siege became a global symbol of defiance.

Why do we still have an embargo? Cuba isn't a military threat. It's not exporting terrorism. The Cold War is over. And yet, the U.S. continues its economic war against the island, largely due to domestic politics. Florida's Cuban-American voting bloc wields disproportionate influence, and U.S. presidents, Democrat and Republican alike, have pandered to it.[6] Lifting the embargo is politically risky, even if it's economically and morally indefensible.

Meanwhile, the rest of the world has moved on. The European Union, Canada, Mexico, and most of Latin America engage openly with Cuba. They invest, trade, and maintain diplomatic relations. The United Nations has condemned the U.S. embargo almost unanimously every year for decades.[7] Only the U.S. and Israel consistently vote to uphold it.

CHAPTER RECAP: GUANTÁNAMO AND THE GHOST OF EMPIRE

The effects on the Cuban people have been devastating. Shortages of medicine, decaying infrastructure, and limited access to modern technology have crippled the economy. But before the embargo, under Batista, Cuba was a deeply unequal society, prosperous on paper, but with systemic poverty and no political freedom. The revolution lifted millions into literacy and basic health, even if it couldn't bring prosperity.

And then there's Guantánamo Bay, a piece of Cuba still occupied by the United States. Seized in 1903 under a "lease" that was never recognized by the revolutionary government[8], it remains a relic of American imperialism. Today, it houses a notorious military prison where the United States keeps "detainees" without trial. If any other country did this, we would call them "political hostages." We imprison them there specifically so that we can deny them any of the rights that they would have in the United States proper. It's a permanent reminder that even as Cuba has tried to rid itself of foreign domination, the empire never really left.

Cuba is not perfect. But its crime was never tyranny, it was resistance. Resistance to a foreign power that demanded obedience. That resistance, however flawed, still burns. And that is why Cuba remains, in the eyes of the empire, unforgivable.

CHAPTER 20:

PANAMA

AMERICAN INTERFERENCE AND THE PURSUIT OF POWER

The story of American involvement in Panama is one of calculated interference, economic opportunism, and political manipulation. When most people hear the word "Panama," they think of the Panama Canal—which makes sense because it is a marvel of engineering—but they rarely understand the country of Panama as a site of American domination. The United States' actions in Panama, from orchestrating political upheaval to imposing economic control, highlight the troubling ways in which the United States prioritizes its own interests at the expense of others' sovereignty and freedom.

THE STRATEGIC IMPORTANCE OF PANAMA

To understand the United States' interest in Panama, one must first look at world geography. Panama's isthmus is the narrowest point between the Atlantic and Pacific Oceans, making it one of the most strategically significant pieces of land in the world. Long before the canal was built, explorers and merchants recognized Panama's potential as a shortcut for global trade. For the United States, expanding its influence across the globe in the late 1800s and early 1900s, control of passage across the North and South American continent was critical.

By the late 1800s, the idea of a canal through Panama wasn't just theoretical. The French, under Ferdinand de Lesseps, attempted to construct a canal in the 1880s[1] but failed due to engineering challenges and rampant disease. That failure left the region ripe for intervention, and the United States quickly seized the opportunity.

AMERICAN MANIPULATION: THE BIRTH OF PANAMA AS A NATION

Panama wasn't always an independent country. What we today recognize as the country of Panama was part of Colombia until its independence in 1903.[2] The Colombian government was reluctant to give up the land, and when they hesitated to approve a treaty granting the United States control over the land needed for the canal, the U.S. decided to take matters into its own hands.

In 1903, the United States orchestrated Panama's secession from Colombia. The plan was simple: encourage and support a local revolt in exchange for favorable terms regarding the canal. On November 3, 1903, Panamanian separatists declared independence, and the United States immediately recognized the new nation, The Republic of Panama, on November 6th.[3]

What is notable is the speed and efficiency of the operation. President Roosevelt ordered U.S. warships to position off both the Pacific and Atlantic coasts of Panama to prevent Colombian forces from suppressing the revolt. American military presence, combined with diplomatic pressure, ensured the success of Panama's independence movement, though the "independence" was hardly organic.

To ensure that the new country would be formed exactly as the United States wanted and to guarantee U.S. control over the canal, the United States effectively pre-wrote a constitution for the Panamanians.[4] This new constitution contained provisions advantageous to the United States, including the provision that the United States had "the right to intervene in any part of Panama, to re-establish public peace and constitutional order," with the United States being the sole arbiter of "public peace" and "constitutional order."

This meant that the newly formed Republic of Panama was essentially a United States client state. A few days after recognizing the new Republic of Panama, the country signed the **Hay-Bunau-Varilla Treaty**[5] with the United States, granting the U.S. control of the Canal Zone, a strip of land stretching across the isthmus. In exchange, the new Panamanian government received $10 million and rent payments for the Canal Zone of $250,000 a year.

Even at the time, these terms were outrageously one-sided: the U.S. gained sovereign rights to a piece of Panamanian land and complete control over the construction, operation, and defense of the canal. Most notably, the treaty wasn't negotiated by a Panamanian representative, but by Philippe Bunau-Varilla, a Frenchman with close ties to American interests. The entire agreement was negotiated in Washington D.C. and New York City and signed the night before the Panamanian delegation even arrived in the United States.

President Theodore Roosevelt, who championed the canal, made no attempt to hide the United States' role in Panama's independence. In a speech years later, he bluntly declared, "I took the Canal Zone and let Congress debate; and while the debate goes on, the canal does also."[6]

It would be difficult to form a more concise statement of indifference to international norms and Panamanian sovereignty.

ECONOMIC DOMINATION AND THE CANAL'S CONSTRUCTION

The construction of the Panama Canal (1904–1914) was a monumental technical achievement, but at significant cost to the Panamanian people. While the United States reaped the economic benefits of the canal, Panama remained on the margins, excluded from decision-making and denied fair compensation.

The Canal Zone was governed by the U.S. and became a stark symbol of American dominance. American administrators ran the zone as a quasi-colony, with laws, infrastructure, and social systems that prioritized American workers over Panamanians. Segregation was rampant. White American employees lived in comfortable housing with modern amenities, while Panamanian workers and Afro-Caribbean laborers, many brought in to work on the canal, endured poor conditions, low wages, and systemic discrimination.

In total, approximately 25,000 workers died building the Panama Canal. Most died in the late 1800s when the French were trying to build the canal, but even under U.S. control, there was an official death toll of 5,609 workers. Many historians believe the number is much higher and doesn't include the tens of thousands of workers who were permanently injured.

Economically, the United States almost exclusively benefited from the canal. Panama, despite hosting one of the world's most important trade routes, saw little of the wealth it generated. The $250,000 annual payment promised by the Hay-Bunau-Varilla Treaty was a pittance compared to the billions of dollars the canal generated for the United States.

THE AMERICAN-LED COUP: POLITICAL MANIPULATION IN THE 20TH CENTURY

One would think that with such one-sided control of the canal, the United States would be content with the status quo. But as in other areas of the world, the beast had to continue to be fed, and independence that might conflict with U.S. interests had to be immediately suppressed. Thus, throughout the 20th century, the United States repeatedly intervened in Panamanian politics to protect its interests, often at the expense of democracy and stability.

The most egregious example of United States interference occurred in 1941, when the U.S. facilitated the ousting of

Panamanian President Arnulfo Arias.[7] Arias, democratically elected by the Panamanian people, was a nationalist who challenged American control over the Canal Zone and sought greater sovereignty for Panama. As part of his desire to see Panama as an independent nation, he attempted to reclaim some of the land in the Canal Zone and renegotiate terms with the United States. This was seen as a direct threat to American interests and needed to be immediately dealt with.

Later, Arias returned to power, but in October 1968 the United States supported a coup that removed him from power once again.[8] Panamanian officials, with covert backing from the U.S. military, orchestrated his ousting just days after he introduced reforms aimed at asserting Panama's independence. Arias' removal sent a clear message to Panamanians and the world: Any leader who dared to challenge American hegemony would face consequences.

The United States supported a successor to Arias named **Omar Torrijos Herrera**. Torrijos was a major in the Panamanian National Guard and attended the notorious **School of the Americas**.[9] Torrijos negotiated the Torrijos-Carter Treaty and the Panama Canal Treaty with U.S. President Carter in 1977, which passed sovereignty of the canal zone back to Panama but retained the U.S. right to protect what it described as the "neutrality of the canal."

In 1979, Torrijos organized the new "Democratic Revolutionary Party," which had ties to socialist international organizations. Again, this did not align with U.S. interests. In July 1981, Torrijos died when a military aircraft carrying him crashed in the middle of the jungle in light weather.[10] Charges of U.S. CIA assassination immediately followed. The Soviet Union claimed that the U.S. had caused Torrijos' death, and a decade later, after the U.S. had ousted Manuel Noriega as the Panamanian leader, Noriega's attorney claimed that "General Noriega has in his possession documents showing attempts to assassinate General Noriega and Mr. Torrijos by agencies of the United States."

For the time being, in the early 1980s, the United States supported an authoritarian regime that prioritized American interests over Panamanian sovereignty—that of General **Manuel Noriega**. Noriega ruled Panama as a military dictator throughout much of the 1980s with tacit U.S. support, until his usefulness ran out.

Noriega worked with the CIA in the 1950s and became one of the CIA's most valuable assets in Central America.[11] He also started building the Panamanian military, and it soon reached a point where it could challenge U.S. forces in Panama.

Noriega was an American tool that allowed the U.S. to control the Panama Canal, but more importantly, to control both drug and arms shipments through Central America. Noriega agreed with the U.S. to train Contra soldiers in preparation for an invasion of Nicaragua in 1986. Noriega also supported U.S. and Israeli efforts to supply the Contras with weapons and was a central figure when all of this blew up in the United States' face with the "Iran-Contra Affair."[12]

Noriega became the scapegoat that the U.S. used to hide its involvement in drugs, arms, and political revolution and was indicted by a U.S. grand jury in 1988. In 1989, Noriega annulled the results of a Panamanian general election, and the U.S., under the guise of promoting democracy, invaded Panama, captured Noriega, and brought him to the U.S. to stand trial, where he was convicted and sentenced to 40 years in prison.[13]

Noriega's attorney claimed that during his time in power, Noriega received approximately $11 million in payments from the CIA.

THE HUMAN COST OF AMERICAN HEGEMONY

While the Panama Canal stands as a testament to American engineering, its legacy for Panamanians is more complex. The economic and political interference that accompanied the canal's construction left deep scars on Panamanian society. Native Panamanians and Afro-Caribbean laborers faced systemic exploitation by the United States, and generations of Panamanians were denied the right to fully benefit from their country's most valuable asset. Panamanians refer to this as the "Generational Struggle."[14]

The Canal Zone itself became a symbol of colonial inequality. While American administrators enjoyed a privileged lifestyle, Panamanians were often treated as second-class citizens in their own land. This inequality sowed resentment and fueled nationalist movements that demanded justice and the return of the Canal Zone to Panama.

RECKONING WITH THE PAST

The United States' actions in Panama reveal a familiar pattern of imperial behavior: economic exploitation, political manipulation, and disregard for sovereignty. While the canal was undoubtedly a strategic asset for the United States, its construction and control came at great cost to Panama.

The legacy of American interference remains. The canal, while now a source of pride and economic opportunity for Panama, serves as a reminder of the unequal relationship that defined U.S.-Panama relations for much of the 20th century. Most recently in 2024, President Trump continued U.S. interference in Panama by stating that the U.S. should "take back" the Canal, completely ignoring that the canal is part of another sovereign nation and not the property of the United States. During a speech to young conservatives in Phoenix, Arizona, Trump commented that if U.S. demands aren't met, "...we will demand that the Panama Canal be returned to the United States. So, to the officials of Panama, please be guided accordingly."

CHAPTER RECAP: LESSONS FROM PANAMA

The United States' actions in Panama provide a sobering lesson about the costs and actions of an empire. The canal, frequently celebrated as a symbol of progress, was built on a foundation of exploitation, inequality, and political manipulation. Panama's story should challenge all of us to rethink the narratives of American exceptionalism and to confront the realities of colonial power that we are part of and that we as a population, at least tacitly, support.

At the very least, we can acknowledge the injustices of the past done in our name and, through acknowledging them, ensure that they are not repeated. For Panama, the struggle for sovereignty was long and arduous, and it seemed to ultimately succeed, but recent comments by President Trump demonstrate that U.S. interference isn't over—it has just been dormant or hidden.

The question remains: How many nations must pay the price for another nation's progress? The answer lies not in the past, but in how we recognize the past, and how we choose to act in the future.

CHAPTER 21:

VENEZUELA

OIL, EMPIRE, AND ENGINEERED CRISIS

If you want to understand U.S. foreign policy, start with oil, then add a dash of anti-communism, a pinch of corporate greed, and a heaping spoonful of hypocrisy. Venezuela, once the wealthiest nation in Latin America, now serves as a case study in what happens when a resource-rich country dares to chart its own course.

For decades, the United States has viewed Venezuela not as a sovereign nation but as a strategic asset. With the world's largest proven oil reserves and a fiercely independent streak, Venezuela became a thorn in Washington's side the moment it began prioritizing national development over foreign profit. And America responded the way empires always do, by trying to break the country until it fell back in line.

CHÁVEZ CROSSES THE LINE

When Hugo Chávez came to power in 1999, he vowed to redistribute wealth, nationalize key industries, and use oil revenues to help the poor.[1] Washington didn't view this as reform, but as rebellion. Chávez's "Bolivarian Revolution" was framed as a dangerous tilt toward socialism, threatening U.S. corporate interests and regional influence. The fact that Venezuela was using its oil wealth to reduce poverty, build schools, and expand healthcare didn't matter. What mattered was that ExxonMobil and Chevron no longer called the shots.

The backlash was swift. In 2002, just three years into Chávez's presidency, a U.S.-backed coup attempt briefly removed him from power.[2] Although he was restored by a popular uprising within 48 hours, the message was clear: independence would not be tolerated. From that moment forward, the U.S. worked to isolate, destabilize, and ultimately topple the Venezuelan government.

ECONOMIC WAR DISGUISED AS POLICY

Sanctions became the weapon of choice. Under both Republican and Democratic administrations, the U.S. imposed layer after layer of economic restrictions, choking off access to global financial markets, freezing assets, and crippling the country's oil exports. The Obama administration laid the groundwork, declaring Venezuela a "national security threat" in 2015,[3] but it was Trump who turned the screws.

During his first term (2017–2021), Trump recognized opposition leader Juan Guaidó as Venezuela's "legitimate president" in a bold but hollow maneuver that most of the world eventually abandoned.[4] His administration labeled Nicolás Maduro a "narcoterrorist," placed sanctions on the country's central bank and state-owned oil company PDVSA, and openly called for regime change.[5] The resulting collapse was catastrophic. Venezuela's economy shrank by over 60%, hyperinflation spiraled, and millions fled the country. A 2019 study by the Center for Economic and Policy Research estimated that U.S. sanctions were responsible for over 40,000 deaths due to lack of access to medicine and medical equipment.[6]

This wasn't humanitarian policy. It was economic warfare. It was engineered suffering in the hopes of manufacturing political change.

TRUMP RETURNS, WITH A VENGEANCE

The Biden administration shifted gears slightly. While maintaining pressure on Maduro, it reopened channels for negotiation and relaxed some oil sanctions in exchange for electoral reforms. Limited oil imports resumed. Temporary Protected Status (TPS) was extended for Venezuelan migrants. There was no love lost between Biden and Maduro, but the approach was pragmatic, aimed at containment rather than collapse.[7]

Then came Trump 2.0.

As of August 2025, the second Trump administration has revived its "maximum pressure" campaign with renewed vigor. The new strategy is the old one on steroids, economic sanctions, military threats, immigration crackdowns, and public designations all aimed at bringing Venezuela to heel.

SANCTIONS, TARIFFS, AND THE OIL CHOKEHOLD

Within weeks of taking office, Trump signed an executive order slapping a 25% tariff on any country that imports Venezuelan crude oil. Effective April 2, 2025, the tariff targeted intermediaries like India and China, who had taken advantage of discounted Venezuelan oil to bypass Western restrictions.[8] The move was framed as a protectionist measure, defending U.S. energy markets from "unfair competition." But the real goal was simpler: cut off Maduro's cash flow.

Oil remains the backbone of Venezuela's economy, accounting for about 61 percent of its total export value in 2023. When the Donald Trump administration imposed new tariffs on Venezuelan crude, the effect on trade was swift. U.S. imports fell from roughly 295,000 barrels per day in late 2024 to just 118,000 by May 2025, signaling a sharp contraction in one of Venezuela's last remaining revenue streams. Contrary to Trump's promises that the move would ease domestic energy costs, global oil prices immediately spiked, with Brent Crude prices hitting $73 per barrel before falling later back to their pre-tariff price of about $70 per barrel in late March and then to the low-$60s by early May.[9] These price changes were attributed more to weak demand forecasts and OPEC output decisions rather than tariffs.

FROM NAVY PRESENCE TO MILITARY POSTURING

Meanwhile, the military escalated its presence. In August 2025, the U.S. Navy deployed three guided-missile destroyers off Venezuela's coast, allegedly to combat drug trafficking.[10] But critics called it what it was: saber-rattling.

Maduro responded by mobilizing Venezuelan forces and appealing to the United Nations. Russia pledged military support. Iran offered to assist in maintaining Venezuela's aging refinery infrastructure. And the region braced for what looked increasingly like a U.S.-manufactured crisis.

MIGRATION AS LEVERAGE

At home, Trump folded Venezuela policy into his broader immigration crackdown. In February 2025, his administration revoked TPS for roughly 500,000 Venezuelans living in the U.S., leaving them vulnerable to deportation.[11] Parole programs for other migrants from Cuba, Haiti, Nicaragua, and Venezuela (CHNV) were also scrapped. Federal courts issued temporary injunctions, but the message was clear: refugees fleeing a crisis partly engineered by U.S. sanctions were no longer welcome.

Then came the symbolic moves. On day one of his second term, Trump designated the Venezuelan gang Tren de Aragua (TdA) as a Foreign Terrorist Organization. The group, originally formed inside Venezuelan prisons, had reportedly expanded into U.S. cities, engaging in extortion and drug trafficking. Whether the gang truly posed a national threat was debatable. But linking it to Maduro served Trump's narrative: that Venezuela was not just a failed state, but a criminal one.

EMPIRE IN ACTION, AGAIN

The administration's rhetoric, driven by returning figures like Secretary of State Mike Pompeo, leaned heavily on the language of national security, anti-communism, and "restoring order to the

Western Hemisphere." But the policies revealed something else—an effort to consolidate domestic political support using a foreign villain, even at the risk of sparking greater international conflict.

Trump's Venezuela playbook is not just a retread of Cold War strategies. It's an extension of a long-running U.S. tradition: use democracy as a pretext, use sanctions as a weapon, and call it leadership when the rubble smokes.

The truth is, Washington doesn't fear Venezuela because of its failings. It fears it because of what it tried to do right. Chávez and Maduro challenged the global oil market, nationalized resources, and partnered with countries outside the U.S. orbit, and that kind of disobedience is punished.

COLLATERAL DAMAGE: THE VENEZUELAN PEOPLE

By mid-2025, the impact of renewed U.S. pressure was already taking shape. Inflation surged. Food and medicine shortages worsened. Hospitals reported critical supply gaps. Once again, like in other countries, the poorest Venezuelans bore the brunt of U.S. foreign policy.

And yet, Maduro remained in power. Despite allegations of fraud, he declared victory in the 2024 elections and retained control of key state institutions. The opposition, fragmented and leaderless after the international community backed away from Juan Guaidó, offered little viable alternative. The more Washington pushed, the more entrenched Maduro became.

GLOBAL PUSHBACK AND RISING TENSIONS

Diplomatically, America's unilateral approach backfired. While Trump framed the campaign as a moral imperative, Latin American allies distanced themselves. Brazil and Mexico called for de-escalation. The European Union, once aligned with U.S. policy, now pushed for dialogue. Global sympathy leaned increasingly toward Venezuela, not because of its government, but because of the obvious double standard: the U.S. claims to support democracy while starving nations that refuse to obey.

At the heart of all of this is a geopolitical reality: Venezuela sits on a sea of oil. China holds billions in Venezuelan debt. Iran wants a strategic ally in the Americas. Russia sees an opportunity to flank the U.S. in its own backyard. Trump's aggressive stance isn't about freedom or human rights. It's about control: control of markets, control of resources, and control of narratives.

CHAPTER RECAP: SAME PLAYBOOK, SAME MISTAKES

The danger is that we've seen this script before: impose sanctions, stir unrest, demonize the leader, and pretend it's all for democracy. But this pattern constantly fails. It has failed from Iraq to Libya to Syria, and in Venezuela, it's failing again.

So why does the U.S. keep playing the same hand?

Because in the imperial mindset, failure is never the fault of the policy, it's the fault of the people being punished. If they resist, we call them terrorists. If they collapse, we call it liberation.

But make no mistake: what's unfolding in Venezuela is not a liberation effort. It's economic siege warfare, and it's being carried out in our name.

CHAPTER 22:

IRAN

AN ENEMY MADE, NOT BORN

The story of U.S.-Iran relations is one of betrayal, intervention, and enduring enmity. Over decades, the United States has vilified Iran as a global threat, yet a closer look reveals a different reality, one shaped by American interests, oil politics, and Cold War paranoia. From orchestrating coups to covert arms deals, and from sanctions to military threats, the United States' actions have undermined Iran's sovereignty and security while claiming to defend freedom and stability.

THE 1953 COUP: THE U.S. OVERTHROWS IRAN'S DEMOCRACY

Modern U.S.-Iranian tensions can be traced back to 1953, when the United States, through the CIA, orchestrated the overthrow of Iran's democratically elected Prime Minister, Mohammad Mossadegh.[1] At the heart of the conflict was oil. Mossadegh had moved to nationalize the Iranian oil industry, taking control from the British-owned Anglo-Iranian Oil Company (AIOC), which had long profited from Iran's resources while leaving Iranians impoverished.

For the United States, Mossadegh's move represented more than just oil, it symbolized a challenge to Western dominance. In the Cold War era, any assertion of independence by a resource-rich nation risked being labeled "communist" or "anti-Western."

The CIA's operation, codenamed **TP-AJAX**, worked to destabilize Mossadegh's government. The agency funded protests, bribed Iranian officials, and spread propaganda to create chaos. In August 1953, Mossadegh was overthrown, and the pro-Western Shah Mohammad Reza Pahlavi was installed as ruler. The Shah, backed by U.S. military and financial aid, ruled Iran with an iron fist for the next 26 years.[2]

"The CIA overthrew Mossadegh in order to protect U.S. oil interests. That coup was the original sin in U.S.-Iranian relations," noted historian Stephen Kinzer.[3]

For Iranians, the coup was a betrayal of democracy and sovereignty. For the United States, it was a successful assertion of control in the Middle East.

THE ISLAMIC REVOLUTION AND THE BIRTH OF AN ENEMY

By the 1970s, resentment toward the Shah's regime had reached a boiling point. The Shah's policies, heavily influenced by U.S. interests, enriched a small elite while much of the population remained impoverished. His secret police, the SAVAK, brutalized dissenters with torture and imprisonment.

In **1979**, Iran erupted in revolution. Led by **Ayatollah Ruhollah Khomeini**, the Iranian people overthrew the Shah and established the **Islamic Republic of Iran**.[4] For the United States, the revolution was a catastrophe: it not only ousted a key ally but also challenged U.S. dominance in the region.

The U.S.-Iranian relationship deteriorated further when, in November 1979, Iranian students seized the U.S. Embassy in Tehran, holding 52 Americans hostage for 444 days.[5] Though driven by anger at decades of American interference, the hostage crisis was seized upon by U.S. leaders as evidence of Iran's hostility and extremism.

THE IRAN-IRAQ WAR: THE U.S. SIDES WITH SADDAM

In 1980, Iraq, led by Saddam Hussein, invaded Iran, triggering a brutal eight-year conflict. The United States, eager to weaken Iran's revolutionary government, backed Iraq. American support included intelligence sharing, economic aid, and covert arms sales.

The war devastated Iran:

- Casualties: Over 500,000 Iranians were killed, including civilians.

- Chemical weapons: Iraq used chemical weapons, supplied with Western materials, against Iranian soldiers and civilians.

- Economic collapse: Iran's oil infrastructure and economy were severely damaged.

The U.S.'s support for Iraq revealed its real agenda: not promoting peace but containing Iran's power.

"We knew Saddam was using chemical weapons. But the U.S. wanted to see Iran weakened," admitted former U.S. officials years later.[6]

For Iranians, American complicity in their suffering further deepened mistrust.

THE IRAN-CONTRA AFFAIR

While the U.S. publicly supported Iraq during the Iran-Iraq War, a shocking revelation emerged in the late 1980s: the Reagan administration had been secretly selling arms to Iran. The scandal, known as the **Iran-Contra Affair**[7], exposed the hypocrisy and covert operations of American foreign policy.

The Scheme

The Iran-Contra Affair was a convoluted scheme with two primary objectives:

1. **Arms-for-hostages:** The Reagan administration sought to secure the release of American hostages held by Hezbollah in Lebanon (a group with ties to Iran).
2. **Funding the Contras:** Proceeds from arms sales to Iran were funneled to the Contras, a U.S.-backed rebel group fighting the leftist Sandinista government in Nicaragua.

The problem? Both arms sales to Iran and funding the Contras were illegal. Congress had passed the Boland Amendment[8], prohibiting U.S. aid to the Contras. Yet the Reagan administration circumvented the law, operating in secret.

THE EXPOSURE AND FALLOUT

In 1986, a Lebanese newspaper exposed the arms sales, triggering a media frenzy. Investigations revealed that the U.S. had sold over $30 million worth of weapons to Iran, including missiles and spare parts.

Key figures, such as National Security Advisor John Poindexter and Marine Colonel Oliver North, were implicated. North famously shredded documents to cover up the scandal, later testifying:

"I was authorized to do everything I did."[9]

The Iran-Contra hearings exposed not just illegal actions but the depth of U.S. hypocrisy. The Reagan administration had labeled Iran a "state sponsor of terrorism" while secretly arming it.

For many, the scandal epitomized American foreign policy: unprincipled, self-serving, and reckless.

WHY THE U.S. CONSIDERS IRAN AN ENEMY

The United States' hostility toward Iran is rooted in three key factors:

1. Loss of a Client State: The 1979 revolution ended U.S. dominance over Iran. America lost control of Iran's oil and a key regional ally.

2. Opposition to U.S. Hegemony: Iran's leadership openly challenges American dominance in the Middle East, supporting groups like Hezbollah and opposing U.S.-backed regimes.

3. Strategic Interests: Iran sits on massive oil reserves and occupies a critical geopolitical location, bordering the Persian Gulf.

Iran's defiance is framed as "aggression," but it is better understood as resistance to American hegemony.

"Iran is being turned into Public Enemy No. 1—not because it threatens anyone, but because it refuses to obey." remarked former CIA analyst Ray McGovern.[10]

IRAN'S GLOBAL POSTURE VS. U.S. IMPERIAL REACH

Contrary to American portrayals of Iran as a global aggressor, Iran's military and foreign presence are minimal. Unlike the United States, which maintains over 750 military bases in more than 80 countries, Iran has modest extra territorial bases.[11]

Iran's military strategy is primarily defensive, aimed at deterring U.S. and Israeli attacks. Instead of overt bases projecting its power, Iran supports regional allies, such as Syria and Hezbollah, it does not engage in global military intervention.

In contrast, the United States uses its vast network of bases to project power, coerce allies, and wage wars. From Afghanistan to Iraq to Libya, U.S. interventions have left destruction and chaos in their wake.

Some argue that Iran is more subtle than the U.S. and prefers to fight proxy wars, and there is some truth to this, but a careful examination of Iranian support reveals that they only support areas directly affected by Zionist aggression, i.e. Syria, Iraq, and Lebanon, or those engaged in resisting Zionist expansion, like the Houthis. They don't engage in projecting power to any other surrounding countries.

CHAPTER RECAP: THE REAL AGGRESSOR

The United States' decades-long hostility toward Iran has been driven by imperial ambitions, not principles. Iran's resistance to American dominance, whether through nationalizing oil, overthrowing the Shah, or opposing U.S. allies, has made it a target. Yet Iran's global actions reveal a nation focused on self-defense, not aggression.

When judged objectively, it becomes clear: Iran is not the threat the U.S. claims it to be. Instead, the United States, with its history of coups, sanctions, and military interventions, emerges as the true aggressor.

For Iran, the struggle is about sovereignty and survival. For the United States, it has always been about power.

CHAPTER 23:

IRAQ

WAR, OIL, AND EMPIRE'S PURSUIT OF POWER

Few nations have borne the brunt of U.S. intervention more severely than Iraq. Over the last few decades, Iraq has been subject to devastating wars, economic collapse, and societal upheaval, all driven primarily by U.S. strategic interests. The Gulf Wars, the false pretenses of weapons of mass destruction (WMDs), and the devastating toll on Iraqi civilians paint a grim picture of American priorities: dominance, resources, and geopolitics. Iraq's suffering was not an accident. It was a calculated cost in the pursuit of American power.

SADDAM HUSSEIN: DICTATOR AND MODERNIZER

The name "Saddam Hussein" has become synonymous in the U.S. with evil despotism, and in some ways that is well deserved. Saddam orchestrated an ongoing campaign against the Kurds that included mass deportations, firing squads, and chemical attacks.[1] There were executions, torture, and disappearances.[2] His sons, Uday and Qusay, were also accused of being sadistic and brutal.[3] They were accused of beating athletes,[4] clubbing a party-goer to death,[5] mass prisoner execution,[6] and overseeing the crackdown after the Gulf War.[7]

Contrasting all of this, Saddam made education mandatory.[8] Literacy rates skyrocketed.[9] He championed women's rights, stringently restricted polygamy, improved divorce rights for women, and supported women in higher education and the workplace.[10] He started a public food distribution system to prevent famine during the sanctions we'll discuss below.[11] He built roads, electric plants, water and sewer systems, schools, universities, cultural facilities, raised the GDP, salaries, and housing—especially during the oil-boom of the 1970s before the later wars and sanctions reversed all of his gains.[12]

Which was it: an Eden or a hell? Like most things, it was a little of both. There were some things, like the treatment of the Kurds, that definitely needed to be addressed by the international community. The U.S. involvement, though, was short-sighted, heavy-handed, and left Iraq, the Middle East, and the United States worse off than before.

THE PRELUDE TO WAR: U.S.-IRAQ RELATIONS AND APRIL GLASPIE'S ASSURANCE

In the 1980s, U.S.-Iraq relations were shaped by pragmatism. During the Iran-Iraq War (1980–1988), the United States supported Saddam Hussein's government despite his known brutality and saw Iraq as a bulwark against the spread of Iran's Islamic Revolution.[13]

Saddam was useful, and American leaders looked the other way as his regime committed atrocities, including the use of chemical weapons against both Iranian soldiers and Kurdish civilians.[14]

However, by 1990, the U.S. relationship with Iraq would take a dramatic turn. Iraq, burdened by war debt and economic stagnation, looked to its oil-rich neighbor, Kuwait, for economic relief. Saddam accused Kuwait of overproducing oil, driving down prices, and effectively sabotaging Iraq's economy. He also claimed Kuwait was slant-drilling into Iraqi oil fields, a claim widely disputed, but one that Saddam used to justify his grievances.

In July 1990, Saddam Hussein met with **U.S. Ambassador April Glaspie** in Baghdad. During the meeting, Glaspie reportedly told Saddam:

"We have no opinion on your Arab-Arab conflicts, like your border disagreement with Kuwait." And "The American people have no interest to go to war for oil."[15]

These words were interpreted by Saddam as a green light for his plans to invade Kuwait. Whether Glaspie's comments were intentional or a diplomatic blunder remains debated, but the result was clear: on August 2, 1990, Iraqi forces invaded and occupied Kuwait.

THE FIRST GULF WAR: OPERATION DESERT STORM

After the Iraqis entered Kuwait, the U.S. swiftly reversed its ambiguous stance. President **George H.W. Bush** condemned the invasion and mobilized a massive international coalition under the banner of the United Nations. Iraq's occupation of Kuwait was framed as a threat to global stability and a violation of sovereignty, a convenient pretext for what would become a devastating military campaign.

By **January 1991**, U.S.-led coalition forces launched **Operation Desert Storm**, an overwhelming air and ground assault aimed at expelling Iraq from Kuwait. The "war" didn't last long. After just 42 days of bombing and ground operations, Iraqi forces were decimated, and Kuwait was "liberated."[16]

The destruction inflicted on Iraq, however, was far out of proportion to its occupation of Kuwait. U.S. airstrikes targeted not only military installations but also civilian infrastructure, power plants, bridges, water treatment facilities, and telecommunications, actions that are illegal and considered war crimes under the Additional Protocols, article 52 of the Fourth Geneva Convention and the Hague Convention, unless they are used for military purposes. The devastation crippled Iraq's economy and caused immense suffering for its people, but who in the world was going to charge the United States with crimes?

THE HUMAN COST OF THE FIRST GULF WAR

- **Military deaths:** An estimated **20,000 to 35,000** Iraqi soldiers were killed.[17]

- **Civilian casualties:** Between **1,000 and 5,000** Iraqi
  civilians died as a result of bombings.[18]

- **Infrastructure destruction:** Iraq's electrical grid and
  water systems were largely destroyed, leading to public
  health crises that lasted for decades.[19]

The war was not just about Kuwait, it was about sending a
message. The United States wanted to demonstrate its dominance
in the post-Cold War world. Iraq, with its vast oil reserves and
defiant leader, was made an example.

THE SANCTIONS ERA: A SILENT WAR ON IRAQ'S CIVILIANS

Following the Gulf War, the U.N., under heavy U.S. influence,
imposed crippling economic sanctions on Iraq. The sanctions were
ostensibly designed to pressure Saddam Hussein into complying
with U.N. resolutions, including disarmament. In practice, they
became a weapon of collective punishment.

Over the next 12 years, the sanctions destroyed Iraq's
economy and caused immense suffering for ordinary Iraqis. Vital
imports such as food, medicine, and spare parts for infrastructure
were restricted or outright banned. U.S. officials insisted the
sanctions were necessary, but their impact was catastrophic:

- **Child mortality:** While the exact figures remain
  disputed, multiple studies documented significant
  increases in child mortality during the sanctions period. A
  1999 UNICEF study estimated substantial excess deaths,
  though later research has questioned some of these
  findings.[20]

- **Health crisis:** Hospitals were left without medicine or
  equipment. Preventable diseases such as cholera and
  typhoid surged as Iraq's water treatment systems lay in
  ruins.[21]

- **Economic collapse:** Iraq's GDP fell by over **75%** during the sanctions period. Poverty and unemployment became widespread.[22]

In a now-infamous interview, **U.S. Secretary of State Madeleine Albright** was asked about the half-million Iraqi children who allegedly died due to sanctions. Her response:

"We think the price is worth it."[23]

This cold admission underscored the true purpose of U.S. policy: Iraq's suffering was collateral damage in America's broader agenda of control.

THE SECOND GULF WAR: WEAPONS OF MASS DECEPTION

By the early 2000s, Iraq was a shattered nation, still reeling from war and sanctions. Yet for the United States, it remained a target. Following the September 11, 2001 terrorist attacks, the Bush administration began building a case for war against Iraq, falsely linking Saddam Hussein to Al-Qaeda and claiming that Iraq possessed weapons of mass destruction (WMDs).

ISRAEL'S ROLE IN PUSHING THE NARRATIVE

Israel, long a vocal opponent of Saddam Hussein, played a significant role in initiating and amplifying the WMD narrative. Israeli leaders, including Prime Minister Ariel Sharon, insisted that Iraq's alleged weapons program posed a grave threat to regional stability. These claims, however, were based on misinformation.[24] Israeli intelligence, alongside the U.S. and British governments, misrepresented Iraq's capabilities to justify military action.

The Bush administration seized on these claims. In 2002, President George W. Bush declared Iraq part of an "Axis of Evil" and began preparing for war. Secretary of State Colin Powell's infamous presentation to the U.N. in February 2003 featured fabricated evidence, including doctored photos of alleged WMD facilities, and analysis that was incorrect and framed to support the decision to go to war that had already been made. The fabricated narrative was clear: Iraq was a threat to global security and had to be neutralized.[25]

THE 2003 INVASION: SHOCK AND AWE

On March 20, 2003, the U.S. and its allies launched the invasion of Iraq, dubbed Operation Iraqi Freedom.[26] The opening salvo, a brutal aerial bombardment known as "Shock and Awe," was intended to overwhelm Iraq's defenses and demonstrate American dominance.

In just three weeks, U.S. forces captured Baghdad, and Saddam Hussein's regime collapsed. President Bush declared "Mission Accomplished" aboard the USS Abraham Lincoln on May 1, 2003. Yet the war was far from over.

THE HUMAN COST OF THE IRAQ WAR

The Second Gulf War and its aftermath unleashed unimaginable suffering on Iraq:

- **Iraqi deaths:** Estimates of Iraqi deaths vary widely, but most credible sources place the toll between **200,000 and 1 million** civilians killed as a result of combat, airstrikes, and sectarian violence.[27]

- **Displacement:** Over **4 million Iraqis** were displaced internally and externally, creating one of the largest refugee crises in modern history.[28]

- **Infrastructure collapse:** Iraq's infrastructure, already weakened by the First Gulf War and sanctions, was further destroyed. Hospitals, schools, and power plants were left in ruins.[29]

WHY IT WAS DONE: OIL, POWER, AND PROFIT

The official justification for the war, WMDs and the fight against terrorism, was a lie. No WMDs were ever found, and Iraq had no operational ties to Al-Qaeda. So why was Iraq targeted?

Oil: Iraq has the world's fifth-largest proven oil reserves. U.S. corporations and policymakers saw control of Iraq's oil as a strategic priority.

- While the 1991 Gulf War was framed as a response to Iraq's invasion of Kuwait, protection of global oil markets, particularly access to Persian Gulf reserves, was central to U.S. motivations.[30]

- In 2003, the Bush administration denied oil was a motive, but internal memos, post-invasion policy decisions, and the swift move to privatize Iraq's oil industry suggest otherwise.[31]

- After the invasion, major U.S. and British oil companies such as ExxonMobil, Chevron, BP, and Shell were awarded favorable contracts to develop Iraq's oil fields, previously off-limits to Western firms for decades.[32]

Power in the Middle East: The United States still maintains military bases on Iraqi soil.

- Following the Cold War, the U.S. sought to reshape the Middle East to reflect its own economic and security interests, and Iraq offered a critical geographic platform between Iran, Syria, and the Persian Gulf.

- The 1990 and 2003 wars provided justification for a long-term U.S. military presence, helping to encircle Iran and influence neighboring Arab regimes.

- The invasion initially established Iraq as a client state in the American security architecture, reinforcing U.S.

hegemony and enabling surveillance, drone operations, and rapid deployment capabilities throughout the region.

Preserving Israeli military dominance: A strong, independent Iraq, particularly under Saddam Hussein, was viewed as a long-term threat to Israel's regional military and political dominance.

- Iraq supported the Palestinian cause, funded resistance movements, and had one of the largest conventional armies in the Arab world.[33]

- In both 1990 and 2003, Israeli officials quietly encouraged U.S. action to neutralize Iraq's power and prevent the emergence of any state capable of challenging Israel's qualitative military edge.[34]

- The removal of Iraq as a potential counterbalance further isolated other regional adversaries like Iran and Syria, aligning with the long-term strategic goals of Israeli policymakers and their allies in Washington.[35]

IRAQ TODAY: A NATION IN RUINS

Two decades after the 2003 invasion, Iraq is still a shadow of its former self. The war unleashed sectarian violence, empowered extremist groups like ISIS, and left millions of Iraqis in poverty. While American corporations and military interests profited, the people of Iraq were left to pick up the pieces of their shattered nation.

The destruction of Iraq was not an accident or a mistake—it was part of a deliberate strategy. The United States, acting as a colonial power, prioritized its economic and geopolitical interests, and those of its closest ally in the Middle East, Israel, over the lives of millions of Iraqis. Iraq's suffering serves as a grim reminder of the human cost of empire.

CHAPTER RECAP: THE UNITED STATES IN IRAQ—A LEGACY OF INTERVENTION

Iraq's history is a case study in American interference and its devastating consequences. From the First Gulf War and sanctions to the Second Gulf War and its aftermath, Iraq was sacrificed on the altar of American hegemony. For the United States, Iraq was not a sovereign nation with its own people and culture—it was a resource to be exploited, a battlefield to be dominated, and a warning to others who dared challenge American power.

As former U.N. weapons inspector **Scott Ritter** put it:

> *"Iraq was never about WMDs. It was about the projection of power. It was about oil. It was about shaping the future of the Middle East."*[36]

In that light, the invasion of Iraq was not a failure, it was a resounding success for American empire. For the Iraqi people, it was a tragedy of unimaginable proportions.

CHAPTER 24:

LIBYA

THE TRUE COST OF "HUMANITARIAN" INTERVENTION

In 2011, the United States, along with NATO allies, launched a military intervention in Libya under the pretext of "humanitarian responsibility." The official justification was to prevent a massacre in Benghazi by Libyan leader **Muammar Gaddafi**. But a closer examination reveals a much deeper and more calculated motive— one that had little to do with saving lives and everything to do with preserving American and Western dominance in Africa and beyond.

Libya, under Gaddafi, was not a perfect nation. No state is. But by regional and even global standards, it had become one of the most prosperous and stable countries in Africa. What made Gaddafi dangerous to U.S. interests was not terrorism or aggression, but his vision for African independence, his challenge to the Western financial system, and his audacity to defy U.S.-led global hegemony.

GADDAFI'S LIBYA: A SUCCESS STORY THE WEST COULDN'T TOLERATE

Before the NATO intervention, Libya had achieved remarkable development indicators that contradicted Western media narratives of a failing dictatorship. Libya's commitment to human development was evident in its comprehensive social programs. Healthcare and education were provided free to all citizens as a constitutional guarantee.[1] International health experts acknowledged that Libya possessed "one of the more comprehensive and effective health care systems in the Arab World."[2]

The numbers were impressive: Libya had 96 hospitals, 25 specialized units, 1,355 basic health centers, and 37 polyclinics.[3] Net enrollment in basic education reached 96% with only a 1% absence rate.[4] Female youth illiteracy dropped to less than 7%.[5] Childhood immunization became virtually universal, and the WHO noted that 11 of 12 global indicators for "Health for All by 2000" were achieved by Libya.[6]

The literacy transformation under Gaddafi's rule tells the story of a society investing in its people. When Libya gained independence in 1951, only 10-25% of the four million population could read and write.[7] By 2010, that figure had soared to 89.9% adult literacy according to the UN Development Programme.[8] UNICEF estimated youth literacy rates at an extraordinary 99.9% for both sexes by 2012.[9] This represented one of the most dramatic literacy improvements in modern history, a transformation from a largely illiterate society to one where virtually every young person could read and write in just four decades.

Libya's economic model represented everything neoliberal capitalism opposes: a nation using its natural resources for the benefit of its people rather than foreign corporations. Libya had achieved something almost unheard of in the developing world: zero external debt.[10] The African Development Bank notes that "historically, Libya has relied little on external borrowing thanks to its abundant foreign reserves from oil and gas exports."[11]

Life expectancy improved dramatically, from approximately 35 years at independence in 1951 to over 76 years by 2010, higher than the United States at the time.[12] By 1979, the average per-capita income had reached $8,170, up from just $40 in 1951, higher than many industrialized countries including Italy and the UK.[13] The state provided extensive social benefits including heavily subsidized electricity and unemployment benefits.[14]

By 2010, Libya consistently ranked as the African nation with the highest Human Development Index (HDI), standing at 0.755— significantly higher than any other African country.[15] The UN Development Programme considered Libya a "high-development country" in the Middle East and North Africa region.[16]

THE REAL THREAT: GADDAFI'S CHALLENGE TO WESTERN FINANCIAL CONTROL

What made Gaddafi unacceptable to Western powers wasn't his authoritarian governance, the U.S. has supported countless dictators who served American interests. What made him dangerous was his vision of African economic independence and his concrete steps toward achieving it.

Gaddafi's most ambitious, and ultimately fatal, project was his proposal for a Pan-African gold-backed currency.[17] He envisioned the creation of the "gold dinar," a unified monetary system that African nations could adopt in place of the U.S. dollar or the French franc (CFA). This wasn't just theoretical. Gaddafi had systematically accumulated the gold reserves necessary to back such a currency. According to leaked diplomatic cables, by 2011 Libya held 143 tons of gold and a similar amount of silver, reserves valued at over $7 billion.[18]

The plan included creating continent-wide African financial institutions: an African Investment Bank and an African Monetary Fund that would replace the International Monetary Fund and World Bank in Africa, providing alternatives to Western-controlled financial systems.

To understand why this threatened Western interests, consider how France maintains economic control over its former African colonies through the CFA franc system. Fourteen African countries use the CFA franc, guaranteed by the French treasury. This system ensures that African countries must deposit 50% of their foreign currency reserves with France, cannot print money without French approval, and must give France first rights to purchase any natural resources discovered.

Gaddafi's gold dinar threatened to break this system. If oil-rich African nations could trade in gold-backed dinars instead of CFA francs or U.S. dollars, it would destabilize both French economic control over Africa and the petrodollar system underpinning American global financial dominance.

The smoking gun for Western economic motivations came through leaked diplomatic cables. A March 2, 2011 email from Sidney Blumenthal to Secretary of State Hillary Clinton explicitly stated that Gaddafi's gold reserves and plan to create a Pan-African currency "were a threat to the French franc (CFA)" and to "the monetary stability of countries dependent on it."[19]

The email revealed that French intelligence had discovered Gaddafi's gold dinar plans shortly after the Libyan uprising began, and that "this was one of the factors that influenced President Nicolas Sarkozy's decision to commit France to the attack on Libya."[20] According to the intelligence briefing, Sarkozy's motivations included: gaining a greater share of Libya's oil production, increasing French influence in North Africa, improving his domestic political situation, providing the French military an opportunity to reassert its position globally, and addressing concerns about Gaddafi's long-term plans to supplant France as the dominant power in Francophone Africa.[21]

LIBYA POSED NO SECURITY THREAT

Despite the narrative of stopping a humanitarian catastrophe, there was no credible evidence that Gaddafi posed any threat to the United States or Western Europe. Following September 11, Libya worked closely with U.S. and British intelligence services. On December 19, 2003, Libya announced its decision to disclose and dismantle all weapons of mass destruction programs and accept international inspectors.[22] Libya fully complied with these commitments. The Organization for the Prohibition of Chemical Weapons (OPCW) verified the complete destruction of Libya's declared chemical weapons stockpiles.[23]

Libya had abandoned nuclear weapons programs, renounced terrorism, re-established diplomatic ties with Western nations, and was providing intelligence cooperation in counterterrorism efforts. Gaddafi had done everything Western powers demanded of him.

Unlike Tunisia or Egypt, Libya's protest movement quickly became an armed rebellion backed by foreign governments. Rather than allowing the African Union to mediate, the U.S. and NATO invoked the "Responsibility to Protect" (R2P) doctrine to justify immediate military intervention.[24] NATO implemented a "no-fly zone" that quickly expanded into a full bombing campaign targeting Libyan government forces and infrastructure. Rather than protecting civilians, NATO became the air force for rebel groups fighting to overthrow the government.

When Gaddafi was captured and brutally executed by NATO-backed rebels on October 20, 2011, Secretary of State Hillary Clinton celebrated the news. Upon hearing of Gaddafi's death during a television interview, Clinton laughed and said, **"We came, we saw, he died."**[25] This callous celebration revealed the true sentiment behind the "humanitarian" intervention, satisfaction that a geopolitical obstacle had been eliminated.

THE AFTERMATH: FROM AFRICA'S SUCCESS STORY TO FAILED STATE

The destruction of Libya provides a textbook example of how modern imperialism operates through destruction rather than occupation. Libya's economy, which had grown by 10.6% in 2010, contracted by 62.1% in 2011 due to the war.[26] The free healthcare system collapsed, the education system fragmented, and social welfare programs disappeared. Libya lost the institutional capacity to maintain the programs that had made it Africa's development leader.

Libya today exists as multiple competing governments with no unified control. Various "governments," tribal councils, and militias control different territories and oil facilities, making it impossible to restore basic services or provide security. Libya became a hub for human trafficking, with desperate African migrants sold in open-air slave markets, a practice eliminated under Gaddafi's rule.[27] Armed extremist groups, including ISIS, gained footholds in the power vacuum. Healthcare and education systems largely collapsed as professionals fled and infrastructure was destroyed.

Libya's weapons stockpiles were looted and distributed throughout the region, fueling conflicts across the Sahel and contributing to regional instability. WikiLeaks cables revealed that Western corporations positioned themselves to claim Libya's resources immediately after Gaddafi's overthrow. French President Sarkozy and British Prime Minister Cameron traveled to Tripoli to negotiate "favorable contracts for French and British energy companies."[28] France negotiated to "reserve as much as 35% of Libya's oil related industry for French firms."[29] These negotiations occurred while Libya was still in chaos, demonstrating that resource extraction took priority over humanitarian concerns or reconstruction.

THE LESSONS OF LIBYA

Libya offers crucial lessons about how American empire operates and why it's incompatible with global justice. Western discourse presents a false choice between supporting Gaddafi's authoritarian rule or supporting democratic revolution. This conceals the real choice: between a functioning state that served its people and chaos that serves Western economic interests.

Libya under Gaddafi was authoritarian but provided healthcare, education, and economic opportunity. The "democracy" that replaced him has provided none of these benefits while offering less political freedom than existed under Gaddafi. The Libya intervention cynically used humanitarian language to justify economic objectives. The rhetoric of "protecting civilians" built public support for military action that had nothing to do with humanitarian concerns. This weaponization of human rights concerns makes genuine humanitarian crises harder to address.

Libya demonstrates the price countries pay for challenging Western economic dominance. Any nation attempting to use its resources for domestic development rather than Western corporate profits becomes a target for destruction. Other African leaders witnessed Gaddafi's fate and learned that cooperation with Western economic interests, however harmful to their people, is safer than independence and self-determination.

Modern imperialism follows a consistent pattern: identify threats to Western economic interests, create humanitarian pretexts for intervention, destroy functioning states, then extract resources from the chaos while preventing genuine reconstruction. Libya revealed that the greatest enemy of democracy and human development isn't dictatorship, it's imperialism. Even flawed governments that serve their people represent a greater threat to Western interests than chaos that allows resource extraction.

Libya demonstrated that meaningful reform of American foreign policy is impossible within the current system. The economic interests that drove Libya's destruction, corporate access to resources, financial system dominance, geopolitical control, are fundamental to how American capitalism operates globally.

Most importantly, Libya proved that an alternative is possible. Despite its flaws, Libya demonstrated that developing countries can use their natural resources for domestic benefit, achieve rapid human development improvements, and maintain independence from Western financial systems. Libya's story places a moral obligation on Americans to confront what their government does in their name. The healthcare workers who lost jobs when hospitals were bombed, the teachers who fled when schools closed, the children who lost access to education, their suffering was caused by American taxpayer-funded bombs.

The lesson of Libya is that American empire is incompatible with global justice, development, and peace. As long as the United States maintains the power to destroy any country that challenges its interests, the world remains trapped in systems of exploitation and violence.

Libya's gold may be gone, looted in the chaos following Gaddafi's murder. Its oil flows again, but to foreign markets under foreign control. Its schools and hospitals remain damaged, its social programs dismantled, its people scattered and traumatized. But Libya's example, of what's possible when a country puts its people before foreign profits, remains. It stands as proof that another world is possible, and as a reminder of what we lose when we allow empire to triumph over humanity.

CHAPTER RECAP

Libya's destruction represents one of the clearest examples of how modern American imperialism operates. Under the guise of humanitarian intervention, NATO destroyed one of Africa's most prosperous nations, not because it threatened American security, but because it threatened American economic control.

Libya's Success Was Its Crime: By 2011, Libya had achieved remarkable development indicators—89% literacy, universal healthcare, zero external debt, and Africa's highest Human Development Index. Libya proved that African nations could use their natural resources for domestic prosperity rather than Western corporate profits.

The Real Threat Was Economic Independence: Gaddafi's plan for a Pan-African gold-backed currency threatened both the French CFA franc system that controls fourteen African economies and the petrodollar system underpinning American global dominance. Leaked diplomatic cables confirm this was a primary motivation for intervention.

Humanitarian Rhetoric Masked Economic Motives: While NATO claimed to protect civilians, the real goals were accessing Libya's oil reserves and preventing African monetary independence. Hillary Clinton's celebratory "We came, we saw, he died" comment revealed the true sentiment behind the "humanitarian" mission.

Destruction, Not Democracy, Was the Goal: Libya today is a failed state with slave markets, competing governments, collapsed infrastructure, and no meaningful democracy. This wasn't an unintended consequence, it was the predictable result of prioritizing resource control over human welfare.

The Pattern Repeats: Libya demonstrates how modern imperialism works: identify threats to Western economic interests, create humanitarian pretexts for intervention, destroy functioning states, then extract resources from the chaos while preventing genuine reconstruction.

Libya's story is both a tragedy and a warning. It shows what happens when empire triumphs over humanity, and what we lose when prosperity becomes a crime punishable by destruction. Most importantly, it proves that another world is possible, if we're willing to confront the forces that destroyed Libya to prevent them from claiming more victims.

CHAPTER 25:

NICARAGUA

AMERICAN PURSUIT OF POWER

Nicaragua's history reveals a devastating pattern of systematic exploitation, political manipulation, and economic coercion at the hands of the United States. Much like other Central American nations, Nicaragua became a key target for American imperial ambitions during the 19th and 20th centuries. Through direct military intervention, support for coups, and the imposition of economic dependencies, the U.S. cemented its dominance over the country, often under the guise of safeguarding economic stability and democracy. In reality, these actions served to enhance American power and corporate interests at the expense of Nicaraguan sovereignty and the welfare of its people.

THE ROOTS OF INTERVENTION: NICARAGUA'S
GEOPOLITICAL AND ECONOMIC IMPORTANCE

Nicaragua's strategic location and economic potential made it an irresistible prize for American interests. Situated between the Pacific Ocean and the Caribbean Sea, the nation offered an alternative route for a transoceanic canal, a vision that loomed large in American foreign policy during the 19th century. Though the Panama Canal would eventually become the chosen site, Nicaragua remained vital for U.S. economic and strategic dominance in Central America.

Additionally, Nicaragua's fertile land, natural resources, and emerging agricultural economy offered immense opportunities for American corporations. By the late 19th century, U.S. businesses, particularly those in the banana and coffee industries, began establishing deep economic ties in the region, exploiting local labor and land to fuel American prosperity.

With these interests at stake, the United States would go to great lengths to ensure political compliance in Nicaragua. If local leaders dared to challenge American hegemony or disrupt business interests, they were quickly met with pressure, coups, or military force.

EARLY INTERVENTIONS AND THE RISE OF DOLLAR DIPLOMACY

American interference in Nicaragua began in earnest during the early 20th century under the banner of "Dollar Diplomacy,"[1] a policy advanced by President William Howard Taft and Secretary of State Philander Knox. Dollar Diplomacy sought to use American financial power to stabilize foreign economies while simultaneously expanding U.S. influence. In practice, it was a tool for controlling smaller nations through debt and dependence.

In Nicaragua, this policy was particularly devastating. By 1912, the U.S. had gained control of Nicaragua's finances, customs, and infrastructure under the guise of helping the country "stabilize" its economy.

When Nicaraguan President José Santos Zelaya refused to play by these rules and challenged American dominance, the United States intervened directly. Zelaya was a nationalist leader who sought to reduce foreign influence and prioritize Nicaraguan sovereignty. Under his leadership, the country began to explore partnerships with European powers to develop its resources and infrastructure.

This move was unacceptable to the United States, which viewed European involvement in the region as a threat to its own interests under the Monroe Doctrine. Using the killing of two American mercenaries as a pretext, the U.S. forced Zelaya to resign in 1909.[2] In his place, the U.S. installed conservative leaders who were far more amenable to American corporate and political influence. From this moment forward, Nicaragua's political landscape became a revolving door of leaders who served American interests while suppressing nationalist movements.

THE U.S. OCCUPATION OF NICARAGUA (1912–1933)

To ensure control over Nicaragua's government and economy, the United States deployed troops in 1912, marking the beginning of a military occupation that would last for more than two decades. The presence of U.S. Marines was justified as a measure to "restore order" and protect American investments, but its real purpose was to prevent any Nicaraguan leaders from challenging U.S. dominance.

The occupation solidified American control over Nicaragua's infrastructure, including railways, ports, and banks. It also protected the interests of American corporations such as the United Fruit Company,[3] which came to dominate the banana trade in the region. Nicaraguan farmers were pushed off their land, forced into low-paying labor, or rendered dependent on foreign-owned plantations.

The human cost of this occupation was immense. Nicaraguan sovereignty was effectively dismantled, and the nation's economy became a tool for American profit. Local resistance was met with brutal force, and dissenters were branded as "bandits" or "anarchists."

One of the most notable figures to emerge during this period was Augusto César Sandino, a revolutionary leader who rejected U.S. imperialism and led a guerrilla campaign against the American occupation. Sandino became a symbol of Nicaraguan resistance, rallying farmers, workers, and indigenous people to fight for their nation's independence. In one of his famous proclamations, Sandino declared: "We will not allow our country to become a colony of any foreign power. We fight for the dignity of Nicaragua and the liberation of our people."[4]

Despite being vastly outgunned, Sandino's forces waged a determined resistance that ultimately contributed to the withdrawal of U.S. troops in 1933. However, this was far from the end of American interference.

THE SOMOZA DYNASTY: A U.S.-BACKED DICTATORSHIP

Following the withdrawal of U.S. forces, the United States sought to maintain control in Nicaragua through political proxies. The opportunity came in the form of Anastasio Somoza García, who rose to power as head of the U.S. trained Nicaraguan National Guard. Somoza quickly consolidated power, assassinated Sandino in 1934, and established a military dictatorship with the full backing of the United States.[5]

Somoza's regime, and later the rule of his sons, became synonymous with corruption, repression, and brutality. The family amassed enormous wealth by exploiting Nicaragua's economy and natural resources while violently suppressing opposition. The United States, in turn, continued to support the Somoza dynasty because it provided political stability and protected American corporate interests.

President Franklin D. Roosevelt's infamous comment about Somoza García epitomized the U.S. attitude toward Nicaragua: **"He may be a son of a bitch, but he's our son of a bitch."**[6]

The Somoza dictatorship lasted for more than four decades, during which time Nicaragua's economy became increasingly dependent on American trade and aid. The country's infrastructure remained underdeveloped, wealth inequality widened, and dissent was met with torture, imprisonment, or execution.

REVOLUTION AND THE SANDINISTAS: A CHALLENGE TO AMERICAN HEGEMONY

By the 1970s, opposition to the Somoza regime had reached a boiling point. The Sandinista National Liberation Front (FSLN), named in honor of Augusto César Sandino, emerged as the leading revolutionary force.[7] The Sandinistas sought to overthrow the dictatorship, end foreign exploitation, and implement social and economic reforms.

In 1979, the Sandinistas succeeded in toppling the Somoza dynasty, marking a dramatic turning point in Nicaraguan history. For the first time in decades, Nicaragua appeared poised to reclaim its sovereignty and chart its own path forward.

However, the United States saw the Sandinista government as a threat. Fearing the spread of socialism and the loss of U.S. influence in the region, the Reagan administration launched a covert campaign to destabilize the Sandinista government. The U.S. funded and armed the Contras, a right-wing rebel group that waged a bloody insurgency against the Sandinistas.[8] The Contras' campaign was marked by atrocities, including attacks on civilians, assassinations, and the destruction of vital infrastructure. The Reagan administration justified its support for the Contras as a fight for "freedom," but the reality was far grimmer.

A leaked CIA manual provided instructions on how the Contras could wage psychological warfare, sabotage public support for the Sandinistas, and undermine Nicaragua's government.[9] The U.S. also imposed economic sanctions, crippling the Nicaraguan economy and exacerbating poverty.

THE SURPRISING SEQUEL

The stories of countries don't just end neatly like a movie or a play. They go on, and sometimes the sequel is more interesting than the original.

Daniel Ortega, the onetime insurgent who helped topple the Somozas, returned to the presidency in 2007 and has since concentrated power through loyal courts, electoral rule changes, and security forces. By 2018, when nationwide protests erupted over social security reforms and broader grievances, the government responded with live fire, mass detentions, and systematic repression. Regional monitors and human-rights groups documented hundreds of deaths and widespread abuses beginning in April 2018.[10]

In 2021, authorities jailed or sidelined nearly all viable opposition candidates ahead of the presidential vote, producing an election that international observers deemed devoid of democratic legitimacy.[11] Repression has intensified rather than eased. The government has shuttered thousands of nongovernmental organizations, seized a Jesuit-run university, and expanded attacks on independent media and the Catholic Church.[12] In early 2023, Managua expelled 222 political prisoners to the United States, and later that year it stripped dozens of dissidents of citizenship and assets.[13]

Has the United States intervened in Nicaragua in the last twenty years the way it once did? No. Washington has not mounted a covert war, nor a military operation. Instead, it has relied on sanctions, visa restrictions, and pressure at multilateral lenders. Congress passed the NICA Act in 2018 and the RENACER Act in 2021, which mandate targeted sanctions and instruct U.S. officials to oppose most new loans to the Nicaraguan government until basic democratic conditions are met.[14] This represents a very different toolkit from the 1980s.

What changed? The strategic calculus is not the same. There is no Cold War proxy fight, no canal at stake, and no armed U.S. client to back. After Iraq and Afghanistan, the political appetite for regime-change gambits in Central America is low. Meanwhile, the economic relationship continues under CAFTA-DR, with Nicaragua remaining inside the U.S. Central America free-trade framework and several billion dollars in annual goods trade.[15]

The irony is hard to miss. A revolutionary who once promised to free Nicaragua from dictatorship now governs as a strongman. A superpower that once treated Nicaragua as a battleground now treats it as a sanctions case file, one of many. For Nicaraguans who hoped 1979 would open a democratic future, the current reality is a closed political space, a battered civil society, and an economy still tethered to external forces.

That is a sequel plot twist worth noting.

CHAPTER RECAP

Nicaragua's tragic history demonstrates how the United States systematically destroyed a nation's sovereignty through military occupation, economic control, and proxy warfare. From the removal of nationalist leader José Santos Zelaya in 1909 to the Contra war of the 1980s, American interventions prioritized corporate profits and geopolitical dominance over Nicaraguan welfare. Even today, Nicaragua remains economically dependent on the United States through trade agreements, showing how imperial control adapts but never truly ends.

This chapter reveals the classic American imperial playbook that we have now seen time and time again: identify strategic targets, install compliant dictators, crush nationalist movements, and maintain control through economic dependency. Nicaragua's experience mirrors U.S. interventions throughout Latin America, from Guatemala to Chile, demonstrating how "promoting democracy" became code for protecting American business interests.

Nicaragua's strategic location between two oceans made it a prime target for over a century of U.S. intervention, beginning with financial control through "Dollar Diplomacy" in 1912 and evolving into direct military occupation from 1912-1933 to protect American corporate interests like the United Fruit Company. The U.S. subsequently installed and supported the brutal Somoza family dictatorship for over four decades, with FDR infamously defending the regime by saying Somoza was "our son of a bitch." Though Augusto César Sandino's early guerrilla resistance inspired the 1979 Sandinista revolution that briefly restored Nicaraguan independence, the Reagan administration responded by funding right-wing Contra death squads and imposing crippling sanctions to destroy the new government.

The modern irony is that Daniel Ortega, once a revolutionary hero, now rules Nicaragua as an authoritarian leader, while U.S. intervention has shifted from military occupation to economic sanctions and diplomatic pressure. This illustrates how American policy consistently prioritized regional dominance and economic control over Nicaraguan sovereignty, leaving a legacy of violence, instability, and the tragic transformation of revolutionary movements into the very authoritarianism they once fought against.

The courage of figures like Augusto César Sandino and the Sandinista revolutionaries proves that resistance to empire is possible, even against overwhelming odds. Their legacy challenges us to recognize that America's global dominance comes at an enormous human cost, and that confronting this reality is the first step toward building a more just world.

CHAPTER 26:

HAITI

THE AMERICAN GRIP ON HAITI, ECONOMICS, POLITICS, AND COLONIAL POWER

The story of Haiti is one of resilience, a small Caribbean nation that rose from the ashes of slavery to proclaim itself the first Black republic in 1804. But Haiti's story is also one of relentless interference, a tale in which foreign powers, particularly the United States, have repeatedly undermined Haiti's sovereignty for their own gain. To fully understand the modern struggles of Haiti, we must examine the United States' calculated actions to exploit Haiti's economy, manipulate its government, and ultimately wield control over its future. This is not a comfortable story to tell, nor is it one we often hear. But it is a story that demands to be told.

THE EARLY DAYS OF HAITIAN INDEPENDENCE: A THORN IN AMERICA'S SIDE

Haiti's independence was revolutionary. It shook the foundations of colonial powers who relied on the enslavement of Black laborers to sustain their economic empires. For the United States, which still clung to slavery in its southern states, Haiti's successful revolt was not just inconvenient, it was dangerous. The fear was simple: if Haiti could free itself, what was stopping enslaved people in the U.S. from doing the same?

Thus, America's first act of interference in Haiti came through silence, a refusal to recognize Haiti's independence. For nearly 60 years, Haiti was treated as a pariah, denied trade relationships and diplomatic acknowledgment. While European powers like France extorted massive reparations from Haiti, crippling its economy for generations, the United States stood by, watching as Haiti

231

floundered under crushing debt. Interestingly, while the United States invoked the Monroe Doctrine in other countries to exert control or justify intervention, it remained silent regarding Haiti even though the French were operating on America's front door.

This denial of recognition was no passive act. It was economic warfare. By isolating Haiti, the U.S. ensured that Haiti could not establish itself as a trading partner, could not attract international investment, and could not build a sustainable economy. This was interference by exclusion, a calculated move to keep Haiti weak while safeguarding American economic and political interests.

THE U.S. OCCUPATION OF HAITI: A TEMPLATE FOR CONTROL

If the 19th century was marked by silence, the early 20th century was marked by direct action. In 1915, the United States invaded Haiti under the pretext of "protecting American interests" and restoring stability.[1] What followed was a nearly two-decade-long military occupation that reshaped Haiti's economy, government, and infrastructure, not for the benefit of the Haitian people, but for the benefit of American business and strategic power.

To understand the full impact of the occupation, one must examine the economic exploitation that defined it. American officials rewrote Haiti's constitution in 1917 to legalize foreign ownership of land, a change that had been forbidden since Haiti's independence.[2] U.S. corporations swooped in, buying up vast tracts of land for agriculture, primarily for sugar, rubber, and other exports that served American markets. Haitian peasants, who had been subsistence farmers, were pushed off their lands and forced into low-wage labor under foreign-owned plantations.

The U.S. occupation also controlled Haiti's finances. The National City Bank of New York, now Citibank, took over the Haitian treasury,[3] diverting funds to pay off loans to American banks, loans that Haiti never had a fair chance to negotiate. Public revenues, which should have funded schools, hospitals, and infrastructure for the Haitian people, were instead funneled to foreign creditors.

And then there was the human cost. Haitians who resisted American rule faced brutal suppression. The U.S. Marines established forced labor systems to build roads and other infrastructure projects. Thousands of Haitians died under this coerced labor, their lives sacrificed to create systems that primarily benefited American business interests.[4]

This was not an occupation to help Haiti. This was an occupation to extract from Haiti. Under the guise of "stability," the United States ensured Haiti's economy was reoriented toward serving American markets, a pattern that would persist long after the troops left Haitian soil.

HAITI'S GOVERNMENT: A PUPPET FOR AMERICAN INTERESTS

U.S. interference in Haiti's government was as deliberate as its economic exploitation. During the occupation, American officials controlled Haiti's legislative and executive branches, ensuring that leaders who complied with U.S. policies remained in power while suppressing those who resisted.

Even after the occupation ended in 1934, America's influence over Haiti's government continued. Throughout the 20th century, the United States supported dictators and regimes that prioritized American economic and geopolitical interests. One such regime was that of François "Papa Doc" Duvalier and later his son, Jean-Claude "Baby Doc" Duvalier. To entrench their power, the Duvaliers built a parallel security apparatus, the Tonton Macoute (officially the Volunteers for National Security), a regime militia used to terrorize and eliminate opponents through disappearances, assassinations, and everyday intimidation.[5]

The Duvalier regimes ruled with an iron fist, committing atrocities against the Haitian people while enjoying American backing as reliable anti-communist partners during the Cold War.[6] The U.S. turned a blind eye to the brutality and corruption of the Duvaliers because, to Washington, stability was more valuable than democracy in Haiti. Stability meant American businesses could continue to operate, and it meant a predictable client on a volatile Caribbean map.

This pattern, supporting leaders who align with American interests while undermining those who challenge them, is not unique to Haiti. But in Haiti, the consequences were devastating. Decades of U.S.-backed authoritarian rule left public institutions hollowed out, the economy stagnant, and society traumatized.[7] Even after the Duvalier dynasty fell in 1986, their legacy of impunity and political violence continued to shadow efforts at democratic reconstruction.

MODERN ECHOES: HAITI AS A PAWN IN U.S. POLICY

American interference in Haiti did not end with the Cold War. Today, the echoes of past policies are still felt in Haiti's economic and political struggles. Trade agreements that favor American markets have stifled local Haitian industries. For example, the influx of subsidized American rice, known as "Miami Rice," decimated Haiti's domestic rice production in the 1990s, leaving Haitian farmers without livelihoods and deepening the country's dependency on imports.[8]

Politically, the United States has continued to exert influence over Haitian elections and governance. In recent decades, Haitian leaders who challenge American economic or political agendas have often found themselves marginalized, while those who comply are rewarded with international support.

This is the reality of Haiti's relationship with the United States: a relationship defined by power imbalances, economic exploitation, and political manipulation. The United States, which prides itself on championing freedom and democracy, has too often denied those very principles to Haiti.

HAITI NOW: A CRISIS THE WORLD WOULD RATHER IGNORE

Haiti is living through its most sustained period of upheaval in modern history. Armed groups control most of Port-au-Prince, state institutions are powerless, and humanitarian needs have surged.[9] Sexual violence has become a weapon of social control. UN agencies and medical NGOs report that children make up a shocking share of survivors, including very young girls and boys. In some datasets from the capital, roughly one in five survivors are under the age of ten.[10] This is a national trauma that will echo for decades.

The United States has not returned to the era of Marines and military occupations. Washington has avoided direct intervention to "put down" the gangs. Instead, it has backed a Kenya-led Multinational Security Support mission authorized by the UN Security Council, provided funding and logistics, and used sanctions and visa restrictions against Haitian and regional actors.[11] That is a different toolkit than the twentieth century. It is also a choice. After Iraq and Afghanistan, there is little appetite for open-ended deployments in the Caribbean, and Haiti's crisis, while devastating, no longer sits inside a Cold War chessboard.

If the United States wants to help rather than harm, the path is both clear and difficult. Support a professional, rights-respecting security effort that protects civilians, not factions. Tie assistance to verifiable improvements in justice, policing, and corruption cases. Expand humanitarian funding targeted to displaced families, clinics that treat sexual-violence survivors, and services for children. Back Haitian-led political arrangements that can actually govern, including credible timelines for elections when basic security allows. And be honest about our history in Haiti, since credibility requires it.

Haiti's people have endured more than most nations could bear. Their strength is the only reason the country still stands. The question is whether outside powers, especially the United States, will choose policies that reduce harm and expand Haitian agency, or whether they will keep treating Haiti as a problem to be managed from afar. Haiti's story is not over. It will be written by Haitians. The rest of us should decide whether we will make that work easier or harder.

CHAPTER RECAP

Haiti's tragic story reveals how American foreign policy systematically destroyed a nation that dared to challenge the global order of white supremacy and economic exploitation. From refusing recognition to military occupation to supporting dictatorships, the United States consistently prioritized corporate profits and regional control over Haitian sovereignty and human rights. The current humanitarian crisis—with gangs controlling the capital and children suffering mass sexual violence—cannot be understood without acknowledging this century-long pattern of American interference.

Haiti's experience demonstrates the intersection of racism and imperialism in American foreign policy. Unlike other Caribbean nations, Haiti faced unique punishment for being the first successful slave revolt, showing how America's imperial agenda was always intertwined with maintaining white supremacist power structures. The pattern of economic extraction, political manipulation, and military intervention in Haiti became a template later applied across Latin America and beyond.

The United States refused to recognize Haiti's independence for 60 years, deliberately isolating the first Black republic economically and diplomatically to ensure its weakness. When the

U.S. finally intervened directly with a 1915-1934 military occupation, it rewrote Haiti's constitution to allow foreign land ownership, enabling American corporations to seize agricultural lands while Citibank took control of Haiti's treasury, diverting public funds from essential services to debt repayment. U.S. Marines established brutal forced labor systems that killed thousands building infrastructure for American business interests, and later the U.S. backed the murderous Duvalier dictatorship for decades because it provided "stability" for American corporations despite massive human rights abuses.

The economic warfare continued into the 1990s when subsidized American rice imports destroyed Haiti's domestic agriculture, forcing farmers off their land and creating deeper dependency on foreign food aid. Today, while avoiding direct military occupation, the U.S. continues to treat Haiti as a crisis to be managed from a distance rather than confronting how over two centuries of American policy—from initial isolation through occupation, financial extraction, support for dictators, and trade policies—created the foundation for Haiti's current instability and poverty.

The resilience of the Haitian people in the face of relentless foreign interference stands as a testament to human dignity and the possibility of resistance. Their ongoing struggle for true independence challenges us to confront how America's global dominance has been built on the systematic exploitation of Black and brown nations and demands that we work toward genuine justice rather than perpetual extraction.

CHAPTER 27:

GUATEMALA

GUATEMALA, UNITED FRUIT, COUPS, AND THE SEEDS OF IMPERIALISM

Guatemala's tragic encounter with U.S. interference serves as one of the most devastating examples of how economic interests, corporate influence, and Cold War paranoia combined to crush a nation's path toward sovereignty and social progress. Beneath the rhetoric of defending freedom and democracy lay a simpler truth: the United States prioritized profits over people, choosing to destabilize Guatemala in service of corporate greed.

Like the story of many other countries affected by the United States, the story of Guatemala is a story of land, power, and betrayal. It is the story of a democratically elected government overthrown, of peasants robbed of their livelihoods, and of a country plunged into decades of violence, all to preserve the fortunes of an American fruit company.

THE UNITED FRUIT COMPANY: LAND, EXPLOITATION, AND POWER

By the early 20th century, the United States had cemented its economic dominance in Central America, and Guatemala was no exception. The United Fruit Company (UFC), an American corporation with sprawling operations across the region, came to symbolize U.S. control.[1] Known locally as "El Pulpo" (the octopus) for its many tentacles that reached into every sector of society, United Fruit controlled vast tracts of land, railroads, ports, and even communications systems.

United Fruit's economic power translated into political influence. By securing preferential treatment from Guatemala's ruling elites, the company gained tax exemptions, monopolized transportation infrastructure, and ensured that land ownership remained concentrated in foreign hands. For the majority of Guatemalans, indigenous farmers and laborers, this meant poverty, exploitation, and dispossession.

The company's business model was built on extraction and inequality. United Fruit paid minimal taxes, employed workers at subsistence wages, and maintained monopolistic control over Guatemala's most vital infrastructure. The banana plantations operated as virtual company towns, where workers lived in company housing, shopped at company stores, and found themselves trapped in cycles of debt that resembled the sharecropping systems of the American South.

In 1950, nearly 72% of Guatemala's arable land was owned by just 2% of the population.[2] The majority of it lay unused, held as speculative assets by wealthy landowners and foreign companies like United Fruit, while indigenous campesinos (farmers) struggled to survive on small, infertile plots of land. This concentration of land ownership wasn't accidental, it was the deliberate result of policies that favored foreign corporations over Guatemalan citizens.

Against this backdrop of inequality and injustice, the seeds of reform began to take root.

JACOBO ÁRBENZ AND THE PATH TO REFORM

In 1951, Guatemala elected Jacobo Árbenz Guzmán as president in what was widely regarded as a free and fair democratic process. Árbenz, a former military officer turned reformer, sought to transform Guatemala into a modern, self-sufficient nation by addressing the country's staggering inequalities. At the heart of his agenda was land reform, a policy that would redistribute unused land to impoverished farmers, empowering them to work for their own livelihoods.

Árbenz's vision was neither radical nor communist, it was simply democratic. He wanted Guatemala to control its own destiny, to build roads and ports that served Guatemalan interests, and to ensure that the country's agricultural wealth benefited its own people rather than foreign shareholders. His administration invested in education, infrastructure, and social programs that had been neglected under previous U.S.-backed regimes.

Decree 900, the centerpiece of Árbenz's reform, sought to expropriate uncultivated land from large landowners and compensate them based on its declared tax value. This move directly challenged the dominance of the United Fruit Company, which owned over 40% of Guatemala's land, much of it not being cultivated.[3] The company had deliberately kept vast tracts of land idle to maintain artificial scarcity and prevent competition, a practice that enriched United Fruit while impoverishing Guatemalan farmers.

To Árbenz and his supporters, the land reforms represented justice for the Guatemalan people, an opportunity to reclaim their dignity and independence. For United Fruit, however, the reforms posed an existential threat to its profits. The company launched a vigorous lobbying campaign in the United States, framing Árbenz's policies as evidence of a growing communist threat in the Western Hemisphere.[4]

THE COLD WAR AND THE MANUFACTURED THREAT OF COMMUNISM

The 1950s were defined by the Cold War, a period when American foreign policy was driven by an obsession with containing communism at all costs. Any attempt at economic redistribution or nationalist reform, no matter how moderate, was branded as a communist plot. This paranoid worldview created opportunities for corporations like United Fruit to manipulate U.S. foreign policy for their own benefit.

United Fruit's lobbyists found sympathetic ears in the Eisenhower administration. Secretary of State John Foster Dulles and his brother Allen Dulles, the director of the CIA, both had close ties to United Fruit.[5] The conflict of interest was blatant: the very officials tasked with shaping U.S. foreign policy had financial and professional incentives to defend the company's interests. John Foster Dulles had worked as a lawyer for United Fruit, while Allen Dulles served on the company's board of directors.

This web of corporate connections extended throughout the U.S. government. Assistant Secretary of State John Moors Cabot was a stockholder in United Fruit, and his family had significant investments in the company. Under Secretary of State Walter Bedell Smith would later join United Fruit's board after leaving government service. The revolving door between corporate boardrooms and government offices ensured that United Fruit's interests were treated as synonymous with American interests.

Under pressure from United Fruit and fueled by Cold War paranoia, the United States branded Árbenz as a communist sympathizer and began plotting his removal, much like today we brand people or groups "terrorists" in order to justify sanctions and actions. This narrative, though unfounded, served as a convenient justification for American intervention. The truth was far simpler: Árbenz threatened corporate profits, and in the 1950s, that was enough to warrant regime change.

OPERATION PBSUCCESS: THE CIA COUP

In 1954, the United States launched Operation PBSUCCESS, a CIA-orchestrated coup to overthrow Jacobo Árbenz.[6] The operation was a textbook example of U.S. imperial strategy, combining economic sabotage, psychological warfare, and military pressure to destabilize the Guatemalan government.

The CIA armed and trained a rebel force led by Carlos Castillo Armas, a right-wing military officer.[7] While the actual invasion was small and militarily insignificant, the psychological impact was immense. The CIA bombed key infrastructure, spread propaganda through radio broadcasts, and created the illusion of a massive uprising. Radio stations controlled by the CIA broadcast fabricated reports of communist atrocities and rebel victories, while psychological warfare experts crafted propaganda designed to demoralize Árbenz's supporters.

The operation also included economic warfare. The CIA organized strikes, sabotaged transportation networks, and pressured other Central American countries to isolate Guatemala diplomatically. These tactics created the impression of widespread opposition to Árbenz's government, when in reality most Guatemalans supported the democratically elected president.

Guatemalan military leaders, convinced that a full-scale U.S. invasion was imminent, abandoned Árbenz. The threat of American military intervention had been made clear through diplomatic channels, and Guatemala's generals understood that resistance would be futile. Facing betrayal and overwhelming pressure, Árbenz resigned on June 27, 1954. In a heartbreaking farewell speech broadcast to the nation, he declared:

> "The United Fruit Company, in collaboration with the governing circles of the United States, are responsible for what is happening to us. The truth is clear: Guatemala is suffering under an imperialist aggression."[8]

THE AFTERMATH: REPRESSION AND VIOLENCE

With Árbenz removed, Carlos Castillo Armas was installed as president, a puppet leader handpicked by the United States. His regime immediately rolled back the land reforms, returning expropriated land to United Fruit and the country's oligarchy. Thousands of campesinos who had begun to farm the redistributed land were evicted, often violently. The brief moment when

Guatemala's indigenous majority had glimpsed economic justice was brutally extinguished.

Political repression followed swiftly. Castillo Armas launched a campaign to eliminate "communist elements," targeting labor leaders, teachers, intellectuals, and anyone suspected of supporting Árbenz's reforms. Mass arrests, torture, and assassinations became tools of governance. Political parties were banned, unions were outlawed, and civil liberties were suspended. The United States celebrated the coup as a victory for freedom and democracy, but for the Guatemalan people, it marked the beginning of decades of suffering.

The new regime also reversed Árbenz's economic policies, eliminating programs that had supported indigenous farmers and returning to the export-oriented model that benefited foreign corporations. Literacy programs were shut down, rural health clinics were closed, and infrastructure projects that would have connected remote communities to national markets were abandoned. Guatemala's brief experiment with inclusive development was replaced by a return to colonial-style extraction.

THE LEGACY OF THE COUP: CIVIL WAR AND GENOCIDE

The 1954 coup had far-reaching consequences for Guatemala. By dismantling Árbenz's reforms and crushing popular movements, the United States laid the groundwork for instability, inequality, and violence that would plague the country for generations. Over the following decades, Guatemala descended into a brutal civil war that lasted from 1960 to 1996.[9]

During the war, the U.S. supported successive right-wing military regimes that waged a scorched-earth campaign against indigenous communities and leftist rebels. The military's counterinsurgency strategy deliberately targeted Maya communities, viewing indigenous identity itself as subversive. Entire villages were wiped out, tens of thousands were forcibly disappeared, and over 200,000 people were killed, the vast majority of them indigenous Maya civilians.[10]

The violence reached genocidal levels during the early 1980s, when U.S.-backed General Efraín Ríos Montt ordered the systematic destruction of Maya communities. The military's "beans and bullets" campaign promised food to those who supported the government and death to those who didn't. Soldiers massacred entire families, burned villages, and destroyed crops and livestock to deny support to guerrilla forces.

The Guatemalan military justified its atrocities as part of the fight against communism, but the real victims were ordinary people who dared to demand justice and dignity. The United States provided training, weapons, and intelligence that enabled these crimes against humanity, all while maintaining that it was defending freedom and democracy.

IN THE END, WHO BENEFITS? WHO SUFFERS?

The United States' intervention in Guatemala was not about defending democracy, it was about defending corporate profits and maintaining geopolitical dominance. The overthrow of Jacobo Árbenz revealed the lengths to which the U.S. would go to protect its economic interests, even at the cost of destabilizing an entire nation and enabling genocide.

For Guatemala, the price of this interference was immense. The country's dreams of progress were crushed, its people subjected to unimaginable violence, and its future shaped by foreign interests. The democratic institutions that Árbenz had sought to strengthen were destroyed, replaced by military rule that served American and elite Guatemalan interests while oppressing the indigenous majority.

Today, Guatemala remains one of the poorest and most unequal nations in Latin America, a direct legacy of the exploitation and imperialism it endured. Land ownership remains concentrated among a small elite, indigenous communities continue to face discrimination and violence, and economic opportunities remain limited for the majority of the population. The social programs and infrastructure investments that Árbenz had planned might have transformed Guatemala into a prosperous, equitable society. Instead, decades of U.S.-backed authoritarianism left the country impoverished and traumatized.

The story of Guatemala forces us to confront uncomfortable truths about American foreign policy. Beneath the rhetoric of freedom lies a darker reality: a nation willing to sacrifice the sovereignty and well-being of others to serve its own ends. The 1954 coup established a template for U.S. interventions throughout Latin America, demonstrating how corporate interests could manipulate national security concerns to justify regime change.

As we look back on this history, one question remains: Can the United States acknowledge its role in Guatemala's suffering, and can we, as global citizens, learn from this legacy of imperial arrogance? For the people of Guatemala, the scars of 1954 remain, and their struggle for justice continues. Their resilience in the face of such overwhelming oppression stands as a testament to the human spirit and a reminder that the pursuit of dignity and self-determination cannot be permanently extinguished, no matter how powerful the forces arrayed against it.

CHAPTER RECAP

Guatemala's tragedy demonstrates how American foreign policy systematically destroyed democracy to protect corporate profits. The 1954 coup wasn't about fighting communism—it was about preserving United Fruit Company's exploitative monopoly over Guatemalan land and labor. When a democratically elected president dared to implement land reforms that would benefit his own people rather than foreign shareholders, the United States orchestrated his overthrow and installed a brutal dictatorship.

The consequences were genocidal. Over 200,000 Guatemalans, mostly indigenous Maya, died in the civil war that followed the coup. The social programs, infrastructure investments, and economic development that Árbenz had planned were abandoned, leaving Guatemala trapped in poverty and inequality that persists today.

Guatemala is just another example of the same playbook that we continue to see in country after country. The revolving door between corporate boardrooms and government offices ensured that American business interests were treated as national security priorities.

The 1954 CIA-orchestrated coup in Guatemala exemplified corporate-government collusion at its worst, with Secretary of State John Foster Dulles and CIA Director Allen Dulles both having direct financial ties to the United Fruit Company, which controlled over 40% of Guatemala's arable land while keeping most deliberately uncultivated. When democratically-elected president Jacobo Árbenz implemented moderate land reforms to redistribute this unused land to peasant farmers—threatening United Fruit's monopolistic profits in a country where just 2% of the population owned 72% of arable land—the U.S. falsely branded him a communist and launched Operation PBSUCCESS, using psychological warfare, economic sabotage, and military pressure to overthrow Guatemala's legitimate government and install a puppet regime that immediately reversed all democratic reforms.

The consequences were catastrophic: the 1954 coup triggered a 36-year civil war that killed over 200,000 people, mostly indigenous Maya civilians, as U.S.-backed military regimes committed systematic genocide against indigenous communities. Guatemala remains one of Latin America's poorest and most unequal nations today, its democratic development and social progress deliberately stunted by decades of U.S.-backed authoritarianism that prioritized corporate profits over human rights, proving that the real threat wasn't communism but rather any government that dared challenge American business interests in the region.

The courage of leaders like Jacobo Árbenz and the resilience of the Guatemalan people prove that resistance to empire is possible, even against overwhelming odds. Árbenz's final speech, naming United Fruit Company and the U.S. government as the architects of Guatemala's suffering, stands as a powerful indictment of American imperialism.

This is the real takeaway for Americans: The Guatemalan story challenges us to recognize that our prosperity may come at the expense of others' freedom, and that confronting this truth is essential for building a more just world.

CHAPTER 28:

AFGHANISTAN

AFGHANISTAN, EMPIRE'S GRAVEYARD AND AMERICA'S UNFINISHED WAR

Afghanistan's history is a tale of resilience, survival, and the crushing weight of foreign intervention. Often called the "Graveyard of Empires,"[1] this mountainous nation has long been a battlefield for those seeking to impose their will. The British Empire, the Soviet Union, and most recently, the United States, have all tried and failed to reshape Afghanistan to suit their own interests.

For the United States, its involvement in Afghanistan represents one of the most glaring examples of foreign policy hubris. Cloaked in the language of security and democracy, America's intervention was marked by violence, shifting goals, and a deep misunderstanding of Afghan society. The consequences have been catastrophic: decades of war, thousands of lives lost, and a nation left to rebuild amid the rubble of broken promises.

THE COLD WAR PRELUDE: AFGHANISTAN AS A PROXY BATTLEFIELD

To understand the U.S. role in Afghanistan, we must begin with the Cold War, a period when the United States and the Soviet Union vied for global dominance. Afghanistan, located at the crossroads of Central and South Asia, became a pawn in this ideological struggle that would shape its destiny for decades to come.

In 1978, the pro-Soviet People's Democratic Party of Afghanistan (PDPA) seized power in a coup, launching a series of radical reforms.[2] The PDPA's policies, such as land redistribution, secular education, and women's rights, were deeply unpopular among Afghanistan's rural, religious population, sparking widespread rebellion. While these reforms might have seemed progressive to Western observers, they were imposed from above without regard for Afghan traditions or consultation with local communities.

The Soviet Union, fearing the collapse of its ally and concerned about the spread of Islamic fundamentalism along its southern border, invaded Afghanistan in December 1979.[3] The invasion ignited a brutal war between Soviet forces and Afghan resistance fighters, known as the Mujahideen.[4] It was in this conflict that the United States first became deeply involved in Afghanistan, not to support democracy or human rights, but to bleed its Cold War rival dry.

THE U.S. AND THE MUJAHIDEEN: ARMING THE RESISTANCE

Under the banner of containing communism, the United States, through the CIA, provided funding, weapons, and training to the Mujahideen fighters. Operation Cyclone,[5] one of the largest covert operations in U.S. history, funneled billions of dollars into Afghanistan. Stinger missiles, rifles, and cash flowed freely into the hands of Afghan warlords and foreign jihadists, turning Afghanistan into a magnet for militants from around the world.

The irony here is almost laughable—the United States was arming and training the very same Islamic fundamentalists who would later become America's enemies. The CIA worked closely with Pakistan's Inter-Services Intelligence (ISI) to channel weapons to the most radical Mujahideen factions, believing that religious zealots would fight more fiercely against the Soviets than moderate nationalists.

The U.S. strategy was clear: turn Afghanistan into a Soviet quagmire. Congressman Charlie Wilson, a key architect of the program, famously declared: "There were 58,000 dead in Vietnam, and we owe the Russians one."[6] This callous calculus treated Afghan lives as expendable tools in a superpower rivalry, setting the stage for decades of suffering.

For the Mujahideen, the war was not about global ideologies but about expelling foreign invaders from their homeland. To the United States, however, Afghanistan was a battlefield of convenience, a place where Soviet forces could be weakened without risking American lives. The human cost to Afghans was irrelevant as long as the strategic objective was achieved.

By 1989, the Soviet Union withdrew from Afghanistan, its military exhausted and its economy strained by the costly occupation.[7] The Mujahideen, now flush with American weapons and battle-hardened by a decade of warfare, declared victory. But rather than investing in Afghanistan's future or helping to rebuild the devastated country, the United States turned its back, leaving Afghanistan awash in arms, warlords, and instability. The lesson was clear: America's support lasted only as long as it served American interests.

THE TALIBAN AND THE RETURN OF EXTREMISM

The power vacuum left by the Soviet withdrawal and American abandonment plunged Afghanistan into chaos. Rival Mujahideen factions, armed with weapons provided by the CIA, turned on each other in a vicious civil war. Kabul was reduced to rubble, millions fled as refugees, and the country descended into anarchy.

Out of this chaos emerged the Taliban, an ultraconservative Islamist group formed by students (or Talibs) from religious schools in Pakistan.[8] Many of these schools, funded by Saudi Arabia and supported by Pakistan, preached an extreme interpretation of Islam that bore little resemblance to traditional Afghan religious practices. The Taliban's leaders were often former Mujahideen commanders who had been armed and trained by the CIA during the Soviet war.

251

The Taliban, with backing from Pakistan's military and intelligence services, promised to restore order and impose a strict interpretation of Islamic law. By 1996, they had seized control of Kabul and most of the country. Their rule was marked by extreme repression: women were banned from schools and workplaces, music and television were forbidden, public executions and amputations became common, and dissent was crushed with brutal efficiency.

Yet during this period, Afghanistan became a safe haven for extremist groups from around the world. Al-Qaeda, led by Osama bin Laden, found refuge under Taliban protection. From training camps in Afghanistan, Al-Qaeda recruited, trained, and equipped terrorists who would carry out attacks across the globe, culminating in the September 11, 2001, attacks against the United States.[9]

The weapons and training provided by the CIA to fight the Soviets had now been turned against America itself. The policy of arming Islamic fundamentalists to serve short-term strategic goals had produced catastrophic long-term consequences.

THE 2001 INVASION: AMERICA'S LONGEST WAR BEGINS

The 9/11 attacks shocked the world and galvanized the United States into action. The Taliban's refusal to surrender bin Laden provided the justification for military intervention. Within weeks, President George W. Bush launched Operation Enduring Freedom,[10] vowing to dismantle Al-Qaeda and overthrow the Taliban regime. The U.S.-led coalition quickly toppled the Taliban, its superior military power overwhelming the poorly equipped militants.

Initially, the invasion enjoyed broad international support, with the Taliban viewed as illegitimate harbors of terrorism and Al-Qaeda seen as a global threat. The mission seemed clear and achievable: capture or kill bin Laden, destroy Al-Qaeda's infrastructure, and prevent Afghanistan from again becoming a terrorist sanctuary.

However, as the years passed, the U.S. mission in Afghanistan began to unravel. The Bush administration, distracted by its invasion of Iraq in 2003, failed to consolidate its early military victories in Afghanistan. Resources and attention were diverted to Iraq, allowing the Taliban to regroup and rebuild. Meanwhile, the U.S.-backed Afghan government led by Hamid Karzai proved corrupt, ineffective, and increasingly unpopular.

Corruption plagued every level of the Afghan government, with billions of dollars in foreign aid vanishing into the pockets of warlords and political elites. Drug trafficking flourished under the noses of American and coalition forces, providing funding for the Taliban insurgency. The very warlords who had been America's allies against the Taliban often proved to be predators who abused their power and alienated the population.

SHIFTING GOALS AND ENDLESS WAR

Over two decades, the U.S. mission in Afghanistan shifted repeatedly, from counterterrorism to nation-building, from promoting women's rights to training Afghan security forces. Each new strategy was presented as the key to victory, but none addressed the fundamental problem: the United States was trying to impose a foreign vision on a society it did not understand.

The military strategy itself was flawed. NATO forces would conduct operations to clear Taliban fighters from an area, attempt to hold it with limited troops, and then try to build government institutions and win local support. But without sufficient forces to maintain security or effective governance to provide services, these areas would inevitably revert to Taliban control once international troops moved on.

Despite spending over $2 trillion and deploying hundreds of thousands of troops, the United States could not defeat the Taliban or create a stable Afghan state.[11] The war became a grim cycle: U.S. forces would clear Taliban-held areas, only for the militants to return once American troops withdrew. Every few years, a new general would arrive with a new strategy, promising that this time would be different.

For Afghans, the war brought unimaginable suffering. Tens of thousands of civilians were killed in airstrikes, bombings, and Taliban attacks. Entire villages were destroyed, millions were displaced, and generations grew up knowing nothing but war. The promised improvements in education, healthcare, and women's rights were largely confined to urban areas and constantly threatened by ongoing violence.

For American forces, the toll was also severe. Over 2,400 U.S. service members died in Afghanistan, with tens of thousands more wounded. Many returned home with traumatic brain injuries, post-traumatic stress disorder, and other invisible wounds of war. The mission's constantly shifting objectives and rules of engagement created confusion and frustration among troops who were asked to fight an enemy they often couldn't identify in a war whose purpose was never clearly defined.

THE WITHDRAWAL AND THE FALL OF KABUL

In February of 2020, after twenty years of fighting, President Trump negotiated "The Doha Agreement" with the Taliban to reduce troops slowly and remove all U.S. troops by May of 2021. Starting in January of 2021 when President Joe Biden took office, the U.S. started accelerating the withdrawal to comply with the agreement.[12] The decision marked the end of America's longest war, but it came at a steep cost. As U.S. forces departed, the Afghan government, hollowed out by corruption and overreliance on foreign support, collapsed almost overnight.

The political finger-pointing that followed was predictable but misguided. Critics blamed Biden for the chaotic withdrawal, but the timeline had been established by his predecessor. Mike Pompeo, Trump's Secretary of State, signed an agreement on February 29, 2020, that committed the U.S. to reduce forces to 8,600 and close five bases by July 2020, with complete withdrawal to be accomplished no later than May 1, 2021.

Troops were reduced and bases closed by July 2020, but nothing more was done by the Trump administration because it was focused on the upcoming election. By the time Biden took office on January 20, 2021, there was little time left to fulfill the agreement he inherited from his predecessor. With the May 2021 deadline fast approaching, and no preparations made during the previous seven months, the only choice was a rapid and complete pullout.

As had occurred in other instances where the U.S. left quickly, a power vacuum was created. In August 2021, the Taliban retook Kabul with shocking speed, effectively erasing two decades of U.S. efforts. Images of desperate Afghans clinging to U.S. evacuation planes became symbols of America's failure, reminiscent of the helicopter evacuations from Saigon in 1975.

The Taliban's return to power raised haunting questions: What had been accomplished during twenty years of war? At what cost? And could the outcome have been different if the U.S. had committed to a more sustainable, long-term approach based on understanding rather than force?

THE HUMAN TOLL OF EMPIRE

The U.S. intervention in Afghanistan was justified as a fight against terrorism and a mission to bring democracy and human rights. Yet for many Afghans, these promises rang hollow. The war devastated Afghanistan's infrastructure, left millions in poverty, and failed to deliver lasting peace or genuine democracy.

Women, who had gained hard-won freedoms in urban areas under the U.S.-backed government, now face a bleak future under renewed Taliban rule. Girls are once again banned from schools, women cannot work or travel freely, and the progress that had been made in gender equality has been brutally reversed. The countryside remains scarred by decades of violence, and Afghanistan's economy teeters on collapse, with millions facing starvation.

For the United States, the war revealed the limits of its military power and the dangers of imperial overreach. Despite overwhelming technological superiority and virtually unlimited resources, America could not achieve its objectives in Afghanistan. The war demonstrated that military force alone cannot create stable, democratic societies, especially when deployed without genuine understanding of local culture, history, and social dynamics.

Thousands of American soldiers were killed, and tens of thousands returned home with physical and psychological wounds. The financial cost to the U.S. was enormous—over $2 trillion that could have been spent on education, healthcare, infrastructure, and other domestic priorities. The opportunity cost of the Afghanistan war may have been America's greatest loss of all.

LESSONS FROM AFGHANISTAN

The U.S. intervention in Afghanistan serves as a cautionary tale of hubris, short-sightedness, and the perils of imposing foreign solutions on complex societies. What began as a mission to defeat terrorism morphed into an unwinnable war, leaving behind a shattered nation and a legacy of suffering.

The war's failure stemmed from fundamental misunderstandings about Afghan society, unrealistic expectations about what military force could achieve, and constantly shifting objectives that reflected American political cycles rather than Afghan realities. The U.S. government's own inspector general concluded that America lacked even "a mediocre understanding of the Afghan environment" and that many mistakes were born from "willful disregard for information that may have been available."[13]

Afghanistan's story challenges us to ask difficult questions: What drives powerful nations to wage war in the name of security? Who benefits, and who pays the price? For Afghans, the cost has been enormous—generations lost to war, a society traumatized by violence, and a future made uncertain by foreign intervention.

As the United States reckons with its failure in Afghanistan, one truth remains: the people of Afghanistan, who have endured the weight of empire after empire, deserve more than empty promises. They deserve peace, dignity, and the chance to determine their own future, free from the interference of foreign powers.

If history has taught us anything, it is this: No empire, no matter how powerful, can subdue a nation forever. Afghanistan, once again, belongs to its people, however uncertain their path forward may be. The lesson for America is equally clear: true security cannot be achieved through endless war, and lasting peace requires understanding, humility, and respect for the sovereignty of other nations.

CHAPTER RECAP

Afghanistan represents the ultimate failure of American imperial hubris, a twenty-year war that achieved none of its objectives despite overwhelming military and financial advantages. The United States entered Afghanistan with legitimate grievances after 9/11 but transformed a focused counterterrorism mission into an impossible nation-building project that ignored Afghan history, culture, and social dynamics.

The war's roots trace back to the Cold War, when America armed the very Islamic fundamentalists who would later attack the United States. This pattern of short-term strategic thinking, supporting extremists when convenient, then fighting them when they become inconvenient, characterizes much of American foreign policy throughout the imperial era.

Afghanistan exemplifies how military force cannot substitute for genuine understanding, sustainable development, or respect for local sovereignty. The same pattern of intervention, mission creep, and eventual withdrawal plagued American efforts in Vietnam, Iraq, and numerous other countries, revealing the fundamental limitations of imperial power.

The U.S. intervention in Afghanistan began as Cold War proxy warfare when the CIA launched Operation Cyclone, one of history's largest covert operations, arming and training Islamic fundamentalists with billions in weapons to bleed the Soviet Union before abandoning the country once that strategic objective was achieved. This short-term thinking produced catastrophic blowback when CIA-trained militants formed the Taliban and harbored Al-Qaeda, leading to 9/11 and a twenty-year war that cost over $2 trillion, killed more than 170,000 people (including 2,400+ U.S. service members), and displaced millions—all while U.S. objectives constantly shifted from counterterrorism to nation-building to women's rights, reflecting American political cycles rather than Afghan realities or achievable goals.

The entire effort was built on a fundamental misunderstanding of Afghan society, with U.S. officials admitting they lacked even "mediocre understanding" of the country while attempting to impose Western institutions without regard for local culture or traditions. The inevitable result was that the U.S.-backed government collapsed within days of American withdrawal because it was built on foreign aid and military support rather than genuine legitimacy or popular support, proving that two decades of war, trillions in spending, and massive human suffering achieved none of America's stated objectives—leaving Afghanistan under Taliban control once again, exactly where the cycle of intervention had begun.

The courage and resilience of the Afghan people, who have resisted empire after empire for centuries, demonstrates that no foreign power can permanently subjugate a determined population. Their struggle reminds us that true security comes not from military dominance but from justice, understanding, and respect for national sovereignty. The Afghanistan war's failure challenges Americans to confront the costs of empire and consider whether our security truly requires endless intervention in other people's countries.

PART IV:

ZIONISM

There comes a point in every search for truth where you encounter something so taboo, so protected by social and political landmines, that to question it is to risk ruin and exile. In American political discourse, that subject is **Zionism**.

This chapter opens a new section of this book, one that stands apart from the others because it reveals the invisible hand that has shaped so much of what American foreign policy has become. No other ideological, religious, or political force, not communism, not terrorism, not oil, not capitalism itself, has embedded itself so deeply into the American bloodstream, especially in Washington, as Zionism.

Let's be clear from the outset: this is not a critique of Judaism or of Jewish people. It is a critique of Zionism, a nationalist political ideology that demands unwavering loyalty to the state of Israel and its expansion, no matter what the cost, and often at the expense of American interests and values. An ideology that claims to represent survival but thrives on domination. An ideology that has weaponized history, exploited religion, and infiltrated foreign governments, not least the United States, to pursue its vision of power and permanence.

CHAPTER 29:
ABOUT ZIONISM

THE UNSPOKEN DRIVER OF U.S. INTERVENTION

Contemporary Zionism extends far beyond the historical movement for Jewish self-determination. In its current manifestation within American political discourse, it represents an ideology demanding unwavering, uncritical support for Israeli policies regardless of their consistency with international law, American strategic interests, or basic human rights principles.[1] This political framework has become one of the most significant, and least examined, influences on American foreign policy over the past half-century, systematically reshaping military interventions, diplomatic positions, and domestic legislation in ways that prioritize Israeli regional dominance over genuine American interests.[2]

When carefully analyzed, many American foreign entanglements that appear disconnected from genuine U.S. strategic interests can be traced directly to pressures and advocacy originating from organizations promoting Israeli regional hegemony.[3] This influence operates through sophisticated networks of lobbying groups, think tanks, and political action committees that have successfully embedded their agenda within American policy-making institutions to an extent that would be considered scandalous if exercised by any other foreign power.[4]

MEDIA NARRATIVES AND INFORMATION CONTROL

One of the most significant achievements of pro-Israel advocacy has been its systematic capture of mainstream American discourse about Middle Eastern affairs.[5] Analysis of major media coverage reveals consistent, documented patterns that favor Israeli perspectives while systematically marginalizing Palestinian and Arab viewpoints.[6] Israel is routinely described as "responding" to threats, while Palestinian actions are invariably labeled as unprovoked "attacks."[7] Israeli military operations are characterized as "precise" and "defensive," while casualties from these operations, including children, are dismissed as unavoidable "collateral damage."[8]

This asymmetric coverage shapes American public opinion by presenting a fundamentally distorted picture of Middle Eastern conflicts. Many Americans can readily identify Hamas but remain systematically uninformed about historical events perpetrated by Israel like the Deir Yassin massacre, the Sabra and Shatila killings, or ongoing settlement expansion in the West Bank that violates international law.[9] This selective information environment has been extensively documented by media analysts and organizations tracking journalistic bias in Middle Eastern coverage.[10]

The capture of American media discourse extends beyond simple bias into active suppression of dissenting voices. Journalists who report critically on Israeli policies face systematic career consequences, while those who maintain pro-Israel positions receive preferential access and advancement.[11] This pattern of information control would be immediately recognized as propaganda if practiced by Russia or China, yet it operates with virtual impunity when serving Israeli interests.[12]

FINANCIAL DIMENSIONS: SUBSIDIZING APARTHEID

Israel receives approximately $3.8 billion annually in U.S. foreign aid, making it the largest recipient of American assistance despite being a developed nation with universal healthcare, advanced technology sectors, and living standards that exceed those of many American communities.[13] This figure excludes additional funding for missile defense systems like Iron Dome, classified military cooperation programs, and the diplomatic costs of vetoing UN resolutions that consistently isolate the United States internationally.[14]

The scope of American financial support becomes even more striking when compared to domestic priorities. This assistance occurs while American cities face infrastructure crises, students accumulate crushing debt, veterans struggle to access adequate healthcare, and millions lack basic medical coverage.[15] The allocation of resources raises fundamental questions about whether this assistance serves American interests or primarily benefits Israeli strategic objectives at the expense of American taxpayers.[16]

Moreover, Israel has consistently used American military aid to advance policies that violate international law, including settlement expansion in occupied territories and military operations that international courts have characterized as war crimes.[17] American taxpayers are thus directly subsidizing violations of international law while their own government struggles to fund basic social services.[18]

POLITICAL INFLUENCE AND INSTITUTIONAL CAPTURE

The extent of pro-Israel influence within American political institutions extends far beyond traditional lobbying into areas that would provoke intense scrutiny if exercised by any other foreign interest.[19] AIPAC alone spent over $100 million in the 2024 election cycle, successfully defeating progressive congresspeople who criticized Israeli policies while supporting candidates who pledged unwavering support for Israeli objectives.[20] This unprecedented financial intervention in American democratic processes represents a level of foreign influence that would be immediately condemned if practiced by any other nation.[21]

Congressional Rituals: American politicians, particularly presidential candidates, routinely travel to Israel to be photographed at religious sites while pledging support for Israeli security, a ritual that has become an informal requirement for serious political candidates.[22] This creates a system where American leaders must demonstrate loyalty to a foreign nation before even assuming power, undermining the basic principle that elected officials should serve American interests first.[23]

Dual Symbols in Government Buildings: Israeli flags appear alongside American flags in congressional buildings with a frequency unmatched by other allied nations, symbolizing a level of integration that fundamentally blurs boundaries between domestic and foreign representation.[24] This symbolic subordination would be inconceivable with any other foreign power, yet has become normalized through the systematic application of pro-Israel political pressure.[25]

Foreign Military Uniforms in Congress: In October 2023, Representative Brian Mast (R-FL) wore his Israeli Defense Forces uniform on the floor of the House of Representatives while declaring his primary loyalty to Israel rather than the United States.[26] This extraordinary breach of protocol would likely provoke calls for treason charges if the uniform belonged to any other foreign military, yet produced minimal criticism, demonstrating the extent to which Israeli influence has been normalized within American political culture.[27]

Unprecedented Foreign Leader Access: When Israeli Prime Minister Benjamin Netanyahu addressed a joint session of Congress in 2015 without presidential invitation, it represented an extraordinary breach of diplomatic protocol that demonstrated the political power of pro-Israel advocacy groups to override executive branch foreign policy.[28] The speech received 26 standing ovations from American lawmakers, who cheered a foreign leader's direct challenge to their own president's diplomatic initiatives.[29]

Constitutional Violations: Criminalizing Dissent

Perhaps most concerning is the passage of anti-BDS (Boycott, Divestment, Sanctions) legislation in 35 states that systematically penalizes American citizens for exercising their First Amendment rights to engage in political boycotts.[30] These laws require individuals and businesses to sign pledges promising not to boycott Israel as a condition of receiving government contracts or public employment, creating loyalty oath requirements to a foreign nation that have no precedent in American constitutional history.[31]

Federal courts have repeatedly ruled these laws unconstitutional, with judges explicitly stating that boycotting Israel constitutes protected political speech under the First Amendment.[32] Despite these clear constitutional violations, states continue to enforce these laws while appealing adverse decisions, demonstrating their commitment to protecting Israeli interests even at the expense of American constitutional principles.[33]

In documented cases, American citizens have lost jobs, contracts, and speaking opportunities for refusing to sign these loyalty oaths to a foreign nation.[34] Speech pathologist Bahia Amawi was terminated from her position in Texas for declining to sign such a pledge, while documentary filmmaker Abby Martin had her speaking engagement canceled at Georgia Southern University for the same reason.[35] These cases represent a systematic erosion of constitutional rights that would provoke intense outrage if the loyalty oaths were demanded by any other foreign power.[36]

The existence of such laws represents an unprecedented level of foreign influence over American domestic policy, creating legal protections for one foreign nation that exist nowhere else in American jurisprudence.[37] The American Civil Liberties Union has filed numerous lawsuits challenging these laws, with their legal director stating that "the right to boycott is fundamental to the First Amendment."[38]

The Intelligence Assessment: Israel as Primary Threat

According to declassified U.S. intelligence documents, American security agencies consistently identify Israel as one of the most aggressive intelligence threats against the United States.[39]

A 2013 National Intelligence Estimate ranked Israel as the third most aggressive intelligence service targeting America, behind only Russia and China.[40] The National Security Agency's Global Capabilities Manager for Countering Foreign Intelligence explicitly identified Israel as a primary threat, noting that "Israel targets us too" despite their intelligence cooperation in other areas.[41]

The National Counterintelligence Center has documented Israel's systematic engagement in economic espionage against American companies and government agencies, stealing technology and trade secrets that provide Israeli companies with unfair competitive advantages.[42] This intelligence assessment reveals the fundamental contradiction in describing Israel as a strategic ally while simultaneously defending against its systematic espionage operations.[43]

CAMPUS SURVEILLANCE AND DOMESTIC OPERATIONS

Recent investigations have revealed extensive Israeli intelligence operations targeting American students and activists on college campuses.[44] The Israel on Campus Coalition has used student informants to spy on pro-Palestinian campus groups, collecting detailed personal information that is then passed to Israeli intelligence services for potential "covert operations" against American citizens.[45]

Israeli private intelligence firm Psy-Group has conducted psychological warfare operations against American activists, using fabricated information to destroy reputations and brand critics of Israeli policies as terrorists.[46] These operations, secretly financed by wealthy donors in the United States, represent direct attacks on American citizens' rights to political expression and association.[47]

The scope of these domestic intelligence operations raises serious questions about Israeli compliance with laws governing foreign agents operating in the United States, yet the FBI has consistently declined to investigate or prosecute these activities.[48] Former counterintelligence officials have expressed frustration with the political barriers preventing proper investigation of Israeli operations, with one stating: "I've brought cases to the Department of Justice on Israel. Cases that were never opened."[49]

ELECTORAL INTERVENTION AND DEMOCRATIC CORRUPTION

AIPAC's transformation from a lobbying organization to a direct electoral intervention force represents a fundamental escalation in foreign influence over American democracy.[50] Their massive financial intervention noted previously in the U.S. 2024 election successfully eliminated Representatives Jamaal Bowman and Cori Bush, two of Congress's most vocal critics of Israeli human rights violations.[51]

The organization's ability to marshal such enormous financial resources demonstrates the extent to which wealthy pro-Israel donors are willing to distort American democratic processes to protect Israeli interests.[52] Billionaire donors like Jan Koum (former WhatsApp CEO) contributed millions to AIPAC's super PAC specifically to eliminate American lawmakers who supported Palestinian rights.[53] This represents a systematic corruption of American democracy by foreign financial interests operating through ostensibly domestic organizations.[54]

AIPAC's electoral strategy involves recruiting primary challengers specifically to target critics of Israeli policies, then flooding these races with millions in outside spending that drowns out local voices and concerns.[55] This approach has proven devastatingly effective at silencing criticism of Israeli policies within Congress, creating a political environment where even mild criticism of Israeli actions becomes politically dangerous for American lawmakers.[56]

THE SCOPE OF INSTITUTIONAL PENETRATION

Pro-Israel advocacy operates through hundreds of organizations that coordinate lobbying, media messaging, and political pressure in ways that qualitatively differ from other foreign influence efforts.[57] Major organizations include AIPAC, the Anti-Defamation League, the American Jewish Committee, Christians United for Israel, and dozens of campus-based groups that work together to advance Israeli interests across multiple sectors of American society.[58]

This network's influence extends into academic institutions, where pro-Israel donors fund programs that promote favorable interpretations of Israeli policies while systematically excluding critical perspectives.[59] Major universities have established Israel studies programs funded by pro-Israel donors who explicitly shape curriculum to support Israeli narratives.[60] Faculty members who criticize Israeli policies face coordinated harassment campaigns designed to damage their careers and silence their research.[61]

The entertainment industry represents another vector of influence, with pro-Israel advocates working systematically to ensure that Hollywood productions present favorable portrayals of Israeli actions while marginalizing Palestinian perspectives.[62] This cultural influence operation shapes American public opinion by controlling the narratives that reach mass audiences through popular media.[63]

CONSTITUTIONAL CRISIS AND DEMOCRATIC EROSION

The cumulative effect of these influence operations represents a constitutional crisis that strikes at the heart of American democratic governance.[64] When foreign interests can successfully punish American citizens for exercising constitutional rights, determine electoral outcomes through massive financial intervention, and shape government policy to serve foreign rather than American objectives, the fundamental premise of democratic self-governance is undermined.[65]

The systematic prioritization of Israeli interests over American constitutional principles, strategic objectives, and citizen welfare represents a form of institutional capture that would be immediately recognized as a national security threat if practiced by any other foreign power.[66] Yet the political costs of acknowledging this reality remain so high that even obvious violations of American sovereignty are ignored or rationalized by political leaders afraid of the consequences of challenging pro-Israel orthodoxy.[67]

CHAPTER RECAP

Pro-Israel advocacy has achieved unprecedented penetration of American institutions through systematic media capture that suppresses Palestinian perspectives, over $100 million in AIPAC spending to eliminate critical lawmakers through massive foreign electoral intervention, and anti-BDS laws in 35 states that unconstitutionally criminalize Americans' First Amendment boycott rights. This influence manifests in extraordinary displays—foreign military uniforms worn in Congress, Israeli flags throughout government buildings—that would be deemed treasonous if practiced by any other nation, while Israel extracts $3.8 billion annually despite being a developed nation with higher living standards than many American communities whose citizens lack basic healthcare, infrastructure, and educational funding.

Beyond political capture, documented evidence reveals ongoing Israeli espionage operations against American interests, with U.S. intelligence agencies ranking Israel as the third most aggressive spy threat facing the U.S. Israel continues to operate within our borders with extensive surveillance networks targeting American students and activists who criticize Israeli policies. This comprehensive institutional capture across media, academia, government, and entertainment creates a system where Israeli interests consistently override American constitutional principles and strategic objectives, forcing loyalty oath requirements to a foreign nation that federal courts have repeatedly ruled unconstitutional and demonstrating a level of foreign influence fundamentally incompatible with national sovereignty.

This represents the most successful foreign capture of American democratic institutions in the nation's history, operating not through dramatic single events but through patient, systematic pressure across multiple institutions simultaneously. By embedding their own narratives in media, college campuses, and political culture while systematically punishing dissent, these organizations have normalized what would be immediately recognized as foreign subversion if practiced by any other nation, creating an environment where American policy consistently serves Israeli objectives regardless of constitutional principles, strategic interests, or citizen welfare.

This pattern reveals fundamental vulnerabilities in our democratic systems that allows organized influence campaigns to operate within legal frameworks while systematically undermining our democratic principles. When criticism of a foreign nation's policies becomes politically dangerous for American lawmakers, when American citizens lose jobs for refusing loyalty oaths to foreign governments, and when foreign intelligence services operate with impunity against American targets, democratic self-governance has been compromised. Yet the courage of journalists who report truthfully despite career consequences and citizens who refuse loyalty oaths despite financial penalties demonstrates that democratic resistance remains possible, challenging all Americans to examine whether their government truly serves American interests or has been systematically captured by a foreign power operating under the protection of political taboos that make honest discussion nearly impossible.

CHAPTER 30:
AIPAC & U.S. GOVERNMENT

If you want to understand how a small foreign country representing less than 0.2% of the global population wields such immense influence over the most powerful nation on Earth, you need only understand three things: money, lobbying, and fear. All three converge in one of the most influential political lobbies in American history: **AIPAC**, the **American Israel Public Affairs Committee**.

Jewish Americans comprise about 2% of the U.S. population. But you wouldn't know that by looking at Capitol Hill.

AIPAC is one of the most powerful lobbying groups in Washington. It spends millions every year to ensure near-unanimous congressional support for Israel, regardless of its actions. It writes legislation. It drafts talking points. It funds campaigns. And it destroys careers of those who dissent.

No other foreign lobby enjoys this level of access and influence. No other foreign country receives standing ovations in Congress for committing acts other nations are sanctioned for. And no other issue has American politicians so terrified to speak honestly.

You're trained not to see it. But once you do, it's impossible to unsee.

Why are Israeli flags hanging in the offices of U.S. lawmakers? Why can a sitting member of Congress enter the chamber wearing the uniform of a foreign military and draw no outrage? Why was the Prime Minister of Israel allowed to bypass the White House entirely and deliver a speech directly to Congress, as Benjamin Netanyahu did in 2015, without even notifying the sitting president?

These aren't symbolic gestures. They are signs of power.

In this chapter, we explore how AIPAC, and by extension the Israeli state, has carved out influence over U.S. politics so entrenched that it shapes everything from foreign aid to domestic discourse. It's not just about lobbying. It's about loyalty tests, campaign financing, and political survival. As detailed in *The Israel Lobby and U.S. Foreign Policy* by John Mearsheimer and Stephen Walt, this isn't a mutual alliance, it's an imbalance that often prioritizes Israeli interests over American ones through financial leverage, not democratic debate.[1]

If you've never questioned it before, that's not your fault. That's how power works, quietly, pervasively, and with the confidence that no one will call it out. But once you start noticing, you'll see it everywhere. And you'll start asking the question that so few dare to voice: who are our representatives really representing?

WHAT IS AIPAC?

AIPAC is a pro-Israel lobbying group founded in the 1950s, originally as a public relations wing to improve U.S.-Israel ties. Today, it is one of the most powerful and feared lobbies in Washington, spending millions annually to influence U.S. lawmakers, draft legislation, and coordinate political donations to candidates who show unwavering support for Israel.

It is **not a political action committee (PAC)** in the traditional sense. It does not directly donate to candidates. Instead, it orchestrates a vast network of donors and affiliated PACs who funnel money to pro-Israel candidates and target opponents for political defeat.

This didn't happen by accident. AIPAC began as the "American Zionist Council," a group explicitly advocating for the interests of a foreign state.[2] In 1962, under pressure from President John F. Kennedy's administration, the organization was ordered to register under the **Foreign Agents Registration Act (FARA)**, which would have required public disclosure of its activities, finances, and affiliations on behalf of a foreign government. Rather than comply, the organization restructured, rebranded, and emerged as AIPAC, now calling itself a domestic lobbying group, free from FARA restrictions.[3]

To maintain the appearance of separation, AIPAC operates through a web of affiliated organizations, each with narrowly defined legal roles. One of the most prominent is the American Israel Education Foundation (AIEF), a registered 501(c)(3) nonprofit that claims to focus on education rather than lobbying.[4] AIEF pays for expensive, guided trips to Israel for U.S. lawmakers and influential figures, shaping their understanding of the conflict through a tightly controlled narrative. Contributions to AIEF are tax-deductible, giving donors a financial incentive to fund pro-Israel advocacy under the cover of education.

FOLLOW THE MONEY

According to OpenSecrets and Federal Election Commission records, AIPAC-affiliated groups and individuals have directed tens of millions of dollars per election cycle to supportive candidates.[5] In the 2022 midterms alone, AIPAC's new PAC, United Democracy Project, spent over $27 million on congressional races, primarily to defeat progressive candidates critical of Israeli policy.[6]

Candidates who question U.S. support for Israel are systematically targeted, often drowned in a flood of negative ads funded by AIPAC's ecosystem. AIPAC does not merely lobby, it coerces. Members of Congress have privately admitted that refusing to follow the AIPAC line can mean political suicide.

LEGAL IMMUNITY BY DESIGN

AIPAC's power grew in part thanks to congressional loopholes. Under U.S. lobbying law, it operates as a nonprofit advocacy organization, not a foreign agent, despite working on behalf of a foreign government's interests. When FARA was strengthened in the 1960s, many thought AIPAC would be reclassified as a foreign agent. It was not. Through quiet lobbying, AIPAC maintained its nonprofit status, allowing it to evade disclosure requirements and avoid restrictions that would cripple any similar organization working for Russia, China, or even Britain.

INSTITUTIONAL CAPTURE

AIPAC's reach goes beyond elections. It writes legislation later introduced in Congress, often by both parties, hosts exclusive conferences where lawmakers pledge fealty to Israeli interests, and crafts pro-Israel talking points distributed to media, think tanks, and academic institutions.

U.S. politicians now routinely put Israel's priorities above their constituents' needs. From military aid to diplomatic protection at the U.N., Israel receives more deference than any U.S. state or ally.

U.S. AID: A ONE-WAY STREET

Since 1948, the U.S. has provided **over $146 billion** in direct aid to Israel, more than any other country in American history. Today, Israel receives $3.8 billion annually, most of it in unconditional military assistance.[7]

This aid comes despite the fact that Israel has universal healthcare,[8] provides free college education,[9] has a higher GDP per capita than many U.S. states,[10] and operates a nuclear arsenal not subject to international oversight.[11]

American cities struggle to fix roads, hospitals are underfunded, and teachers work second jobs, but Congress passes record military aid packages to Israel without debate. Recent legislation proposes billions more in supplemental aid to "defend Israeli sovereignty."[12]

THE HUMAN COST

This alignment doesn't just cost money, it costs lives, credibility, and moral standing. U.S. foreign policy is viewed globally as an extension of Israeli interests. Meanwhile, opposing Israeli policies has become a red line in American politics. University professors are fired for criticizing Israel,[13] activists are surveilled under anti-BDS laws,[14] and elected officials face primary challenges funded by AIPAC-aligned groups if they dissent.[15]

In 2022, Representative Andy Levin, a progressive Jewish member of Congress and strong supporter of Israeli-Palestinian peace, lost his primary to an AIPAC-funded opponent. The message was clear: there is no room for nuance. Only obedience.[16]

BREAKING THE SILENCE

The Israel Lobby and U.S. Foreign Policy by Mearsheimer and Walt laid bare this dynamic in academic terms. The authors faced enormous backlash and accusations of anti-Semitism, even though their research was meticulously sourced and widely supported by intelligence professionals. Other books, including *Against Our Better Judgment* by Alison Weir and *Big Israel* by Grant F. Smith, have explored the machinery of influence, how money, fear, and narrative control maintain a stranglehold on American policy.[17]

And yet, Congress has never held hearings. No investigation. No reclassification. Nothing.

A NATION IN DECLINE, STILL FUNDING A NATION IN CONTROL

The tragedy is not just geopolitical—it's personal. Americans are paying more in taxes, receiving fewer services, and living shorter, sicker, poorer lives than Israeli citizens, all while Israel grows stronger, richer, and more insulated from accountability.

We are not supporting an ally. We are funding our own decline so another nation can flourish.

AMERICA TODAY: THE COST OF CAPTIVITY

AIPAC does not operate in the shadows. It operates in broad daylight, daring anyone to name what it is. And few do. Because to name it is to face consequences. Because to resist it is to lose funding. Because to oppose it is to be cast as a pariah.

But the truth is this: **Israel's influence over the U.S. government is not a conspiracy. It is not a theory. It is a documented fact**. It is corrosive, extractive, and anti-democratic. And until Americans demand independence from this grip, we will continue to act not as a sovereign nation, but as a client state under foreign management.

CHAPTER RECAP

• **AIPAC wields unprecedented foreign influence** over U.S. policy through a sophisticated network of money, lobbying, and political intimidation

• **The organization circumvented foreign agent registration requirements** in the 1960s by restructuring from the American Zionist Council to AIPAC, avoiding transparency obligations

• **Financial coercion drives policy compliance**: AIPAC's affiliated PACs spend tens of millions targeting candidates who question Israeli policies, effectively ending political careers

• **U.S. taxpayers fund Israeli prosperity while American infrastructure crumbles**: Over $146 billion in aid to a country with universal healthcare, free education, and higher GDP per capita than many U.S. states

• **Democratic debate has been eliminated**: Criticizing Israeli policies results in career destruction, surveillance, and social ostracism across academia, politics, and civil society

• **America operates as a client state**: U.S. foreign policy prioritizes Israeli interests over American sovereignty, making us complicit in policies that damage our global credibility and moral standing

This chapter exposes the uncomfortable truth that American democracy has been captured by foreign interests operating in plain sight. Until we confront this reality and demand accountability, we remain not a sovereign nation but a client state funding our own decline while another country prospers at our expense.

The human cost of this captured foreign policy becomes devastatingly clear when we examine what American tax dollars and diplomatic protection have enabled in Palestine and Gaza— where decades of unconditional support have funded an ongoing humanitarian catastrophe that implicates every American taxpayer in systematic oppression and violence.

CHAPTER 31:

PALESTINE AND GAZA

While the world's attention is currently focused on Gaza, it's critical to understand that Gaza is just one part of Palestine. The Israeli state's campaign of ethnic cleansing did not begin in 2023, it has been ongoing since the very foundation of Israel in 1948. What we are witnessing today is not an isolated event or a "war" in the conventional sense. It is the continuation of a decades-long, systematic effort to eliminate the Palestinian people from their land.

Gaza, often referred to as the world's largest open-air prison, was never meant to be a safe haven for Palestinians. It was designed as a containment zone, a densely populated strip where millions of Palestinians were forcibly pushed, trapped, and blockaded. This forced confinement has allowed the Israeli state to carry out its genocidal campaign more efficiently, away from the international spotlight that often ignores what happens beyond Gaza's borders.

From the Nakba in 1948, to the relentless settlement expansion in the West Bank, to the suffocating siege of Gaza, Israel has pursued a continuous policy of dispossession, dehumanization, and erasure of Palestinian life and identity. The Nakba, Arabic for "catastrophe," refers to the forced expulsion of over 700,000 Palestinians during the establishment of the Israeli state. Entire villages were destroyed, civilians were killed, and families were displaced into permanent exile. This was not an unintended side effect of war, but a foundational step in the Zionist project to secure a Jewish majority on land already inhabited by Palestinians.

What we are witnessing today is not some sudden escalation or isolated conflict. It is the logical, brutal outcome of a decades-long colonial enterprise that has treated Palestinian presence as a problem to be solved through walls, bombs, blockades, and bureaucracy. The violence is not accidental. It is strategic. And it has always been aimed at achieving one goal: to remove, suppress, or silence the indigenous people of Palestine.

A BRIEF HISTORY

Palestine has been ruled by various empires throughout history, including the Ottomans, who controlled the region from 1517 to 1917. Following World War I, the League of Nations granted Britain a mandate over Palestine, during which tensions escalated between the indigenous Arab population and a growing influx of European Jews arriving as part of the Zionist movement.[1]

The 1917 British Balfour Declaration promised a "national home for the Jewish people" in a land already home to hundreds of thousands of Palestinians, while stating that "nothing shall be done which may prejudice the civil and religious rights of existing non-Jewish communities in Palestine."[2] As more Jewish settlers arrived with foreign funding and political backing, Palestinians were steadily pushed out of political, economic, and eventually physical space. The escalating tensions culminated in the 1947 UN Partition Plan proposing to divide the land into separate Jewish and Arab states, leading to the establishment of Israel in 1948 and the subsequent "Nakba.""

Deep history

c. 1200–1000 BCE: Coastal city-states of **Philistia** form (Gaza, Ashkelon, Ashdod, Ekron, Gath). Gaza is a major Philistine center and trade hub.

8th–6th c. BCE: **Neo-Assyrian** then **Neo-Babylonian** control; Gaza cycles between imperial vassalage and direct rule.

539–332 BCE: **Achaemenid Persian** province (part of *Eber-Nari*); Gaza remains a key node on the coastal road.

332 BCE: **Alexander the Great** besieges and captures Gaza; Hellenistic era follows—first **Ptolemaic**, later **Seleucid** control.

63 BCE – 4th c. CE: Roman rule (after Pompey). Gaza is rebuilt and prospers; later part of the Roman province that Hadrian re-names **Syria Palaestina** (2nd c. CE).

4th–7th c. CE: **Byzantine** period; strong Christian/monastic communities around Gaza and along the coast.

638 CE: **Rashidun** armies take Gaza; successive **Umayyad** and **Abbasid** caliphates administer the region.

1099–1187: **Crusader** control on and off within the Kingdom of Jerusalem; **Saladin** and the **Ayyubids** retake the area.

1250–1517: **Mamluk** period; Gaza serves as a provincial center on the Cairo–Damascus route.

Modern Transitional Period

1517–1917: **Ottoman** rule over Palestine/Gaza (with brief Egyptian control under **Muhammad Ali** 1831–1840, then Ottoman restoration).

1917–1948: **British Mandate for Palestine**; Gaza falls under British civil administration after WWI.

Modern Gaza Timeline

1948: Israel declares independence without following UN Resolution 181 guidelines, beginning massive land seizures. President Truman recognizes Israel within minutes. An

	Arab-Israeli war follows, resulting in 700,000+ Palestinian refugees.
1949:	UN creates the United Nations Relief and Works Agency for Palestine Refugees (UNRWA) to provide assistance to displaced Palestinians.[3]
1948-1967:	Egypt administers Gaza, housing significant numbers of Palestinian refugees.
1967:	Israel captures Gaza during the Six-Day War, initiating prolonged military occupation.
1987-1993:	The First Intifada, a Palestinian uprising against Israeli occupation, begins in Gaza.
2006:	HAMAS wins Palestinian legislative elections in both Gaza and the West Bank, observed by international monitors including former President Jimmy Carter.[4] Following the victory, international aid is cut and Israel, the U.S., and EU refuse to recognize the government.
2007:	After clashes with Fatah, the ruling party in the West Bank, HAMAS takes control of Gaza, leading to territorial split with the West Bank.
2008-present:	Multiple Israeli military operations devastate Gaza infrastructure and kill thousands of civilians, each supported by billions in U.S. military aid and diplomatic protection.

HAMAS: CONTEXT BEYOND THE LABEL

HAMAS was democratically elected by Palestinians in both Gaza and the West Bank during the 2006 legislative elections, winning 74 out of 132 seats in the Palestinian Legislative Council.[5] The organization gained prominence through grassroots social services, including schools, hospitals, and welfare programs, earning considerable support among Palestinians where the Palestinian Authority was seen as corrupt or ineffective.

While designated a terrorist organization by the United States, Israel, and some allies, the majority of the world's nations do not share this classification. Many see HAMAS as a resistance movement born from decades of Israeli occupation and military aggression.[6] Notably, HAMAS operations have been confined to Israel and occupied Palestinian territories, it has not carried out attacks on foreign soil against other nations' civilians.

In contrast, Israel maintains an expansive program of extraterritorial assassinations, as documented in Ronen Bergman's *Rise and Kill First*, detailing hundreds of assassinations across Europe, the Middle East, and beyond.[7] The September 2024 "Pager Attack" exemplifies this approach: Israel killed 42 people and injured 3,500 to eliminate 2 confirmed Hezbollah members, casualty ratios that would be called terrorism if executed by any other nation.

Just as this book is going to print in September of 2025, Israel launched an attack on a house in Qatar where Israel claimed HAMAS negotiators were meeting to discuss a U.S. proposed ceasefire. Six people were killed. Clearly, there are no ongoing negotiations for a ceasefire when one side has attempted to assassinate the negotiation team of the other side.[8] Prior to this in July of 2024, Israel assassinated Ismail Haniyeh, another negotiator for HAMAS when he was in Tehran for the inauguration of President Masoud Pezeshkian.[9]

THE SCALE OF DESTRUCTION

In recent campaigns, Israel dropped over 29,000 bombs on Gaza within weeks. According to Palestinian health officials and international observers, over 70% of those killed were civilians, including thousands of women and children.[10] Entire neighborhoods have been leveled, hospitals destroyed, and refugee camps bombed. The UN reports no safe place remains in Gaza.

The tonnage of explosives dropped on Gaza exceeded what was dropped on Dresden, Hamburg, and Hiroshima during World War II. While Hiroshima's atomic bomb delivered approximately 15 kilotons of TNT equivalent, Gaza bombings (2023-2024) used an estimated equivalent of over 100 kilotons of high explosives, equivalent to **more than six Hiroshima-sized atomic bombs**.[11]

The disparity in military power between Israel and the Palestinians is stark. Israel possesses one of the world's most advanced militaries, supported by billions in U.S. aid, cutting-edge technology, a nuclear arsenal, and compulsory military service. Palestine has no standing army, air force, navy, or armored divisions. The confrontation is between a powerful, high-tech state and a largely defenseless, occupied population.

AMERICAN FINGERPRINTS ON EVERY BOMB

Israel does not manufacture the bulk of its weapons, the United States does it for them. Nearly all of the $3.8 Billion given to Israel each year is directed toward weapons systems.[12] According to the Congressional Research Service, over 60% of all Israeli military equipment is American-made. During high-conflict periods, the U.S. rushes emergency weapon shipments to replenish Israeli stockpiles.[13]

The bombs falling on apartment complexes are made in America. The F-16s and F-35s carrying out airstrikes are funded by U.S. tax dollars. The artillery shells leveling schools and hospitals are manufactured by American defense contractors. This is not passive support, it is active complicity.

WAR CRIMES IN BROAD DAYLIGHT

The Geneva Conventions prohibit collective punishment, attacks on civilian infrastructure, disproportionate force, and targeting medical personnel and journalists. Israel has violated all these principles without consequence. Human Rights Watch, Amnesty International, and the United Nations have documented what they describe as war crimes and crimes against humanity.[14]

Israel severely limits news reporting by targeting media personnel. At this book's printing, 242 journalists have been killed trying to report on Israeli actions in Palestine, the deadliest period for journalists since the Committee to Protect Journalists began collecting data in 1992.[15]

Despite these findings, the U.S. has repeatedly vetoed UN Security Council resolutions calling for ceasefires or independent investigations, blocking international accountability while providing more weapons and diplomatic immunity.[16]

GLOBAL CONDEMNATION, AMERICAN COMPLICITY

Across the world, from South Africa to Ireland, from Brazil to Malaysia, Israel is increasingly viewed as a pariah state. Dozens of countries have recalled ambassadors, imposed trade restrictions, and called for war crimes tribunals. The global consensus is clear: Israel operates as an apartheid regime engaged in ethnic cleansing.

Yet the United States remains its most fervent defender, providing over $146 billion in direct aid since 1948, more than any other country in American history.[17] That money could have eliminated medical debt for every American, funded universal pre-K and tuition-free college, or rebuilt critical infrastructure across all 50 states. Instead, it funds the systematic destruction of Palestinians and defense of a regime that spies on us, manipulates our politics, and endangers our global standing.

THE COST TO AMERICA

Supporting Israel's destruction of Gaza has weakened America's global influence. Arab and Muslim countries see the U.S. not as a peace broker but as an enemy. European allies increasingly distance themselves from U.S. positions at the United Nations. American embassies worldwide face protests and attacks, not because of who we are, but because of what we support.

The moral cost is equally damning. Americans are told we value freedom, human rights, and democracy, yet we defend a state that imposes apartheid, kills children, and demolishes homes with bulldozers and bombs. Israel has prevented virtually all aid from reaching Palestinians inside Gaza, including potable water, food, and medical supplies. People are dying of starvation while thousands of tons of food sit miles away, blocked by Israeli forces.[18]

We sanction countries like Iran and North Korea for far less. We invaded Iraq on false pretenses, killing over 500,000 people, but Israel's actual weapons of mass destruction, its nuclear arsenal, drones, and indiscriminate bombing campaigns, receive not scrutiny but subsidy.

THE ILLUSION OF ALLYSHIP

Israel is not an ally, it is a liability. It spies on us, sells our technology to rival nations including China, undermines our foreign policy objectives, and inflames regional tensions that draw us into endless wars. An ally does not commit acts of terrorism in your name, manipulate your media and politicians, or make you an accessory to genocide.

GAZA AS MIRROR

Gaza is not just a human rights catastrophe, it is a moral and political mirror reflecting who we have become as a nation. A country so entangled in Zionist influence, so corrupted by weapons contractors and political fear, that it will defend mass murder if the right flag is attached.

We must stop pretending this is about defense. Gaza has no air force, no navy, no tanks, and no shelters. It is a trapped population being bombarded into dust. Every American weapon that explodes there carries our name. Every building leveled, every child buried, every life erased, is done with our approval and our money.

THE AMERICAN LEGACY: GENOCIDE BY PROXY

History will remember Gaza, the bombs, the smoke, the screams, the starvation, and the endless pleas for help. It will also remember who ignored the victims' pleas and who armed the killers instead.

The United States has become a state sponsor of genocide, not through direct action but through proxy militarism. Unlike previous empires, we cannot claim ignorance. We have livestreams, satellite images, journalistic reports, and testimonies. We know exactly what is happening.

The question is not whether Israel is committing war crimes. The question is: how long will America keep writing the checks? Because until we stop, Gaza will remain a graveyard of our values, and every American citizen will carry the weight of a war they did not choose but are forced to fund.

CHAPTER RECAP

The assault on Gaza represents the most documented genocide in human history, broadcast in real-time as Israeli forces systematically destroy an entire population with American weapons, American funding, and American diplomatic protection. What makes this moment distinct is not the brutality—ethnic cleansing has defined the Israeli project since 1948—but rather the complete transparency of the operation and America's singular role as the sole enabler preventing international intervention. Understanding Gaza requires confronting how deeply American complicity runs through every aspect of this catastrophe.

- **Gaza represents the continuation of 75+ years of systematic ethnic cleansing** that began with the 1948 Nakba, not an isolated conflict but the logical outcome of a colonial project designed to eliminate Palestinian presence

- **American complicity is total and documented**: Over $146 billion in aid since 1948, with 60%+ of Israeli military equipment being American-made, making every bomb and bullet a product of U.S. taxpayer funding

- **The scale of destruction exceeds WWII bombing campaigns**: Israel dropped over 100 kilotons of explosives on Gaza, equivalent to more than six Hiroshima atomic bombs, against a population with no air force, navy, or standing army

- **War crimes are committed with U.S. protection**: Despite documented violations of Geneva Conventions and targeting of journalists (242 killed), the U.S. has vetoed UN ceasefire resolutions while rushing emergency weapon shipments to Israel

- **Global isolation exposes American moral bankruptcy**: While dozens of countries recall ambassadors and impose sanctions on Israel, the U.S. remains the sole defender of an apartheid regime, damaging our credibility and making us complicit in genocide

- **The illusion of allyship masks strategic liability**: Israel spies on the U.S., sells our technology to rivals, and inflames regional tensions that drag us into endless wars, behavior no true ally would exhibit

This chapter forces Americans to confront an uncomfortable truth: our tax dollars fund systematic destruction of Palestinian lives while our government provides diplomatic immunity for war crimes. We cannot claim ignorance about Gaza's destruction because we are not passive observers—we are active participants in genocide by proxy, and history will judge us accordingly.

CHAPTER 32:

LEBANON

When the average American thinks of Lebanon, they don't think of a country under siege. They might not think of Lebanon at all. But for decades, Israel has waged a campaign of intimidation, destruction, and occupation in southern Lebanon, often under the guise of security, but in truth, to enforce regional dominance. And the United States, once again, is complicit, not because Lebanon threatens us, but because Israel commands it.

In recent escalations, Israel has made clear its intention to establish a "buffer zone", not within its own borders, but inside Lebanese territory. This would amount to a de facto annexation of part of a sovereign country. The world calls this illegal. Israel calls it "security," and the United States blindly parrots the Israeli narrative.

THE PATTERN OF AGGRESSION

Israel's military involvement in Lebanon spans decades of invasions, bombings, and occupations that have devastated the country while creating the very threats Israel claims to fight.

1978 - Operation Litani: Israel invaded southern Lebanon under the pretense of stopping PLO attacks, displacing over 265,000 Lebanese civilians and establishing a permanent military presence in violation of UN Resolution 425, which demanded immediate withdrawal.[1]

1982 - Full-Scale Invasion: Israel launched a comprehensive invasion that led to the siege of Beirut and the **Sabra and Shatila massacre**, where Israeli-allied Phalangist militias slaughtered up to 3,500 Palestinian refugees while Israeli forces provided perimeter security and illumination flares.[2] The Israeli occupation of southern Lebanon that followed directly led to the creation of

WE ARE THE BAD GUYS

Hezbollah in 1985, meaning Israel's occupation created the very organization it now claims poses an existential threat.

2006 - 34-Day War: After Hezbollah captured two Israeli soldiers, Israel launched a massive bombing campaign that killed over 1,200 Lebanese, mostly civilians, while destroying key infrastructure including airports, roads, power stations, and bridges. The UN estimated that 90% of casualties were civilians.[3] Israel dropped over 4 million cluster bombs on southern Lebanon during the final 72 hours alone, contaminating farmland for years.[4]

Each operation was framed as defensive necessity. Each left Lebanon more broken and vulnerable than before. This is not coincidence—it is strategy.

THE CURRENT CRISIS: MANUFACTURING A BUFFER ZONE

Recent statements by Israeli officials, including Defense Minister Yoav Gallant, openly declare their intention to establish a buffer zone stretching several kilometers into Lebanon. This isn't speculation, it's official policy being implemented through systematic destruction of border villages and forced civilian displacement.[5]

The pretext remains the same: ongoing clashes with Hezbollah. But the reality is strategic. Israel's goal is permanent regional superiority achieved by destabilizing neighboring states that might pose symbolic or actual resistance. Lebanon, fractured by economic collapse and political paralysis, presents the easiest target.

Israeli operations have intensified along the border, targeting what they call "Hezbollah assets" while regularly striking homes, farms, schools, and entire villages. Thousands of Lebanese civilians have been displaced from border areas, creating the demographic clearing necessary for an eventual "buffer zone" that would effectively annex Lebanese territory under the guise of security needs.

AMERICAN COMPLICITY: BEYOND FUNDING TO ACTIVE FACILITATION

Beyond funding Israel, American complicity extends to direct operational support that makes Israeli aggression possible.

The U.S. military regularly transports weapons and munitions to Israeli ports using American ships and aircraft. During active conflicts, American pilots fly weapons directly to Israeli airfields, while U.S. intelligence agencies provide real-time targeting data for Israeli operations.[6] According to a 2024 investigation by The Intercept, U.S. military aircraft carried thousands of tons of laser-guided bombs, artillery shells, and bunker-busters to Israel for operations in Gaza and Lebanon.[7]

Congressional legislation has further entrenched this relationship:

H.R. 8034 - Israel Security Supplemental Appropriations Act (2024): Provided over $14 billion in additional aid to Israel, including expedited weapons transfers for "regional stability." This became Public Law 118-50 on April 24, 2024.[8]

Presidential Memorandum NSM-20 (2024): On February 8, 2024, President Biden signed a memorandum requiring countries receiving U.S. arms to certify they would not be used in violation of international humanitarian law or to restrict humanitarian aid.[9]

Executive Order (2025): One year later, on February 21, 2025, President Trump rescinded NSM-20, explicitly allowing arms shipments to Israel despite documented war crimes and civilian casualties in Gaza and Lebanon.[10]

This legislative pattern reveals the depth of American commitment to Israeli military operations regardless of their legality or humanitarian impact.

LEBANON POSES NO THREAT TO AMERICA

Lebanon does not threaten the United States. It possesses no long-range missiles capable of reaching American territory. Its military is one of the weakest in the region, focused primarily on internal security rather than external projection of power. The country's economy has collapsed, with the Lebanese pound losing over 95% of its value since 2019. Lebanese citizens struggle with electricity shortages, water scarcity, and basic survival needs.

Yet the U.S. acts as Israel's proxy in Lebanese affairs, defending Israeli ambitions rather than American interests. Our complicity is measured in Lebanese lives lost to American-made weapons and American diplomatic protection of Israeli actions.

GLOBAL ISOLATION: AMERICA STANDS ALONE

The international community has widely condemned Israel's repeated aggressions against Lebanon. The United Nations Human Rights Council describes Israel's bombing campaigns as "collective punishment" violating the Fourth Geneva Convention. European nations, including France, Ireland, and Belgium, have called for immediate de-escalation and respect for Lebanese sovereignty.[11]

But the U.S. has blocked multiple U.N. Security Council resolutions seeking to censure Israeli actions or establish monitoring mechanisms for Lebanese border violations. Our systematic obstruction of international accountability mechanisms has isolated America diplomatically while protecting Israeli impunity.[12]

As Time Magazine noted: "In the longstanding U.S.-Israel alliance... it acts as Israel's chief defender at international forums such as the U.N. Security Council, where Washington routinely uses its veto power to block resolutions critical of Israel."[13]

THE DOMESTIC COST OF FOREIGN MILITARISM

Every American weapon used against Lebanese civilians represents a choice about national priorities that devastates both countries. While Israeli operations are rearmed with American munitions, American veterans sleep on streets. While the Iron Dome receives upgrades, American children go without insulin due to cost. While foreign borders are militarized with American equipment, U.S. infrastructure decays from decades of deferred investment.

The $14 billion supplemental aid package to Israel equals the annual budget needed to end homelessness among American veterans. The $3.8 billion in yearly military aid could provide free school meals to over 2 million American children. These are not abstract trade-offs, they represent deliberate choices to prioritize Israeli military superiority over American human needs.

This is not charity or alliance management. It is strategic self-sabotage that weakens America while strengthening a foreign military that operates with impunity across the Middle East.

A RELATIONSHIP BUILT ON COERCION, NOT PARTNERSHIP

True alliances involve mutual consultation, shared decision-making, and respect for each partner's interests. The U.S.-Israel relationship operates differently. Israel threatens consequences if demands are not met, while American politicians, particularly those dependent on AIPAC and related organizations, deliver without question, fearing electoral retribution and media campaigns.

This dynamic resembles coercion more than cooperation. It reflects the behavior of a client state that believes it owns its patron rather than an independent ally respecting mutual sovereignty.

Every Israeli strike in Lebanon becomes another test of how far America will go to justify the unjustifiable. So far, we are passing with flying colors while failing morally.

LEBANON AS STRATEGIC WARNING

Lebanon's destruction serves Israeli regional strategy while advancing no legitimate American interest. The country has no significant oil reserves, no nuclear weapons program, and no capacity for power projection beyond its borders. Its only "crime" is existing beside Israel while maintaining minimal sovereignty.

But Israel's long-term vision is transparent: destabilize, destroy, divide, then establish "security zones" inside foreign borders backed by American diplomatic protection and military supplies. Lebanon represents a test case for this strategy of incremental annexation disguised as defensive necessity.

America provides the bulldozers, bombs, and diplomatic cover that make this expansion possible. We are not passive observers of Middle Eastern conflicts, we are active participants funding and facilitating Israeli territorial ambitions at the expense of regional stability and international law.

The next time American officials speak of the "special relationship" with Israel, ask yourself: who benefits from the relationship, and who pays the costs? Because Lebanon's destruction is not in American interests. But it is being done in our name, with our weapons, and with our protection.

CHAPTER RECAP

Israel's assault on Lebanon follows the same pattern visible in Gaza: systematic destabilization justified by security threats that Israeli aggression itself created, all enabled by unconditional American support that transforms the United States into an active participant rather than a neutral ally. Lebanon poses zero threat to American security, yet U.S. military aircraft transport weapons to Israel, American intelligence provides targeting data, and American diplomacy shields Israeli operations from international accountability—making every Lebanese civilian death a product of deliberate American policy choices that sacrifice our credibility and resources for Israeli territorial ambitions.

- **Israel has systematically destabilized Lebanon through decades of invasions and occupations** that created the very security threats Israel now claims to fight—demonstrating how Israeli aggression generates its own justifications for further aggression

- **American complicity extends far beyond financial aid to direct operational support**: U.S. military aircraft transport weapons to Israel, American intelligence provides targeting data, and U.S. diplomatic protection shields Israeli operations from international accountability

- **Lebanon poses zero threat to American security** yet the U.S. acts as Israel's proxy, defending Israeli territorial ambitions while ignoring Lebanese sovereignty and civilian casualties caused by American-made weapons

- **Congressional legislation demonstrates unconditional support regardless of Israeli actions**: Even when President Biden attempted minimal oversight through NSM-20, Trump immediately rescinded these protections, revealing the depth of American subservience to Israeli demands

- **Global isolation exposes American moral bankruptcy**: While European allies and international bodies condemn Israeli aggression against Lebanon, the U.S. systematically blocks accountability measures and provides diplomatic immunity for war crimes

- **Domestic costs reveal misplaced priorities**: The $14 billion in supplemental Israeli aid could end veteran homelessness, while annual military aid could feed millions of American children, exposing how Israeli militarism is prioritized over American human needs

This chapter demonstrates how Israel uses American resources to destabilize neighboring countries while expanding its territorial control through "buffer zones" and "security operations." Lebanon's experience reveals the true nature of the U.S.-Israel relationship: America serves as an enabler of Israeli regional domination while sacrificing both international credibility and domestic priorities to maintain this destructive alliance.

CHAPTER 33:

WITH FRIENDS LIKE THIS. . .

Supporters of Israel in the United States often repeat the line that "Israel is our only friend in the Middle East," a phrase designed to evoke loyalty and justify billions in military and diplomatic aid. But history tells a different story. Allies don't spy on your leaders, attack your Navy vessels, or entangle your foreign policy in endless regional conflicts. Yet Israel has done all of the above.

From the Lavon Affair, where Israeli agents staged attacks on American targets to manipulate U.S. policy, to the bombing of the USS Liberty that killed 34 American sailors, Israel's actions have repeatedly betrayed rather than bolstered the alliance. Add the Jonathan Pollard spy case, the AIPAC espionage scandal, and surveillance of U.S. officials by Israel's elite cyber intelligence Unit 8200, and the narrative of loyal partnership unravels completely.

Far from being a dependable ally, Israel has repeatedly acted to undermine U.S. sovereignty and security, all while continuing to receive unconditional support from American taxpayers and politicians alike.

As Thomas Jefferson wrote in the Declaration of Independence when listing King George's actions that compelled American independence: "To Prove this, let Facts be submitted to a candid World."

THE LAVON AFFAIR: STATE-SPONSORED TERRORISM AGAINST AMERICA

In 1954, Israel launched an operation so audacious that it should have redefined how Americans viewed their supposed ally. Instead, the incident was buried under diplomatic silence and media erasure. **Operation Susannah**, better known as The Lavon Affair, was a covert Israeli plan to commit terrorist attacks against U.S. and British interests in Egypt, blame them on local Arabs, and sabotage Western-Egyptian relations.[1]

This was not a rogue operation. This was state-sponsored terrorism, orchestrated by Israeli military intelligence and approved at the highest levels of Israeli leadership. The goal? To maintain British and American presence in Egypt by making it appear Western facilities were under attack by Arab nationalists.

Let that sink in: **Israel, America's "closest ally," devised a plot to kill American and British citizens, destroy American property, and drag the United States into confrontation with Egypt under false pretenses.**

OPERATION SUSANNAH: BETRAYAL DISGUISED AS SECURITY

The plan was methodical. A group of Egyptian Jews, recruited and trained by Israeli military intelligence, were instructed to plant bombs in American and British cultural centers, libraries, and cinemas in Cairo and Alexandria. While timed to minimize casualties, the psychological purpose was clear: create fear, foster division, and halt British withdrawal from the Suez Canal.

On July 2, 1954, bombs exploded at a post office in Alexandria and the U.S. Information Agency library. But the plan unraveled when one operative was caught after explosives ignited in his pocket. Under interrogation, he confessed, revealing the full extent of Israeli involvement.

When Egyptian authorities exposed the plot and tried the Israeli operatives, Israel denied responsibility, claiming the men acted independently. But evidence mounted, including direct communications with Israeli handlers, making the lie untenable. The scandal led to Israeli Defense Minister Pinhas Lavon's resignation, though Prime Minister David Ben-Gurion may have authorized the operation.[2]

In the United States? Barely a whisper. Newspaper coverage was muted. There was no congressional inquiry, no diplomatic reprimand, no statement of condemnation. The American government, eager to maintain its growing alliance with Israel, looked the other way.

The Lavon Affair set a precedent: Israel would act unilaterally, even treacherously, to advance its agenda, and American leadership would remain silent even when caught in the crossfire.

USS LIBERTY: DELIBERATE ATTACK, DELIBERATE COVER-UP

On June 8, 1967, during the Six-Day War, the U.S. Navy intelligence ship **USS Liberty** was attacked in international waters by Israeli air and naval forces. Thirty-four American sailors were killed and 171 wounded in a relentless assault lasting over an hour involving rockets, torpedoes, and napalm.[3]

The USS Liberty was an intelligence-gathering vessel monitoring communications during the Israeli-Arab conflict. On a clear day in international waters, with American flags visible, the ship posed no threat. Israeli reconnaissance had flown over the Liberty multiple times that morning, there was no chance of mistaking it for an Egyptian vessel.

Without warning, Israeli Mirage jets strafed the ship with cannon fire and rockets, targeting communications equipment and the bridge. Israeli torpedo boats joined the assault, launching torpedoes that blew massive holes in the hull. Napalm was dropped to ignite fires. Most shockingly, lifeboats were machine-gunned, a war crime under any definition.[4]

The Liberty's distress call reached the U.S. Sixth Fleet, and aircraft were launched to defend the ship. But those planes were recalled twice on orders from the White House. President Lyndon Johnson reportedly said, "I will not embarrass an ally."[5]

Despite overwhelming evidence, survivor testimony, intercepted communications, and physical evidence, the U.S. government accepted Israel's apology and the claim of "mistaken identity." The official investigation was rushed, key witnesses were silenced, and survivors were ordered never to speak publicly under threat of court-martial.[6]

The likely motive, supported by declassified documents and intelligence officials, was Israeli fear that the Liberty would intercept radio transmissions exposing violations of international law, including execution of Egyptian prisoners of war.[7] The ship had to be neutralized.

In the entire history of the United States, no other foreign country has ever attacked a U.S. naval vessel, killed American service members, and suffered no consequences. Israel not only escaped punishment but continued receiving unprecedented U.S. aid. The lesson was clear: America will absorb betrayal to maintain the illusion of alliance.

JONATHAN POLLARD: ESPIONAGE REWARDED WITH HONORS

In 1985, civilian intelligence analyst Jonathan Pollard was arrested for spying for Israel. Over 18 months, he passed tens of thousands of pages of highly classified documents to Israeli agents, including material so sensitive that parts remain classified today.[8]

Instead of marking a crisis in U.S. Israeli relations, the affair was managed, downplayed, and ultimately forgiven. Israel eventually admitted its role but never expressed meaningful contrition. Instead, it celebrated Pollard as a hero and lobbied for his release for decades.[9]

Working at Naval Intelligence Command with top-secret clearance, Pollard secretly copied and delivered over 800 classified documents containing thousands of pages to Israeli handlers. The information included satellite imagery, technical specifications of U.S. weapons systems, and electronic surveillance programs.

According to former CIA Director George Tenet, the damage was devastating, possibly the worst inflicted by any single individual on U.S. intelligence.[10] Some information Pollard gave Israel was traded to the Soviet Union in exchange for exit visas for Soviet Jews, further harming American interests. Again, don't just pass this by too quickly. **Israel spied on the U.S., exfiltrated highly classified U.S. military documents, and then gave those documents to our arch-enemy.**

Initially, Israel claimed the operation was "unauthorized," blaming rogue agents. Declassified documents revealed this was false, Pollard was recruited and directed by senior Israeli intelligence officials in a coordinated operation involving multiple handlers, safe houses, and diplomatic support.

When Pollard fled to the Israeli embassy seeking asylum, Israeli officials turned him over to U.S. authorities, hoping to contain diplomatic fallout. After Pollard's arrest and life sentence, Israel began a decades-long campaign to free him, involving AIPAC pressure, letters from Israeli Prime Ministers, and Knesset resolutions calling him a "Jewish patriot."

In 2020, after serving 30 years, Pollard traveled to Israel and was greeted as a returning hero, receiving a private meeting with Prime Minister Netanyahu, a state-funded apartment, and citizenship.[11] The image of an American traitor being celebrated by Israeli leadership should have prompted reassessment of U.S.-Israeli relations. Instead, American politicians said nothing.

AIPAC ESPIONAGE SCANDAL: LOBBYING AS INTELLIGENCE OPERATION

In the mid-2000s, Pentagon analyst Larry Franklin was arrested for passing classified information about Iran's nuclear program to AIPAC officials Steve Rosen and Keith Weissman. The intelligence reportedly reached Israeli officials through this channel. Franklin pled guilty and was sentenced to over 12 years in prison.[12]

AIPAC denied wrongdoing and fired Rosen and Weissman. Charges against them were eventually dropped after years of legal battles. Despite clear evidence of intelligence-sharing with a foreign power, AIPAC emerged unscathed, and the scandal was buried beneath political amnesia.

This wasn't traditional lobbying, it was espionage through influence, an end-run around democratic deliberation using classified leaks and foreign channels. The case exposed how Israeli influence extends beyond public diplomacy into intelligence operations and political manipulation.

UNIT 8200: SURVEILLANCE OF AMERICAN OFFICIALS

In 2015, The Wall Street Journal revealed that Israel had been spying on confidential U.S. negotiations with Iran using its elite signals intelligence agency, Unit 8200. While the U.S. and world powers engaged in sensitive nuclear talks with Iran, Israel chose surveillance over diplomacy.

Their targets weren't Iranian negotiators—they were American ones.

Israel intercepted private communications, including classified briefings and diplomatic updates, then relayed that intelligence to members of Congress and pro-Israel lobbying groups to undermine the Obama administration's policy and kill the Iran nuclear deal.[13]

This wasn't just espionage, it was sabotage. Israeli officials privately acknowledged the surveillance, justifying it on grounds that "Israel had a right to know." In their logic, this included a right to spy on the government providing them with over $3 billion annually in military aid.

The Obama administration, aware of the espionage, chose not to make a public case. There were no expulsions, no sanctions, no public rebukes. The story received brief media attention, then vanished. No hearings, no accountability, no consequences.

THE PATTERN OF BETRAYAL

These incidents are not isolated events. They form a clear pattern. Israel operates not as an ally but as an entity with its own agenda, and pursuing that agenda even when it means:

- Attacking American military personnel (USS Liberty)

- Staging false flag operations to manipulate U.S. policy (Lavon Affair)

- Stealing American intelligence and trading it to adversaries (Pollard)

- Infiltrating American lobbying organizations for espionage purposes (AIPAC)

- Spying on American officials to sabotage U.S. diplomacy (Unit 8200)

In each case, the American response was the same: silence, excuses, and continued support. This is not how alliances work. This is how client states with leverage operate.

THE COST OF WILLFUL BLINDNESS

Every act of Israeli betrayal that goes unpunished sends a message: America will absorb any insult, any attack, any espionage operation rather than risk the political cost of confronting Israeli actions. This pattern has created a relationship where:

- Israel acts with impunity, knowing American protection is guaranteed

- American sovereignty is routinely violated without consequence

- U.S. intelligence assets are compromised to serve Israeli interests

- American lives are expendable when they conflict with Israeli objectives

The "special relationship" is indeed special. It is the only alliance in American history where one partner can repeatedly betray, attack, and spy on the other while receiving increased support in return.

REDEFINING THE RELATIONSHIP

When supporters claim "Israel is our only friend in the Middle East," the quick and flippant answer is "Prior to 1948 we didn't have any enemies in the Middle East," but the factual response is just as simple: true friends don't behave this way. Friends don't:

- Plan terrorist attacks against your citizens

- Sink your naval vessels and kill your sailors

- Steal your most sensitive intelligence

- Spy on your diplomatic negotiations

- Celebrate your traitors as heroes

The evidence is overwhelming and undeniable. Israel has repeatedly demonstrated that it views America not as a partner but as a resource to be exploited, manipulated, and when necessary, betrayed.

The question Americans must ask is not whether Israel is our friend, the evidence clearly answers that. The question is why we continue pretending otherwise, and what it costs us to maintain that fiction.

CHAPTER RECAP

The relationship between the United States and Israel is unique in American diplomatic history—no other nation has attacked American military assets, conducted massive espionage operations against the U.S. government, or planned false-flag terrorist attacks against American targets while continuing to receive billions in unconditional aid and unwavering political support. This pattern of systematic betrayal, followed by American cover-ups and continued alliance, reveals a relationship built not on mutual benefit but on Israeli leverage over American political institutions that prioritize avoiding domestic political consequences over defending American sovereignty and security.

- **Israel has repeatedly committed acts of aggression against the United States** including planned terrorist attacks (Lavon Affair), deliberate military assault (USS Liberty), massive espionage operations (Pollard), and surveillance of American officials (Unit 8200)

- **American government response demonstrates systematic cover-up and complicity**: Rather than holding Israel accountable, U.S. officials have consistently silenced victims, classified evidence, and maintained unconditional support despite documented betrayals

- **The pattern reveals a relationship based on Israeli leverage, not mutual benefit**: Israel operates with impunity because American politicians fear political retribution more than they value American sovereignty or the lives of American service members

- **Israeli celebration of American traitors exposes the relationship's true nature**: When Israel welcomes convicted spy Jonathan Pollard as a hero while receiving billions in American aid, it demonstrates complete contempt for American interests and security

309

- **No other ally has ever attacked, spied on, and betrayed the United States with such consistency**: The "special relationship" is special only in its one-sided tolerance for actions that would end any other alliance immediately

- **The cost of willful blindness continues to mount**: Every unpunished Israeli betrayal emboldens further aggression while compromising American intelligence assets, diplomatic credibility, and national security interests

This chapter exposes the fundamental lie underlying U.S.-Israel relations: the notion that Israel is a loyal ally deserving trust. The documented evidence reveals systematic betrayal from false-flag terrorism to naval attacks to espionage operations, all protected by American political cover and media silence. The relationship serves Israeli interests while consistently harming American security, sovereignty, and credibility—proving that with friends like Israel, America truly doesn't need enemies.

PART V:

THE FUTURE OF THE
UNITED STATES

The evidence is in. The case has been made. Across hundreds of pages, we have documented the machinery of American empire: the propaganda that blinds us, the economic weapons that enslave nations, the military interventions that destroy lives, and the ideological forces that drive it all forward. The question that remains is not whether America has been the villain in countless stories across the globe—the record speaks for itself. The question is what comes next.

Every empire in history has faced this moment: the recognition that its power is finite, its methods unsustainable, and its legitimacy crumbling. Rome fell to barbarian invasions after centuries of overextension. Britain retreated from empire after two world wars bankrupted its treasury. The Soviet Union collapsed under the weight of its own contradictions and military quagmires. Spain's gold ran out, and with it, its global dominance.

America now stands at that same crossroads, though most Americans remain oblivious to the choice before them. The national debt approaches $34 trillion. Military commitments span the globe while infrastructure crumbles at home. Trust in institutions has eroded to historic lows. International coalitions increasingly exclude or oppose American leadership. The tools of empire, economic coercion, military intervention, propaganda— are losing their effectiveness as the world builds alternatives to American systems.

This final section examines the fork in the road ahead: **transformation or collapse**. Can Americans confront the truth about their nation's actions and choose a different path? Can the republic be saved from the empire that has consumed it? Or will America follow the predictable trajectory of every empire before it, clinging to power until that power destroys both the nation and its people?

The future is not predetermined, but it is rapidly approaching. And the choice—however uncomfortable, however difficult— remains ours to make.

CHAPTER 34:

THE WARNING OF HISTORY

LESSONS FROM FALLEN EMPIRES

In the grand theater of human ambition, empires rise like titans, casting long shadows over the world, only to crumble under the weight of their own excesses. The story of American exceptionalism isn't just a tale of triumph; it's a cautionary epic laced with the ghosts of predecessors who once dominated the globe. History doesn't repeat itself exactly, but it rhymes with eerie precision, whispering warnings about overreach, economic hemorrhage, and the erosion of legitimacy.

The Roman Empire, the British Empire, the Soviet Union, and the Spanish Empire offer stark mirrors to the United States today. Each fell not from a single cataclysmic blow, but from a slow poison of internal rot and external strain—much like the fiscal and moral dilemmas we face now.

ROME: THE PRICE OF OVEREXTENSION

At its peak in the 2nd century CE, Rome controlled vast swaths of Europe, North Africa, and the Middle East, its legions enforcing "Pax Romana" across three continents. But by the 3rd and 4th centuries, the cracks widened into chasms.

Edward Gibbon, in his monumental *The History of the Decline and Fall of the Roman Empire*, identifies internal corruption as the empire's Achilles' heel.[1] While emperors like Diocletian attempted reforms, the elite class—senators and landowners equivalent to today's congressmen and corporations—hoarded wealth from taxes, leaving the legions that guarded the frontiers starved and demoralized.[2]

Overextension compounded the problem: Rome maintained an estimated 400,000 troops stretched thin across borders from the

Rhine to the Euphrates, facing barbarian incursions and Persian threats. Modern historians emphasize economic factors like debased currency and endless civil wars that reflected elite self-interest over imperial stability.[3] By 476 CE, when the last Western emperor was deposed, Rome's fall wasn't just military, it was a legitimacy crisis where the people no longer believed in the system's promise of security and prosperity.

BRITAIN: COLONIAL RESISTANCE AND ECONOMIC COLLAPSE

At its peak after World War I, Britain ruled a quarter of the world's land and population. Yet as Niall Ferguson details in *Empire: The Rise and Demise of the British World Order*, the seeds of decline were sown through unsustainable expansion and economic burdens.[4]

Colonial resistance proved decisive. In India, Gandhi's nonviolent movement, culminating in the Salt March of 1930 and the Quit India campaign of 1942, exposed the empire's moral bankruptcy.[5] In Kenya, the Mau Mau uprising (1952-1960) represented brutal armed revolt against land dispossession, killing thousands and draining British resources.

The coup de grâce came from World War II: Britain's war debt ballooned to an equivalent of about $650 billion in today's currency, crippling its economy and forcing reliance on American loans.[6] By 1947, with India's independence, Britain retreated, its legitimacy shattered by the realization that maintaining empire was no longer viable.

SOVIET UNION: IDEOLOGY MEETS REALITY

The USSR's implosion in 1991 provides a recent example of ideological fracture meeting fiscal crisis. The 1979 invasion of Afghanistan proved disastrous, costing an estimated 15,000 Soviet lives and billions in rubles while fighting the mujahideen resistance backed by the U.S.[7]

Declassified Politburo documents reveal how the war bankrupted Moscow, diverting 2-3% of GDP annually from domestic needs and fueling public discontent.[8] This external quagmire intertwined with internal dissent, notably Poland's Solidarity movement. Launched in 1980 as a trade union led by Lech Wałęsa, Solidarity grew into nationwide resistance challenging communist orthodoxy and inspiring dissent across the Warsaw Pact.[9]

Gorbachev's perestroika reforms, intended to revitalize the system, instead accelerated its unraveling as economic strain from Afghanistan and suppressed dissent exposed the regime's hollow core. The USSR's fall wasn't just economic, it was a crisis of faith where citizens rejected the narrative of proletarian paradise.

SPAIN: THE RESOURCE CURSE

The Spanish Empire's collapse illustrates the perils of resource-driven overconfidence. Emerging from Columbus's voyages in 1492, Spain amassed vast New World domains, flooding Europe with gold and silver from Potosí and Mexico—over 180 tons annually by the 16th century.[10] This influx sparked catastrophic inflation: prices in Spain quadrupled between 1500 and 1600, eroding purchasing power while the rigid mercantilist economy stagnated.[11]

Colonial revolts compounded the problems. In Latin America, figures like Simón Bolívar led independence wars from 1810 to 1825, while Spain's involvement in Napoleonic Wars diverted troops, leaving viceroyalties vulnerable. By 1898, with the loss of Cuba and the Philippines, Spain's empire had fragmented, its gold-fueled grandeur reduced to economic ruin.

AMERICA 2025: ECHOING THE PAST

These historical patterns resonate strikingly in today's America. Our national debt has surged to $33 trillion, a figure approaching unsustainable levels.[12] The base defense budget of $886 billion for fiscal year 2025 funds a global military footprint echoing Rome's legions, with over 750 bases in 80 countries.[13]

Economic strain mounts as interest payments on existing debt approach $1 trillion annually, rivaling defense spending and squeezing domestic priorities like infrastructure and healthcare. Legitimacy wanes through rising inequality—the top 1% hoarding wealth like Roman elites—while endless wars erode public trust.

THE PATTERN OF DECLINE

To visualize this pattern, consider how imperial declines unfold:

Empire	Peak	Fall	Key Factors	Modern Parallel
Rome	117 CE	476 CE	Military overextension, elite corruption, currency debasement	750+ U.S. bases, $33T debt, political dysfunction
Spain	1580s	1825	Resource curse inflation, colonial revolts	Resource dependency, inequality-fueled unrest
Britain	1920s	1947	War debt, colonial resistance	Post-war fiscal burdens, anti-imperial movements
Soviet Union	1960s	1991	Afghan War costs, internal dissent	Forever wars, domestic polarization

This is a roadmap drawn from history's lessons. If Rome fell to overextension, Britain to debt, and the USSR to military quagmires, what challenges await America?

LEARNING FROM THE MIRROR

Each fallen empire believed in its exceptionalism until the end. Romans thought their civilization eternal, the British believed their empire civilizing, the Soviets saw their ideology as inevitable, and the Spanish trusted their gold would last forever.

Americans today face a choice: acknowledge these patterns and change course, or repeat history's most predictable tragedy. The warning signs are visible—unsustainable debt, military overextension, domestic division, and eroding legitimacy. But unlike previous empires, we have their examples as guides.

The question isn't whether empires fall—history proves they do. The question is whether Americans have the wisdom to transform our republic before it's too late, learning from those who didn't.

CHAPTER RECAP

• **Historical empires follow predictable patterns of decline** through military overextension, fiscal crisis, internal corruption, and legitimacy collapse—patterns clearly visible in Rome, Britain, Spain, and the Soviet Union

• **America exhibits identical warning signs** including $33 trillion national debt, 750+ overseas military bases, rising inequality, and domestic political dysfunction that mirror the terminal phases of previous empires

• **Military overextension proves consistently fatal** as seen in Rome's 400,000 troops across continents, Britain's unsustainable colonial commitments, and Soviet Afghanistan costs—paralleling America's global military footprint and endless wars

• **Economic collapse follows fiscal irresponsibility** when interest payments consume increasing portions of imperial budgets, as happened to debt-crushed Britain and inflation-devastated Spain—now threatening America with trillion-dollar annual debt service

317

- **Legitimacy crises destroy empires from within** when populations lose faith in imperial promises, from Roman citizens abandoning the system to Soviet citizens rejecting communist ideology—reflected in declining American trust in institutions
- **Colonial resistance accelerates imperial decline** through organized opposition that drains resources and exposes moral contradictions, from Gandhi's campaigns against Britain to mujahideen resistance against Soviets—echoing global opposition to American interventions

This chapter demonstrates that American exceptionalism cannot exempt us from historical patterns that have destroyed every previous empire. The choice facing Americans is stark: learn from these examples and transform our approach to global power, or repeat the same predictable trajectory toward imperial collapse that history has documented with devastating consistency.

CHAPTER 35:

CREEPING TO THE EDGE

WARNING SIGNS OF DECLINE

Rome's legions overreached; Spain's gold drained dry; Britain's colonies rebelled. America's turn is here, and the signs are screaming. Seven warning signs—endless wars, economic fragility, surveillance, democratic illusion, moral bankruptcy, division, and climate blowback—show an empire teetering on a precipice.

ENDLESS WARS: THE QUICKSAND STRATEGY

We're stuck in quicksand, fighting wars that never end. In 2025, Syria's still burning after more than a decade of conflict. Israeli airstrikes, backed by U.S. intelligence and weaponry, continue hitting Damascus, with civilian casualties mounting into the hundreds.[1] Yemen presents an even starker picture. The U.S.-backed Saudi campaign has displaced over 4 million people—a humanitarian catastrophe tied directly to our arms sales and diplomatic approval.[2]

These are part of a pattern: Iraq, Afghanistan, Libya, Somalia, Syria, Yemen. Each intervention promised swift victory and democratic transformation. Each delivered prolonged occupation and regional instability. Over 1 million killed in our post-9/11 wars according to Brown University's Costs of War project, with civilian deaths comprising nearly 400,000 of that total.

The Pentagon's 2025 budget exceeds is more than the next ten countries combined, yet Americans are demonstrably less secure.[3] Each dollar spent on overseas military operations represents resources diverted from domestic infrastructure, education, and healthcare. We've spent over $8 trillion on post-9/11 conflicts while our bridges collapse and schools decay.

International perception reflects this strategic failure. Pew Research's 2025 survey shows only 35% of our allies trust American leadership, a precipitous decline from 64% a decade ago.[4]

ECONOMIC FRAGILITY: HOUSE OF CARDS IN A HURRICANE

Our economy resembles a house of cards in a hurricane. The Congressional Budget Office projects a $1.5 trillion deficit for 2025, pushing our debt-to-GDP ratio to 99%—dangerously close to the 100% threshold economists consider unsustainable.[5]

The American Society of Civil Engineers graded U.S. infrastructure a D+ in 2025, estimating $9.1 trillion needed in the next decade to address critical deficiencies.[6] Our roads, bridges, water systems, and electrical grids decay while we spend nearly $1 trillion annually on military and intelligence operations.

Meanwhile, China's Belt and Road Initiative has invested over $1 trillion in global infrastructure projects, building influence through construction rather than destruction.[7] Chinese engineers build ports in Pakistan while American engineers repair bombed bridges in countries we've "liberated."

Interest payments on existing debt now approach $1 trillion annually, consuming resources that could modernize our economy. Like Spain flooding Europe with gold while its domestic economy stagnated, we flood the world with military hardware while our competitive advantages erode.

SURVEILLANCE STATE: WHEN BIG BROTHER WEARS STARS AND STRIPES

George Orwell's Big Brother has arrived wearing American flags. The NSA's 2025 surveillance revelations reveal expanded domestic spying operations that dwarf anything Orwell imagined.[8] Phone metadata, social media interactions, smart home devices, GPS locations, financial transactions—all swept up without warrants through programs that supposedly target foreign threats but inevitably capture American citizens.

The Fourth Amendment's protection against unreasonable searches becomes meaningless when every digital interaction is monitored and stored indefinitely. The infrastructure of totalitarianism exists; only political restraint prevents its full deployment.

THE ILLUSION OF DEMOCRACY: THEATER WITH EXPENSIVE TICKETS

We call it democracy, but it's elaborate theater where corporations write the script and citizens buy increasingly expensive tickets to watch predetermined outcomes. OpenSecrets reports that $14 billion was spent on the 2024 elections—corporate and billionaire investments in political outcomes rather than grassroots democratic participation.[9]

Federal Election Commission data shows barely 50% of eligible Americans bothered voting in 2024, reflecting widespread recognition that the system serves elite interests regardless of electoral outcomes.[10] Why participate when lobbying budgets dwarf campaign contributions, when corporate-written legislation passes regardless of public opinion, and when the same foreign policy establishment manages global interventions under both parties?

AIPAC alone spent over $100 million in 2024 elections, systematically targeting candidates who questioned Israeli policies. Defense contractors fund think tanks that advocate for military spending. The revolving door between government service and corporate employment ensures policy continuity regardless of electoral changes.

While Americans oppose endless wars by substantial margins in polling, Congress approves military budgets with bipartisan enthusiasm. The disconnect between public preferences and policy outcomes exposes the fundamental hollowness of American democratic institutions.

MORAL BANKRUPTCY: FUNDING ATROCITIES WHILE PREACHING RIGHTS

Empires collapse when they lose their moral foundation, when the gap between proclaimed values and actual behavior becomes impossible to ignore. The 2024-2025 Gaza escalation provides stark evidence of American moral bankruptcy. UN reports document over 40,000 Palestinian deaths, mostly civilians, as Israel's U.S.-backed campaign intensifies with American-supplied weapons and diplomatic protection.[11]

America's response reveals our moral degeneration. We've vetoed UN Security Council resolutions calling for ceasefires three times in 2024 alone, despite nearly universal international support for ending the bloodshed.[12] We provide the bombs, block accountability mechanisms, and then express concern about humanitarian conditions we helped create.

This pattern extends beyond Gaza. Our drone strikes kill wedding parties while claiming to target terrorists. Our sanctions collectively punish civilians while supposedly pressuring government change. Our silence on systematic ethnic cleansing while we lecture other nations about human rights.

Young people globally see these contradictions most clearly. They watch Palestinian children die from American bombs while American politicians claim to support human rights. They witness climate destruction from American military emissions while American leaders pledge environmental stewardship.

INTERNAL DIVISION: A HOUSE DIVIDED

We're tearing ourselves apart from within, exhibiting the internal fractures that historically precede imperial collapse. Gallup's 2025 polling shows 80% of Americans distrust our core institutions—government, media, courts, even elections themselves.[13] This isn't partisan skepticism but systemic legitimacy crisis affecting the entire political structure.

Political violence has increased 20% since 2020, manifesting in everything from Capitol riots to street clashes between opposing political movements.[14] The social fabric that holds diverse societies together—shared narratives, common institutions, mutual respect—has frayed to the breaking point.

Urban and rural Americans inhabit different information ecosystems, economic realities, and cultural frameworks. They consume different media, trust different authorities, and hold incompatible visions of American identity. These aren't policy differences but civilizational conflicts within a single nation.

The federal response has been characteristically imperial: deploy military force to manage internal dissent. American troops now patrol American cities under the rhetoric of fighting crime, normalizing military solutions to political problems. When empires turn their military apparatus inward, the end approaches rapidly.

CLIMATE BLOWBACK: THE EMPIRE THAT COOKED THE WORLD

Our military machine isn't just destroying other countries—it's destroying the planet. The U.S. military burns 340,000 barrels of oil daily, making it a larger greenhouse gas emitter than many entire nations.[15] Those emissions drive climate chaos that threatens global stability.

The United Nations projects 200 million climate migrants by 2050, fleeing floods, droughts, and storms worsened by emissions from American military operations.[16] These aren't abstract future problems but current realities creating instability that justifies further military intervention, creating a vicious cycle of climate destruction and military response.

In 2025, wildfires rage across California, hurricanes batter Gulf Coast communities, and drought devastates agricultural regions. Yet our response remains characterized by military thinking: deploy troops for disaster response rather than address emissions causing the disasters.

THE INTERCONNECTED CRISIS

These warning signs aren't independent problems but interconnected elements of systemic imperial decay. Endless wars drain economic resources needed for infrastructure investment. Economic fragility necessitates increased surveillance to manage domestic unrest. Democratic dysfunction prevents course corrections while moral bankruptcy erodes international legitimacy.

Each warning sign amplifies the others in a cascade of imperial decline. Military overstretch weakens economic competitiveness, requiring increased domestic control to manage resulting social tensions. Loss of international legitimacy reduces soft power effectiveness, necessitating increased reliance on military coercion.

CHAPTER RECAP

The American empire displays seven interconnected warning signs of terminal decline that mirror the patterns visible in every previous empire before collapse—from Rome's fiscal crises to Britain's imperial overstretch to the Soviet Union's moral bankruptcy. These are not isolated policy failures that can be corrected through electoral politics or technical reforms, but rather symptoms of systemic imperial decay where military overextension, economic fragility, surveillance expansion, democratic dysfunction, moral bankruptcy, internal division, and environmental destruction reinforce each other in accelerating cycles of decline that historically prove irreversible once fully established.

- **Seven interconnected warning signs indicate systematic imperial decline** resembling patterns that destroyed previous empires: endless wars, economic fragility, surveillance expansion, democratic dysfunction, moral bankruptcy, internal division, and environmental destruction

- **Military overextension continues draining resources** with $850+ billion annual defense spending producing strategic failures, declining international trust (35% ally confidence), and millions of displaced civilians from American-backed conflicts
- **Economic foundations crumble under imperial costs** as $1.5 trillion deficits push debt to 99% of GDP while domestic infrastructure receives D+ grades, mirroring the fiscal crises that bankrupted previous empires
- **Constitutional protections collapse under surveillance expansion** with NSA domestic spying programs normalizing authoritarian control mechanisms that mirror technologies first deployed overseas
- **Democratic institutions serve elite interests rather than popular will** through $14 billion election spending, 50% voter turnout, and corporate-written legislation that ignores public preferences on foreign policy and domestic priorities
- **Moral bankruptcy destroys international credibility** as American weapons kill thousands of civilians while U.S. diplomats veto ceasefire resolutions, exposing hypocrisy between proclaimed values and actual behavior
- **Internal divisions threaten social cohesion** with 80% of Americans distrusting core institutions, 20% increases in political violence, and geographic polarization creating incompatible visions of national identity

These warning signs operate as interconnected elements of imperial decay rather than isolated problems. Military overstretch weakens economic competitiveness, requiring increased domestic surveillance to manage resulting social tensions. The cascade of decline accelerates as each crisis amplifies the others, creating the systemic breakdown that historically precedes imperial collapse.

CHAPTER 36:

BRAIN DRAIN AND GLOBAL REJECTION

The United States is hemorrhaging talent—engineers, scientists, artists, entrepreneurs who'd rather build the future elsewhere than navigate America's increasingly hostile environment for innovation and creativity. The numbers tell a stark story of decline: we're slipping in innovation rankings, educational achievement, and creative freedom while other nations eagerly recruit the talent we're pushing away.

This isn't merely brain drain, it's future drain. The minds that built Silicon Valley, pioneered American research universities, and created our cultural dominance are choosing other destinations. Meanwhile, the world that once looked to America for leadership increasingly turns away, seeking alternatives to our military-backed economic system.

THE INNOVATION EXODUS: LOSING OUR TECHNOLOGICAL EDGE

America's technological supremacy, built on attracting the world's best minds, is crumbling under policy failures and cultural hostility toward expertise. The Global Innovation Index ranks the U.S. third in 2025, down from first place in 2000, trailing Switzerland and Sweden in innovation capacity.[1] This decline represents a fundamental shift in global innovation patterns.

Indian AI engineers, once Silicon Valley's backbone, increasingly choose Bangalore's startup ecosystem over American visa uncertainties. India's technology sector grew by 8.4% in 2024, driven partly by returning expatriates who bring Silicon Valley experience to Indian companies.[2] The World Economic Forum reports that Bangalore now hosts over 4,000 technology startups, creating a competitive alternative to American tech hubs without the bureaucratic obstacles facing foreign workers in the U.S.[3]

Chinese researchers face even starker choices. OECD data shows significant declines in Chinese graduate student enrollment at American universities, driven by visa restrictions, political tensions, and expanding opportunities in China's state-backed research institutions.[4] Beijing's massive investments in artificial intelligence research—reportedly exceeding $15 billion annually, provide compelling alternatives to American academic and corporate positions.

The H-1B visa system, designed to attract high-skilled workers, has become a barrier rather than a bridge. Annual caps remain artificially low while bureaucratic processing creates years-long uncertainties. Meanwhile, Canada's streamlined immigration system attracted increasing numbers of skilled workers previously destined for the United States.[5]

EDUCATIONAL DECLINE: FAILING THE NEXT GENERATION

America's educational system, once the global gold standard, now struggles to maintain international competitiveness. The Programme for International Student Assessment (PISA) consistently ranks U.S. students in the middle tier of developed nations in mathematics and science, behind countries like Estonia, Poland, and Vietnam.[6] This educational mediocrity creates pipeline problems for innovation and technical leadership.

While Asian nations steadily improve educational outcomes through systematic reforms, American performance stagnates amid political conflicts over curriculum, funding, and educational philosophy. The politicization of education—from evolution to climate science to historical analysis—drives away qualified teachers and creates hostile environments for rigorous academic inquiry.

International student enrollment, a traditional source of talent and innovation, has declined due to visa restrictions, political climate, and competition from other English-speaking countries. Universities that once attracted global talent now compete with institutions in Canada, Australia, and the UK that offer clearer paths to permanent residence.

The STEM pipeline shows particular weakness. While China graduates twice as many engineering PhDs as the United States, American programs struggle with both domestic student interest and international accessibility.[7]

CULTURAL BRAIN DRAIN: SILENCING CREATIVE VOICES

The exodus extends beyond technical fields to creative and cultural domains. PEN America documents over 3,000 book titles targeted for bans, predominantly works by authors from marginalized communities.[8] This cultural censorship creates chilling effects that extend far beyond specific banned books.

Writers, artists, and cultural producers increasingly seek environments offering greater creative freedom. The American literary and artistic communities that once attracted global talent now compete with cities like Toronto, Berlin, and Barcelona that provide both creative freedom and economic opportunity.

When established creators leave, emerging talent loses mentorship opportunities and institutional support, creating cascading effects on cultural production. Content creators, researchers, and journalists face systematic restrictions that drive talent toward platforms and publishers in jurisdictions with stronger free expression protections.

GLOBAL REJECTION: THE WORLD TURNS AWAY

Parallel to losing individual talent, America faces systematic rejection by nations and institutions that once aligned with American leadership. This rejection manifests across economic, political, and cultural dimensions, creating alternatives to American-dominated global systems.

ECONOMIC DIVERSIFICATION: BEYOND THE DOLLAR

The most significant trend involves gradual reduction in dollar dependence through alternative financial arrangements. China's Belt and Road Initiative includes financing mechanisms that bypass dollar-denominated transactions, particularly for infrastructure projects across Asia and Africa.[9]

Saudi Arabia's exploration of non-dollar oil trading arrangements represents a fundamental challenge to the petrodollar system that has anchored American financial dominance since the 1970s. While these changes occur gradually, they reflect strategic decisions by major economies to reduce vulnerability to American financial coercion.[10]

The BRICS expansion, incorporating major economies like Saudi Arabia, demonstrates growing appetite for alternatives to American-dominated international institutions. These countries represent over 40% of global population and substantial portions of world GDP, making their coordinated policies increasingly significant.

TECHNOLOGICAL INDEPENDENCE: BREAKING FREE FROM SILICON VALLEY

European digital sovereignty initiatives represent systematic efforts to reduce dependence on American technology platforms and services. The European Union's digital regulations, including the Digital Markets Act and Digital Services Act, specifically target American technology companies while promoting European alternatives.[11]

These policies extend beyond regulation to active industrial policy supporting European technology development. Government contracts, research funding, and procurement preferences increasingly favor European companies over American alternatives, creating protected markets for local innovation.

Similar patterns emerge across Asia, where countries develop indigenous technology capabilities rather than relying on American systems. China's technology sector operates largely independent of American platforms, while countries like India develop domestic alternatives to American services and applications.

CULTURAL AND SOFT POWER DECLINE

America's cultural influence faces systematic challenges as other countries develop competitive cultural industries. Korean popular culture, Chinese media production, and European artistic movements increasingly capture global audiences without American intermediation.

International education patterns reflect this shift. European universities attract increasing numbers of international students, particularly from regions where American institutions previously dominated. These students return home with different cultural references and professional networks, gradually reducing American cultural influence.

THE INTERCONNECTED CRISIS

Brain drain and global rejection operate as interconnected phenomena. When talented individuals leave America, they strengthen competitors while weakening American capabilities. When countries reduce dependence on American systems, they create alternative opportunities that attract even more talent away from American institutions.

This creates cascading effects. Economic competitors become stronger, making their employment opportunities more attractive. Educational alternatives improve, reducing demand for American universities. Cultural alternatives emerge, providing creative professionals with viable career paths outside American institutions.

The feedback loops accelerate decline. As America becomes less attractive to talent, innovation suffers, making the country even less competitive globally. As global influence wanes, the soft power advantages that historically attracted talent diminish further.

STRATEGIC IMPLICATIONS

The combined impact of brain drain and global rejection threatens long-term American competitiveness across multiple dimensions. Technical innovation, cultural production, economic influence, and political leadership all depend on attracting and retaining top talent while maintaining global partnerships.

Historical precedents suggest these trends, once established, prove difficult to reverse. Britain's decline from global dominance occurred partly through similar processes, talent exodus, reduced global influence, and systematic development of alternatives by competitors. The timelines extended over decades, but the fundamental patterns remain consistent.

America's response to these challenges will determine whether current trends represent temporary adjustments or permanent shifts in global power structures. The window for effective policy responses remains open, but the trends documented here suggest urgent action is required to prevent irreversible decline.

CHAPTER RECAP

The American empire's most dangerous vulnerability is not military defeat or economic collapse, but rather the quiet exodus of talent, capital, and legitimacy as the world systematically builds alternatives to American-dominated systems. What distinguishes this moment from previous periods of American weakness is the coordinated, global nature of the rejection—from individual scientists choosing Toronto over Boston to entire nations constructing dollar-independent financial architectures—creating feedback loops where each defection strengthens alternatives while accelerating America's relative decline in ways that cannot be reversed through military spending or diplomatic pressure.

- **America's innovation leadership erodes as top talent chooses alternative destinations** with the U.S. falling from first to third in global innovation rankings while competitors like India and China aggressively recruit American-trained professionals

- **Educational decline creates pipeline problems for future competitiveness** as U.S. students perform in the middle tier of developed nations in mathematics and science while Asian countries steadily improve through systematic reforms

- **Cultural censorship drives creative talent abroad** with over 3,000 book titles banned and artists, writers, and intellectuals seeking environments with greater creative freedom in Canada, Europe, and other destinations

- **Visa restrictions and bureaucratic obstacles push skilled workers toward competitors** as streamlined immigration systems in Canada, Australia, and other countries attract talent previously destined for the United States

- **Global economic diversification reduces American financial dominance** through alternative trading arrangements, expanded BRICS membership, and systematic efforts to create dollar-independent financial systems

- **Technological independence movements challenge Silicon Valley's dominance** as European digital sovereignty initiatives, Chinese technology development, and indigenous innovation capabilities reduce dependence on American systems

- **Cultural soft power declines as alternatives emerge globally** with Korean, Chinese, and European cultural industries capturing international audiences while American universities lose market share to international competitors

This chapter documents interconnected crises where individual talent exodus and systematic global rejection reinforce each other in accelerating cycles of decline. As talented individuals choose other destinations, they strengthen competitors while weakening American capabilities. As countries reduce dependence on American systems, they create alternative opportunities that attract even more talent away from American institutions, creating the feedback loops that historically characterize imperial decline.

CHAPTER 37:

THE ROAD AHEAD

MANAGED DECLINE OR A NEW PATH

The United States stands at a crossroads. Its global dominance is fraying under mounting pressures of economic overreach, technological competition, social division, and eroding international trust. The empire is not collapsing overnight, but the cracks are widening across multiple domains. Current trends, if left unchanged, point toward managed decline rather than renewal. From escalating debt burdens to losing technological advantages, from increasing domestic unrest to international isolation, the data suggests a slow unraveling of American hegemony.

The question facing Americans is stark: Will we follow the path of Rome in 476 CE, or can we rewrite the script before it's too late?

ECONOMIC PRESSURES: THE DEBT TRAP

The U.S. economy faces unprecedented fiscal pressures that threaten long-term sustainability. Federal debt has grown from 35% of GDP in 1980 to over 120% today, with interest payments consuming an increasing share of government resources.[1] The Congressional Budget Office projects that interest payments alone will reach $1 trillion annually by 2034 under current policies, rivaling defense spending for budgetary priority.[2]

This debt trajectory constrains policy flexibility precisely when major investments in infrastructure, education, and climate adaptation are needed to repair our aging and failing infrastructure.[3]

High debt levels reduce fiscal space for responding to crises, limit domestic investment capacity, and create vulnerabilities to interest rate fluctuations. When debt service consumes increasing portions of federal revenue, spending on productive investments necessarily declines, weakening long-term competitiveness.

International economic patterns compound domestic pressures. China's economy has grown from 11% of global GDP in 2000 to over 17% today, while the U.S. share has declined from 31% to 24%.[4] This isn't necessarily problematic—other countries developing successfully benefits global prosperity. However, it does represent a fundamental shift in economic power that affects everything from trade relationships to currency arrangements.

TECHNOLOGICAL COMPETITION: THE INNOVATION CHALLENGE

Matching the brain drain, America's technological leadership faces unprecedented challenges from international competitors, particularly China. The semiconductor industry exemplifies these dynamics. While the U.S. maintains advantages in design and manufacturing equipment, actual chip production has largely moved to Asia. Taiwan Semiconductor Manufacturing Company produces over 60% of global semiconductors and over 90% of the most advanced chips.[5]

Recent export controls on advanced semiconductors to China represent attempts to maintain technological advantages, but they also fragment global supply chains and reduce market access for American companies. Nvidia, for example, has had to develop special versions of its AI chips that comply with export restrictions, potentially losing competitive advantages to Chinese alternatives.[6]

The broader innovation ecosystem shows concerning trends. While the U.S. still leads in total research and development spending, China has rapidly increased its investments, growing from 0.6% of GDP in 1996 to 2.4% by 2020.[7] More concerning, the pipeline of technical talent shows vulnerabilities. International students comprise about 40% of doctoral recipients in engineering and computer science at U.S. universities, but visa restrictions and political tensions reduce America's attractiveness to global talent.[8]

China's approach differs fundamentally from America's market-driven model. State-directed investments in strategic technologies, coordinated industrial policies, and long-term planning horizons create systematic advantages in emerging fields like renewable energy, electric vehicles, and artificial intelligence. While this approach has limitations, it demonstrates that alternative models can compete effectively with American technological dominance.

SOCIAL FRAGMENTATION: THE TRUST CRISIS

American society exhibits dangerous levels of fragmentation that threaten democratic governance and social cohesion. Trust in institutions has declined precipitously across all major categories. Only 7% of Americans express "a great deal" of confidence in Congress, while trust in media, courts, and even elections has reached historic lows.[9]

This trust deficit has practical consequences. When citizens don't believe in institutional legitimacy, democratic governance becomes nearly impossible. Policy implementation suffers when bureaucracies lack public confidence. Economic performance weakens when social capital, the networks of relationships and trust that facilitate cooperation, erodes.

Political polarization exacerbates these problems. Geographic sorting has created communities with increasingly homogeneous political views, while social media algorithms amplify extreme positions and conspiracy theories. The result is a society where different groups not only disagree on policy but inhabit completely different information ecosystems.

Violence indicators show concerning trends. The FBI reports that hate crimes reached a 12-year high in 2021, while domestic terrorism cases have increased substantially.[10] Political violence, once unthinkable in American politics, has become normalized in some communities. When political disagreement becomes existential conflict, democratic institutions cannot function effectively.

INTERNATIONAL ISOLATION: THE CREDIBILITY GAP

America's international influence has declined significantly since its post-Cold War peak. The Iraq War damaged American credibility regarding intelligence and military intervention. The 2008 financial crisis raised questions about American economic management. Recent political dysfunction, including the January 6th Capitol attack, has damaged America's democratic reputation globally.

Polling data reflects this credibility decline. Pew Research shows that global confidence in American leadership dropped from 64% under Obama to 20% under Trump, recovering only partially to 49% under Biden.[11] Even traditional allies express doubts about American reliability and judgment.

China's Belt and Road Initiative exemplifies how other countries are creating alternative international systems. With over $1 trillion committed to infrastructure projects across Asia, Africa, and Latin America, China offers economic development partnerships without the political conditions typically attached to American aid.[12] While these arrangements have their own problems, they provide alternatives to American-dominated institutions.

Regional powers increasingly pursue independent foreign policies rather than following American leadership. Turkey, a NATO ally, purchased Russian air defense systems despite American objections. Saudi Arabia, a traditional American partner, has strengthened relationships with China and Russia. Even European allies pursue "strategic autonomy" policies that reduce dependence on American decision-making.

THE PATH FORWARD: REFORM OR DECLINE

These trends point toward two possible futures: managed decline or transformative reform. Managed decline would involve gradual reduction of American global commitments as domestic pressures and international competition make current approaches unsustainable. This path would avoid catastrophic collapse but would also mean accepting reduced influence and living standards.

Transformative reform would require fundamental changes in priorities, policies, and approaches to both domestic and international challenges. Such reform would be difficult and politically contentious but could potentially reverse decline and create sustainable foundations for prosperity.

A REFORM AGENDA: TEN STRATEGIC PRIORITIES

Transformative reform requires systematic changes across multiple policy domains. The following ten priorities address the most critical challenges facing American society:

1. Fiscal Restructuring: Sustainable Public Finance

Current fiscal trajectory is unsustainable and must change. This requires both spending reforms and revenue increases. Defense spending offers the largest opportunities for reductions without compromising actual security needs. The U.S. spends more on defense than the next ten countries combined, yet faces no existential military threats requiring such massive expenditures.

A 25% reduction in defense spending would save approximately $200 billion annually while maintaining capabilities far exceeding any potential adversary. These resources could fund infrastructure improvements, educational investments, and debt reduction that would strengthen long-term competitiveness.

Revenue increases are also necessary. Tax rates on high incomes and wealth remain below historical levels and international standards. Closing tax loopholes and ensuring effective taxation of multinational corporations could generate

339

substantial additional revenue while improving economic efficiency.

2. Infrastructure Investment: Building Competitive Foundations

American infrastructure requires massive investment to maintain economic competitiveness. The American Society of Civil Engineers graded U.S. infrastructure a D+ in 2025, estimating $9.1 trillion needed in the next decade to address critical deficiencies.[13] This investment would create jobs, improve productivity, and provide foundations for sustained economic growth.

Priority areas include transportation networks, broadband communications, electrical grid modernization, and water systems. These investments have high economic returns and create employment in sectors that cannot be outsourced to other countries.

Financing could combine federal investment with innovative public-private partnerships. Infrastructure banks, long-term bonds, and user fees can spread costs over time while ensuring adequate funding for critical projects.

3. Educational Excellence: Developing Human Capital

Education represents the most important investment in long-term competitiveness. American educational performance has stagnated while other countries have systematically improved. The Programme for International Student Assessment (PISA) shows American 15-year-olds performing in the middle tier of developed countries in mathematics and science.[14]

Reform priorities include early childhood education, STEM programs, vocational training, and teacher development. Educational technology can improve access and effectiveness while reducing costs. Community colleges and trade schools deserve particular attention for providing practical skills needed in modern economies.

Higher education affordability has become a crisis, with student debt exceeding $1.7 trillion nationally.[15] Reform approaches could include expanded public funding, income-based repayment programs, and stronger accountability for educational outcomes.

4. Healthcare Efficiency: Improving Outcomes While Controlling Costs

American healthcare represents the most glaring policy failure among developed countries. The U.S. spends nearly twice as much per capita as other developed countries while achieving inferior health outcomes.[16] Administrative costs alone consume over $800 billion annually, more than most countries spend on entire healthcare systems.

Reform must address both coverage and cost issues. Universal coverage through single-payer or mixed systems could improve outcomes while reducing total costs. Price controls for prescription drugs, medical procedures, and insurance premiums could eliminate excessive profits that burden both individuals and the economy.

Healthcare employment represents over 12% of total jobs, so reforms must consider transition assistance for workers in eliminated administrative roles while expanding clinical and caregiving positions.

5. Climate Action: Avoiding Catastrophic Environmental Costs

Climate change represents an existential threat requiring immediate systematic action. The costs of inaction, sea level rise, extreme weather, agricultural disruption, and refugee flows, far exceed the costs of prevention. The military implications alone, as Pentagon analyses recognize, threaten national security through multiple pathways.[17]

Clean energy transition offers economic opportunities as well as environmental benefits. Renewable energy costs have declined dramatically, making clean technologies economically competitive with fossil fuels in many applications. Government policies can accelerate adoption while ensuring just transitions for affected communities.

International leadership on climate action could restore American soft power while addressing global challenges that affect all countries. Climate cooperation provides opportunities for constructive engagement even with strategic competitors.

6. Technology Policy: Maintaining Innovation Leadership

Maintaining technological leadership requires balancing security concerns with innovation needs. Export controls and investment restrictions may protect specific advantages but can also limit market access and technological development for American companies.

Immigration policy represents a critical tool for technological competitiveness. The U.S. has historically attracted global talent through educational opportunities and employment pathways. Visa restrictions and political hostility toward immigration undermine these advantages and benefit competitor countries.

Antitrust enforcement can prevent monopolization that stifles innovation while ensuring fair competition. Large technology platforms have acquired potential competitors and established market dominance that may limit technological development.

Research and development investment, both public and private, requires sustained support. Basic research particularly benefits from public funding since private companies cannot capture all returns from fundamental discoveries.

7. Campaign Finance Reform: Restoring Democratic Accountability

Political dysfunction partly results from campaign finance systems that prioritize wealthy donors and corporate interests over broader public preferences. Reform approaches could include public campaign financing, strict contribution limits, and transparency requirements for political spending.

Lobbying regulation needs strengthening to prevent undue influence by special interests. The Foreign Agents Registration Act (FARA) requires better enforcement to prevent foreign manipulation of American politics.

Electoral systems could benefit from reforms like ranked-choice voting, open primaries, and redistricting reforms that reduce gerrymandering. These changes could moderate political incentives and improve representation.

8. Criminal Justice Reform: Addressing Systemic Problems

American incarceration rates exceed all other developed countries, creating enormous social and economic costs. Mass incarceration disproportionately affects minority communities while failing to improve public safety. Reform approaches could include sentencing reform, drug decriminalization, police accountability measures, and rehabilitation programs.

These reforms could reduce costs while improving outcomes for both individuals and communities. Resources freed from excessive incarceration could fund education, mental health services, and economic development programs that address crime causes rather than just punishment.

9. Immigration Policy: Attracting Global Talent

Immigration has historically provided demographic, economic, and cultural advantages for the United States. Current policies often drive away talented individuals who could contribute to American prosperity and innovation.

Reform priorities include expanded high-skilled immigration, pathways to legal status for undocumented residents, and humane asylum processes. Immigration benefits the economy through entrepreneurship, innovation, and demographic balance as American birth rates decline.

10. International Cooperation: Multilateral Problem-Solving

Global challenges require cooperative solutions that no country can achieve independently. Climate change, pandemic prevention, economic stability, and technological governance all benefit from multilateral approaches.

American leadership in international institutions could advance both American interests and global welfare. This requires accepting constraints on unilateral action in exchange for enhanced influence through legitimate institutions.

THE COSTA RICA MODEL: DEMILITARIZATION SUCCESS

Costa Rica provides a remarkable example of successful demilitarization and reallocation of resources. In 1948, following a civil war, Costa Rica abolished its military and redirected resources toward education, healthcare, and environmental protection.[18]

The results have been impressive. Costa Rica consistently ranks among the top countries globally in education, health outcomes, and environmental performance. GDP per capita has grown steadily, life expectancy exceeds that of the United States, and the country has achieved nearly 100% renewable electricity generation.[19]

Costa Rica's approach demonstrates that military spending is not necessary for either security or prosperity. The country has avoided the military coups, civil wars, and international conflicts that have plagued other Central American countries. Resources that would have gone to military spending have instead built human capital and sustainable development.

While Costa Rica's small size and geography provide advantages not available to larger countries, the basic principle remains valid: resources devoted to military purposes could often generate higher returns through productive investments in education, infrastructure, and environmental protection.

IMPLEMENTATION CHALLENGES AND POLITICAL REALITIES

These reforms face substantial political obstacles. Entrenched interests benefit from current arrangements and will resist changes that threaten their advantages. Defense contractors, healthcare companies, fossil fuel industries, and financial institutions have enormous political influence that they will use to prevent reforms.

Public opinion polling suggests that many Americans support individual reform elements, but comprehensive change requires sustained political coalitions that can overcome organized opposition. Building such coalitions requires combining immediate benefits with long-term vision.

International examples provide both hope and caution. Countries like Germany, Denmark, and South Korea have successfully reformed major policy areas, but change required decades of sustained effort and often occurred during crisis periods that created reform opportunities.

INDIVIDUAL ACTION: WHAT READERS CAN DO

While systematic reform requires political change, individuals can take meaningful action to support transformation:

Economic Choices: Divest from industries that profit from dysfunction—defense contractors, private prisons, fossil fuel companies. Support businesses that prioritize employee welfare, environmental responsibility, and community development.

Political Engagement: Support candidates who advocate for comprehensive reform rather than incremental changes that preserve fundamental problems. Participate in primary elections where reform candidates often face their greatest challenges.

Education and Advocacy: Learn about policy issues and communicate with others about the need for systematic change.

Social media, community organizations, and personal networks all provide opportunities to build support for reform.

Lifestyle Changes: Reduce consumption patterns that depend on unsustainable resource use. Support renewable energy, public transportation, and sustainable agriculture through personal choices that create market demand for better alternatives.

Community Building: Strengthen local institutions and relationships that can provide resilience during transition periods. Community organizations, mutual aid networks, and local governance structures all contribute to social capital that enables reform.

CHAPTER RECAP

The United States stands at a critical juncture where interconnected crises—unsustainable debt, technological competition, social fragmentation, and collapsing international credibility—threaten national viability, yet the scale of the challenges also creates rare political opportunities for transformative reform that addresses systemic problems rather than symptoms. Unlike previous moments of American crisis that could be resolved through increased military spending or diplomatic maneuvering, current challenges require fundamental restructuring of fiscal priorities, democratic institutions, and international relationships in ways that directly confront the imperial model that created these interconnected failures.

- **America faces interconnected crises requiring systematic reform** including unsustainable debt trajectories, technological competition from China, social fragmentation, and declining international credibility that together threaten long-term viability

- **Current fiscal policies are unsustainable** with federal debt exceeding 120% of GDP and interest payments approaching $1 trillion annually, constraining investment in productive infrastructure, education, and climate adaptation

- **Technological leadership faces unprecedented challenges** as China rapidly increases R&D investment while American visa restrictions and political tensions reduce access to global talent that historically drove innovation

- **Social trust has collapsed across institutions** with only 7% of Americans expressing confidence in Congress while political polarization creates incompatible information ecosystems that make democratic governance nearly impossible

- **International influence has declined significantly** as allies pursue independent policies, competitors offer alternative partnership models, and American credibility suffers from military failures and political dysfunction

- **Ten strategic reform priorities offer pathways to renewal** including fiscal restructuring, infrastructure investment, educational excellence, healthcare efficiency, climate action, technology policy, campaign finance reform, criminal justice reform, immigration policy, and international cooperation

- **Costa Rica's demilitarization provides a successful model** showing how redirecting military spending toward education, healthcare, and environmental protection can achieve superior outcomes in human development and economic growth

This chapter demonstrates that while American decline appears likely under current trajectories, transformative reform remains possible through systematic policy changes that address root causes rather than symptoms. The choice between managed decline and national renewal depends on Americans' willingness to confront entrenched interests and implement comprehensive reforms that prioritize long-term sustainability over short-term advantages.

CHAPTER 38:

THE FUTURE OF AMERICA

Empires don't fall in a day. They wither away in silence, in delusion, and in the dead weight of their own contradictions.

I learned that lesson not in a classroom at the Naval Academy, but looking at the dust-choked streets of Iraq during Desert Storm. There, along what would later be called "the highway of death," amid the roar of tanks and scattered carcasses of civilian cars, I saw the raw might of American power—hundreds of bases scattered like iron fists across the globe,[1] an economy that bent the world's trade and finance to its will, and an intelligence web of satellites and proxies that pierced every border, unseen and unaccountable.

We were the unchallenged giant, the self-proclaimed beacon of freedom and democracy. But even then, I glimpsed the fragility beneath the surface: locals who viewed us not as liberators but as occupiers, allies who whispered doubts about our endless interventions, and a growing sense that our "victories" sowed seeds of resentment that would one day bloom into isolation.

The United States today remains the most powerful nation in human history, militarily, financially, technologically, and culturally. Our military budget alone dwarfs the combined spending of the next ten countries.[2] We boast over 750 overseas bases, an economy intertwined with global systems that extract wealth from distant lands, and a surveillance apparatus unseen and unaccountable in its reach. With that dominance comes responsibility and costs, but we are failing in our responsibility to promote worldwide peace and cooperation, and the costs we have inflicted on others—shattered regions, displaced millions, manipulated markets—we now begin to inflict on ourselves.[3]

This book has chronicled the bloody footprint of U.S. imperialism: from the Middle East to Latin America, from

Southeast Asia to Africa, from the forced submission of sovereign nations to the manipulation of global markets and information. And always, beneath it, the myth of exceptionalism—the belief that we are always the good guys.

We are not.

I'm not a fortune teller and I don't have a crystal ball, but I do have a broad vision of what is happening in the world, and I have the examples of history. When you lay one over the other, the path is clear. It doesn't take clairvoyance to predict the future; it just takes not ignoring the facts and trends that are there in full view.

From a worldwide perspective, we are frequently the bad guys. If we stay on this path, we will suffer the same fate as every other empire that forgot its place in the human story.[4] Like a fortress built on sand, America's dominance looks invincible from afar, but it rests on contradictions: freedom preached abroad while control tightens at home, democracy exported through bombs while elections are bought by corporations.[5] In my years as a Marine officer and pilot, I proudly "defended" these ideals, echoing slogans like "Freedom isn't free." But deployments to the Philippines in 1989 and the Gulf in 1991 showed me the dissonance: grateful faces were rare, replaced by looks of resignation and distrust.

What I saw then has only intensified. Recent policies accelerate our isolation rather than address underlying weaknesses. Trade wars that cripple allies and inflate costs at home demonstrate how short-term thinking undermines long-term stability.[6] Immigration restrictions that reduce talent inflows while demanding global leadership reveal the contradiction at our empire's core.[7] Meanwhile, the Congressional Budget Office projects federal deficits equivalent to over 6% of GDP, with national debt climbing toward 100% of GDP, fueled by unchecked military spending that hollows out our future.[8]

This section peers into that future, peeling back the illusions we've examined throughout this book to reveal the ticking clock of decline. We'll revisit the warning signs: endless wars yielding diminishing returns, economic fragility masked by military brawn, a culture of surveillance turned inward, the hollow shell of democracy, moral bankruptcy on the global stage, and the fractures of internal division that threaten to shatter us from within. We'll examine the brain drain already underway, where the innovators who built our technological empire are fleeing to calmer shores, eroding our cognitive capital and innovation edge. Then, we'll confront the road ahead: a slow unraveling marked by global rejection, domestic unrest, cultural erosion, economic instability, and moral irrelevance, as nations turn to alternatives like China's coalitions and BRICS alliances.

But this isn't a tale of inevitable doom. Empires fall, but nations can evolve, *if* we have the courage to tell ourselves the truth and dismantle the myths that bind us.

How long can we call ourselves heroes while the world sees villains? The choice is ours, but it's getting late. In the pages that follow, we'll chart the precipice we teeter on and map a path back from the edge, one that honors the ideals we claim but rarely live by, transforming our republic from an empire in denial to a force for genuine good.

A BRIEF ACCOUNTING

This book has been a reckoning, a peeling back of the myths we tell ourselves to justify the American empire's march across the globe. As a Marine officer, I once stood on the deck of a carrier in the Western Pacific, believing we were the world's shield, delivering freedom with every sortie. But the faces in the countries I visited told a different story: fear, not gratitude; distrust, not liberation. The truth hit me like our missiles hit those people. Our actions, cloaked in ideals, have left a trail of ruin, and the cost is now coming home. Here, we tally that cost, drawing from the chapters of *We Are the Bad Guys* to lay bare the machinery of imperialism and its toll on the world and ourselves.

We began with "Part I: The American Bubble," exposing the illusion of American liberty and the geographic isolation that blinds us to global realities. At home, we boast of free speech and democracy, yet rank 57th in press freedom globally, behind nations we dismiss as "lesser."[9] Our elections, drowned in $14 billion of corporate money in 2024, mock the idea of a people's voice.[10] Meanwhile, we export "freedom" through regime change and sanctions, leaving nations like Venezuela and Cuba choked. Venezuela's GDP fell 65% from 2013 to 2023 under U.S. sanctions, pushing 7 million to flee.[11] As a pilot, I flew missions we called "support," but the bombed-out markets and refugee streams below told of control, not liberation.

Our examination of historical events, including the betrayals in the Middle East, reveals the human toll of our alliances and interventions. Since 9/11, U.S. wars in Iraq, Afghanistan, and beyond have cost $8 trillion and killed over 1 million people, including 400,000 civilians, detailed in Brown University's Costs of War.[12] In Iraq, our depleted uranium munitions left soil and water toxic, with cancer rates in Fallujah rising 15-fold since 2004.[13]

In 2025, we continue airstrikes in Syria, displacing 2 million more, while Yemen's U.S.-backed Saudi campaign has left 4 million homeless, and U.S.-backed Israel continues its unrelenting illegal occupation and genocide of Palestine.[14] These aren't accidents; they're the wages of empire, amplified by the pattern of Israeli actions like the AIPAC scandal and Unit 8200 surveillance that undermine our own security.

Economic coercion, as seen in cases from Haiti to Chile to Venezuela, binds the world to our will. The IMF and World Bank, led by the U.S., have saddled nations like Haiti with debt, $2.2

billion since 2000, tripling its burden while forcing austerity that cut healthcare access by 30%.[15] We sanction dissenters, freezing $300 billion in Russian assets in 2022, a move echoed in 2025 against Chinese firms, escalating trade tensions.[16] Our SWIFT system, controlling global finance, ensures compliance, or starvation. You can see this in Haiti's slums, where U.S. policies propped up elites while families scavenged for food.

The influence of Zionism, unpacked in the betrayals like the Lavon Affair and Pollard case, distorts our moral compass. U.S. aid to Israel, even in 2025, fuels occupation, with 60,000 Palestinian deaths in Gaza since 2023, per UN reports.[17] We veto UN resolutions calling for peace, shielding apartheid while preaching human rights.[18] In my service, I heard officers justify this as "strategic," but the blood on our hands betrays that lie. Our complicity undermines global trust, as 60% of the Global South now prefers China's model, per Pew 2025.[19]

The military-industrial complex, traced in "Part I: The American Bubble" and the broader driving forces, keeps this cycle spinning. Lockheed Martin and Raytheon reap billions while Congress approves ever larger defense budgets, dwarfing education and healthcare.[20]

Below is a snapshot of our interventions' toll:

Region	Cost ($T)	Deaths (Est.)	Displaced (M)	Source
Middle East	6.0	1,000,000	37	Costs of War, 2025[12]
Latin America	0.5	100,000	8	UNHCR, 2025[11]
Africa	1.0	200,000	5	UN, 2025[14]

This accounting isn't just numbers—it's lives, nations, and our own soul. We've spent trillions to dominate, yet face a world turning away, allies wavering, and a homeland fracturing under debt and division. The myth of exceptionalism has blinded us, but the ledger is clear: on the international stage, we are the bad guys. Change begins with facing that truth.

THE STAKES: REFORM OR IRRELEVANCE

The window for voluntary reform is narrowing. As domestic problems intensify and international competitors strengthen, the costs of maintaining current approaches will become prohibitive. Reform becomes more difficult as options narrow and crises intensify.

Historical precedents suggest that failing empires rarely reform successfully. More often, they continue existing approaches until external pressures or internal collapse forces change. The question is whether Americans have the wisdom and political capacity to choose reform before circumstances eliminate alternatives.

The choice is ours, but time is running out. We can choose transformation, or transformation will be forced upon us.

ENDNOTES

CHAPTER 1:

THE NATIONALISTIC BUBBLE

[1] United Nations. "Member States." 2023. https://www.un.org/en/about-us/member-states. Accessed September 6, 2025. Accessed September 06, 2025.

[2] National Geographic Society and Roper Public Affairs. "2002 Global Geographic Literacy Survey." Washington, DC: National Geographic Society, 2002.

[3] Defense Casualty Analysis System. "U.S. Military Casualties - Operation Enduring Freedom (OEF) Casualty Summary by Casualty Category." U.S. Department of Defense. Accessed September 6, 2025. https://dcas.dmdc.osd.mil/dcas/pages/report_oef_deaths.xhtml. Accessed September 6, 2025.

[4] Council on Foreign Relations and National Geographic Society. "U.S Adults' Knowledge About the World: A Survey on Global Literacy." 2019. https://www.cfr.org/report/us-adults-knowledge-about-world. Accessed September 6, 2025.

[5] Berlin, Isaiah. *Two Concepts of Liberty* Oxford University Press, 1958. Accessed September 14, 2025.

[6] Simons, Daniel J., and Christopher F. Chabris. "Gorillas in Our Midst: Sustained Inattentional Blindness for Dynamic Events." *Perception* 28, no. 9 (1999): 1059-1074. Accessed September 14, 2025.

[7] The Future of Free Speech. "Who in the World Supports Free Speech? Findings from a Global Survey." Nashville, TN: The Future of Free Speech, March 2025. https://futurefreespeech.org/wp-content/uploads/2025/03/Who-In-The-World-Supports-Free-Speech-The-Future-of-Free-Speech.pdf. Accessed October 04, 2025.

[8] Reporters Without Borders, "2023 World Press Freedom Index," 2023, https://rsf.org/en/index. Accessed September 14, 2025.

[9] Pew Research Center, "Restrictions on Religion Among the 25 Most Populous Countries," September 30, 2021, https://www.pewresearch.org/religion/2024/03/05/restrictions-on-religion-in-the-worlds-25-most-populous-countries-in-2021/. Accessed September 14, 2025.

[10] Economist Intelligence Unit, "Democracy Index 2023," 2023, https://www.eiu.com/n/campaigns/democracy-index-2023/. Accessed September 14, 2025.

[11] World Population Review. "https://worldpopulationreview.com/country-rankings/most-free-countries." 2025. Accessed September 14, 2025.

[12] Freedom House. "https://freedomhouse.org/report/freedom-world." 2025. Accessed September 14, 2025.

CHAPTER 2:

THE PATRIOTISM BUBBLE

[1] Eric Foner, The Fiery Trial: Abraham Lincoln and American Slavery (New York: W. W. Norton, 2010), 87-92, 156-164; Ellen Carol DuBois, Suffrage: Women's Long Battle for the Vote (New York: Simon & Schuster, 2020), 234-251; Martin Luther King Jr., "Letter from Birmingham Jail," April 16, 1963, in A Testament of Hope: The Essential Writings and Speeches of Martin Luther King, Jr., ed. James M. Washington (San Francisco: Harper & Row, 1986), 289-302.

[2] Twain, Mark. "The Czar's Soliloquy." *The North American Review* 180, no. 580 (March 1905): 321–326. https://archive.org/details/sim_north-american-review_1905-03_180_580/page/320/mode/2up. Accessed September 14, 2025.

[3] Thomas Jefferson, *The Declaration of Independence* (Philadelphia: Continental Congress, July 4, 1776).

[4] George Washington, "Farewell Address," September 19, 1796, in The Papers of George Washington, Retirement Series, vol. 4, ed. Dorothy Twohig (Charlottesville: University Press of Virginia, 1999), 319-320. For the scholarly interpretation, see: Joseph J. Ellis, His Excellency: George Washington (New York: Knopf, 2004), 234-235.

[5] James Madison to W. T. Barry, August 4, 1822, in The Writings of James Madison, vol. 9, ed. Gaillard Hunt (New York: G. P. Putnam's Sons, 1910), 103-104.

[6] Thomas Paine, *Common Sense* (Philadelphia: W. and T. Bradford, 1776), 5.

[7] Eric Hobsbawm, Nations and Nationalism Since 1780 (Cambridge: Cambridge University Press, 1990), 163-183; Robert O. Paxton, The Anatomy of Fascism (New York: Knopf, 2004), 41-84.

[8] Dwight D. Eisenhower, "Remarks at the Centennial Celebration Banquet of the National Education Association," April 4, 1957, Washington, DC, in Public Papers of the Presidents of the United States: Dwight D. Eisenhower, 1957 (Washington, DC: Government Printing Office, 1958), 225-226.

[9] Abraham Lincoln, *Gettysburg Address*, November 19, 1863, in *The Collected Works of Abraham Lincoln*, vol. 7, ed. Roy P. Basler (New Brunswick, NJ: Rutgers University Press, 1953), 23.

[10] Wendell Phillips, "Speech Before the Massachusetts Antislavery Society," January 28, 1852, in Speeches, Lectures, and Letters (Boston: Lee and Shepard, 1884), 13.

[11] Nancy Chang, Silencing Political Dissent: How Post-September 11 Anti-Terrorism Measures Threaten Our Civil Liberties (New York: Seven Stories Press, 2002), 45-78; David Cole, Enemy Aliens: Double Standards and Constitutional Freedoms in the War on Terrorism (New York: New Press, 2003), 112-135.

CHAPTER 3:

THE INFORMATION BUBBLE:

INTRODUCTION

[1] Mahzarin R. Banaji and Anthony G. Greenwald, *Blind Spot: Hidden Biases of Good People* (New York: Delacorte Press, 2013).

[2] Seph Fontane Pennock, "The Science of Persuasion: NLP Techniques for Effective Influence," Quenza (blog), accessed September 10,

2025, https://quenza.com/blog/nlp-techniques-for-influence/.
Accessed September 14, 2025.

[3] People Shift, "Cialdini's 6 Principles of Persuasion: A Simple Summary," People Shift, accessed September 10, 2025, https://people-shift.com/articles/cialdinis-6-principles-of-persuasion/ Accessed September 14, 2025.

[4] Robert Jay Lifton, *Thought Reform and the Psychology of Totalism* (New York: Norton, 1961)

[5] Herbert A. Simon, "Designing Organizations for an Information-Rich World," in *Computers, Communications, and the Public Interest*, ed. Martin Greenberger (Baltimore: Johns Hopkins Press, 1971), 40-41.

[6] David Tigabu, "Colin Kaepernick and How Americans Feel About National Anthem Protests," *PRRI Spotlight*, September 15, 2018, https://www.prri.org/spotlight/colin-kaepernick-nike-americans-feel-about-national-anthem-protests-stats/ Accessed September 14, 2025.

[7] "Four Years Later, Roger Goodell Says He Wishes He'd Listened to Colin Kaepernick," *Vanity Fair*, August 24, 2020, https://www.vanityfair.com/style/2020/08/roger-goodell-colin-kaepernick-comments. Accessed September 14, 2025.

[8] *Encyclopaedia Britannica*, s.v. "Pentagon Papers," last modified August 1, 2025, https://www.britannica.com/topic/Pentagon-Papers. Accessed September 14, 2025.

[9] "The Pentagon Papers Case Today," *Harvard Law School*, June 21, 2021, https://hls.harvard.edu/today/the-pentagon-papers-case-today/, Accessed September 14, 2025.

CHAPTER 4:

THE INFORMATION BUBBLE:

MANIPULATION

[1] For analysis of intelligence failures across multiple countries, see: Charles Duelfer, Comprehensive Report of the Special Advisor to the DCI on Iraq's WMD (Washington, DC: Central Intelligence Agency, 2004); Brigadier General Shlomo Brom, "The War in Iraq: An Intelligence Failure," Strategic Assessment, November 2003.

[2] U.S. Customs and Border Protection, Report of Investigation: Mounted Border Patrol Agents, July 8, 2022.

[3] Lisa K. Fazio, Nadia M. Brashier, B. Keith Payne, and Elizabeth J. Marsh, "Knowledge does not protect against illusory truth," Journal of Experimental Psychology: General 144, no. 5 (2015): 993-1002.

[4] Rutgers University, "Nearly Half of Americans Still Unsure About Popular Vaccine Misinformation," Rutgers Today, February 15, 2022.

[5] U.S. Army, FM 3-05.301 Psychological Operations Process Tactics, Techniques, and Procedures (2003).

[6] David Ogilvy, Ogilvy on Advertising (New York: Vintage, 1983).

[7] Robert B. Cialdini, Influence: The Psychology of Persuasion, Revised edition (New York: Harper Business, 2006).

[8] For accurate analysis of Nazi propaganda techniques, see: Jeffrey Herf, The Jewish Enemy: Nazi Propaganda During World War II and the Holocaust (Cambridge, MA: Harvard University Press, 2006).

CHAPTER 5:

THE INFORMATION BUBBLE:

CONTROL

[1] Andrei Lankov, The Real North Korea: Life and Politics in the Failed Stalinist Utopia (Oxford University Press, 2013).

[2] James Griffiths, The Great Firewall of China: How to build and control an alternative version of the internet (Zed Books, 2019).

[3] Bipan Chandra et al., India's Struggle for Independence, 1857-1947 (New Delhi: Penguin Books, 1989).

[4] +972 Magazine, "Israel sees unprecedented spike in media censorship," May 2, 2025, https://www.972mag.com/israeli-military-censor-media-2024/, Accessed September 14, 2025.

[5] Daniel Boguslaw, "CNN runs Gaza coverage past Jerusalem team operating under shadow of IDF censor," The Intercept, January 4,

2024, https://theintercept.com/2024/01/04/cnn-israel-gaza-idf-censorship/, Accessed September 14, 2025.

6 Freedom House, "Freedom in the world 2023: Saudi Arabia," 2023, https://freedomhouse.org/country/saudi-arabia/freedom-world/2023, Accessed September 14, 2025.

7 Chicago Booth School of Business, "How media consolidation affects the news you see" (Mar 2025), https://www.chicagobooth.edu/review/how-media-consolidation-affects-news-you-see, Accessed September 14, 2025.

8 Revelio Labs, "Media consolidation is leaving middle America dry" (2024), https://www.reveliolabs.com/news/business/no-local-paper-and-no-local-journalists-media-consolidation-is-leaving-middle-america-dry, Accessed September 14, 2025.

9 University of North Carolina Hussman School of Journalism, The Expanding News Desert report (updated 2022), https://www.usnewsdeserts.com/reports/expanding-news-desert/loss-of-local-news/bigger-and-bigger-they-grow/, Accessed September 14, 2025.

10 Olivia Rubin, "What Fox News hosts allegedly said privately versus on-air about false election fraud claims," ABC News, Apr 24 2023, https://abcnews.go.com/Politics/fox-news-hosts-allegedly-privately-versus-air-false/story, Accessed September 14, 2025.

11 U.S. Senate Select Committee to Study Governmental Operations, Intelligence Activities and the Rights of Americans. Book II: Final Report (Washington, DC: U.S. Government Printing Office, 1976).

12 U.S. Senate Select Committee on Intelligence, Project MKUltra, the CIA's Program of Research in Behavioral Modification (Washington, DC: U.S. Government Printing Office, 1977).

13 Centers for Disease Control and Prevention, "U.S. Public Health Service Syphilis Study at Tuskegee," 2021.

14 Glenn Greenwald, No Place to Hide: Edward Snowden, the NSA, and the U.S. Surveillance State (New York: Metropolitan Books, 2014).

CHAPTER 6:

THE INFORMATION BUBBLE:

ILLUSIONS

[1] Siva Vaidhyanathan, Antisocial Media: How Facebook Disconnects Us and Undermines Democracy (Oxford University Press, 2018).

[2] Sam Levin, "Palestinian Harvard student says he was barred from US over friends' social media posts

," The Guardian, August 27, 2019, https://www.theguardian.com/education/2019/aug/27/palestinian-harvard-barred-us-friends-social-media, Accessed on September 11, 2025.

[3].S. Press Freedom Tracker, "CBP Agent Asks British Journalist Entering US If He's Part of the 'Fake News Media,'" U.S. Press Freedom Tracker, February 14, 2018, https://pressfreedomtracker.us/all-incidents/cbp-agent-asks-british-journalist-entering-us-if-hes-part-of-the-fake-news-media/, Accessed on September 11, 2025.

[4] Democracy Now!, "Israel Bars One of Its Most Prominent Critics, Norman Finkelstein, for Ten Years," Democracy Now!, May 29, 2008, https://www.democracynow.org/2008/5/29/israel_bars_one_of_its_most, Accessed on September 11, 2025.

[5] Reporters Without Borders, "US: Leaked database shows US government has been secretly monitoring journalists at the US-Mexico border," March 7, 2019, https://rsf.org/en/us-leaked-database-shows-us-government-has-been-secretly-monitoring-journalists-us-mexico-border, Accessed on September 11, 2025.

[6] Glenn Greenwald, No Place to Hide: Edward Snowden, the NSA, and the U.S. Surveillance State (New York: Metropolitan Books, 2014).

[7] The Intercept, "Canary Mission's Blacklist of Pro-Palestine Activists Is Taking a Toll", 2018, https://theintercept.com/2018/11/22/israel-boycott-canary-mission-blacklist/, Accessed on September 11, 2025.

CHAPTER 7:

THE PROPAGANDA BUBBLE

[1] Roger Daniels, Prisoners Without Trial: Japanese Americans in World War II (New York: Hill and Wang, 1993).

[2] Nectar Gan, "Netflix blockbuster '3 Body Problem' divides opinion and sparks nationalist anger in China," CNN, March 22, 2024.

[3] Fred Halliday, The Soviet Union and the Afghan Revolution (New York: Oxford University Press, 1987).

[4] Douglas Kellner, Media Spectacle and the Crisis of Democracy: Terrorism, War, and Election Battles (Boulder, CO: Paradigm Publishers, 2005).

[5] Mark Hampton, "The Fourth Estate Ideal in Journalism History," in The Routledge Companion to News and Journalism, ed. Stuart Allan (London: Routledge, 2010), 19–29, https://commons.ln.edu.hk/sw_master/3196, Accessed on September 14, 2025.

[6] Robert W. McChesney, Rich Media, Poor Democracy: Communication Politics in Dubious Times (New York: New Press, 2015).

[7] "How the Media Iced Out Bernie Sanders & Helped Donald Trump Win," Democracy Now!, December 1, 2016, https://www.democracynow.org/2016/12/1/how_the_media_iced_out_bernie, Accessed on September 11, 2025.

[8] David Cole, Enemy Aliens: Double Standards and Constitutional Freedoms in the War on Terrorism (New York: New Press, 2003).

[9] George W. Bush, "President Delivers 'State of the Union,'" speech, U.S. Capitol, Washington, DC, January 29, 2002, The White House Archives, https://georgewbush-whitehouse.archives.gov/news/releases/2002/01/20020129-11.html, Accessed on September 11, 2025.

[10] Christina Zhao, " Alexandria Ocasio-Cortez Warns, 'World Is Going to End in 12 Years,' Reiterating Claims of Recent U.N. Climate Change Report,'" News Week, January 22, 2019, https://www.newsweek.com/alexandria-ocasio-cortez-climate-change-

world-will-end-12-years-un-report-1300873, Accessed on September 11, 2025.

[11] Tom Cohen, "GOP Lawmaker Warns of Terror Babies Plot," CNN, July 16, 2010, https://transcripts.cnn.com/show/acd/date/2010-08-11/segment/02, Accessed on September 7, 2025.

CHAPTER 8:

THE LIFESTYLE BUBBLE

[1] Helliwell, John F., Richard Layard, Jeffrey Sachs, and Jan-Emmanuel De Neve, eds. *World Happiness Report 2024*. New York: Sustainable Development Solutions Network, 2024.

[2] OECD. "Average annual hours actually worked per worker." OECD Employment Database, 2023.

[3] U.S. Census Bureau. "Health Insurance Coverage in the United States: 2023." September 2024.

[4] U.S. News & World Report, "Countries with the Longest and Shortest Life Expectancies," *U.S. News & World Report*, accessed September 14, 2025, https://www.usnews.com/news/best-countries/articles/countries-with-the-longest-and-shortest-life-expectancies, Accessed on September 14, 2025.

[5] Himmelstein, David U., et al. "Medical Bankruptcy: Still Common Despite the Affordable Care Act." *American Journal of Public Health* 109, no. 3 (2019): 431-433, https://pmc.ncbi.nlm.nih.gov/articles/PMC6366487/, Accessed on September 11, 2025.

[6] Federal Reserve. "Consumer Credit Outstanding." Statistical Release G.19, 2024.

[7] Mapping Police Violence. "Police Violence Report 2023." mappingpoliceviolence.org.

[8] World Population Review, "Safest Countries in the World 2025," accessed September 14, 2025, https://worldpopulationreview.com/country-rankings/safest-countries-in-the-world, Accessed on September 14, 2025.

[9] Woolf, Steven H., and Heidi Schoomaker. "Life Expectancy and Mortality Rates in the United States, 1959-2017." *JAMA* 322, no. 20 (2019): 1996-2016, https://jamanetwork.com/journals/jama/article-abstract/2756187, Accessed on September 11, 2025.

[10] Stockholm International Peace Research Institute. "SIPRI Military Expenditure Database 2024."

CHAPTER 9:

THE SELF-DETERMINATION BUBBLE

[1] Piff, Paul K., Michael W. Kraus, Stéphane Côté, Bonnie Hayden Cheng, and Dacher Keltner. "Having Less, Giving More: The Influence of Social Class on Prosocial Behavior." *Journal of Personality and Social Psychology* 99, no. 5 (2010): 771-784. https://doi.org/10.1037/a0020092, Accessed on September 11, 2025.

[2] Chetty, Raj, Nathaniel Hendren, Patrick Kline, Emmanuel Saez, and Nicholas Turner. "Is the United States Still a Land of Opportunity? Recent Trends in Intergenerational Mobility." *American Economic Review* 104, no. 5 (2014): 141-147. https://doi.org/10.1257/aer.104.5.141, Accessed on September 11, 2025.

[3] Chetty, Raj, David J. Deming, and John N. Friedman. "Diversifying Society's Leaders? The Determinants and Consequences of Admission to Highly Selective Colleges." *Opportunity Insights*, July 2023. https://opportunityinsights.org/wp-content/uploads/2023/07/CollegeAdmissions_Paper.pdf, Accessed on September 11, 2025.

[4] Pew Charitable Trusts. "Pursuing the American Dream: Economic Mobility Across Generations." The Pew Charitable Trusts, 2012. https://www.pew.org/~/media/legacy/uploadedfiles/pcs_assets/2012/pursuingamericandreampdf.pdf, Accessed on September 11, 2025.

[5] Mischel, Walter. *The Marshmallow Test: Mastering Self-Control*. New York: Little, Brown and Company, 2014.

[6] Watts, Tyler W., Greg J. Duncan, and Haonan Quan. "Revisiting the Marshmallow Test: A Conceptual Replication Investigating Links

Between Early Delay of Gratification and Later Outcomes." *Psychological Science* 29, no. 7 (2018): 1159-1177. https://doi.org/10.1177/0956797618761661, Accessed on September 11, 2025.

[7] Chetty, Raj, Matthew O. Jackson, Theresa Kuchler, Johannes Stroebel, Nathaniel Hendren, Robert B. Fluegge, Sara Gong, et al. "Social Capital I: Measurement and Associations with Economic Mobility." *Nature* 608 (2022): 108-121. https://doi.org/10.1038/s41586-022-04996-4, Accessed on September 11, 2025.

[8] National Center for Education Statistics. "Public School Revenue Sources." U.S. Department of Education, 2023. https://nces.ed.gov/programs/coe/indicator/cma, Accessed on September 11, 2025.

[9] U.S. Department of Education. "Title I and the Elementary and Secondary Education Act." Washington, DC: Department of Education, 2009. https://www2.ed.gov/policy/elsec/leg/esea02/index.html, Accessed on September 11, 2025.

[10] Dee, Thomas S., and Brian A. Jacob. "The Impact of No Child Left Behind on Student Achievement." *Journal of Policy Analysis and Management* 30, no. 3 (2011): 418-446. https://www.jstor.org/stable/23018959, Accessed September 14, 2025.

[11] Centers for Disease Control and Prevention. "Health, United States Report: Life Expectancy." Atlanta, GA: CDC, 2023. https://www.cdc.gov/nchs/nvss/life-expectancy.htm, Accessed on September 11, 2025.

[12] Alexander, Michelle. *The New Jim Crow: Mass Incarceration in the Age of Colorblindness*. New York: The New Press, 2010.

[13] Centers for Disease Control and Prevention. "Youth Risk Behavior Survey Data Summary & Trends Report: 2009-2019." Atlanta, GA: CDC, 2021. https://www.cdc.gov/healthyyouth/data/yrbs/index.htm, Accessed on September 11, 2025.

[14] U.S. Department of Health and Human Services. *Protecting Youth Mental Health: The U.S. Surgeon General's Advisory*. Washington, DC: HHS, 2021. https://www.hhs.gov/surgeongeneral/reports-and-publications/youth-mental-health/index.html, Accessed on September 11, 2025.

[15] Deloitte. *2023 Gen Z and Millennial Survey*. Deloitte Insights, 2023. https://www2.deloitte.com/global/en/pages/about-deloitte/articles/genzmillennialsurvey.html, Accessed on September 11, 2025.

[16] Hickman, Caroline, et al. "Climate Anxiety in Children and Young People and Their Beliefs About Government Responses to Climate Change: A Global Survey." *The Lancet Planetary Health* 5, no. 12 (2021): e863-e873. https://doi.org/10.1016/S2542-5196(21)00278-3, Accessed on September 11, 2025.

[17] Twenge, Jean M. *iGen: Why Today's Super-Connected Kids Are Growing Up Less Rebellious, More Tolerant, Less Happy—and Completely Unprepared for Adulthood*. New York: Atria Books, 2017.

[18] National Child Traumatic Stress Network. *Trauma Among Youth Experiencing Homelessness*. Los Angeles, CA, and Durham, NC: National Center for Child Traumatic Stress, 2017. https://www.nctsn.org/what-child-trauma-populations-risk/youth-who-experience-homelessness, Accessed on September 11, 2025.

[19] Tali Te'eni Harari, Yaron Sela, and Liad Bareket-Bojmel, "Gen Z during the COVID-19 Crisis: A Comparative Analysis of the Differences between Gen Z and Gen X in Resilience, Values and Attitudes," Current Psychology 42, no. 28 (October 1, 2023): 24223–24232, https://doi.org/10.1007/s12144-022-03501-4, Accessed September 14, 2025.

[20] E. Jane Costello, William Copeland, and Adrian Angold, "Trends in Psychopathology across the Adolescent Years: What Changes When Children Become Adolescents, and When Adolescents Become Adults?," *Journal of Child Psychology and Psychiatry* 52, no. 10 (October 2011): 1015–25, https://doi.org/10.1111/j.1469-7610.2011.02446.x, Accessed on September 11, 2025.

[21] Fineman, Stephen, Yiannis Gabriel, and David Sims. *Understanding Emotion at Work*. 2nd ed. London: SAGE Publications, 2010.

CHAPTER 10:

THE GOVERNMENT & TAXES BUBBLE

[1] OpenSecrets.org. "Cost of Election." Center for Responsive Politics, 2024. https://www.opensecrets.org/elections-overview/cost-of-election, Accessed on September 11, 2025.

[2] Gilens, Martin, and Benjamin I. Page. "Testing Theories of American Politics: Elites, Interest Groups, and Average Citizens." *Perspectives on Politics* 12, no. 3 (2014): 564-581. https://doi.org/10.1017/S1537592714001595, Accessed on September 11, 2025.

[3] Reuters. "U.S. Political Ad Spending to Soar in 2024 with TV Media Biggest Winner: Report." Reuters, January 11, 2024. https://www.reuters.com/world/us/us-political-ad-spending-soar-2024-with-tv-media-biggest-winner-report-2024-01-11/, Accessed on September 11, 2025.

[4] OpenSecrets. "Winning vs. Spending in Congressional Elections." Center for Responsive Politics, 2024. https://www.opensecrets.org/elections-overview/winning-vs-spending, Accessed on September 11, 2025.

[5] Sharp, Jeremy M. *U.S. Foreign Aid to Israel*. Washington, DC: Congressional Research Service, 2024. https://crsreports.congress.gov/product/pdf/RL/RL33222, Accessed on September 11, 2025.

[6] OECD. *OECD Economic Surveys: Israel 2024*. Paris: OECD Publishing, 2024. https://www.oecd.org/en/publications/2024/12/oecd-economic-outlook-volume-2024-issue-2_67bb8fac/full-report/israel_f19fef21.html, Accessed September 14, 2025. Accessed on September 11, 2025.

[7] Rauch, Jonathan. *Government's End: Why Washington Stopped Working*. New York: PublicAffairs, 1999.

[8] U.S. Department of the Treasury. "Debt to the Penny." TreasuryDirect, 2025. https://www.treasurydirect.gov/NP_WS/debt/current Accessed on September 11, 2025.

9 U.S. Department of the Treasury. *Monthly Treasury Statement of Receipts and Outlays of the United States Government*. Washington, DC: U.S. Department of the Treasury, 2024. https://fiscal.treasury.gov/reports-statements/mts/ Accessed on September 11, 2025.

10 Congressional Budget Office. *The Distribution of Household Income, 2019*. Washington, DC: CBO, 2022. https://www.cbo.gov/publication/58533, Accessed on September 11, 2025.

11 Tax Policy Center. *An Analysis of the Tax Cuts and Jobs Act*. Washington, DC: Urban Institute & Brookings Institution, 2017. https://www.brookings.edu/articles/effects-of-the-tax-cuts-and-jobs-act-a-preliminary-analysis/, Accessed on September 11, 2025.

12 Hanson, Melanie. "How Much Would Free College Cost?" Education Data Initiative, Feruary 15, 2025. https://educationdata.org/how-much-would-free-college-cost Accessed on September 11, 2025, Accessed September 14, 2025.

13 Center for American Progress. *A Blueprint for Child Care Reform*. Washington, DC: Center for American Progress, 2018. https://www.americanprogress.org/article/blueprint-child-care-reform/, Accessed on September 11, 2025.

14 Jacobson, Mark Z., et al. "100% Clean and Renewable Wind, Water, and Sunlight All-Sector Energy Roadmaps for 50 United States." *Energy & Environmental Science* 8, no. 7 (2015): 2093-2117. https://doi.org/10.1039/C5EE01283J, Accessed on September 11, 2025.

CHAPTER 11:

THE MILITARY BUBBLE

1 Johnson, Chalmers. "America's Empire of Bases." *Harper's Magazine* 308, no. 1847 (2004): 31-42.

2 Vine, David. *The United States of War: A Global History of America's Endless Conflicts, from Columbus to the Islamic State*. Oakland: University of California Press, 2020.

3 U.S. Department of Defense. *Military and Civilian Personnel by Service/Agency by State/Country*. Washington, DC: Department of Defense, 2024. https://dwp.dmdc.osd.mil/dwp/app/dod-data-reports/workforce-reports, Accessed on September 11, 2025.

4 Stockholm International Peace Research Institute. *SIPRI Military Expenditure Database 2024*. https://sipri.org/databases/milex, Accessed on September 11, 2025.

5 Stockholm International Peace Research Institute. "Trends in World Military Expenditure, 2024." SIPRI Fact Sheet, April 2025. https://www.sipri.org/sites/default/files/2025-04/2504_fs_milex_2024.pdf, Accessed on September 11, 2025.

6 U.S. Government Accountability Office. *DOD Financial Management: Continued Efforts Needed to Improve Audit Readiness*. Washington, DC: GAO, 2023. https://www.gao.gov/products/gao-23-106864, Accessed on September 11, 2025.

7 United States Government Accountability Office. Military Readiness: Actions Needed to Further Implement the Strategy to Mitigate Challenges in the Management of the Basic Allowance for Housing Program. GAO-24-105750. Washington, DC: Government Printing Office, 2024.

8 Herring, George C. *America's Longest War: The United States and Vietnam, 1950-1975*. 4th ed. New York: McGraw-Hill, 2002, Accessed on September 11, 2025.

9 Special Inspector General for Iraq Reconstruction. *Hard Lessons: The Iraq Reconstruction Experience*. Washington, DC: U.S. Government Printing Office, 2009. https://apps.dtic.mil/sti/citations/ADA493696, Accessed on September 11, 2025.

10 Special Inspector General for Afghanistan Reconstruction. *Quarterly Report to the United States Congress*. Arlington, VA: SIGAR, October 2021. https://www.sigar.mil/Portals/147/Files/Reports/Quarterly-Reports/2021-07-30qr.pdf, Accessed on September 11, 2025.

11 Chivvis, Christopher S. *Toppling Qaddafi: Libya and the Limits of Liberal Intervention*. Cambridge: Cambridge University Press, 2014.

[12] Eisenhower, Dwight D. "Farewell Address to the Nation." January 17, 1961. Eisenhower Presidential Library. https://www.eisenhowerlibrary.gov/research/online-documents/farewell-address, Accessed on September 11, 2025.

[13] Stockholm International Peace Research Institute. "Trends in International Arms Transfers, 2023." SIPRI Fact Sheet, March 2024. https://www.sipri.org/sites/default/files/2024-03/fs_2403_at_2023.pdf ,Accessed on September 11, 2025.

[14] U.S. Government Accountability Office. *School Facilities: Condition of America's Public School Facilities*. Washington, DC: GAO, 2020. https://www.gao.gov/products/gao-20-494, Accessed on September 11, 2025.

[15] National Alliance to End Homelessness. *The State of Homelessness in America 2023*. Washington, DC: National Alliance to End Homelessness, 2023. https://endhomelessness.org/wp-content/uploads/2024/10/StateOfHomelessness_2023.pdf, Accessed on September 11, 2025.

[16] U.S. Department of the Treasury. *The Economics of Child Care Supply in the United States*. Washington, DC: U.S. Department of the Treasury, 2021. https://home.treasury.gov/system/files/136/The-Economics-of-Childcare-Supply-09-14-final.pdf, Accessed on September 11, 2025.

[17] Pollin, Robert, and Jeffrey Thompson. *The Economic Analysis of the Green New Deal*. Amherst, MA: Political Economy Research Institute, University of Massachusetts Amherst, 2019. https://prospect.org/topics/bonus-issue-2019-green-new-deal/, Accessed on September 11, 2025.

[18] Sharp, Jeremy M. *U.S. Foreign Aid to Israel*. Washington, DC: Congressional Research Service, 2024. https://crsreports.congress.gov/product/pdf/RL/RL33222, Accessed on September 11, 2025.

[19] National Priorities Project. *The Federal Budget in 2023: Where Does Your Tax Dollar Go?* Northampton, MA: National Priorities Project, 2023. https://www.nationalpriorities.org/analysis/2023/tax-day-2023/, Accessed on September 11, 2025.

CHAPTER 12:

THE LAW ENFORCEMENT BUBBLE

[1] U.S. Bureau of Labor Statistics, "National Census of Fatal Occupational Injuries in 2022," December 19, 2023, https://www.bls.gov/news.release/cfoi.nr0.htm, Accessed on September 12, 2025.

[2] U.S. Bureau of Labor Statistics, "National Census of Fatal Occupational Injuries in 2022."

[3] National Law Enforcement Officers Memorial Fund, "Law Enforcement Deaths in 2023," https://www.nleomf.org/facts-figures/law-enforcement-facts, Accessed on September 12, 2025.

[4] Anthony A. Braga and David Weisburd, "The Effects of Focused Deterrence Strategies on Crime: A Systematic Review and Meta-Analysis of the Empirical Evidence," *Journal of Research in Crime and Delinquency* 49, no. 3 (2012): 323-358.

[5] International Association of Fire Chiefs, "Fire Service-Based Emergency Medical Services," 2021, https://www.iafc.org/topics-and-tools/resources/resource/iafc-position-fire-based-emergency-medical-services, Accessed on September 12, 2025.

[6] Joyful Heart Foundation, "Eliminating the backlog of untested rape kits and preventing a backlog from ever occurring again," https://www.joyfulheartfoundation.org/our-work/policy-and-advocacy/end-the-backlog/, Accessed on September 12, 2025.

[7] Texas House of Representatives Investigative Committee, *Robb Elementary School Shooting Report*, July 2022, https://www.house.texas.gov/pdfs/committees/reports/interim/87interim/Robb-Elementary-Investigative-Committee-Report-update.pdf, Accessed on September 12, 2025.

[8] Marjory Stoneman Douglas High School Public Safety Commission, *Initial Report*, January 2019, http://www.fdle.state.fl.us/msdhs/commissionreport.pdf, Accessed on September 12, 2025.

[9] Frank Edwards, Hedwig Lee, and Michael Esposito, "Risk of Being Killed by Police Use of Force in the United States by Age, Race-Ethnicity, and Sex," *Proceedings of the National Academy of Sciences* 116, no. 34 (2019): 16793-16798.

[10] U.S. Department of Defense, "1033 Program Overview," https://www.dla.mil/Disposition-Services/Offers/Law-Enforcement/Program-FAQs/, Accessed on September 12, 2025.

[11] American Civil Liberties Union, *War Comes Home: The Excessive Militarization of American Policing*, 2014, https://www.aclu.org/publications/war-comes-home-excessive-militarization-american-police, Accessed on September 12, 2025.

[12] U.S. Department of Defense, "1033 Program Data," 2021.

[13] Federal Bureau of Investigation, "Crime in the United States, 2022," https://www.fbi.gov/news/press-releases/fbi-releases-2022-crime-in-the-nation-statistics, Accessed on September 12, 2025.

[14] OECD, "Government at a Glance 2023: Public Expenditure on Law Enforcement," https://www.oecd.org/content/dam/oecd/en/publications/reports/2023/06/government-at-a-glance-2023_da193b0d/3d5c5d31-en.pdf, Accessed on September 12, 2025.

[15] Institute for Justice, "Policing for Profit: The Abuse of Civil Asset Forfeiture," 2020, https://ij.org/report/policing-for-profit-3/, Accessed on September 12, 2025.

[16] United States Department of the Treasury. Treasury Forfeiture Fund Fiscal Year 2024 Performance and Accountability Report. Washington, DC: Office of Strategic Planning and Performance Management, 2024.

[17] Roy Walmsley, *World Prison Population List*, 13th ed., 2023, https://www.prisonstudies.org/world-prison-brief, Accessed on September 12, 2025.

[18] World Prison Brief, "Highest to Lowest—Prison Population Rate," 2023, https://www.prisonstudies.org/highest-to-lowest/prison_population_rate, Accessed on September 12, 2025.

[19] Brigette Sarabi and Edwin Bender, *The Prison Payoff: The Role of Politics and Private Prisons in the Incarceration Boom*, November

2000,
https://www.prisonpolicy.org/scans/Prison_Payoff_Report_WPP_200
0.pdf Accessed on September 12, 2025.

[20] Federal Bureau of Investigation, "Crime in the United States, 2022:
Clearance Rates,"
https://cde.ucr.cjis.gov/LATEST/webapp/#/pages/explorer/crime/crim
e-trend, Accessed on September 12, 2025.

[21] Federal Bureau of Investigation, "Crime in the United States, 2022:
Clearance Rates."

[22] Mapping Police Violence, "Police Violence Report 2023,"
https://mappingpoliceviolence.org Accessed on September 12, 2025.

[23] American Civil Liberties Union, "The War on Marijuana in Black and
White," 2013, https://www.aclu.org/report/war-marijuana-black-and-
white, Accessed on September 12, 2025.

CHAPTER 13:

ECONOMIC AND FINANCIAL IMPERIALISM

[1] Eric Toussaint, *The World Bank: A Critical Primer* (London: Pluto
Press, 2008), 12.

[2] Joseph E. Stiglitz, *Globalization and Its Discontents* (New York: W. W.
Norton, 2002), 38.

[3] John Perkins, *Confessions of an Economic Hit Man* (San Francisco:
Berrett-Koehler, 2004), 27.

[4] Barry Eichengreen, *Exorbitant Privilege: The Rise and Fall of the
Dollar and the Future of the International Monetary System* (Oxford:
Oxford University Press, 2011), 3.

[5] Benn Steil, *The Battle of Bretton Woods* (Princeton: Princeton
University Press, 2013), 64.

[6] Michael Hudson, *Super Imperialism: The Economic Strategy of
American Empire* (London: Pluto Press, 2003), 55.

[7] Ngaire Woods, *The Globalizers: The IMF, the World Bank, and Their Borrowers* (Ithaca: Cornell University Press, 2006), 42.

[8] John Perkins, *Confessions of an Economic Hit Man* (San Francisco: Berrett-Koehler, 2004), 68.

[9] Eric Toussaint and Damien Millet, *Debt, the IMF, and the World Bank: Sixty Questions, Sixty Answers* (New York: Monthly Review Press, 2010), 27.

[10] Joseph E. Stiglitz, *Globalization and Its Discontents* (New York: W. W. Norton, 2002), 39.

[11] Benn Steil, *The Battle of Bretton Woods* (Princeton: Princeton University Press, 2013), 89.

[12] Ngaire Woods, *The Globalizers: The IMF, the World Bank, and Their Borrowers* (Ithaca, NY: Cornell University Press, 2006), 52.

[13] Toussaint and Millet, *Debt, the IMF, and the World Bank*, 58.

[14] Sebastian Mallaby, "The Frothing Conspiracy Theorist," *The Washington Post*, January 30, 2005; "Confessions of an Economic Hit Man," *Boston Magazine*, February 2005 Accessed September 11, 2025.

[15] John Perkins, *Confessions of an Economic Hit Man* (San Francisco: Berrett-Koehler, 2004), 15.

[16] Eric Toussaint, *The World Bank: A Critical Primer* (London: Pluto Press, 2008), 45.

[17] Ngaire Woods, *The Globalizers: The IMF, the World Bank, and Their Borrowers* (Ithaca, NY: Cornell University Press, 2006), 59.

[18] Benn Steil, *The Battle of Bretton Woods* (Princeton: Princeton University Press, 2013), 152.

[19] Joseph E. Stiglitz, *Globalization and Its Discontents* (New York: W. W. Norton, 2002), 57.

[20] Michael Hudson, *Killing the Host: How Financial Parasites and Debt Destroy the Global Economy* (Petoskey, MI: CounterPunch Books, 2015), 113.

[21] John Perkins, *Confessions of an Economic Hit Man* (San Francisco: Berrett-Koehler, 2004), 34.

[22] Eric Toussaint and Damien Millet, *Debt, the IMF, and the World Bank: Sixty Questions, Sixty Answers* (New York: Monthly Review Press, 2010), 38.

[23] Joseph E. Stiglitz, *Globalization and Its Discontents* (New York: W. W. Norton, 2002), 44.

[24] Michael Hudson, *Super Imperialism: The Economic Strategy of American Empire* (London: Pluto Press, 2003), 68.

[25] Susan George, *A Fate Worse Than Debt* (London: Penguin, 1988), 119.

[26] David Harvey, *A Brief History of Neoliberalism* (Oxford: Oxford University Press, 2005), 77.

[27] John Perkins, *Confessions of an Economic Hit Man* (San Francisco: Berrett-Koehler, 2004), 25.

[28] Naomi Klein, *The Shock Doctrine: The Rise of Disaster Capitalism* (New York: Metropolitan Books, 2007), 115.

[29] Michael Witter and Kari Levitt, *Jamaica: The IMF and Structural Adjustment* (Kingston: University of the West Indies Press, 1992), 14.

[30] Yanis Varoufakis, *Adults in the Room: My Battle with Europe's Deep Establishment* (London: Bodley Head, 2017), 98.

[31] Stathis Kouvelakis, *The Greek Cauldron: The Left, the Crisis, and the Prospects for Change* (London: Verso, 2014), 77.

[32] Mark Weisbrot and Jeffrey Sachs, *Economic Sanctions as Collective Punishment: The Case of Venezuela* (Washington, DC: Center for Economic and Policy Research, 2019), 4.

33 Human Rights Watch, *Venezuela's Humanitarian Crisis: Severe Medical and Food Shortages, Inadequate and Repressive Government Response* (New York: HRW, 2016), 8.

34 Joy Gordon, *Invisible War: The United States and the Iraq Sanctions* (Cambridge, MA: Harvard University Press, 2010), 15.

35 Louis A. Pérez Jr., *Cuba and the United States: Ties of Singular Intimacy* (Athens: University of Georgia Press, 2003), 254.

36 Human Rights Watch, *"Maximum Pressure": U.S. Economic Sanctions Harm Iran's Right to Health* (New York: HRW, 2019), 3.

37 Chad P. Bown, *US-China Trade War Tariffs: An Up-to-Date Chart* (Washington, DC: Peterson Institute for International Economics, 2020).

38 Mary E. Lovely and Yang Liang, "Trump Tariffs Hurt U.S. Workers," *Peterson Institute for International Economics Policy Brief* (2018), 2.

39 Naomi Klein, *The Shock Doctrine: The Rise of Disaster Capitalism* (New York: Metropolitan Books, 2007), 215.

40 Naomi Klein, *The Shock Doctrine: The Rise of Disaster Capitalism* (New York: Metropolitan Books, 2007), 154.

41 Susan George, *A Fate Worse Than Debt* (London: Penguin, 1988), 97.

42 Joseph E. Stiglitz, *Globalization and Its Discontents* (New York: W. W. Norton, 2002), 106.

43 John Perkins, *Confessions of an Economic Hit Man* (San Francisco: Berrett-Koehler, 2004), 42.

44 Michael Hudson, *Killing the Host: How Financial Parasites and Debt Destroy the Global Economy* (Petoskey, MI: CounterPunch Books, 2015), 177.

45 Ha-Joon Chang, *Kicking Away the Ladder: Development Strategy in Historical Perspective* (London: Anthem Press, 2002), 13.

46 Timothy A. Wise, *Eating Tomorrow: Agribusiness, Family Farmers, and the Battle for the Future of Food* (New York: The New Press, 2019), 47.

[47] Chad P. Bown, *US-China Trade War Tariffs: An Up-to-Date Chart* (Washington, DC: Peterson Institute for International Economics, 2020).

[48] Susan K. Sell, *Private Power, Public Law: The Globalization of Intellectual Property Rights* (Cambridge: Cambridge University Press, 2003), 67.

[49] Public Citizen, *"The WTO COVID-19 TRIPS Waiver: Why It Matters"* (Washington, DC: Public Citizen, 2021).

[50] John Perkins, *Confessions of an Economic Hit Man* (San Francisco: Berrett-Koehler, 2004), 59.

[51] Joseph E. Stiglitz, *Globalization and Its Discontents* (New York: W. W. Norton, 2002), 114.

[52] Oliver Stuenkel, *The BRICS and the Future of Global Order* (Lanham, MD: Lexington Books, 2015), 14.

[53] Kevin Gallagher, *The BRICS and the Financing Mechanisms They Created* (Boston: Boston University Global Development Policy Center, 2016).

[54] "How Would a New BRICS Currency Affect the US Dollar?" *Investing News Network*, January 10, 2025, https://investingnews.com/brics-currency/, Accessed September 11, 2025.

[55] Ibid.

[56] Barry Eichengreen, *Exorbitant Privilege: The Rise and Fall of the Dollar and the Future of the International Monetary System* (Oxford: Oxford University Press, 2011), 5.

[57] Michael Hudson, *Killing the Host: How Financial Parasites and Debt Destroy the Global Economy* (Petoskey, MI: CounterPunch Books, 2015), 212.

[58] Patrick Bond, *BRICS: An Anti-Capitalist Critique* (London: Pluto Press, 2013), 67.

[59] Vijay Prashad, *The Darker Nations: A People's History of the Third World* (New York: New Press, 2007), 189.

[60] Michael Hudson, *Super Imperialism: The Economic Strategy of American Empire* (London: Pluto Press, 2003), 212.

[61] Naomi Klein, *The Shock Doctrine: The Rise of Disaster Capitalism* (New York: Metropolitan Books, 2007), 215.

[62] Joseph E. Stiglitz, *Globalization and Its Discontents* (New York: W. W. Norton, 2002), 122.

[63] John Perkins, *Confessions of an Economic Hit Man* (San Francisco: Berrett-Koehler, 2004), 25.

[64] Eric Toussaint and Damien Millet, *Debt, the IMF, and the World Bank: Sixty Questions, Sixty Answers* (New York: Monthly Review Press, 2010), 66.

CHAPTER 14:

DIGITAL AND SURVEILLANCE IMPERIALISM

[1] Shoshana Zuboff, *The Age of Surveillance Capitalism* (New York: PublicAffairs, 2019), 9.

[2] Tim Wu, *The Master Switch: The Rise and Fall of Information Empires* (New York: Vintage, 2010), 243.

[3] Yasha Levine, *Surveillance Valley: The Secret Military History of the Internet* (New York: PublicAffairs, 2018), 76.

[4] Glenn Greenwald, *No Place to Hide: Edward Snowden, the NSA, and the U.S. Surveillance State* (New York: Metropolitan Books, 2014), 31.

[5] Shoshana Zuboff, *The Age of Surveillance Capitalism*, 17.

[6] Yasha Levine, *Surveillance Valley: The Secret Military History of the Internet* (New York: PublicAffairs, 2018), 212.

[7] Shoshana Zuboff, *The Age of Surveillance Capitalism* (New York: PublicAffairs, 2019), 327.

[8] Ronald J. Deibert, *Black Code: Surveillance, Privacy, and the Dark Side of the Internet* (Toronto: Signal, 2013), 198.

[9] Evgeny Morozov, *To Save Everything, Click Here* (New York: PublicAffairs, 2013), 149.

[10] Edward Snowden, *Permanent Record* (New York: Metropolitan Books, 2019), 211.

[11] Glenn Greenwald, *No Place to Hide: Edward Snowden, the NSA, and the U.S. Surveillance State* (New York: Metropolitan Books, 2014), 4.

[12] Barton Gellman and Laura Poitras, "U.S., British Intelligence Mining Data from Nine U.S. Internet Companies in Broad Secret Program," *Washington Post*, June 6, 2013 Accessed September 11, 2025.

[13] Luke Harding, *The Snowden Files: The Inside Story of the World's Most Wanted Man* (London: Vintage, 2014), 215.

[14] Shoshana Zuboff, *The Age of Surveillance Capitalism* (New York: PublicAffairs, 2019), 347.

[15] Yasha Levine, *Surveillance Valley: The Secret Military History of the Internet* (New York: PublicAffairs, 2018), 287.

[16] Ward Churchill and Jim Vander Wall, *Agents of Repression: The FBI's Secret Wars Against the Black Panther Party and the American Indian Movement* (Boston: South End Press, 2002), 61.

[17] Shoshana Zuboff, *The Age of Surveillance Capitalism* (New York: PublicAffairs, 2019), 23.

[18] Nick Srnicek, *Platform Capitalism* (Cambridge: Polity, 2017), 45.

[19] Evgeny Morozov, *To Save Everything, Click Here* (New York: PublicAffairs, 2013), 102.

[20] Yasha Levine, *Surveillance Valley: The Secret Military History of the Internet* (New York: PublicAffairs, 2018), 241.

[21] Ronald J. Deibert, *Black Code: Surveillance, Privacy, and the Dark Side of the Internet* (Toronto: Signal, 2013), 219.

[22] Tim Wu, *The Master Switch: The Rise and Fall of Information Empires* (New York: Vintage, 2010), 255.

23 Philip N. Howard and Muzammil M. Hussain, *Democracy's Fourth Wave? Digital Media and the Arab Spring* (Oxford: Oxford University Press, 2013), 27.

24 Siva Vaidhyanathan, *Antisocial Media: How Facebook Disconnects Us and Undermines Democracy* (Oxford: Oxford University Press, 2018), 133.

25 Shoshana Zuboff, *The Age of Surveillance Capitalism* (New York: PublicAffairs, 2019), 285.

26 David Kirkpatrick, *The Facebook Effect: The Inside Story of the Company That Is Connecting the World* (New York: Simon & Schuster, 2010), 212.

27 Yochai Benkler, Robert Faris, and Hal Roberts, *Network Propaganda: Manipulation, Disinformation, and Radicalization in American Politics* (Oxford: Oxford University Press, 2018), 74.

28 Evgeny Morozov, *The Net Delusion: The Dark Side of Internet Freedom* (New York: PublicAffairs, 2011), 5.

29 Glenn Greenwald, *No Place to Hide: Edward Snowden, the NSA, and the U.S. Surveillance State* (New York: Metropolitan Books, 2014), 87.

30 Luke Harding, *The Snowden Files: The Inside Story of the World's Most Wanted Man* (London: Vintage, 2014), 223.

31 Siva Vaidhyanathan, *Antisocial Media: How Facebook Disconnects Us and Undermines Democracy* (Oxford: Oxford University Press, 2018), 179.

32 Shoshana Zuboff, *The Age of Surveillance Capitalism* (New York: PublicAffairs, 2019), 365.

33 Yasha Levine, *Surveillance Valley: The Secret Military History of the Internet* (New York: PublicAffairs, 2018), 142.

34 Spencer Ackerman, *Reign of Terror: How the 9/11 Era Destabilized America and Produced Trump* (New York: Viking, 2021), 189.

35 Marwa Fatafta, "Exporting Surveillance: U.S. and European Technologies in the Middle East," Access Now Policy Brief, 2019 Accessed September 11, 2025.

[36] Parminder Jeet Singh, "Digital Colonization: Facebook's Free Basics in Africa and Asia," *IT for Change* (2016) Accessed September 11, 2025.

[37] Shoshana Zuboff, *The Age of Surveillance Capitalism* (New York: PublicAffairs, 2019), 401.

[38] Yasha Levine, *Surveillance Valley: The Secret Military History of the Internet* (New York: PublicAffairs, 2018), 265.

[39] Rashida Richardson, Jason M. Schultz, and Kate Crawford, "Dirty Data, Bad Predictions: How Civil Rights Violations Impact Police Data, Predictive Policing Systems, and Justice," *New York University Law Review* 94 (2019): 21.

[40] Natasha Singer, "Palantir Knows Everything About You," *New York Times*, October 21, 2018 Accessed September 11, 2025.

[41] Ronald J. Deibert, *Black Code: Surveillance, Privacy, and the Dark Side of the Internet* (Toronto: Signal, 2013), 227.

[42] American Friends Service Committee, "Palantir Technologies Inc.," AFSC Investigate, accessed September 17, 2025, https://investigate.afsc.org/company/palantir-technologies. Accessed September 11, 2025.

[43] James Bamford, "How US Intelligence and an American Company Feed Israel's Killing Machine in Gaza," *The Nation*, April 12, 2024 Accessed September 11, 2025.

[44] "Palantir response to allegations over its complicity in war crimes amid Israel's war in Gaza," Business & Human Rights Resource Centre, https://www.business-humanrights.org/en/latest-news/palantir-response-to-the-allegations-over-its-complicity-in-war-crimes-amid-israels-war-in-gaza/, Accessed September 11, 2025.

[45] "Companies Profiting from the Gaza Genocide," American Friends Service Committee, https://afsc.org/gaza-genocide-companies, Accessed September 11, 2025.

[46] Ali Winston, "Palantir Has Secretly Been Using New Orleans to Test Its Predictive Policing Technology," *The Verge*, February 27, 2018 Accessed September 11, 2025.

[47] Shoshana Zuboff, *The Age of Surveillance Capitalism* (New York: PublicAffairs, 2019), 411.

[48] Glenn Greenwald, *No Place to Hide: Edward Snowden, the NSA, and the U.S. Surveillance State* (New York: Metropolitan Books, 2014), 198.

[49] Yasha Levine, *Surveillance Valley: The Secret Military History of the Internet* (New York: PublicAffairs, 2018), 243.

[50] Ronald J. Deibert, *Black Code: Surveillance, Privacy, and the Dark Side of the Internet* (Toronto: Signal, 2013), 276.

[51] Edward Snowden, *Permanent Record* (New York: Metropolitan Books, 2019), 257.

[52] Tim Wu, *The Master Switch: The Rise and Fall of Information Empires* (New York: Vintage, 2010), 302.

CHAPTER 15:

CULTURAL IMPERIALISM

[1] Edward Said, *Culture and Imperialism* (New York: Vintage, 1993), xix.

[2] Herbert Schiller, *Communication and Cultural Domination* (New York: International Arts and Sciences Press, 1976), 9.

[3] Joseph Nye, *Soft Power: The Means to Success in World Politics* (New York: PublicAffairs, 2004), 54.

[4] Ariel Dorfman and Armand Mattelart, *How to Read Donald Duck: Imperialist Ideology in the Disney Comic* (New York: International General, 1975), 14.

[5] Edward Said, *Culture and Imperialism* (New York: Vintage, 1993), 287.

[6] Roger Stahl, *Militainment, Inc.: War, Media, and Popular Culture* (New York: Routledge, 2010), 22.

[7] Toby Miller et al., *Global Hollywood 2* (London: British Film Institute, 2005), 8.

[8] Ariel Dorfman and Armand Mattelart, *How to Read Donald Duck: Imperialist Ideology in the Disney Comic* (New York: International General, 1975), 41.

[9] Herbert Schiller, *Communication and Cultural Domination* (New York: International Arts and Sciences Press, 1976), 15.

[10] Naomi Klein, *No Logo* (New York: Picador, 2000), 3.

[11] Benjamin Barber, *Consumed: How Markets Corrupt Children, Infantilize Adults, and Swallow Citizens Whole* (New York: W. W. Norton, 2007), 24.

[12] Herbert Schiller, *Communication and Cultural Domination* (New York: International Arts and Sciences Press, 1976), 52.

[13] Victoria de Grazia, *Irresistible Empire: America's Advance through Twentieth-Century Europe* (Cambridge: Harvard University Press, 2005), 112.

[14] Richard P. Tucker, *Insatiable Appetite: The United States and the Ecological Degradation of the Tropical World* (Berkeley: University of California Press, 2000), 178.

[15] Robert Phillipson, *Linguistic Imperialism* (Oxford: Oxford University Press, 1992), 47.

[16] Toby Miller et al., *Global Hollywood 2* (London: British Film Institute, 2005), 23.

[17] Edward Said, *Covering Islam: How the Media and the Experts Determine How We See the Rest of the World* (New York: Vintage, 1997), 12.

[18] Phillip Altbach, *Global Perspectives on Higher Education* (Baltimore: Johns Hopkins University Press, 2016), 91.

[19] Herbert Schiller, *Culture, Inc.: The Corporate Takeover of Public Expression* (New York: Oxford University Press, 1989), 14.

[20] Noam Chomsky, *Hegemony or Survival: America's Quest for Global Dominance* (New York: Metropolitan Books, 2003), 128.

[21] William Easterly, *The White Man's Burden: Why the West's Efforts to Aid the Rest Have Done So Much Ill and So Little Good* (New York: Penguin, 2006), 19.

[22] Gerald Sussman, *Branding Democracy: U.S. Regime Change in Post-Soviet Eastern Europe* (New York: Peter Lang, 2010), 44.

[23] Butler, Desmond, Jack Gillum, and Alberto Arce. "U.S. Secretly Created 'Cuban Twitter' to Stir Unrest." Associated Press, April 2, 2014. AP News. https://apnews.com/article/technology-cuba-united-states-government-5661cee3232a4fd09c930e1548861be3, Accessed September 11, 2025.

[24] Rajiv Shah, *Transforming Foreign Aid: U.S. Policy and the Future of Development* (Washington, DC: Brookings Institution Press, 2016), 62.

[25] Jack Gillum, "U.S. Secretly Created 'Cuban Twitter' to Stir Unrest," *Associated Press*, April 3, 2014.

[26] Francis Nyamnjoh, *Africa's Media: Democracy and the Politics of Belonging* (London: Zed Books, 2005), 122.

[27] Edward Said, *Covering Islam: How the Media and the Experts Determine How We See the Rest of the World* (New York: Vintage, 1997), 115.

[28] Edward Said, *Culture and Imperialism* (New York: Vintage, 1993), 287.

[29] Herbert Schiller, *Communication and Cultural Domination* (New York: International Arts and Sciences Press, 1976), 64.

[30] Naomi Klein, *No Logo* (New York: Picador, 2000), 134.

[31] Ariel Dorfman and Armand Mattelart, *How to Read Donald Duck: Imperialist Ideology in the Disney Comic* (New York: International General, 1975), 59.

[32] Phillip Altbach, *Global Perspectives on Higher Education* (Baltimore: Johns Hopkins University Press, 2016), 103.

[33] Robert Phillipson, *Linguistic Imperialism* (Oxford: Oxford University Press, 1992), 183.

CHAPTER 16:

POLICING AND SECURITY IMPERIALISM

[1] Stuart Schrader, *Badges Without Borders: How Global Counterinsurgency Transformed American Policing* (Berkeley: University of California Press, 2019), 3.

[2] Kristian Williams, *Our Enemies in Blue: Police and Power in America* (Brooklyn: Soft Skull Press, 2004), 25.

[3] U.S. Department of State, *Bureau of International Narcotics and Law Enforcement Affairs: Fact Sheet*, 2021 Accessed September 11, 2025.

[4] Amnesty International, *Deadly Force: Police Use of Lethal Force in the United States*, 2015, and *Annual Human Rights Reports on U.S. Security Assistance Recipients*, 2018 Accessed September 11, 2025.

[5] Radley Balko, *Rise of the Warrior Cop: The Militarization of America's Police Forces* (New York: PublicAffairs, 2013), 229.

[6] Radley Balko, *Rise of the Warrior Cop: The Militarization of America's Police Forces* (New York: PublicAffairs, 2013), 8.

[7] "Federal Militarization of Law Enforcement Must End," American Civil Liberties Union, https://www.aclu.org/news/criminal-law-reform/federal-militarization-of-law-enforcement-must-end, Accessed September 11, 2025.

[8] "Ferguson's Police Got Free Military Gear Straight From The Pentagon," Talking Points Memo, August 14, 2014, https://talkingpointsmemo.com/dc/ferguson-missouri-militarized-police-1033-program, Accessed September 11, 2025.

[9] "Providing police with military gear does not reduce crime or protect officers: Studies," ABC News, December 9, 2020, https://abcnews.go.com/US/providing-police-military-gear-reduce-crime-protect-officers/story?id=74518923, Accessed September 11, 2025.

[10] ACLU, *War Comes Home: The Excessive Militarization of American Policing*, 2014, 5.

[11] Michelle Alexander, *The New Jim Crow: Mass Incarceration in the Age of Colorblindness* (New York: The New Press, 2010), 130.

[12] Stuart Schrader, *Badges Without Borders: How Global Counterinsurgency Transformed American Policing* (Berkeley: University of California Press, 2019), 11.

[13] Jeremy Kuzmarov, *Modernizing Repression: Police Training and Nation-Building in the American Century* (Amherst: University of Massachusetts Press, 2012), 42.

[14] Noam Chomsky and Edward Herman, *The Washington Connection and Third World Fascism* (Boston: South End Press, 1979), 129.

[15] Human Rights Watch, *Smoke and Mirrors: Colombia's Demobilization of Paramilitary Groups*, 2005 Accessed September 11, 2025.

[16] Amnesty International, *Bahrain: Tear Gas Misuse in Dispersing Protests*, 2012, and *Philippines: "If You Are Poor, You Are Killed"*, 2017 Accessed September 11, 2025.

[17] Martha Huggins, *Political Policing: The United States and Latin America* (Durham: Duke University Press, 1991), 214.

[18] P. W. Singer, *Corporate Warriors: The Rise of the Privatized Military Industry* (Ithaca: Cornell University Press, 2003), 49.

[19] Jeremy Scahill, *Blackwater: The Rise of the World's Most Powerful Mercenary Army* (New York: Nation Books, 2007), 239.

[20] Anna Leander, "The Market for Force and Public Security: The Destabilizing Consequences of Private Military Companies," *Journal of Peace Research* 42, no. 5 (2005): 606.

[21] Alleen Brown, Will Parrish, and Alice Speri, "Leaked Documents Reveal Counterterrorism Tactics Used at Standing Rock to 'Defeat Pipeline Insurgencies,'" *The Intercept*, May 27, 2017 Accessed September 11, 2025.

22 Stuart Schrader, *Badges Without Borders: How Global Counterinsurgency Transformed American Policing* (Berkeley: University of California Press, 2019), 211.

23 Human Rights Watch, " On Their Watch Evidence of Senior Army Officers' Responsibility for False Positive Killings in Colombia," June 24, 2015, https://www.hrw.org/report/2008/06/24/breaking-hourglass/increased-political-violence-against-afro-descendant-communities, Accessed September 12, 2025.

24 David Shirk, *The Drug War in Mexico: Confronting a Shared Threat* (New York: Council on Foreign Relations, 2011), 16.

25 Amnesty International, "Jamaica: A Long Road to Justice? Human Rights Violations under the State of Emergency," November 2011, https://www.amnesty.org/en/documents/amr38/004/2011/en/, Accessed January 15, 2025.

26 Michelle Alexander, *The New Jim Crow: Mass Incarceration in the Age of Colorblindness* (New York: The New Press, 2010), 112.

27 Stuart Schrader, *Badges Without Borders: How Global Counterinsurgency Transformed American Policing* (Berkeley: University of California Press, 2019), 274.

28 U.S. Department of State, "Anti-Terrorism Assistance Program Fact Sheet," Bureau of Counterterrorism, 2020, https://www.state.gov/wp-content/uploads/2024/05/ATA-Fact-Sheet-January-2024.pdf, Accessed September 12, 2025.

29 Jeremy Kuzmarov, *Modernizing Repression: Police Training and Nation-Building in the American Century* (Amherst: University of Massachusetts Press, 2012), 118.

30 Noura Erakat, *Justice for Some: Law and the Question of Palestine* (Stanford: Stanford University Press, 2019), 202.

31 Alex de Waal, *The Real Politics of the Horn of Africa: Money, War and the Business of Power* (Cambridge: Polity, 2015), 156.

32 Radley Balko, *Rise of the Warrior Cop: The Militarization of America's Police Forces* (New York: PublicAffairs, 2013), 243.

[33] Patrick Cockburn, *The Occupation: War and Resistance in Iraq* (London: Verso, 2006), 112.

[34] Anand Gopal, *No Good Men Among the Living: America, the Taliban, and the War through Afghan Eyes* (New York: Metropolitan Books, 2014), 198.

[35] Jeremy Kuzmarov, *Modernizing Repression: Police Training and Nation-Building in the American Century* (Amherst: University of Massachusetts Press, 2012), 156.

[36] Stuart Schrader, *Badges Without Borders: How Global Counterinsurgency Transformed American Policing* (Berkeley: University of California Press, 2019), 301.

[37] Radley Balko, *Rise of the Warrior Cop: The Militarization of America's Police Forces* (New York: PublicAffairs, 2013), 278.

[38] Jeremy Scahill, *Blackwater: The Rise of the World's Most Powerful Mercenary Army* (New York: Nation Books, 2007), 252.

[39] Michelle Alexander, *The New Jim Crow: Mass Incarceration in the Age of Colorblindness* (New York: The New Press, 2010), 144.

[40] Amnesty International, "Deadly Force: Police Use of Lethal Force in the United States," June 2015, https://www.amnestyusa.org/reports/deadly-force-police-use-of-lethal-force-in-the-united-states/, Accessed September 12, 2025.

[41] Human Rights Watch, "Smoke and Mirrors: Colombia's Demobilization of Paramilitary Groups," July 2005, https://www.hrw.org/report/2005/07/31/smoke-and-mirrors/colombias-demobilization-paramilitary-groups, Accessed September 12, 2025.

[42] Kristian Williams, *Our Enemies in Blue: Police and Power in America* (Brooklyn: Soft Skull Press, 2004), 322.

CHAPTER 17:

ENVIRONMENTAL IMPERIALISM

[1] Naomi Klein, *This Changes Everything: Capitalism vs. The Climate* (New York: Simon & Schuster, 2014), 78.

2 Neta C. Crawford, *Pentagon Fuel Use, Climate Change, and the Costs of War*, Watson Institute for International and Public Affairs, Brown University, June 12, 2019.

3 Protect Our Winters, "IPCC WGIII Report: The Time to Act Is Now," Protect Our Winters, accessed September 11, 2025, https://protectourwinters.org/ipcc-wgiii-report-the-time-to-act-is-now/, Accessed on September 12, 2025.

4 Bruce Rich, *Mortgaging the Earth: The World Bank, Environmental Impoverishment, and the Crisis of Development* (Boston: Beacon Press, 1994), 41.

5 Neta C. Crawford, *Pentagon Fuel Use, Climate Change, and the Costs of War*, Watson Institute for International and Public Affairs, Brown University, June 12, 2019.

6 David Vine, *Base Nation: How U.S. Military Bases Abroad Harm America and the World* (New York: Metropolitan Books, 2015), 7.

7 Michael Klare, *All Hell Breaking Loose: The Pentagon's Perspective on Climate Change* (New York: Metropolitan Books, 2019), 48.

8 Joseph Masco, *The Theater of Operations: National Security Affect from the Cold War to the War on Terror* (Durham: Duke University Press, 2014), 189.

9 U.S. Department of Defense, "Report on Effects of a Changing Climate to the Department of Defense," January 2019, https://media.defense.gov/2019/Jan/29/2002084200/-1/-1/1/CLIMATE-CHANGE-REPORT-2019.PDF, Accessed on September 12, 2025.

10 Michael Klare, *Resource Wars: The New Landscape of Global Conflict* (New York: Metropolitan Books, 2001), 29.

11 Antonia Juhasz, *The Tyranny of Oil: The World's Most Powerful Industry and What We Must Do to Stop It* (New York: HarperCollins, 2008), 197.

12 Vijay Prashad, *The Poorer Nations: A Possible History of the Global South* (London: Verso, 2012), 176.

[13] Mahmood Mamdani, *Saviors and Survivors: Darfur, Politics, and the War on Terror* (New York: Pantheon, 2009), 214.

[14] Naomi Klein, *This Changes Everything: Capitalism vs. The Climate* (New York: Simon & Schuster, 2014), 164.

[15] United Nations High Commissioner for Refugees, "Global Trends: Forced Displacement in 2021," June 2022, https://www.unhcr.org/publications/brochures/62a9d1494/global-trends-report-2021.html, Accessed on September 12, 2025.

[16] Naomi Klein, *This Changes Everything: Capitalism vs. The Climate* (New York: Simon & Schuster, 2014), 129.

[17] Todd Miller, *Storming the Wall: Climate Change, Migration, and Homeland Security* (San Francisco: City Lights, 2017), 46.

[18] U.S. Department of Defense, "2014 Climate Change Adaptation Roadmap," June 2014, https://www.war.gov/News/Releases/Release/Article/605221/dod-releases-2014-climate-change-adaptation-roadmap/, Accessed on September 12, 2025.

[19] Christian Parenti, *Tropic of Chaos: Climate Change and the New Geography of Violence* (New York: Nation Books, 2011), 198.

[20] Naomi Klein, *This Changes Everything: Capitalism vs. The Climate* (New York: Simon & Schuster, 2014), 194.

[21] Robert Brulle, "The Climate Lobby: A Sectoral Analysis of Lobbying Spending on Climate Change in the U.S., 2000–2016," *Climatic Change* 149 (2018): 289, https://link.springer.com/article/10.1007/s10584-018-2241-z, Accessed on September 12, 2025.

[22] "Trump finalizes plan to allow drilling on Arctic National Wildlife Refuge's coastal plain," *Washington Post*, August 17, 2020, https://www.washingtonpost.com/climate-environment/2020/08/17/trump-drilling-arctic-national-wildlife-refuge-alaska/, Accessed on September 12, 2025.

[23] "Forest Service Rejects Oil, Gas Leasing in Nevada's Ruby Mountains," Center for Biological Diversity, March 14, 2019, https://www.biologicaldiversity.org/news/press_releases/2019/ruby-

mountains-fracking-03-14-2019.php, Accessed on September 12, 2025.

[24] "Trump clears way for toxic mine in Boundary Waters watershed," The Wilderness Society, June 29, 2020, https://www.wilderness.org/articles/press-release/trump-clears-way-toxic-mine-boundary-waters-watershed, Accessed on September 12, 2025.

[25] Leah Stokes, *Short Circuiting Policy: Interest Groups and the Battle over Clean Energy and Climate Policy in the American States* (Oxford: Oxford University Press, 2020), 12.

[26] Neta C. Crawford, *Pentagon Fuel Use, Climate Change, and the Costs of War*, Watson Institute for International and Public Affairs, Brown University, June 12, 2019.

[27] Michael Maniates, "Individualization: Plant a Tree, Buy a Bike, Save the World?" *Global Environmental Politics* 1, no. 3 (2001): 31, https://www.mitpressjournals.org/doi/abs/10.1162/152638001316881395, Accessed on September 12, 2025.

[28] Naomi Klein, *This Changes Everything: Capitalism vs. The Climate* (New York: Simon & Schuster, 2014), 312.

[29] Michael Klare, *All Hell Breaking Loose: The Pentagon's Perspective on Climate Change* (New York: Metropolitan Books, 2019), 221.

[30] Todd Miller, *Storming the Wall: Climate Change, Migration, and Homeland Security* (San Francisco: City Lights, 2017), 132.

[31] Robert Brulle, "The Climate Lobby: A Sectoral Analysis of Lobbying Spending on Climate Change in the U.S., 2000–2016," *Climatic Change* 149 (2018): 293, https://link.springer.com/article/10.1007/s10584-018-2241-z, Accessed on September 12, 2025.

[32] Christian Parenti, *Tropic of Chaos: Climate Change and the New Geography of Violence* (New York: Nation Books, 2011), 245.

[33] Neta C. Crawford, *Pentagon Fuel Use, Climate Change, and the Costs of War*, Watson Institute for International and Public Affairs, Brown University, June 12, 2019.

CHAPTER 18:

HAWAII

[1] Lilikala Kameʻeleihiwa, *Native Land and Foreign Desires: Pehea Lā E Pono Ai?* (Honolulu: Bishop Museum Press, 1992), 78-124. The Great Māhele formally divided Hawaiian lands in 1848, with approximately 28,000 acres awarded to Native Hawaiian commoners out of Hawaii's total 4 million acres. Most Native Hawaiians, unfamiliar with Western property concepts, failed to secure claims.

[2] Jonathan Kay Kamakawiwoʻole Osorio, *Dismembering Lāhui: A History of the Hawaiian Nation to 1887* (Honolulu: University of Hawaiʻi Press, 2002), 201-225. The 1887 constitution was forced on King Kalākaua by armed American businessmen, stripping the monarchy of executive power.

[3] U.S. Senate Committee on Foreign Relations, "Report on the Hawaiian Islands" (Blount Report), 53rd Congress, 2nd Session (Washington: Government Printing Office, 1894), https://catalog.hathitrust.org/Record/001261378 Accessed on September 12, 2025.

[4] Noenoe K. Silva, *Aloha Betrayed: Native Hawaiian Resistance to American Colonialism* (Durham: Duke University Press, 2004), 140-172. The Kūʻē Petitions gathered 21,269 signatures opposing annexation, representing over half the Indigenous adult population.

[5] Michael Dougherty, *To Steal a Kingdom: Probing Hawaiian History* (Waimanalo: Island Style Press, 2008), 187-201.

[6] Gavan Daws, *Shoal of Time: A History of the Hawaiian Islands* (Honolulu: University of Hawaii Press, 1968), 285-320. The "Big Five" corporations were C. Brewer & Co., Alexander & Baldwin, Castle & Cooke, American Factors (now Amfac), and Theo H. Davies & Co.

[7] U.S. Public Law 103-150, "Joint Resolution to acknowledge the 100th anniversary of the January 17, 1893 overthrow of the Kingdom of Hawaii," November 23, 1993, https://www.govinfo.gov/app/details/STATUTE-107/STATUTE-107-Pg1510, Accessed on September 12, 2025.

CHAPTER 19:

CUBA

[1] Robert A. Schwartz, "The Mob on the Island: Fulgencio Batista, U.S. Gangsters, and the Cuban Dictatorship," *Havana Review* 12, no. 3 (2011): 45-67.

[2] Hugh Thomas, *Cuba: The Pursuit of Freedom* (London: Picador, 1998), 924-958.

[3] Peter Wyden, *Bay of Pigs: The Untold Story* (New York: Simon & Schuster, 1979), 187-223.

[4] U.S. Senate Select Committee to Study Governmental Operations, "Alleged Assassination Plots Involving Foreign Leaders," November 1975 (Washington: U.S. Government Printing Office), 71-180.

[5] U.S. Department of State, memorandum from Deputy Assistant Secretary Lester D. Mallory, "The Decline and Fall of Castro," Secret, April 6, 1960, *Foreign Relations of the United States, 1958–1960, Cuba, Volume VI*, Document 499, Office of the Historian, U.S. Department of State, accessed September 12, 2025, https://history.state.gov/historicaldocuments/frus1958-60v06/d499. This memo states that every available means should be employed to "make the greatest inroads in denying money and supplies to Cuba, to decrease monetary and real wages, to bring about hunger, desperation and overthrow of the government."

[6] William M. LeoGrande and Peter Kornbluh, *Back Channel to Cuba: The Hidden History of Negotiations between Washington and Havana* (Chapel Hill: University of North Carolina Press, 2014), 412-445.

[7] United Nations General Assembly, "Necessity of ending the economic, commercial and financial embargo imposed by the United States of America against Cuba," Resolution 77/7, November 3, 2022, https://digitallibrary.un.org/record/4024066?v=pdf, Accessed on September 12, 2025.

[8] Maria Garcia, *Guantánamo: An American History* (New Haven: Yale University Press, 2014), 78-102.

CHAPTER 20:

PANAMA

[1] David McCullough, The Path Between the Seas: The Creation of the Panama Canal, 1870–1914 (New York: Simon & Schuster, 1977), 145-189.

[2] Ronn Pineo, Colombia and the United States: War, Unrest and Destabilization (New York: Routledge, 2003), 78-104.

[3] Walter LaFeber, The Panama Canal: The Crisis in Historical Perspective (New York: Oxford University Press, 1989), 28-45.

[4] Lawrence A. Yates, The U.S. Military Intervention in Panama: Origins, Planning, and Crisis Management, June 1987–December 1989 (Washington: U.S. Army Center of Military History, 2008), 23-34.

[5] Walter LaFeber, The Panama Canal: The Crisis in Historical Perspective (New York: Oxford University Press, 1978), 34-56.

[6] Theodore Roosevelt, Theodore Roosevelt: An Autobiography (New York: Macmillan, 1913), 518. Available at https://www.gutenberg.org/files/3335/3335-h/3335-h.htm, Accessed on September 12, 2025.

[7] Steve C. Ropp, Panamanian Politics: From Guarded Nation to National Guard (New York: Praeger, 1982), 45-67.

[8] Dana Priest, The Mission: Waging War and Keeping Peace with America's Military (New York: W. W. Norton, 2003), 234-256.

[9] Lesley Gill, The School of the Americas: Military Training and Political Violence in the Americas (Durham: Duke University Press, 2004), 145-167.

[10] Grace Livingstone, America's Backyard: The United States and Latin America from the Monroe Doctrine to the War on Terror (London: Zed Books, 2009), 178-201.

[11] John Dinges, Our Man in Panama: How General Noriega Used the United States—and Made Millions in Drugs and Arms (New York: Random House, 1990), 87-124. Dinges documented Noriega's

recruitment by the CIA in the 1950s while he was a student, continuing through his rise to power in the 1980s.

[12] Lawrence E. Walsh, Final Report of the Independent Counsel for Iran/Contra Matters (Washington: U.S. Government Printing Office, 1993), Volume 1, 234-267.

[13] U.S. District Court for the Southern District of Florida, United States v. Noriega, Case No. 88-0079-CR-HOEVELER, Sentencing Memorandum (Miami, 1992).

[14] Robert C. Harding, The History of Panama (Westport: Greenwood Press, 2006), 145-178.

CHAPTER 21:

VENEZUELA

[1] Gregory Wilpert, Changing Venezuela by Taking Power: The History and Policies of the Chávez Government (London: Verso, 2007), 78-124.

[2] Eva Golinger, The Chávez Code: Cracking U.S. Intervention in Venezuela (Havana: Editorial José Martí, 2005), 145-178.

[3] Barack Obama, "Executive Order 13692—Blocking Property and Suspending Entry of Persons Contributing to the Situation in Venezuela," Federal Register 80, no. 44 (March 11, 2015): 12747–51, https://www.federalregister.gov/documents/2015/03/11/2015-05677/blocking-property-and-suspending-entry-of-persons-contributing-to-the-situation-in-venezuela, Accessed on September 12, 2025.

[4] Donald J. Trump, "Statement from President Donald J. Trump Recognizing Venezuelan National Assembly President Juan Guaidó as the Interim President of Venezuela," The White House, January 23, 2019, https://trumpwhitehouse.archives.gov/briefings-statements/statement-president-donald-j-trump-recognizing-venezuelan-national-assembly-president-juan-guaido-interim-president-venezuela/, Accessed on September 12, 2025.

[5] U.S. Department of Justice, "Nicolás Maduro Moros and 14 Current and Former Venezuelan Officials Charged with Narco-Terrorism, Corruption, Drug Trafficking and Other Criminal Charges," Press Release, March 26, 2020, https://www.justice.gov/opa/pr/nicol-s-maduro-moros-and-14-current-and-former-venezuelan-officials-charged-narco-terrorism, Accessed on September 12, 2025.

[6] Mark Weisbrot and Jeffrey Sachs, "Economic Sanctions as Collective Punishment: The Case of Venezuela," Center for Economic and Policy Research, April 2019, https://cepr.net/images/stories/reports/venezuela-sanctions-2019-04.pdf ,Accessed on September 12, 2025.

[7] Jake Sullivan, "Remarks of National Security Adviser Jake Sullivan at the 54th Washington Conference on the Americas Luncheon," The White House Archives, May 7, 2024, https://bidenwhitehouse.archives.gov/briefing-room/speeches-remarks/2024/05/07/remarks-of-national-security-adviser-jake-sullivan-54th-washington-conference-on-the-americas-luncheon/, Accessed on September 12, 2025.

[8] *Imposing Tariffs on Countries Importing Venezuelan Oil*, Executive Order No. 14245, 90 Fed. Reg. [page] (Mar. 27, 2025., sec. 2(a), https://www.whitehouse.gov/presidential-actions/2025/03/imposing-tariffs-on-countries-importing-venezuelan-oil/ ,Accessed on September 15, 2025.

[9] International Trade Centre, "Trade Performance HS: Exports of Venezuela (2023)," Trade Competitiveness Map, accessed September 15, 2025, https://tradecompetitivenessmap.intracen.org/TP_EP_CI.aspx?RP=862&Yr=2023, Accessed September 14, 2025.

; U.S. Energy Information Administration, "U.S. Imports from Venezuela of Crude Oil (Thousand Barrels per Day), Monthly," EIA, accessed September 15, 2025, https://www.eia.gov/dnav/pet/hist/LeafHandler.ashx, Accessed September 14, 2025.

; U.S. Energy Information Administration, "Europe Brent Spot Price FOB (Dollars per Barrel)," EIA, release date July 23, 2025, accessed September 15, 2025, https://www.eia.gov/dnav/pet/hist/rbrted.htm, Accessed on September 15, 2025.

¹⁰ Steve Holland and Phil Stewart, "U.S. deploys warships near Venezuela to combat drug threats, sources say," *Reuters*, August 18, 2025, accessed September 15, 2025, https://www.reuters.com/world/americas/us-deploys-warships-near-venezuela-combat-drug-threats-sources-say-2025-08-18/, Accessed on September 15, 2025.

¹¹ Rebecca Santana, "Trump administration ends temporary deportation protection for 350,000 Venezuelans," *Associated Press*, February 3, 2025, https://apnews.com/article/b7e2213c50ee11fca54613702cdaa964 , Accessed on September 15, 2025.

CHAPTER 22:

IRAN

¹ Stephen Kinzer, All the Shah's Men: An American Coup and the Roots of Middle East Terror (Hoboken: John Wiley & Sons, 2008), 89-134.

² Stephen Kinzer, All the Shah's Men: An American Coup and the Roots of Middle East Terror (Hoboken: John Wiley & Sons, 2008), 178-201.

³ Stephen Kinzer, All the Shah's Men: An American Coup and the Roots of Middle East Terror (Hoboken: John Wiley & Sons, 2008), 87.

⁴ Nikki R. Keddie, Modern Iran: Roots and Results of Revolution (New Haven: Yale University Press, 2003), 231-267.

⁵ Gary Sick, All Fall Down: America's Tragic Encounter with Iran (New York: Random House, 1985), 234-289

⁶ Patrick E. Tyler, "Officers Say U.S. Aided Iraq Despite Use of Gas," New York Times, August 18, 2002, https://www.nytimes.com/2002/08/18/world/officers-say-us-aided-iraq-in-war-despite-use-of-gas.html, Accessed on September 12, 2025.

⁷ Lawrence E. Walsh, Final Report of the Independent Counsel for Iran/Contra Matters (Washington: U.S. Government Printing Office, 1993), Volume 1, 234-267.

⁸ U.S. Congress, "Boland Amendments to Foreign Assistance Appropriations Acts, 1982–1984," Congressional Record, https://www.congress.gov/search?q=%7B%22source%22%3A%22leg

islation%22%2C%22search%22%3A%22boland+amendment%22%7
D, Accessed on September 12, 2025.

[9] Oliver North and William Novak, Under Fire: An American Story (New York: HarperCollins, 1991), 345.

[10] Ray McGovern, "Pretexts for an Attack on Iran," Consortium News, May 15, 2019, https://consortiumnews.com/2019/05/15/pretexts-for-an-attack-on-iran/, Accessed on September 12, 2025.

[11] David Vine, The United States of War: A Global History of America's Endless Conflicts, from Columbus to the Islamic State (Berkeley: University of California Press, 2020), 234-267.

CHAPTER 23:

IRAQ

[1] Human Rights Watch, "Genocide in Iraq: The Anfal Campaign Against the Kurds," July 1993, https://www.hrw.org/report/1993/07/01/genocide-iraq/anfal-campaign-against-kurds, Accessed on September 12, 2025.

[2] Human Rights Watch/Middle East Watch, Endless torment: The 1991 uprising in Iraq and its aftermath (New York: HRW, June 1992).

[3] "Son Of Saddam: As Iraq's top Olympic official, Uday Hussein is accused of the torture and murder of athletes who fail to win," Sports Illustrated, March 24, 2003, https://vault.si.com/vault/2003/03/24/son-of-saddam-as-iraqs-top-olympic-official-uday-hussein-is-accused-of-the-torture-and-murder-of-athletes-who-fail-to-win, Accessed on September 12, 2025.

[4] "IOC Panel Proposes Sanctions for Iraq," Washington Post, May 8, 2003, https://www.washingtonpost.com/archive/sports/2003/05/08/ioc-panel-proposes-sanctions-for-iraq/e6b60554-13c8-40ec-9ce7-83c75b1fb603/, Accessed on September 12, 2025.

[5] Hussein Orders Son to Be Tried in Aide's Slaying, Los Angeles Times, November 21, 1988, archived by the Los Angeles Times, accessed September 12, 2025, https://www.latimes.com/archives/la-xpm-1988-11-21-mn-469-story.html, Accessed on September 12, 2025.

[6] U.S. Department of State, "Iraq," in *Country reports on human rights practices for 1997* (Washington: Government Printing Office, 1998), 1245-1267.

[7] Human Rights Watch/Middle East Watch, *Endless torment* (on the regime's 1991 post-war crackdown), 234-256.

[8] World Education News & Reviews, "Education in Iraq: Compulsory Until Age 12 Under Saddam Hussein's Regime," *WENR*, October 17, 2017, https://wenr.wes.org/2017/10/education-in-iraq, Accessed on September 11, 2025.

[9] "Empty classrooms and black market textbooks," ReliefWeb, December 16, 2016, https://reliefweb.int/report/iraq/empty-classrooms-and-black-market-textbooks Accessed on September 12, 2025. By 1987, Iraq's literacy rate had increased to 80%, up from 52% in 1977.

[10] Human Rights Watch, *Background on Women's Status in Iraq Prior to the Fall of the Saddam Hussein Government*, Human Rights Watch Briefing Paper, November 2003, pp. 1–2

[11] World Bank, *The Public Distribution System in Iraq: Reform options to improve efficiency, equity, and household welfare* (Washington: World Bank, 2012), 34-67.

[12] Congressional Research Service, Iraq's Economy: Past, Present, Future, CRS Report RL31944 (Washington, DC: U.S. Government Printing Office, June 3, 2003), 1, https://www.everycrsreport.com/reports/RL31944.html, Accessed on September 11, 2025.

[13] Stephen C. Pelletiere, *Iraq and the International Oil System: Why America Went to War in the Gulf* (Washington: Praeger, 2001), 89-124.

[14] Patrick E. Tyler, "Officers Say U.S. Aided Iraq Despite Use of Gas," *New York Times*, August 18, 2002, https://www.nytimes.com/2002/08/18/world/officers-say-us-aided-iraq-in-war-despite-use-of-gas.html, Accessed on September 12, 2025.

[15] Stephen C. Pelletiere, *Iraq and the International Oil System: Why America Went to War in the Gulf* (Washington: Praeger, 1990), 156-178.

[16] Lawrence Freedman and Efraim Karsh, *The Gulf Conflict, 1990–1991: Diplomacy and War in the New World Order* (Princeton: Princeton University Press, 1993), 234-289.

[17] "High Toll Seen Among Iraqi Forces in Gulf War," *Washington Post*, March 10, 1991.

[18] Project on Defense Alternatives, "The Wages of War: Iraqi Combatant and Noncombatant Fatalities in the 2003 Conflict," Cambridge, MA, 2003.

[19] Human Rights Watch, "Needless Deaths in the Gulf War: Civilian Casualties During the Air Campaign and Violations of the Laws of War," New York, 1991.

[20] The 1999 UNICEF study reported significant child mortality increases, but later research questioned the methodology and suggested possible data manipulation by the Iraqi government. See Tim Dyson and Valeria Cetorelli, "Changing views on child mortality and economic sanctions in Iraq: a history of lies, damned lies and statistics," *BMJ Global Health* 2, no. 2 (2017): e000311, https://gh.bmj.com/content/2/2/e000311, Accessed on September 12, 2025.

[21] Richard M. Garfield, "Morbidity and Mortality Among Iraqi Children from 1990 through 1998: Assessing the Impact of Economic Sanctions," *BMJ* 321, no. 7271 (2000): 1230–1235.

[22] International Monetary Fund, "Iraq: Statistical Appendix," IMF Country Report No. 01/132, 2001.

[23] Lesley Stahl, "Punishing Saddam," *60 Minutes*, CBS News, May 12, 1996.

[24] James Bamford, *A Pretext for War: 9/11, Iraq, and the Abuse of America's Intelligence Agencies* (New York: Doubleday, 2004), 267-298.

[25] Stephen C. Pelletiere, *Iraq and the International Oil System: Why America Went to War in the Gulf* (Washington: Praeger, 1990), 234-267.

[26] Stephen A. Carney, Allied Participation in Operation Iraqi Freedom (Washington, DC: Center of Military History, United States Army, 2011), CMH Pub 59–3–1, https://history.army.mil/portals/143/Images/Publications/catalog/59-3-1.pdf, Accessed on September 12, 2025.

[27] Gilbert Burnham et al., "Mortality after the 2003 invasion of Iraq: a cross-sectional cluster sample survey," *The Lancet* 368, no. 9545 (2006): 1421–1428.

[28] Kathleen Newland and Karen O'Donnell, The Iraqi Refugee Crisis: The Need for Action (Washington, DC: Migration Policy Institute, January 2008), 1, https://www.migrationpolicy.org/pubs/MPI-The_Iraqi_Refugee_Crisis_The_Need_for_Action_011808.pdf, Accessed on September 12, 2025.

[29] Special Inspector General for Iraq Reconstruction (SIGIR), *Hard Lessons: The Iraq Reconstruction Experience* (Washington: U.S. Government Printing Office, 2009), Chapter 1,

[30] Michael T. Klare, *Blood and Oil: The Dangers and Consequences of America's Growing Petroleum Dependency* (New York: Metropolitan Books, 2004), 134-167.

[31] Antonia Juhasz, *The Bush Agenda: Invading the World, One Economy at a Time* (New York: HarperCollins, 2006), 178-201.

[32] Matthew Weaver, "British and U.S. companies win Iraq oil contracts," The Guardian, June 30, 2008, https://www.theguardian.com/world/2008/jun/30/iraq.oil, Accessed on September 12, 2025.

[33] Charles Tripp, *A History of Iraq* (3rd ed.) (Cambridge: Cambridge University Press, 2007), 234-267.

[34] John J. Mearsheimer and Stephen M. Walt, *The Israel Lobby and U.S. Foreign Policy* (New York: Farrar, Straus and Giroux, 2007), 267-298.

[35] Gareth Porter, *Manufactured Crisis: The Untold Story of the Iran Nuclear Scare* (Charlottesville: Just World Books, 2014), 145-178.

[36] Scott Ritter, *Iraq Confidential: The Untold Story of the Intelligence Conspiracy to Undermine the UN and Overthrow Saddam Hussein* (New York: Nation Books, 2005), 298.

CHAPTER 24:

LIBYA

[1] The Borgen Project, "Education in Libya During and After Gaddafi," May 30, 2024, https://borgenproject.org/education-in-libya-gaddafi/, Accessed on September 12, 2025.

[2] The Borgen Project, "10 Facts About Life Expectancy in Libya," May 30, 2024, https://borgenproject.org/10-facts-about-life-expectancy-in-libya/, Accessed on September 12, 2025.

[3] National Center for Biotechnology Information, "Libyan National Health Services The Need to Move to Management-by-Objectives," Libyan Journal of Medicine, June 1, 2008, https://pmc.ncbi.nlm.nih.gov/articles/PMC3074293/ ,Accessed on September 12, 2025.

[4] Ibid.

[5] Ibid.

[6] Ibid.

[7] The Borgen Project, "Education in Libya During and After Gaddafi," May 30, 2024, https://borgenproject.org/education-in-libya-gaddafi/, Accessed on September 12, 2025.

[8] The Global Economy, "Libya Literacy rate," https://www.theglobaleconomy.com/Libya/literacy_rate/, Accessed on September 12, 2025.

[9] The Borgen Project, "Education in Libya During and After Gaddafi," May 30, 2024, https://borgenproject.org/education-in-libya-gaddafi/, Accessed on September 12, 2025.

[10] African Development Bank Group, "Libya Economic Outlook," July 1, 2024, https://www.afdb.org/en/countries/north-africa/libya/libya-economic-outlook, Accessed on September 12, 2025.

[11] Ibid.

[12] ISS African Futures, "Libya," https://futures.issafrica.org/geographic/countries/libya,/ Accessed on September 12, 2025.

[13] Multiple international sources confirm these per-capita income figures from official economic data.

[14] Google Groups, "Re:Beyond Emotions: Just the Record. Myths of the Gaddafi regime Explained," https://groups.google.com/g/usaafricadialogue/c/iDqMbP8nNxE, Accessed on September 12, 2025.

[15] Black Agenda Report, "Libya: Before and After Muammar Gaddafi," https://blackagendareport.com/libya-and-after-muammar-gaddafi, Accessed on September 12, 2025.

[16] Ibid.

[17] William Blum, *Killing Hope: U.S. Military and CIA Interventions Since World War II* (Monroe, ME: Common Courage Press, 2004).

[18] WikiLeaks, "Hillary Clinton Email Archive," April 2, 2011, https://wikileaks.org/clinton-emails/emailid/6528, Accessed on September 12, 2025.

[19] Ibid.

[20] Ibid.

[21] Ibid.

[22] Congressional Research Service, "Disarming Libya: Weapons of Mass Destruction," September 22, 2006, https://www.everycrsreport.com/reports/RS21823.html, Accessed on September 12, 2025.

23 Organisation for the Prohibition of Chemical Weapons, "Libya and the OPCW," https://www.opcw.org/media-centre/featured-topics/libya-and-opcw, Accessed on September 12, 2025.

24 United Nations, "About the Responsibility to Protect," https://www.un.org/en/genocide-prevention/responsibility-protect/about ,Accessed on September 12, 2025.

25 CBS News, "Clinton on Qaddafi: 'We Came, We Saw, He Died,'" October 20, 2011, https://www.cbsnews.com/news/clinton-on-qaddafi-we-came-we-saw-he-died/ ,Accessed on September 12, 2025.

26 African Development Bank Group, "Libya Economic Outlook," July 1, 2024, https://www.afdb.org/en/countries/north-africa/libya/libya-economic-outlook, Accessed on September 12, 2025.

27 Multiple international news organizations, including CNN, Reuters, and the BBC, have documented the existence of slave markets in Libya since 2017.

28 Mint Press News, "Wikileaks: Hillary Clinton Helped Topple Gadhafi While France & UK Fought Over Libya's Oil," March 28, 2016, https://www.mintpressnews.com/wikileaks-hillary-clinton-helped-topple-gadhafi-france-uk-fought-libyas-oil/215104/, Accessed on September 12, 2025.

29 Ibid.

CHAPTER 25:

NICARAGUA

1 Walter LaFeber, *Inevitable Revolutions: The United States in Central America*, 2nd ed. (New York: W.W. Norton & Company, 1993).

2 LaFeber, *Inevitable Revolutions*.

3 Marcelo Bucheli, *Bananas and Business: The United Fruit Company in Colombia, 1899–2000* (New York: NYU Press, 2005).

4 Stephen Kinzer, *Blood of Brothers: Life and War in Nicaragua* (Cambridge, MA: Harvard University Press, 2007).

5 LaFeber, *Inevitable Revolutions*.

[6] Kinzer, *Blood of Brothers*.

[7] John A. Booth and Thomas W. Walker, *Understanding Central America: Global Forces, Rebellion, and Change*, 6th ed. (Boulder, CO: Westview Press, 2015).

[8] Peter Kornbluh, *The Iran-Contra Scandal: The Declassified History* (New York: The New Press, 1993).

[9] Central Intelligence Agency, *Psychological Operations in Guerrilla Warfare*, leaked manual reported by The New York Times, October 1984.

[10] Inter-American Commission on Human Rights, *Gross Human Rights Violations in the Context of Social Protests in Nicaragua* (Washington, DC: OAS/IACHR, 2018), https://www.oas.org/en/iachr/reports/pdfs/Nicaragua2018-en.pdf, Accessed on September 12, 2025.

[11] Human Rights Watch, "Nicaragua: Crackdown on Critics Ahead of Election," June 22, 2021, https://www.hrw.org/news/2021/06/22/nicaragua-crackdown-critics-ahead-election, Accessed on September 12, 2025.

[12] Reuters, "Nicaragua Shuts Down Jesuit University in Latest Crackdown," August 16, 2023, https://www.reuters.com/world/americas/nicaragua-shuts-down-jesuit-university-latest-crackdown-2023-08-16/, Accessed on September 12, 2025.

[13] Associated Press, "Nicaragua Frees 222 Opponents of Ortega, Sends Them to US," February 9, 2023, https://apnews.com/article/politics-united-states-government-daniel-ortega-nicaragua-caribbean-6e407b6d8c1c278a022d40328aa4a828, Accessed on September 12, 2025.

[14] U.S. Congress, *Nicaragua Investment Conditionality Act of 2018*, Public Law 115-335; U.S. Congress, *RENACER Act*, Public Law 117-54, 2021.

[15] Office of the United States Trade Representative, "Nicaragua Trade Summary," https://ustr.gov/countries-regions/americas/nicaragua, Accessed on September 12, 2025.

CHAPTER 26:
HAITI

[1] Mary A. Renda, Taking Haiti: Military Occupation and the Culture of U.S. Imperialism, 1915–1940 (Chapel Hill: University of North Carolina Press, 2001).

[2] Renda, Taking Haiti.

[3] Raymond C. Offenheiser and Susan H. Holcombe, "Challenges and Opportunities in Haiti," The Nation 277, no. 11 (2003): 11–15.

[4] Hans Schmidt, The United States Occupation of Haiti, 1915–1934 (New Brunswick, NJ: Rutgers University Press, 1995).

[5] Robert Debs Heinl and Nancy Heinl, Written in Blood: The Story of the Haitian People, 1492–1995 (Boston: Houghton Mifflin, 1996), 646–58.

[6] Paul Farmer, The Uses of Haiti, rev. ed. (Monroe, ME: Common Courage Press, 2003), 102–10; Laurent Dubois, Haiti: The Aftershocks of History (New York: Metropolitan Books, 2012).

[7] Dubois, Haiti: The Aftershocks of History, 276–85; Farmer, The Uses of Haiti, 110–18.

[8] Farmer, The Uses of Haiti.

[9] United Nations Office of the High Commissioner for Human Rights, "Haiti: Over 5,600 killed in gang violence in 2024, UN figures show," January 7, 2025, https://www.ohchr.org/en/press-releases/2025/01/haiti-over-5600-killed-gang-violence-2024-un-figures-show, Accessed on September 12, 2025.

[10] United Nations Children's Fund (UNICEF), "Haiti's children under siege: The staggering rise of child abuse and recruitment by armed groups," February 7, 2025, https://www.unicef.org/press-releases/haitis-children-under-siege-staggering-rise-child-abuse-and-recruitment-armed-groups, Accessed on September 12, 2025.

[11] United Nations Security Council, Resolution 2699 (2023), https://documents-dds-

ny.un.org/doc/UNDOC/GEN/N23/237/74/PDF/N2323774.pdf
Accessed on September 12, 2025.

CHAPTER 27:

GUATEMALA

[1] Peter Chapman, Bananas: How the United Fruit Company Shaped the World (Edinburgh: Canongate, 2007).

[2] Piero Gleijeses, Shattered Hope: The Guatemalan Revolution and the United States, 1944–1954 (Princeton: Princeton University Press, 1991).

[3] Stephen Schlesinger and Stephen Kinzer, Bitter Fruit: The Story of the American Coup in Guatemala, rev. ed. (Cambridge, MA: Harvard University, David Rockefeller Center for Latin American Studies, 2005).

[4] Richard H. Immerman, The CIA in Guatemala: The Foreign Policy of Intervention (Austin: University of Texas Press, 1982).

[5] Stephen Kinzer, The Brothers: John Foster Dulles, Allen Dulles, and Their Secret World War (New York: Henry Holt and Company, 2013).

[6] Nick Cullather, Secret History: The CIA's Classified Account of Its Operations in Guatemala, 1952–1954 (Stanford: Stanford University Press, 1999).

[7] Schlesinger and Kinzer, Bitter Fruit.

[8] Schlesinger and Kinzer, Bitter Fruit.

[9] Greg Grandin, The Blood of Guatemala: A History of Race and Nation (Durham: Duke University Press, 2000).

[10] Commission for Historical Clarification, Guatemala: Memory of Silence (Guatemala City: UN-backed Truth Commission, 1999).

CHAPTER 28:

AFGHANISTAN

[1] Martin Ewans, Afghanistan: A Short History of Its People and Politics (New York: HarperCollins, 2002).

[2] Anthony Arnold, Afghanistan: The Soviet Invasion in Perspective (Stanford: Hoover Institution Press, 1983).

[3] M. Hassan Kakar, Afghanistan: The Soviet Invasion and the Afghan Response, 1979–1982 (Berkeley: University of California Press, 1995).

[4] U.S. Department of State, Soviet Invasion of Afghanistan (Washington, DC: Historical Office Bulletin, 1980).

[5] George Crile, Charlie Wilson's War: The Extraordinary Story of the Largest Covert Operation in History (New York: Grove Press, 2003).

[6] Crile, Charlie Wilson's War.

[7] Odd Arne Westad, The Global Cold War: Third World Interventions and the Making of Our Times (Cambridge: Cambridge University Press, 2005).

[8] Ahmed Rashid, Taliban: Militant Islam, Oil and Fundamentalism in Central Asia (New Haven: Yale University Press, 2000).

[9] Peter L. Bergen, The Osama Bin Laden I Know: An Oral History of Al Qaeda's Leader (New York: Free Press, 2006).

[10] GlobalSecurity.org, "Operation Enduring Freedom: Official Summary," U.S. Department of Defense, 2001.

[11] Special Inspector General for Afghanistan Reconstruction (SIGAR), *What We Need to Learn: Lessons from Twenty Years of Afghanistan Reconstruction* (Arlington, VA: SIGAR, August 2021), https://www.sigar.mil/Portals/147/Files/Reports/Lessons-Learned/SIGAR-21-46-LL.pdf ,Accessed on September 12, 2025.

[12] *Agreement for Bringing Peace to Afghanistan between the Islamic Emirate of Afghanistan ... and the United States of America*, February 29, 2020, § Title page and signatory page, U.S. Department of State, https://www.state.gov/wp-content/uploads/2020/02/Agreement-For-Bringing-Peace-to-Afghanistan-02.29.20.pdf, Accessed on September 15, 2025.

[13] Special Inspector General for Afghanistan Reconstruction, *What We Need to Learn: Lessons from Twenty Years of Afghanistan Reconstruction* (SIGAR-21-46-LL), August 2021: https://www.sigar.mil/Portals/147/Files/Reports/Lessons-Learned/SIGAR-21-46-LL.pdf ,Accessed on September 15, 2025.

CHAPTER 29:

ABOUT ZIONISM

[1] John J. Mearsheimer and Stephen M. Walt, *The Israel Lobby and U.S. Foreign Policy* (New York: Farrar, Straus and Giroux, 2007), 3-12.

[2] Grant F. Smith, *Big Israel: How Israel's Lobby Moves America* (Washington, DC: Institute for Research: Middle Eastern Policy, 2016), 15-28.

[3] Stephen J. Sniegoski, *The Transparent Cabal: The Neoconservative Agenda, War in the Middle East, and the National Interest of Israel* (Norfolk, VA: Enigma Editions, 2008), 45-67.

[4] James Petras, *The Power of Israel in the United States* (Atlanta: Clarity Press, 2006), 89-112.

[5] Robert I. Friedman, "The Israeli Lobby's Thought Police," *The Nation*, May 15, 1989.

[6] Greg Philo and Mike Berry, *More Bad News from Israel* (London: Pluto Press, 2011), 234-267.

[7] Rashid Khalidi, *Brokers of Deceit: How the US Has Undermined Peace in the Middle East* (Boston: Beacon Press, 2013), 67-89.

[8] Norman Finkelstein, *Beyond Chutzpah: On the Misuse of Anti-Semitism and the Abuse of History* (Berkeley: University of California Press, 2005), 123-145.

[9] Benny Morris, *The Birth of the Palestinian Refugee Problem Revisited* (Cambridge: Cambridge University Press, 2004), 234-289.

[10] Paul Findley, *They Dare to Speak Out: People and Institutions Confront Israel's Lobby* (Westport, CT: Lawrence Hill & Company, 1985), 167-189.

[11] Alison Weir, *Against Our Better Judgment: The Hidden History of How the U.S. Was Used to Create Israel* (CreateSpace Independent Publishing, 2014), 89-112.

[12] Max Blumenthal, *Goliath: Life and Loathing in Greater Israel* (New York: Nation Books, 2013), 234-267.

[13] Jeremy M. Sharp, *U.S. Foreign Aid to Israel* (Washington, DC: Congressional Research Service, 2023), https://crsreports.congress.gov/product/pdf/RL/RL33222 Accessed on September 12, 2025.

[14] Center for Strategic and International Studies, "U.S. Security Assistance to Israel," November 2023.

[15] Economic Policy Institute, "The State of Working America," 2024 edition.

[16] Institute for Research: Middle Eastern Policy, "U.S. Foreign Aid to Israel: The Numbers," 2024.

[17] Human Rights Watch, "A Threshold Crossed: Israeli Authorities and the Crimes of Apartheid and Persecution," April 2021.

[18] Amnesty International, "Israel's Apartheid Against Palestinians," February 2022.

[19] The Intercept, "How Does AIPAC Shape Washington? We Tracked Every Dollar," October 24, 2024, https://theintercept.com/2024/10/24/aipac-spending-congress-elections-israel/, Accessed on September 12, 2025.

[20] Common Dreams, "'Very Bad Sign for Democracy': AIPAC Has Spent Over $100 Million on 2024 Elections," September 6, 2024, https://www.commondreams.org/news/aipac-100-million, Accessed on September 12, 2025.

[21] OpenSecrets, "American Israel Public Affairs Committee Profile," https://www.opensecrets.org/orgs/american-israel-public-affairs-cmte/summary?id=D000046963, Accessed on September 12, 2025.

[22] Peter Baker and Michael D. Shear, "Trump Visits Western Wall," The New York Times, May 22, 2017,

https://www.nytimes.com/2017/05/22/world/middleeast/trump-israel-western-wall.html Accessed on September 12, 2025.

[23] Remarks by President Biden, First Lady Jill Biden, and Second Gentleman Douglas Emhoff at a Celebration of Jewish American Heritage Month, The White House Archives, May 16, 2023, https://bidenwhitehouse.archives.gov/briefing-room/speeches-remarks/2023/05/16/remarks-by-president-biden-first-lady-jill-biden-and-second-gentleman-douglas-emhoff-at-a-celebration-of-jewish-american-heritage-month/, Accessed on September 12, 2025.

[24] U.S. Department of State, "Secretary Antony J. Blinken and Israeli Prime Minister Netanyahu Remarks to the Press," May 25, 2021, U.S. Department of State, https://it.usembassy.gov/secretary-antony-j-blinken-and-israeli-prime-minister-benjamin-netanyahu/, Accessed on September 12, 2025.

[25] Mitchell Bard, *The Arab Lobby: The Invisible Alliance That Undermines America's Interests in the Middle East* (New York: Harper, 2010), 234-267.

[26] The Hill, "GOP lawmaker wears Israeli military uniform to Capitol Hill," October 13, 2023, https://thehill.com/homenews/house/4254384-brian-mast-israeli-military-uniform-capitol-hill/, Accessed on September 12, 2025.

[27] Washington Times, "Rep. Brian Mast dons Israeli military uniform in Capitol," October 13, 2023, https://www.washingtontimes.com/news/2023/oct/13/rep-brian-mast-dons-israeli-military-uniform-in-ca/, Accessed on September 12, 2025.

[28] Emily Harris, "Israelis Hope Obama-Netanyahu Rift Will Result In Change," WOSU Public Media, March 25, 2015, https://www.wosu.org/2015-03-25/israelis-hope-obama-netanyahu-rift-will-result-in-change, Accessed on September 12, 2025.

[29] Washington Post, "Netanyahu's Speech to Congress," March 3, 2015.

[30] Palestine Legal, *Anti-BDS Legislation* (Chicago: Palestine Legal, 2023), https://palestinelegal.org/righttoboycott, Accessed on September 12, 2025.

[31] American Civil Liberties Union, "Third Federal Court Blocks Anti-BDS Law as Unconstitutional," April 24, 2019, https://www.aclu.org/press-releases/third-federal-court-blocks-anti-bds-law-unconstitutiona,l Accessed on September 12, 2025.

[32] Foundation for Middle East Peace, "Constitutionality Issues & BDS Legislation," May 10, 2024, https://fmep.org/resource/constitutionality-issues-bds-legislation-expert-views/, Accessed on September 12, 2025.

[33] Al Jazeera, "Top US court refuses to review anti-BDS law," February 22, 2023, https://www.aljazeera.com/news/2023/2/21/top-us-court-refused-to-review-anti-bds-law-heres-what-it-means, Accessed on September 12, 2025.

[34] Lee, Trymaine. "Israel-Texas Anti-BDS Law: First Amendment Tests." The Intercept, December 17, 2018. Accessed September 15, 2025. https://theintercept.com/2018/12/17/israel-texas-anti-bds-law/, Accessed on September 12, 2025.

[35] DAWN, "Anti-BDS Laws in the U.S. Are an Unconstitutional Attack on Free Speech," April 21, 2022, https://dawnmena.org/anti-bds-laws-in-the-u-s-are-an-unconstitutional-attack-on-free-speech/, Accessed on September 12, 2025.

[36] National Coalition Against Censorship, "Anti-BDS Laws Move to Federal Courts," August 3, 2024, https://ncac.org/news/blog/anti-bds-laws-move-to-federal-courts, Accessed on September 12, 2025.

[37] Rosenberg, Eli. "Bahia Amawi Would Not Sign a Pro-Israel Pledge, and It Cost Her Her Job." Washington Post, December 18, 2018. https://www.washingtonpost.com/nation/2018/12/18/she-lost-her-school-job-after-refusing-sign-pro-israel-pledge-now-shes-filing-lawsuit/, Accessed on September 12, 2025.

[38] Mitchell Hamline Law Review, "A Look at the Rise of Anti-BDS Laws in the United States," September 3, 2024, https://mhlawreview.org/amicus-curiae/a-look-at-the-rise-of-anti-bds-laws-in-the-united-states/, Accessed on September 12, 2025.

[39] Eurasia Review, "Israel's Covert Economic Espionage Against Its Strategic Ally, US," June 7, 2024, https://www.eurasiareview.com/07062024-israels-covert-economic-

espionage-against-its-strategic-ally-us-oped/ ,Accessed on September 12, 2025.

[40] *Foreign Policy*, "Spy vs. Spy, America and Israel Edition," March 24, 2015, https://foreignpolicy.com/2015/03/24/spy_vs_spy_america_and_israel_edition/ Accessed on September 12, 2025.

[41] Glenn Greenwald, "How Israel Receives Weapons and Covers from the U.S.," *The Intercept*, August 19, 2014.

[42] Middle East Research and Information Project, "Israeli Spies in the US," May 8, 2017, https://merip.org/1986/01/israeli-spies-in-the-us/, Accessed on September 12, 2025.

[43] Prof. Hatem Bazian, "Israeli Spies Caught in the US-Top Three Cases," *Medium*, March 6, 2023, https://medium.com/@Prof.hatembazian/israeli-spies-caught-in-the-us-top-three-cases-ae9ef07a1da, Accessed on September 12, 2025.

[44] James Bamford, "Israel's War on American Student Activists," *The Nation*, November 21, 2023, https://www.thenation.com/article/world/israel-spying-american-student-activists/, Accessed on September 12, 2025.

[45] Ibid.

[46] Ibid.

[47] Ibid.

[48] Ibid.

[49] Ibid.

[50] Sludge, "Here Is All the Money AIPAC Spent on the 2024 Elections," January 24, 2025, https://readsludge.com/2025/01/24/here-is-all-the-money-aipac-spent-on-the-2024-elections/, Accessed on September 12, 2025.

[51] *The Intercept*, "How Does AIPAC Shape Washington?" October 24, 2024.

[52] Track AIPAC, "Track Your Congressmembers' Connections to the Israel Lobby," https://www.trackaipac.com/congress, Accessed on September 12, 2025.

[53] *Common Dreams*, "'Very Bad Sign for Democracy': AIPAC Has Spent Over $100 Million," September 6, 2024.

[54] AIPAC PAC, "The largest pro-Israel PAC in America," https://www.aipacpac.org/, Accessed on September 12, 2025.

[55] Politico. "AIPAC to Spend Big in Democratic Primaries to Back Pro-Israel Candidates." Politico, March 3, 2024. https://www.politico.com/news/2024/03/03/aipac-israel-spending-democratic-primaries-00144552, Accessed on September 12, 2025.

[56] Al Jazeera, "US bill to ban Israel boycotts faces right-wing backlash," May 5, 2025, https://www.aljazeera.com/news/2025/5/5/us-bill-to-ban-israel-boycotts-faces-right-wing-backlash-over-free-speech ,Accessed on September 12, 2025.

[57] Mearsheimer and Walt, *The Israel Lobby and U.S. Foreign Policy*, 167-234.

[58] Grant F. Smith, *Big Israel*, 89-156

[59] William A. Cook, *The Plight of the Palestinians* (New York: Palgrave Macmillan, 2010), 123-167.

[60] Joel Kovel, *Overcoming Zionism* (London: Pluto Press, 2007), 234-289.

[61] Steven Salaita, *The Uncultured Wars: Arabs, Muslims, and the Poverty of Liberal Thought* (London: Zed Books, 2008), 145-189.

[62] Jack G. Shaheen, *Reel Bad Arabs: How Hollywood Vilifies a People* (Northampton, MA: Olive Branch Press, 2001), 234-267.

[63] Ibid., 289-334.

[64] Chas W. Freeman Jr., *America's Continuing Misadventures in the Middle East* (Charlottesville, VA: Just World Books, 2016), 167-189.

[65] Richard Falk, *Palestine's Horizon: Toward a Just Peace* (London: Pluto Press, 2017), 123-145.

[66] James Petras, *The Power of Israel in the United States*, 234-289.

[67] Paul Findley, *They Dare to Speak Out*, 289-334.

CHAPTER 30:
AIPAC & U.S. GOVERNMENT

[1] John J. Mearsheimer and Stephen M. Walt, *The Israel Lobby and U.S. Foreign Policy* (New York: Farrar, Straus and Giroux, 2007).

[2] Grant F. Smith, *Big Israel: How Israel's Lobby Moves America* (Washington, DC: Institute for Research: Middle Eastern Policy, 2016).

[3] Mearsheimer and Walt, *The Israel Lobby and U.S. Foreign Policy*.

[4] "American Israel Education Foundation," OpenSecrets.org, https://www.opensecrets.org/orgs/american-israel-education-foundation/summary?id=D000046963, Accessed on September 12, 2025.

[5] "Pro-Israel," OpenSecrets.org, https://www.opensecrets.org/industries/indus.php?ind=Q05, Accessed on September 12, 2025.

[6] "United Democracy Project," OpenSecrets.org, https://www.opensecrets.org/political-action-committees-pacs/american-israel-public-affairs-cmte/C00797670/summary/2024, Accessed on September 12, 2025.

[7] Jeremy M. Sharp, "U.S. Foreign Aid to Israel," Congressional Research Service, updated November 16, 2023, https://crsreports.congress.gov/product/pdf/RL/RL33222, Accessed on September 12, 2025.

[8] "Israel: Country Health Profile 2021," OECD/European Observatory on Health Systems and Policies, https://www.oecd.org/en/countries/israel.html, Accessed on September 12, 2025.

[9] "Education Policy Outlook: Israel," OECD, https://www.oecd.org/content/dam/oecd/en/about/projects/edu/educati

on-policy-outlook/398023-Education-Policy-Outlook-Country-Profile-Israel.pdf, Accessed on September 12, 2025.

[10] "GDP per capita (current US$) - Israel," World Bank, https://data.worldbank.org/indicator/NY.GDP.PCAP.CD?locations=IL, Accessed on September 12, 2025.

[11] Avner Cohen, *Israel and the Bomb* (New York: Columbia University Press, 1998).

[12] "Israel Security Supplemental Appropriations Act, 2024," U.S. Congress, https://www.congress.gov/bill/118th-congress/house-bill/6126, Accessed on September 12, 2025.

[13] "Academic Freedom and Tenure: University of Illinois at Urbana-Champaign," *AAUP Bulletin* 101, no. 2 (2015): 52-71.

[14] " Laws Suppressing Boycotts of Israel Don't Prevent Discrimination — They Violate Civil Liberties," American Civil Liberties Union, https://www.aclu.org/news/free-speech/laws-suppressing-boycotts-israel-dont-prevent-discrimination-they-violate-civil, Accessed on September 12, 2025.

[15] l Saha News, "AIPAC's Meteoric Rise: From Obscurity to a Political Powerhouse," July 27, 2023, https://www.alsafanews.com/article/19914-aipacs-meteoric-rise-from-obscurity-to-a-political-powerhouse ,Accessed on September 12, 2025.

[16] Lerer, "How AIPAC Morphed into a Political Powerhouse."

[17] Alison Weir, *Against Our Better Judgment: The Hidden History of How the U.S. Was Used to Create Israel* (CreateSpace Independent Publishing, 2014); Grant F. Smith, *Big Israel: How Israel's Lobby Moves America* (Washington, DC: Institute for Research: Middle Eastern Policy, 2016).

CHAPTER 31:

PALESTINE AND GAZA

[1] Ilan Pappé, *The Ethnic Cleansing of Palestine* (Oxford: Oneworld Publications, 2006).

[2] Jonathan Schneer, *The Balfour Declaration: The Origins of the Arab-Israeli Conflict* (New York: Random House, 2010).

[3] United Nations General Assembly, "Assistance to Palestine Refugees," A/RES/302 (IV), December 8, 1949, https://docs.un.org/en/A/RES/302%20(IV) ,Accessed on September 12, 2025.

[4] Carter Center, "Final Report on Observing the Palestinian Legislative Council Elections," 2006, https://www.cartercenter.org/resources/pdfs/news/peace_publications/election_reports/palestine2006-ndi-final.pdf, Accessed on September 12, 2025.

[5] Hamas wins huge majority, Al Jazeera, January 26, 2006, https://www.aljazeera.com/news/2006/1/26/hamas-wins-huge-majority, Accessed on September 12, 2025.

[6] Benedetta Berti, *Armed Political Organizations: From Conflict to Integration* (Baltimore: Johns Hopkins University Press, 2013).

[7] Ronen Bergman, *Rise and Kill First: The Secret History of Israel's Targeted Assassinations* (New York: Random House, 2018).

[8] "Angered by Israel's Attack in Qatar, Arab Leaders Meet to Weigh Response." New York Times, September 15, 2025. https://www.nytimes.com/2025/09/15/world/middleeast/qatar-arab-leaders-israel.html, Accessed on September 15, 2025.

[9] Bergman, Ronen, and Farnaz Fassihi. "How Hamas Leader Ismail Haniyeh Was Killed in Iran." New York Times, August 4, 2024. https://www.nytimes.com/2024/08/01/world/middleeast/how-hamas-leader-haniyeh-killed-iran-bomb.html, Accessed on September 15, 2025.

[10] United Nations Office for the Coordination of Humanitarian Affairs (OCHA), "Hostilities in the Gaza Strip and Israel: Flash Update," https://www.ochaopt.org, Accessed on September 12, 2025.

[11] Samuel Glasstone and Philip J. Dolan, The Effects of Nuclear Weapons, 3rd ed. (Washington, DC: U.S. Department of Energy, 1977), accessed [Date], https://www.osti.gov/biblio/6852629, Accessed on September 12, 2025.

[12] Jeremy M. Sharp, "U.S. Foreign Aid to Israel," Congressional Research Service, updated November 16, 2023, https://crsreports.congress.gov/product/pdf/RL/RL33222 Accessed on September 12, 2025.

[13] Sharp, "U.S. Foreign Aid to Israel."

[14] Human Rights Watch, "A Threshold Crossed: Israeli Authorities and the Crimes of Apartheid and Persecution," 2021, https://www.hrw.org/report/2021/04/27/threshold-crossed/israeli-authorities-and-crimes-apartheid-and-persecution, Accessed on September 12, 2025.

[15] Committee to Protect Journalists, "Journalist Casualties in the Israel-Gaza War," https://cpj.org/2024/06/journalist-casualties-in-the-israel-gaza-war https://cpj.org/full-coverage-israel-gaza-war/, Accessed on September 12, 2025.

[16] Middle East Eye, "The 49 Times the US Used Veto Power Against UN Resolutions on Israel," November 20, 2024, https://www.middleeasteye.net/news/49-times-us-has-used-veto-power-against-un-resolutions-israel, Accessed on September 12, 2025.

[17] Sharp, "U.S. Foreign Aid to Israel."

[18] United Nations Office for the Coordination of Humanitarian Affairs, "Hostilities in the Gaza Strip and Israel | Flash Update #218," August 8, 2024, https://www.unocha.org/publications/report/occupied-palestinian-territory/humanitarian-situation-update-218-gaza-strip, Accessed on September 12, 2025.

CHAPTER 32:

LEBANON

[1] United Nations Interim Force in Lebanon, "UNIFIL Background," https://unifil.unmissions.org/unifil-background, Accessed on September 12, 2025.

[2] Amnesty International, "Israel/Lebanon: Evidence of War Crimes in Beirut," August 2006, https://www.amnesty.org/en/documents/mde02/033/2006/en/, Accessed on September 12, 2025.

[3] Human Rights Watch, "Fatal Strikes: Israel's Indiscriminate Attacks Against Civilians in Lebanon," August 2006, https://www.hrw.org/reports/2006/lebanon0806/ Accessed on September 12, 2025.

[4] United Nations Mine Action Service, "Lebanon: Cluster Bomb Impact Assessment," 2007, https://www.un.org/unispal/document/auto-insert-202156/, Accessed on September 12, 2025.

[5] Legal Agenda, Lebanon's Frontline Villages: 600 Days of Erasure, September 2, 2025, https://english.legal-agenda.com/lebanons-frontline-villages-600-days-of-erasure/, Accessed on September 12, 2025.

[6] Jeremy M. Sharp, "U.S. Foreign Aid to Israel: Overview and Developments since October 7, 2023," Congressional Research Service, May 28, 2025, https://www.everycrsreport.com/reports/RL33222.html, Accessed on September 12, 2025.

[7] Reuters (open access): "US has sent Israel thousands of 2,000-pound bombs since Oct. 7." https://www.reuters.com/world/us-has-sent-israel-thousands-2000-pound-bombs-since-oct-7-2024-06-28/, Accessed on September 12, 2025.

[8] U.S. Congress, "H.R. 8034 - Israel Security Supplemental Appropriations Act, 2024," https://www.congress.gov/bill/118th-congress/house-bill/8034, Accessed on September 12, 2025.

[9] The White House, "National Security Memorandum on Safeguards and Accountability With Respect to Transferred Defense Articles and Defense Services," February 8, 2024, https://bidenwhitehouse.archives.gov/briefing-room/presidential-actions/2024/02/08/national-security-memorandum-on-safeguards-and-accountability-with-respect-to-transferred-defense-articles-and-defense-services/, Accessed on September 12, 2025.

[10] The Times of Israel, "Trump Rips Up Biden Memo Aimed at Israel on Rights Abuses Using US Arms," February 25, 2025, https://www.timesofisrael.com/trump-rips-up-biden-memo-aimed-at-israel-on-rights-abuses-using-us-arms/, Accessed on September 12, 2025.

[11] Office of the High Commissioner for Human Rights, "UN Experts Alarmed by Israel-Lebanon Conflict, Strongly Condemn Escalation and Urge Immediate Protection for Civilians," September 30, 2024, https://www.ohchr.org/en/press-releases/2024/09/un-experts-alarmed-israel-lebanon-conflict-strongly-condemn-escalation-and,, Accessed on September 12, 2025.

[12] Edith M. Lederer, "UN Security Council Urges Ceasefire in Gaza, End to Civilian Suffering," Associated Press, June 10, 2024, https://apnews.com/article/gaza-ceasefire-un-security-council-e14ee5e3dc7e8e9a161f058f0381513d Accessed on September 12, 2025.

[13] "What Gaza Reveals About the Limits of American Power," Time Magazine, February 16, 2024, https://time.com/6696023/biden-gaza-israel-us/, Accessed on September 12, 2025.

CHAPTER 33:

WITH FRIENDS LIKE THIS. . .

[1] Tom Segev, 1967: Israel, the War, and the Year That Transformed the Middle East (New York: Metropolitan Books, 2007); Ian Black and Benny Morris, Israel's Secret Wars: A History of Israel's Intelligence Services (New York: Grove Press, 1991).

[2] Black and Morris, Israel's Secret Wars.

[3] James M. Ennes Jr., Assault on the Liberty: The True Story of the Israeli Attack on an American Intelligence Ship (New York: Random House, 1979).

[4] James Bamford, Body of Secrets: Anatomy of the Ultra-Secret National Security Agency (New York: Anchor Books, 2001).

[5] Ennes, Assault on the Liberty.

[6] Ennes, Assault on the Liberty.

[7] Bamford, Body of Secrets.

[8] Howard Blum, The Spy Who Knew Too Much: An Ex-CIA Officer's Quest Through a Legacy of Betrayal (New York: HarperCollins, 2022).

[9] Patrick Kingsley, "Jonathan Pollard, Spy for Israel, Lands in Israel to Hero's Welcome," The New York Times, December 30, 2020 https://www.nytimes.com/2020/12/30/world/middleeast/jonathan-pollard-israel-us-spy.html Accessed on September 12, 2025.

[10] George Tenet with Bill Harlow, At the Center of the Storm: My Years at the CIA (New York: HarperCollins, 2007).

[11] Kingsley, "Jonathan Pollard, Spy for Israel, Lands in Israel to Hero's Welcome."

[12] Scott Shane, "Pentagon Analyst Gets Prison Time in Israel Spy Case," The New York Times, January 21, 2006, https://www.nytimes.com/2006/01/20/politics/pentagon-analyst-gets-12-years-for-disclosing-data.html, Accessed on September 12, 2025.

[13] Adam Entous and Danny Yadron, "Israel Spied on Iran Talks with U.S.," *The Wall Street Journal*, March 23, 2015, https://www.wsj.com/articles/israel-spied-on-iran-talks-1427164201, Accessed on September 12, 2025.

CHAPTER 34:

THE WARNING OF HISTORY

[1] Edward Gibbon, The History of the Decline and Fall of the Roman Empire, vol. 1 (London: Strahan & Cadell, 1776), 89-102.

[2] Edward Gibbon, The History of the Decline and Fall of the Roman Empire, vol. 2 (London: Strahan & Cadell, 1781), 234-247.

[3] Peter Heather, The Fall of the Roman Empire: A New History of Rome and the Barbarians (New York: Oxford University Press, 2006), 112-125.

[4] Niall Ferguson, Empire: The Rise and Demise of the British World Order and the Lessons for Global Power (New York: Basic Books, 2003), 185-204.

[5] Judith M. Brown, Gandhi: Prisoner of Hope (New Haven: Yale University Press, 1989), 231-248.

[6] Richard Overy, The Bombing War: Europe 1939-1945 (London: Allen Lane, 2013), 622-630.

[7] Rodric Braithwaite, Afgantsy: The Russians in Afghanistan, 1979-1989 (New York: Oxford University Press, 2011), 145-167.

[8] National Security Archive, "Soviet Deliberations on Afghanistan, 1979-1989," Electronic Briefing Book No. 272, https://nsarchive2.gwu.edu/NSAEBB/NSAEBB272/, Accessed on September 12, 2025.

[9] Timothy Garton Ash, The Polish Revolution: Solidarity (New Haven: Yale University Press, 2002), 89-112.

[10] J. H. Elliott, Empires of the Atlantic World: Britain and Spain in America, 1492-1830 (New Haven: Yale University Press, 2006), 123-139.

[11] Earl J. Hamilton, American Treasure and the Price Revolution in Spain, 1501-1650 (Cambridge, MA: Harvard University Press, 1934), 201-218.

[12] Congressional Budget Office, "The Budget and Economic Outlook: 2025 to 2035," https://www.cbo.gov/publication/59946, Accessed on September 12, 2025.

[13] U.S. Department of Defense, "Fiscal Year 2025 Defense Budget," https://www.defense.gov/News/Releases/Release/Article/3703410/, Accessed on September 12, 2025.

CHAPTER 35:

CREEPING TO THE EDGE

[1] Syrian Observatory for Human Rights, "Israeli Military Operations in Syria," July 2025, via https://www.securitycouncilreport.org/whatsinblue/2025/07/syria-emergency-briefing-following-israeli-airstrikes.php, Accessed on September 12, 2025.

[2] Atlantic Council, "Yemen Analysis," March 2025, https://www.atlanticcouncil.org/region/yemen/, Accessed on September 12, 2025.

[3] U.S. Department of Defense, "Fiscal Year 2025 Defense Budget," March 2024, https://www.defense.gov/News/Releases/Release/Article/3703410/ Accessed on September 12, 2025.

[4] Pew Research Center, "Global Attitudes Toward U.S. Leadership," June 2025, https://www.pewresearch.org/global/2025/06/11/views-of-the-united-states/, Accessed on September 12, 2025.

[5] Congressional Budget Office, "The Budget and Economic Outlook: 2025 to 2035," February 2025, https://www.cbo.gov/publication/60870, Accessed on September 12, 2025.

[6] American Society of Civil Engineers, "2025 Infrastructure Report Card," https://www.infrastructurereportcard.org Accessed on September 12, 2025. Accessed September 14, 2025. Different aspects of infrastructure (roads, bridges, airports, etc.) were graded between a "B" and a "D." The "D+" rating cited is an average of all independent ratings.

[7] Council on Foreign Relations, "China's Belt and Road Initiative," 2025, https://www.cfr.org/backgrounder/chinas-massive-belt-and-road-initiative ,Accessed on September 12, 2025.

[8] Electronic Frontier Foundation, "NSA Surveillance Programs," August 2025, https://www.eff.org/nsa-spying Accessed on September 12, 2025, Accessed September 14, 2025.

[9] OpenSecrets, "2024 Election Spending Totals," https://www.opensecrets.org/elections-overview/cost-of-election Accessed on September 12, 2025.

[10] U.S. Election Assistance Commission, "2024 Election Administration and Voting Survey," https://www.eac.gov/sites/default/files/2025-06/2024_EAVS_Report_508c.pdf, Accessed on September 12, 2025.

[11] United Nations Office for the Coordination of Humanitarian Affairs, "Occupied Palestinian Territory Humanitarian Update," https://www.ochaopt.org/, Accessed on September 12, 2025.

[12] Security Council Report, "UN Security Council Resolutions 2024-2025," https://www.securitycouncilreport.org/monthly-forecast/2025-01/, Accessed on September 12, 2025.

[13] Gallup, "Confidence in Institutions," 2025, https://news.gallup.com/poll/394283/confidence-institutions-down-average-new-low.aspx, Accessed on September 12, 2025.

[14] Armed Conflict Location & Event Data Project, "Political Violence in the United States," https://acleddata.com/region/united-states-and-canada, Accessed on September 12, 2025.

[15] Brown University, "The Pentagon, Climate Change, and War," Costs of War Project, https://watson.brown.edu/costsofwar/papers/ClimateChangeandCostofWar, Accessed on September 12, 2025.

[16] UNHCR, "Climate Change and Displacement," https://www.unhcr.org/climate-change-and-disasters.html, Accessed on September 12, 2025.

CHAPTER 36:

BRAIN DRAIN AND GLOBAL REJECTION

[1] World Intellectual Property Organization, "Global Innovation Index 2025," https://www.wipo.int/en/web/global-innovation-index/2025/innovation-clusters, Accessed on September 12, 2025.

[2] NASSCOM, "Indian Technology Industry Strategic Review 2024," https://nasscom.in/knowledge-center/publications/technology-sector-india-strategic-review-2025, Accessed on September 12, 2025.

[3] World Economic Forum, "Future of Work in Technology Report," 2025, https://www.weforum.org/publications/the-future-of-jobs-report-2025/, Accessed on September 12, 2025.

[4] OECD, "Education at a Glance 2025," https://www.oecd.org/education/education-at-a-glance/, Accessed on September 12, 2025.

[5] Statistics Canada, "Immigration and Ethnocultural Diversity Statistics," https://www.statcan.gc.ca/en/subjects-

start/immigration_and_ethnocultural_diversity, Accessed on
September 12, 2025.

[6] OECD, "Programme for International Student Assessment (PISA)
2024 Results," https://www.oecd.org/pisa/, Accessed on September
12, 2025.

[7] National Science Foundation, "Science and Engineering Indicators
2024," https://ncses.nsf.gov/pubs/nsb20241, Accessed on September
12, 2025.

[8] PEN America, "Banned in the USA: The Growing Movement to
Censor Books in Schools," https://pen.org/report/banned-usa-
growing-movement-to-censor-books-in-schools/, Accessed on
September 12, 2025.

[9] Council on Foreign Relations, "China's Belt and Road: Implications for
the United States," https://www.cfr.org/backgrounder/chinas-massive-
belt-and-road-initiative, Accessed on September 12, 2025.

[10] Atlantic Council, "The Future of the United States Dollar,"
https://www.atlanticcouncil.org/wp-content/uploads/2020/12/The-
Future-of-the-US-Dollar-Report-web-v3.pdf, Accessed on September
12, 2025.

[11] European Commission, "Digital Markets Act,"
https://commission.europa.eu/strategy-and-policy/priorities-2019-
2024/europe-fit-digital-age/digital-markets-act-ensuring-fair-and-
open-digital-markets_en, Accessed on September 12, 2025.

CHAPTER 37:

THE ROAD AHEAD

[1] Congressional Budget Office, "The Budget and Economic Outlook:
2024 to 2034," February 2024,
https://www.cbo.gov/publication/59946, Accessed on September 12,
2025.

[2] Congressional Budget Office, "The Budget and Economic Outlook:
2024 to 2034."

[3] American Society of Civil Engineers, "2021 Infrastructure Report
Card," https://www.infrastructurereportcard.org, Accessed on

September 12, 2025. Different aspects of infrastructure (roads, bridges, airports, etc.) were graded between a "B" and a "D." The "D+" rating cited is an average of all independent ratings.

[4] World Bank, "GDP (current US$) - China, United States," https://data.worldbank.org/indicator/NY.GDP.MKTP.CD?locations=CN-US, Accessed on September 12, 2025.

[5] Semiconductor Industry Association, " Semiconductor Market Research Reports," 2024, https://www.semi.org/en/products-services/purchase-market-reports, Accessed September 14, 2025.

[6] Reuters, " Nvidia modifies H20 chip for China to overcome US export controls,," October 2023, https://www.reuters.com/world/china/nvidia-modifies-h20-chip-china-overcome-us-export-controls-sources-say-2025-05-09/, Accessed on September 12, 2025.

[7] OECD, "Research and Development Statistics," https://www.oecd.org/sti/rd-statistics.htm, Accessed on September 12, 2025.

[8] National Science Foundation, "Science and Engineering Indicators 2024," https://ncses.nsf.gov/pubs/nsb20241, Accessed on September 12, 2025.

[9] Gallup, "Confidence in Institutions," 2024, https://news.gallup.com/poll/508169/confidence-us-institutions-2024.aspx ,Accessed on September 12, 2025.

[10] FBI, "Hate Crime Statistics, 2021," https://www.fbi.gov/news/press-releases/fbi-releases-2021-hate-crime-statistics, Accessed on September 12, 2025.

[11] Pew Research Center, "Global Attitudes Survey 2024," https://www.pewresearch.org/expertise/international-attitudes/,, Accessed on September 12, 2025.

[12] Council on Foreign Relations, "China's Belt and Road Initiative," https://www.cfr.org/backgrounder/chinas-massive-belt-and-road-initiative Accessed on September 12, 2025.

[13] American Society of Civil Engineers, "2021 Infrastructure Report Card."

[14] OECD, "Programme for International Student Assessment (PISA) 2022 Results," https://www.oecd.org/pisa/, Accessed on September 12, 2025.

[15] Federal Reserve Bank of New York, "Quarterly Report on Household Debt and Credit," 2024, https://www.newyorkfed.org/microeconomics/hhdc, Accessed on September 12, 2025.

[16] Commonwealth Fund, "Mirror, Mirror 2021: Reflecting Poorly," https://www.commonwealthfund.org/publications/fund-reports/2021/aug/mirror-mirror-2021-reflecting-poorly, Accessed on September 12, 2025.

[17] U.S. Department of Defense, " DOD Analysis Highlights Geostrategic Risks of Climate Change," 2021, https://www.war.gov/news/news-stories/article/article/2818343/dod-analysis-highlights-geostrategic-risks-of-climate-change/, Accessed on September 12, 2025.

[18] World Bank, "Costa Rica Overview," https://www.worldbank.org/en/country/costarica/overview, Accessed on September 12, 2025.

[19] World Bank, "Costa Rica Overview."

CHAPTER 38: THE FUTURE OF AMERICA

[1] Neta C. Crawford, The Pentagon, Climate Change, and War: Charting the Rise and Fall of U.S. Military Emissions (Cambridge, MA: MIT Press, 2022), 45-50.

[2] Stockholm International Peace Research Institute, "Military Expenditure Database," 2025, https://www.sipri.org/databases/milex ,Accessed on September 12, 2025.

[3] United Nations High Commissioner for Refugees, "Global Trends: Forced Displacement in 2024," June 2024, https://www.unhcr.org/global-trends-report-2024, Accessed on September 12, 2025.

[4] Chalmers Johnson, Blowback: The Costs and Consequences of American Empire, 2nd ed. (New York: Metropolitan Books, 2004), 15-30.

[5] Reporters Without Borders, "World Press Freedom Index 2025," April 2025, https://rsf.org/en/index, Accessed on September 12, 2025.

[6] Tax Foundation, "Trump Tariffs: Tracking the Economic Impact of the Trump Trade War," 2025, https://taxfoundation.org/research/all/federal/trump-tariffs-trade-war/, Accessed on September 12, 2025.

[7] Ayelet Shachar, "The Race for Talent: Highly Skilled Migrants and Competitive Immigration Regimes," New York University Law Review 81, no. 1 (April 2006): 148-149, https://www.nyulawreview.org/wp-content/uploads/2018/08/11.pdf ,Accessed on September 12, 2025.

[8] Congressional Budget Office, "The Budget and Economic Outlook: 2025 to 2035," January 2025, https://www.cbo.gov/publication/59946, Accessed on September 12, 2025.

[9] Reporters Without Borders, "World Press Freedom Index 2025," April 2025, https://rsf.org/en/rsf-world-press-freedom-index-2025-economic-fragility-leading-threat-press-freedom, Accessed on September 12, 2025.

[10] OpenSecrets, "2024 Election Spending," January 2025, https://www.opensecrets.org/elections-overview, Accessed on September 12, 2025.

[11] United Nations High Commissioner for Refugees, "Venezuela Regional Refugee Response," August 2025, https://www.unhcr.org/venezuela-emergency.html, Accessed on September 12, 2025.

[12] Brown University, Costs of War, "Human and Budgetary Costs to Date of the U.S. War in Afghanistan, Iraq, and Syria," August 2025, https://watson.brown.edu/costsofwar/, Accessed on September 12, 2025.

[13] Dahr Jamail, "Fallujah Babies: Under a New Born Sun of Suffering, Birth Defects Blamed on U.S. Weapons," Truthout, December 31,

2012, https://truthout.org/articles/fallujah-babies-birth-defects-blamed-on-us-weapons/ ,Accessed on September 12, 2025.

[14] United Nations Office for the Coordination of Humanitarian Affairs, "Yemen Humanitarian Response Plan," 2025, https://www.unocha.org/yemen, Accessed on September 12, 2025.

[15] World Bank, "Haiti: Joint World Bank-IMF Debt Sustainability Analysis," April 2023, https://documents.worldbank.org/en/publication/documents-reports/documentdetail/738961592861004930/haiti-joint-world-bank-imf-debt-sustainability-analysis, Accessed on September 12, 2025.

[16] U.S. Treasury Department, "Sanctions Programs and Country Information," 2025, https://ofac.treasury.gov/sanctions-programs-and-country-information, Accessed on September 12, 2025.

[17] United Nations Office for the Coordination of Humanitarian Affairs, "Occupied Palestinian Territory: Humanitarian Needs Overview," 2025, https://www.ochaopt.org/, Accessed on September 12, 2025.

[18] Human Rights Watch, "How the UN Can Help End Israeli Apartheid and Persecution," Human Rights Watch, May 19, 2021, https://www.hrw.org/news/2021/05/19/how-un-can-help-end-israeli-apartheid-and-persecution, Accessed on September 12, 2025.

[19] Pew Research Center, "Global Attitudes Survey 2025," June 2025, https://www.pewresearch.org/global/, Accessed on September 12, 2025.

[20] Congressional Budget Office, "The Budget and Economic Outlook: 2025 to 2035," January 2025, https://www.cbo.gov/publication/59946, Accessed on September 12, 2025.